Visual C++ 6 Distributed

The Cram Sheet

This Cram Sheet contains the distilled, key facts about the Visual C++ 6 Distributed exam. Review this information last thing before entering the test room, paying special attention to those areas where you feel you need the most review. You can transfer any of the facts onto a blank piece of paper before beginning the exam.

DEVELOPMENT ENVIRONMENT

1. Compiler switches control the stack construction for function call definitions:
   - */Gd*—Use **__cdecl**, which specifies the C calling convention (the default setting).
   - */Gr*—Use **__fastcall**, which specifies that arguments are passed in registers.
   - */Gz*—Use **__stdcall**, which specifies that arguments are pushed on the stack from right to left.

2. Compiler switch /GZ can help catch release build errors in debug.

3. The SourceSafe **Share** command allows a single instance of a component to be used with multiple projects.

4. The SourceSafe **Branch** command allows tracking the individual directions of a file as a project. The Branch command breaks any sharing links.

5. Pinning a SourceSafe file prevents you from making changes to the file.

6. Use **Share**, **Pin**, and **Branch** to create service pack projects (bug fixes).

MFC ARCHITECTURE—DOCUMENT/VIEW

7. The AppWizard-generated **InitInstance** function in a **CWinApp**-derived class initiates the creation of the main frame window, the document, and the view. The document template ties together these three objects. Each combination of frame window, document, and view types requires a unique document template. Each document template creates and manages all the documents of its type.

8. The document object stores the applications data. **CDocument**, derived from **CCmdTarget**, is the base class for document objects.

9. The view object displays a visible representation of the data. **CView**, derived from **CWnd**, is the base class for view objects.

10. MFC supports two types of threads: user interface (UI) threads, which have a message pump, and worker threads, which don't. Use **AfxBeginThread()** to launch a new thread. **CWinThread** objects encapsulate threads of execution. **CWinThread** is derived from **CCmdTarget**.

MFC ARCHITECTURE—DYNAMIC LINK LIBRARIES

11. An MFC regular DLL exports C-style functions and can be used by Visual Basic, Delphi, and other languages that can call C-style functions.

12. MFC extension DLLs are used to export functions and classes that enhance MFC. Use the **AFX_EXT_CLASS** macro to export a class or function.

13. The preprocessor symbol **_AFXEXT** must be defined for extension DLLs.

MFC ARCHITECTURE—USER INTERFACE

14. The **CMainFrame::OnCreate** function, generated by the AppWizard, creates and docks the standard status bar and toolbar. Here, you will normally add toolbars and modify the status bar configuration.

15. Menus, keyboard accelerators, toolbar buttons, and other UI objects generate command messages (**WM_COMMAND**).

16. **WM_COMMAND** messages sent to an SDI frame window are routed through the active view object, the active view's document object, the document object's document template, the main frame window object, the application object, and the default window procedure.

17. Regular window messages go directly to the window for which they are intended.

18. Use **CreateEx()** to create toolbar objects when extended styles need to be present during the construction of the embedded control.

19. After creating a toolbar, four more actions are required to place a dockable toolbar in your application: load the toolbar resource, enable docking for the toolbar, enable docking for the frame window, and dock the toolbar to the frame window.

20. Add ToolTips to a toolbar by adding **CBRS_TOOLTIPS** to the toolbar style, creating string table resources containing the ToolTip text, and setting the string resource IDs so that they match the toolbar buttons.

21. Use **CStatusbar::SetIndicators ()** to specify the number of panes a status bar will contain.

22. Use **CStatusBar::SetPaneText()** or **CCmdUI::SetText()** to display text in a status bar pane.

23. Standard controls, such as **CButton** and **CEdit**, send notifications to their parents by using **WM_COMMAND**.

24. Most common controls, such as **CProgressCtrl** and **CSpinButtonCtrl**, enclose their notifications in **WM_NOTIFY**.

25. **CDataExchange** provides dialog data exchange and validation (DDX/DDV).

26. Override **DoDataExchange()** and use **DDX_** functions to transfer data between controls and data members. Use **DDV_** functions to validate the values entered into controls.

27. Register new ActiveX controls by running RegSvr32, passing it the control's file name on the command line.

28. To create an ActiveX control at runtime, insert the component into the project, add an embedded ActiveX control wrapper class member to the appropriate window class, add an ID for the control, add code to call the control's **Create()** function, add the event sink declaration and definition macros, and add the necessary event message handlers and prototypes.

MFC ARCHITECTURE—DRAWING, PRINTING, AND PRINT PREVIEW

29. A **CView**-derived class overrides **OnDraw**. Whenever the framework receives a **WM_PAINT**, it creates a **CPaintDC** object and calls **OnDraw**, passing it a pointer to the **CPaintDC** object.

30. **OnDraw** can be used for displaying to a window, printing, and print previewing.

31. The framework calls five **CView** virtual functions at various stages of the printing process.

    - **OnPreparePrinting**—Override to call **DoPreparePrinting()**, which is responsible for displaying the Print dialog box and creating the printer DC. This function is called at the beginning of the print job.
    - **OnBeginPrinting**—Override to allocate fonts and other resources needed for the print job. You can also set the maximum page count here. This function is called just before printing starts.
    - **OnPrepareDC**—Override to modify the device context. This function is called before each page is printed.
    - **OnPrint**—Override to print headers, footers, and other page elements that are not drawn by **OnDraw** or to do all printing here instead of in **OnDraw**. This function is called to print (or preview) one page.
    - **OnEndPrinting**—Override to deallocate resources allocated in **OnBeginPrinting**. This function is called when printing ends.

COMPONENT OBJECT MODEL (COM)

32. All interfaces must be derived directly or indirectly from **IUnknown**, which has three methods: **QueryInterface()**, **AddRef()**, and **Release()**.

MCSD
Visual C++ 6
Distributed

James M. Lacey

MCSD Visual C++ 6 Distributed Exam Cram

Limits Of Liability And Disclaimer Of Warranty

The author and publisher of this book have used their best efforts in preparing the book and the programs contained in it. These efforts include the development, research, and testing of the theories and programs to determine their effectiveness. The author and publisher make no warranty of any kind, expressed or implied, with regard to these programs or the documentation contained in this book.

The author and publisher shall not be liable in the event of incidental or consequential damages in connection with, or arising out of, the furnishing, performance, or use of the programs, associated instructions, and/or claims of productivity gains.

Trademarks

Trademarked names appear throughout this book. Rather than list the names and entities that own the trademarks or insert a trademark symbol with each mention of the trademarked name, the publisher states that it is using the names for editorial purposes only and to the benefit of the trademark owner, with no intention of infringing upon that trademark.

The Coriolis Group, LLC
14455 N. Hayden Road
Suite 220
Scottsdale, Arizona 85260

480/483-0192
FAX 480/483-0193
http://www.coriolis.com

Library of Congress Cataloging-in-Publication Data
Lacey, James, 1943-
    MCSD Visual C++ 6 distributed exam cram / by James Lacey.
        p.   cm.
    Includes index.
    ISBN 1-57610-372-2
    1. Electronic data processing personnel--Certification.   2. Microsoft software--Examinations--Study guides.   3. Microsoft Visual C++.   I. Title.
QA76.3.L34   2000
005.26'8--dc21   99-055320
                                                          CIP

Printed in the United States of America
10 9 8 7 6 5 4 3 2 1

President, CEO
Keith Weiskamp

Publisher
Steve Sayre

Acquisitions Editor
Shari Jo Hehr

Marketing Specialist
Cynthia Caldwell

Project Editor
Meredith Brittain

Technical Reviewer
Nathan Lewis

Production Coordinator
Kim Eoff

Cover Designer
Jesse Dunn

Layout Designer
April Nielsen

CORIOLIS

14455 North Hayden Road • Suite 220 • Scottsdale, Arizona 85260

Coriolis: The Training And Certification Destination™

Thank you for purchasing one of our innovative certification study guides, just one of the many members of the Coriolis family of certification products.

Certification Insider Press™ has long believed that achieving your IT certification is more of a road trip than anything else. This is why most of our readers consider us their *Training And Certification Destination*. By providing a one-stop shop for the most innovative and unique training materials, our readers know we are the first place to look when it comes to achieving their certification. As one reader put it, "I plan on using your books for all of the exams I take."

To help you reach your goals, we've listened to others like you, and we've designed our entire product line around you and the way you like to study, learn, and master challenging subjects. Our approach is *The Smartest Way To Get Certified ™*.

In addition to our highly popular *Exam Cram* and *Exam Prep* guides, we have a number of new products. We recently launched *Exam Cram Audio Reviews*, which are audiotapes based on *Exam Cram* material. We've also developed *Practice Tests Exam Crams* and *Exam Cram Flash Cards*, which are designed to make your studying fun as well as productive.

Our commitment to being the *Training And Certification Destination* does not stop there. We just introduced *Exam Cram Insider*, a biweekly newsletter containing the latest in certification news, study tips, and announcements from Certification Insider Press. (To subscribe, send an email to **eci@coriolis.com** and type "subscribe insider" in the body of the email.) We also recently announced the launch of the Certified Crammer Society and the Coriolis Help Center—two new additions to the Certification Insider Press family.

We'd like to hear from you. Help us continue to provide the very best certification study materials possible. Write us or email us at **cipq@coriolis.com** and let us know how our books have helped you study, or tell us about new features that you'd like us to add. If you send us a story about how we've helped you, and we use it in one of our books, we'll send you an official Coriolis shirt for your efforts.

Good luck with your certification exam and your career. Thank you for allowing us to help you achieve your goals.

Keith Weiskamp

Keith Weiskamp
President and CEO

Look For These Other Books From The Coriolis Group:

MCSD Visual C++ Desktop Exam Cram
by James M. Lacey

MCSD Architectures Exam Cram
by Donald Brandt

MCSD Architectures Exam Prep
by Keith Morneau

To Ann, my loving wife

About The Author

James M. Lacey is a software developer and technical trainer specializing in C++, COM, Windows, client/server, and n-tier software development. He has more than 25 years of experience in the computer industry in both hardware and software engineering. This experience includes embedded systems, operating systems, compilers, graphic applications, client/server applications, and database systems.

James is a Microsoft Certified Solution Developer and Trainer. In addition to his own consulting practice, James teaches at Boston University and Worcester Polytechnic Institute. He prefers the challenge of designing and developing total solutions for small- to medium-sized businesses. His consulting practice keeps him abreast of current technology trends and allows him to bring real-world experience to the classroom.

James and his wife, Ann, live in central Massachusetts. He can be contacted at **jlacey@rclink.net**.

Acknowledgments

I would like to acknowledge and say thank you to all the people who supported me and helped me in writing this book. To all the folks at The Coriolis Group starting with Shari Jo Hehr, Acquisitions Editor: Thank you for bringing me on board and staying with me through the entire project. To Meredith Brittain, Project Editor, who was helpful in providing guidance when assistance was needed and always had a positive attitude that was much appreciated. To Catherine Oliver, Copy Editor, for asking pointed questions and making excellent suggestions that helped clarify my writing. To Nathan Lewis, Technical Reviewer, for his work to ensure technical accuracy by providing suggestions, asking for clarification, and finding outright mistakes in my writing.

I'd also like to thank all the people behind the scenes with whom I never had direct contact but who were instrumental in getting the book to press: Kim Eoff, Production Coordinator; Cynthia Caldwell, Marketing Specialist; Jesse Dunn, for cover design; and April Nielsen, for interior design.

A special thank you to Gene Olafsen and Phil Janus for the chapters they provided.

Finally, to my wife, Ann, for her loving support.

Contents At A Glance

Table Of Contents

Introduction

Welcome to *MCSD Visual C++ 6 Distributed Exam Cram*! This book aims to help you get ready to take—and pass—the Microsoft certification test numbered 70-015, "Designing and Implementing Distributed Applications with Microsoft Visual C++ 6.0." This Introduction explains Microsoft's certification programs in general and talks about how the *Exam Cram* series can help you prepare for Microsoft's certification exams.

Exam Cram books help you understand and appreciate the subjects and materials you need to pass Microsoft certification exams. *Exam Cram* books are aimed strictly at test preparation and review. They do not teach you everything you need to know about a topic (such as the ins and outs of C++ programming and database development or all the nitty-gritty details involved in using the Visual C++ 6 integrated development environment [IDE] and Visual SourceSafe). Instead, *Exam Cram* books present and dissect the questions and problems I've found that you're likely to encounter on a test. I've worked from Microsoft's own training materials, preparation guides, and tests, as well as from a battery of third-party test preparation tools and practice exams. My aim is to bring together as much information as possible about Microsoft certification exams.

Nevertheless, to completely prepare yourself for any Microsoft test, I recommend that you begin by taking the Self-Assessment included in this book immediately following this Introduction. This tool will help you evaluate your knowledge base against the requirements for an MCSD under both ideal and real circumstances.

Based on what you learn from that exercise, you might decide to begin your studies with some classroom training or by reading one of the many study guides available. I also strongly recommend that you install, configure, and work with the software or environment that you'll be tested on, because nothing beats hands-on experience and familiarity when it comes to understanding the questions you're likely to encounter on a certification test. Book learning is essential, but hands-on experience is the best teacher of all.

The Microsoft Certified Professional (MCP) Program

The MCP program currently includes the following separate tracks, each of which boasts its own special acronym (as a would-be certificant, you need to have a high tolerance for alphabet soup of all kinds):

➤ *MCP (Microsoft Certified Professional)*—This is the least prestigious of all the certification tracks from Microsoft. Passing any of the major Microsoft exams (except the Networking Essentials exam) qualifies an individual for the MCP credential. Individuals can demonstrate proficiency with additional Microsoft products by passing additional certification exams.

➤ *MCP+SB (Microsoft Certified Professional + Site Building)*—This certification program is designed for individuals who are planning, building, managing, and maintaining Web sites. Individuals with the MCP+SB credential will have demonstrated the ability to develop Web sites that include multimedia and searchable content and Web sites that connect to and communicate with a back-end database. It requires passing two of the following three exams: "Designing and Implementing Commerce Solutions with Microsoft Site Server 3.0, Commerce Edition," "Designing and Implementing Web Sites with Microsoft FrontPage 98," and "Designing and Implementing Web Solutions with Microsoft Visual InterDev 6.0."

➤ *MCSD (Microsoft Certified Solution Developer)*—The MCSD credential reflects the skills required to create multitier, distributed, and COM-based solutions, in addition to desktop and Internet applications, using new technologies. To obtain an MCSD, an individual must demonstrate the ability to analyze and interpret user requirements; select and integrate products, platforms, tools, and technologies; design and implement code and customize applications; and perform necessary software tests and quality assurance operations.

To become an MCSD, you must pass a total of four exams: three core exams and one elective exam. Each candidate must choose one of these three desktop application exams—"70-016: Designing and Implementing Desktop Applications with Microsoft Visual C++ 6.0," "70-156: Designing and Implementing Visual FoxPro 6.0," or "70-176: Designing and Implementing Visual Basic 6.0"—*plus* one of these three distributed application exams—"70-015: Designing and Implementing Distributed Applications with Microsoft Visual C++ 6.0," "70-155: Designing and Implementing Distributed Applications with Visual FoxPro 6.0," or "70-175: Designing and Implementing Distributed Applications with Visual

Basic 6.0." The third core exam is "70-100: Analyzing Requirements and Defining Solution Architectures."

Elective exams cover specific Microsoft applications and languages, including Visual Basic, Visual C++ 6 Distributed (the subject of this book), the Microsoft Foundation Classes, Access, SQL Server, Excel, and more. You cannot use the same exam to satisfy two requirements. For example, if you take and pass "Designing and Implementing Distributed Applications with Microsoft Visual C++ 6.0" to satisfy the core "Distributed Application Development" requirement, you cannot also use the exam to satisfy your elective requirement.

If you're on your way to becoming an MCSD and have already taken some exams, visit **www.microsoft.com/train_cert/** for information about how to proceed with your MCSD certification under this new track. Table 1 shows the requirements for MCSD certification.

➤ *MCDBA (Microsoft Certified Database Administrator)*—The MCDBA credential reflects the skills required to implement and administer Microsoft SQL Server databases. To obtain an MCDBA, an individual must demonstrate the ability to derive physical database designs, develop logical data models, create physical databases, create data services by using Transact-SQL, manage and maintain databases, configure and manage security, monitor and optimize databases, and install and configure Microsoft SQL Server.

To become an MCDBA, you must pass a total of five exams: four core exams and one elective exam. The required core exams are "Administering Microsoft SQL Server 7.0," "Designing and Implementing Databases with Microsoft SQL Server 7.0," "Implementing and Supporting Microsoft Windows NT Server 4.0," and "Implementing and Supporting Microsoft Windows NT Server 4.0 in the Enterprise."

The elective exams that you can choose from cover specific uses of SQL Server and include "Designing and Implementing Distributed Applications with Visual Basic 6.0," "Designing and Implementing Distributed Applications with Visual C++ 6.0," "Designing and Implementing Distributed Applications with Microsoft Visual FoxPro 6.0," "Designing and Implementing Data Warehouses with Microsoft SQL Server 7.0," and two exams that relate to Windows NT: "Internetworking with Microsoft TCP/IP on Microsoft Windows NT 4.0" and "Implementing and Supporting Microsoft Internet Information Server 4.0."

Note that the exam covered by this book can be used as the elective for the MCDBA certification. Table 2 shows the requirements for the MCDBA certification.

Table 1 MCSD Requirements*

Core

Choose 1 from the desktop applications development group	
Exam 70-016	Designing and Implementing Desktop Applications with Microsoft Visual C++ 6.0
Exam 70-156	Designing and Implementing Desktop Applications with Microsoft Visual FoxPro 6.0
Exam 70-176	Designing and Implementing Desktop Applications with Microsoft Visual Basic 6.0
Choose 1 from the distributed applications development group	
Exam 70-015	Designing and Implementing Distributed Applications with Microsoft Visual C++ 6.0
Exam 70-155	Designing and Implementing Distributed Applications with Microsoft FoxPro 6.0
Exam 70-175	Designing and Implementing Distributed Applications with Microsoft Visual Basic 6.0
This solution architecture exam is required	
Exam 70-100	Analyzing Requirements and Defining Solution Architectures

Elective

Choose 1 from this group	
Exam 70-015	Designing and Implementing Distributed Applications with Microsoft Visual C++ 6.0
Exam 70-016	Designing and Implementing Desktop Applications with Microsoft Visual C++ 6.0
Exam 70-019	Designing and Implementing Data Warehouses with Microsoft SQL Server 7.0
Exam 70-024	Developing Applications with C++ Using the Microsoft Foundation Class Library
Exam 70-025	Implementing OLE in Microsoft Foundation Class Applications
Exam 70-029	Designing and Implementing Databases with Microsoft SQL Server 7.0
Exam 70-055	Designing and Implementing Web Sites with Microsoft FrontPage 98
Exam 70-057	Designing and Implementing Commerce Solutions with Microsoft Site Server 3.0, Commerce Edition
Exam 70-069	Application Development with Microsoft Access for Windows 95 and the Microsoft Access Developer's Toolkit
Exam 70-091	Designing and Implementing Solutions with Microsoft Office 2000 and Microsoft Visual Basic for Applications
Exam 70-097	Designing and Implementing Database Applications with Microsoft Access 2000
Exam 70-105	Designing and Implementing Collaborative Solutions with Microsoft Outlook 2000 and Microsoft Exchange Server 5.5
Exam 70-152	Designing and Implementing Web Solutions with Microsoft Visual InterDev 6.0
Exam 70-155	Designing and Implementing Distributed Applications with Microsoft FoxPro 6.0
Exam 70-156	Designing and Implementing Desktop Applications with Microsoft Visual FoxPro 6.0
Exam 70-165	Developing Applications with Microsoft Visual Basic 5.0
Exam 70-175	Designing and Implementing Distributed Applications with Microsoft Visual Basic 6.0
Exam 70-176	Designing and Implementing Desktop Applications with Microsoft Visual Basic 6.0

*This is not a complete listing—you can still be tested on some earlier versions of these products. However, we have tried to include the most recent versions so that you may test on these versions and thus be certified longer. We have not included any tests that are scheduled to be retired.

Core exams that can also be used as elective exams can be counted only once toward certification. The same test cannot be used as both a core and an elective exam.

Table 2   MCDBA Requirements

Core

All 4 of these are required	
Exam 70-028	Administering Microsoft SQL Server 7.0
Exam 70-029	Designing and Implementing Databases with Microsoft SQL Server 7.0
Exam 70-067	Implementing and Supporting Microsoft Windows NT Server 4.0
Exam 70-068	Implementing and Supporting Microsoft Windows NT Server 4.0 in the Enterprise

Elective

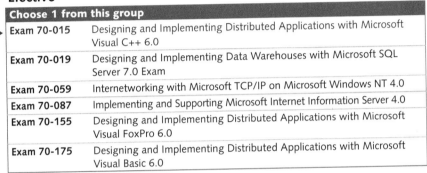

Choose 1 from this group	
Exam 70-015	Designing and Implementing Distributed Applications with Microsoft Visual C++ 6.0
Exam 70-019	Designing and Implementing Data Warehouses with Microsoft SQL Server 7.0 Exam
Exam 70-059	Internetworking with Microsoft TCP/IP on Microsoft Windows NT 4.0
Exam 70-087	Implementing and Supporting Microsoft Internet Information Server 4.0
Exam 70-155	Designing and Implementing Distributed Applications with Microsoft Visual FoxPro 6.0
Exam 70-175	Designing and Implementing Distributed Applications with Microsoft Visual Basic 6.0

➤ *MCSE (Microsoft Certified Systems Engineer)*—Anyone who has a current MCSE is warranted to possess a high level of expertise with Windows NT (version 3.51 or 4) and other Microsoft operating systems and products. This credential is designed to prepare individuals to plan, implement, maintain, and support information systems and networks built around Microsoft Windows NT and its BackOffice family of products.

To obtain an MCSE, an individual must pass four core operating system exams, plus two elective exams. The operating system exams require individuals to prove their competence with desktop and server operating systems and networking components.

You must pass at least two Windows NT-related exams to obtain an MCSE: "Implementing and Supporting Microsoft Windows NT Server" (version 3.51 or 4) and "Implementing and Supporting Microsoft Windows NT Server in the Enterprise" (version 3.51 or 4). These tests demonstrate an individual's knowledge of Windows NT in smaller, simpler networks and in larger, more complex, and heterogeneous networks, respectively.

Note: The Windows NT 3.51 version will be retired by Microsoft on June 30, 2000.

You must pass two additional tests as well. These tests relate to networking and desktop operating systems. At present, the networking requirement can be satisfied only by passing the Networking Essentials test. The desktop operating system test can be satisfied by passing a Windows 95, Windows NT Workstation (the version must match whichever core Windows NT curriculum you are pursuing), or Windows 98 test.

The two remaining exams are electives. An elective exam may fall in any number of subject or product areas, primarily BackOffice components. However, it's also possible to test out on electives by taking advanced networking tests such as "Internetworking with Microsoft TCP/IP on Microsoft Windows NT" (but the version of Windows NT involved must match the version for the core requirements). If you are on your way to becoming an MCSE and have already taken some exams, visit **www.microsoft.com/mcp/certstep/mcse.htm** for information about how to complete your MCSE certification.

In September 1999, Microsoft announced its Windows 2000 track for MCSE and also announced retirement of Windows NT 4 MCSE core exams on 12/31/2000. Individuals who wish to remain certified MCSEs after 12/31/2001 must "upgrade" their certifications on or before 12/31/2001. The details are too complex to discuss here; to obtain those details, please visit **www.microsoft.com/mcp/certstep/mcse.htm**.

Whatever mix of tests is completed toward MCSE certification, individuals must pass six tests to meet the MCSE requirements. It's not uncommon for the entire process to take a year or so, and many individuals find that they must take a test more than once to pass. The primary goal of the *Exam Cram* series is to make it possible, given proper study and preparation, to pass all Microsoft certification tests on the first try.

➤ *MCT (Microsoft Certified Trainer)*—Microsoft Certified Trainers are deemed able to deliver elements of the official Microsoft curriculum based on technical knowledge and instructional ability. Therefore, it's necessary for an individual seeking MCT credentials (which are granted on a course-by-course basis) to pass the related certification exam for a course and to take the official Microsoft training on the subject, as well as to demonstrate an ability to teach. MCT candidates must also possess a current MCSE.

The teaching skill criterion may be satisfied by proving that one has already attained training certification from Novell, Banyan, Lotus, the Santa Cruz Operation, or Cisco, or by taking a Microsoft-sanctioned workshop on instruction. Microsoft makes it clear that MCTs are important cogs in the Microsoft training channels. Instructors must be MCTs before Microsoft will allow them to teach in any of its official training channels, including Microsoft's affiliated Certified Technical Education Centers (CTECs) and its online training partner network.

Microsoft has announced that the MCP+I and MCSE+I credentials will not be continued when the MCSE exams for Windows 2000 are in full swing because the skill set for the Internet portion of the program has been included in the new MCSE program. Therefore, details on these tracks are not provided here; go to **www.microsoft.com/train_cert/** if you need more information.

Once a Microsoft product becomes obsolete, MCPs typically have 12 to 18 months in which to recertify on current versions. (If individuals do not recertify within the specified time period, their certification becomes invalid.) Because technology keeps changing and new products continually supplant old ones, this should come as no surprise. This explains why Microsoft has announced that MCSEs have 12 months past the scheduled retirement date for the Windows NT 4 exams to recertify on Windows 2000 topics. (Note that this means taking at least two exams, if not more.)

The best place to keep tabs on the MCP program and its related certifications is on the Web. The current URL for the MCP program is at **www.microsoft. com/mcp/certstep/mcps.htm**. However, Microsoft's Web site changes frequently, so if this URL doesn't work, try using the search tool on Microsoft's site with either "MCP" or the quoted phrase "Microsoft Certified Professional program" as the search string. This will help you find the latest and most accurate information about the company's certification programs.

Taking A Certification Exam

Alas, testing is not free. Each computer-based MCP exam costs $100, and if you do not pass, you may retest for an additional $100 for each additional try. In the United States and Canada, tests are administered by Sylvan Prometric and Virtual University Enterprises (VUE). Here's how you can contact them:

➤ *Sylvan Prometric*—You can sign up for a test through the company's Web site at **www.slspro.com**. You can also register by phone at 800-755-3926 (within the United States or Canada) or at 410-843-8000 (outside the United States and Canada).

➤ *Virtual University Enterprises*—You can sign up for a test or get the phone numbers for local testing centers through the Web page at **www.microsoft.com/train_cert/mcp/vue_info.htm**.

To sign up for a test, you must possess a valid credit card or contact either company for mailing instructions to send it a check (in the United States). Only when payment is verified, or a check has cleared, can you actually register for a test.

To schedule an exam, call Sylvan or VUE, or sign up online at least one day in advance. To cancel or reschedule an exam, you must call by 7 P.M. pacific standard time the day before the scheduled test (or you may be charged, even if you don't appear to take the test). When you want to schedule a test, have the following information ready:

➤ Your name, organization, and mailing address.

➤ Your Microsoft test ID. (Inside the United States, this is your Social Security number; citizens of other nations should call ahead to find out what type of identification number is required to register for a test.)

➤ The name and number of the exam you wish to take.

➤ A method of payment. (As already mentioned, a credit card is the most convenient method, but alternate means can be arranged in advance, if necessary.)

After you sign up for a test, you'll be informed as to when and where the test is scheduled. Try to arrive at least 15 minutes early. You must supply two forms of identification—one of which must be a photo ID—to be admitted into the testing room.

All exams are completely "closed book." In fact, you will not be permitted to take anything with you into the testing area. However, you will be furnished with a blank sheet of paper and a pen. I suggest that you immediately write down on that sheet of paper all the information you've memorized for the test. In *Exam Cram* books, this information appears on a tear-out sheet inside the front cover of each book. You'll have some time to compose yourself, record this information, and take a sample orientation exam before you must begin the real thing. I suggest you take the orientation test before taking your first exam, but because they're all more or less identical in layout, behavior, and controls, you probably won't need to do this more than once.

When you complete a Microsoft certification exam, the software will tell you whether you've passed or failed. Results are broken into several topic areas. Even if you fail, I suggest you ask for—and keep—the detailed report that the test administrator should print for you. You can use this report to help you prepare for another go-round, if needed.

If you need to retake an exam, you'll have to call Sylvan Prometric or VUE, schedule a new test date, and pay another $100.

 The first time you fail a test, you can retake the test the next day. However, if you fail a second time, you must wait 14 days before retaking that test. The 14-day waiting period remains in effect for all retakes after the first failure.

If you do fail, I do not recommend taking the exam again the next day unless you just missed a passing grade. To me, a week seems about ideal—it gives you enough time to bone up on those areas in which you had problems while also making sure that the types of questions you encountered are fresh in your mind.

Tracking MCP Status

As soon as you pass any Microsoft exam (other than Networking Essentials), you'll attain Microsoft Certified Professional (MCP) status. Microsoft also generates transcripts that indicate which exams you have passed and your corresponding test scores. You can order a transcript by email at any time by sending an email addressed to **mcp@msprograms.com**. You can also obtain a copy of your transcript by downloading the latest version of the MCT guide from the Web site and consulting the section titled "Key Contacts" for a list of telephone numbers and related contacts.

Once you pass the necessary set of exams, you'll be certified. Official certification normally takes anywhere from four to six weeks, so don't expect to get your credentials overnight. When the package for a qualified certification arrives, it includes a Welcome Kit that contains a number of elements:

➤ A certificate, suitable for framing, along with a Professional Program Membership card and lapel pin.

➤ A license to use the MCP logo, thereby allowing you to use the logo in advertisements, promotions, and documents, as well as on letterhead, business cards, and so on. Along with the license comes an MCP logo sheet, which includes camera-ready artwork. (Note that before using any of the artwork, individuals must sign and return a licensing agreement that indicates they'll abide by its terms and conditions.)

➤ A subscription to *Microsoft Certified Professional Magazine*, which provides ongoing data about testing and certification activities, requirements, and changes to the program.

➤ A one-year subscription to the Microsoft Beta Evaluation program. This subscription will get you all beta products from Microsoft for the next year. (This does not include developer products. You must join the MSDN program or become an MCSD to qualify for developer beta products. To join the MSDN program, go to **http://msdn.microsoft. com/developer/join/**.)

Many people believe that the benefits of MCP certification go well beyond the perks that Microsoft provides to newly anointed members of this elite group. I'm starting to see more job listings that request or require applicants to have an MCP, MCP+SB, MCSD, and so on, and many individuals who complete the program can qualify for increases in pay and/or responsibility. As an official recognition of hard work and broad knowledge, one of the MCP credentials is a badge of honor in many IT organizations.

How To Prepare For An Exam

Preparing for any Microsoft product-related test (including Visual C++ 6 Distributed) requires that you obtain and study materials designed to provide comprehensive information about the product and its capabilities, plus Web site design and maintenance techniques that will appear on the specific exam for which you are preparing. The following list of materials will help you study and prepare:

➤ The Visual C++ 6 product CD-ROM includes comprehensive online documentation and related materials; it should be a primary resource when you are preparing for the test.

➤ The Microsoft TechNet CD-ROM delivers numerous electronic titles on Visual C++ 6. Its offerings include Product Manuals, Product Facts, Technical Notes, Tips and Techniques, Tools and Utilities, and information on how to access the Seminars Online training materials for Visual C++ 6. A subscription to TechNet costs $299 per year but is well worth the price. Visit **ww.microsoft.com/technet/** and check out the information under the "TechNet Subscription" menu entry for more details. Don't ignore the Microsoft Developer's Network CD-ROM that comes with the Enterprise edition of Visual C++ 6. You can get the latest version online at **www.msdn.microsoft.com**—the materials include technical articles, Knowledge Base tips, books, and more.

➤ Find, download, and use the exam preparation materials, practice tests, and self-assessment exams on the Microsoft Training And Certification Download page (**www.microsoft.com/train_cert/download/downld.htm**).

In addition, you'll probably find any or all of the following materials useful in your quest for Visual C++ 6 expertise:

➤ *Microsoft Training Kits*—Although there's no training kit currently available from Microsoft Press for Visual C++ 6, many other topics have such kits. It's worthwhile to check to see if Microsoft has come out with anything by the time you need this information.

➤ *Study Guides*—Several publishers—including Certification Insider Press—offer learning materials necessary to pass the tests. The Certification Insider Press series includes:

➤ *The Exam Cram series*—These books give you information about the material you need to know to pass the tests.

➤ *The Exam Prep series*—These books provide a greater level of detail than the *Exam Cram* books.

Together, the two series make a perfect pair.

➤ *Multimedia*—These Coriolis Group materials are designed to support learners of all types—whether you learn best by listening, reading, or doing:

➤ *Practice Tests Exam Cram series*—Provides the most valuable test preparation material: practice exams. Each exam is followed by a complete set of answers, as well as explanations of why the right answers are right and the wrong answers are wrong. Each book comes with a CD that contains one or more interactive practice exams.

➤ *Exam Cram Flash Card series*—Offers practice questions on handy cards you can use anywhere. The question and its possible answers appear on the front of the card, and the answer, explanation, and a valuable reference appear on the back of the card. The set also includes a CD with an electronic practice exam to give you the feel of the actual test—and more practice!

➤ *Exam Cram Audio Review series*—Offers a concise review of key topics covered on the exam, as well as practice questions.

➤ *Classroom Training*—CTECS, online partners, and third-party training companies (such as Wave Technologies, American Research Group, Learning Tree, Data-Tech, and others) all offer classroom training on Visual C++ 6. These companies aim to help prepare developers to use Visual C++ 6 to pass the Visual C++ 6 Distributed exam. Although such training runs upwards of $350 per day in class, most of the individuals lucky enough to partake find them to be quite worthwhile.

➤ *Other Publications*—You'll find direct references to other publications and resources in this text, but there's no shortage of materials available about Visual C++ 6. To help you sift through some of the publications out there, I end each chapter with a "Need To Know More?" section that provides pointers to more complete and exhaustive resources covering the chapter's information. This should give you an idea of where I think you should look for further discussion.

By far, this set of required and recommended materials represents a nonpareil collection of sources and resources for Visual C++ 6 and related topics. I anticipate that you'll find that this book belongs in this company. In the section that follows, I explain how this book works, and I give you some good reasons why this book counts as a member of the required and recommended materials list.

About This Book

Each topical *Exam Cram* chapter follows a regular structure, along with graphical cues about important or useful information. Here's the structure of a typical chapter:

➤ *Opening Hotlists*—Each chapter begins with a list of the terms, tools, and techniques that you must learn and understand before you can be fully conversant with that chapter's subject matter. I follow the hotlists with one or two introductory paragraphs to set the stage for the rest of the chapter.

➤ *Topical Coverage*—After the opening hotlists, each chapter covers a series of topics related to the chapter's subject title. Throughout this section, I highlight topics or concepts likely to appear on a test using a special Exam Alert layout, like this:

This is what an Exam Alert looks like. Normally, an Exam Alert stresses concepts, terms, software, or activities that are likely to relate to one or more certification test questions. For that reason, I think any information found offset in Exam Alert format is worthy of unusual attentiveness on your part. Indeed, most of the information that appears on The Cram Sheet appears as Exam Alerts within the text.

Pay close attention to material flagged as an Exam Alert; although all the information in this book pertains to what you need to know to pass the exam, I flag certain items that are really important. You'll find what appears in the meat of each chapter to be worth knowing, too, when preparing for the test. Because this book's material is very condensed, I recommend that you use this book along with other resources to achieve the maximum benefit.

In addition to the Exam Alerts, I have provided tips that will help you build a better foundation for Visual C++ 6 knowledge. Although the information may not be on the exam, it's certainly related and will help you become a better test-taker.

This is how tips are formatted. Keep your eyes open for these, and you'll become a Visual C++ 6 guru in no time!

➤ *Practice Questions*—Although I talk about test questions and topics throughout each chapter, this section presents a series of mock test questions and explanations of both correct and incorrect answers. I also try to point out especially tricky questions by using a special icon, like this:

Ordinarily, this icon flags the presence of a particularly devious inquiry, if not an outright trick question. Trick questions are calculated to be answered incorrectly if not read more than once—and carefully at that. Although they're not ubiquitous, such questions make regular appearances on the Microsoft exams. That's why I say exam questions are as much about reading comprehension as they are about knowing your material inside out and backwards.

➤ *Details And Resources*—Every chapter ends with a section titled "Need To Know More?". This section provides direct pointers to Microsoft and third-party resources offering more details on the chapter's subject. In addition, these sections try to rank or at least rate the quality and thoroughness of the topic's coverage by each resource. If you find a resource you like in this collection, use it, but don't feel compelled to use all the resources. On the other hand, I recommend only resources I use on a regular basis, so none of my recommendations will be a waste of your time or money (but purchasing them all at once probably represents an expense that many network administrators and would-be MCSDs might find hard to justify).

The bulk of the book follows this chapter structure slavishly, but there are a few other elements I'd like to point out. Chapter 13 is a sample test that provides a good review of the material presented throughout the book to ensure you're ready for the exam. Chapter 14 is an answer key to the sample test that appears in Chapter 13. Additionally, you'll find the Glossary, which explains terms, and an index that you can use to track down terms as they appear in the text.

Finally, the tear-out Cram Sheet attached next to the inside front cover of this *Exam Cram* book represents a condensed and compiled collection of facts, figures, and tips that I think you should memorize before taking the test. Because you can dump this information out of your head onto a piece of paper before taking the exam, you can master this information by brute force—you need to remember it only long enough to write it down when you walk into the test room. You might even want to look at it in the car or in the lobby of the testing center just before you walk in to take the test.

How To Use This Book

If you're prepping for a first-time test, I've structured the topics in this book to build on one another. Therefore, some topics in later chapters make more sense after you've read earlier chapters. That's why I suggest you read this book from front to back for your initial test preparation. If you need to brush up on a topic or you have to bone up for a second try, use the index or table of contents to go straight to the topics and questions that you need to study. Beyond helping you prepare for the tests, I think you'll find this book useful as a tightly focused reference to some of the most important aspects of Visual C++ 6.

If your goal is to be an MCSD, I encourage you to study for and take the Desktop exam first. There is a considerable amount of overlap between the Desktop objectives and the Distributed objectives, and the coverage of the material that appears on both sets of objectives is covered in more depth in the *MCSD C++ 6 Desktop Exam Cram*. In my view, the Desktop exam tests your knowledge of the technology foundation that is further developed in the Distributed exam. If you are reading this book first, I recommend that you put it aside until you have completed your Desktop preparation. If your goal is to be an MCDBA, I encourage you to read this book and consult the "Need To Know More?" sections at the ends of the chapters for supplementary references, if necessary.

Given all the book's elements and its specialized focus, I've tried to create a tool that will help you prepare for—and pass—Microsoft Exam 70-015, "Designing and Implementing Distributed Applications with Microsoft Visual C++ 6.0." Please share your feedback on the book with us, especially if you have ideas about how I can improve it for future test-takers. I'll consider everything you say carefully, and I'll respond to all suggestions.

Please send your questions or comments to me at **jlacey@rclink.net** or the publisher at **cipq@coriolis.com**. Please remember to include the title of the book in your message; otherwise, I'll be forced to guess which book you're writing about. And I don't like to guess—I want to *know*! Also, be sure to check out the Web pages at **www.certificationinsider.com**, where you'll find information updates, commentary, and certification information.

Thanks, and enjoy the book!

Self-Assessment

Based on recent statistics from Microsoft, as many as 400,000 individuals are at some stage of the certification process but haven't yet received an MCP or other Microsoft certification. I also know that three or four times that number may be considering whether or not to obtain a Microsoft certification of some kind. That's a huge audience!

The reason I included a Self-Assessment in this *Exam Cram* book is to help you evaluate your readiness to tackle MCSD certification. It should also help you understand what you need to know to master the topic of this book namely, Exam 70-015, "Designing and Implementing Distributed Applications with Microsoft Visual C++ 6.0." But before you tackle this Self-Assessment, let's talk about concerns you may face when pursuing an MCSD, and what an ideal MCSD candidate might look like.

MCSDs In The Real World

In the next section, I describe an ideal MCSD candidate, knowing full well that only a few real candidates will meet this ideal. In fact, the description of that ideal candidate might seem downright scary. But take heart: Although the requirements to obtain an MCSD may seem formidable, they are by no means impossible to meet. However, be keenly aware that it does take time, involves some expense, and requires real effort to get through the process.

You can get all the real-world motivation you need from knowing that many others have gone before, so you will be able to follow in their footsteps. If you're willing to tackle the process seriously and do what it takes to obtain the necessary experience and knowledge, you can take—and pass—all the certification tests involved in obtaining an MCSD. In fact, these *Exam Crams*, and the companion *Exam Preps*, are designed to make it as easy on you as possible to prepare for these exams. But prepare you must!

The same, of course, is true for other Microsoft certifications, including:

➤ MCSE, which is aimed at network engineers and requires four core exams and two electives for a total of six exams.

➤ Other Microsoft certifications, whose requirements range from one test (MCP) to several tests (MCP+SB and MCDBA).

The Ideal MCSD Candidate

Just to give you some idea of what an ideal MCSD candidate is like, here are some relevant statistics about the background and experience such an individual might have. Don't worry if you don't meet these qualifications, or don't come that close—this is a far from ideal world, and where you fall short is simply where you'll have more work to do.

➤ Academic or professional training in application design and development, as well as relevant database design and usage.

➤ Typically, six years of professional development experience (33 percent of MCSDs have less than 4 years of experience, 20 percent have 5 to 8 years of experience, and 47 percent have 8+ years of experience). This experience includes development tools such as Visual Basic, Visual C++, and so on. This must include application design, requirements analysis, debugging, distribution, and an understanding of the Microsoft Services Model.

➤ Three-plus years in a relational database environment designing and using database tools such as SQL Server and Access. The ideal MCSD will have performed both logical and physical database designs, from entity modeling through normalization and database schema creation.

➤ A thorough understanding of issues involved in the creation and deployment of distributed applications to include knowledge of COM and DCOM, issues involved in the usage of in-process and out-of process components, and the logical and physical design of those components.

➤ An understanding of both operating system architectures (Windows 9x, NT) as they relate to application as well as network issues to include Internet architectures. (You will not, of course, be expected to demonstrate the level of knowledge that a network engineer needs to have. Instead, you want to be familiar with the issues that networks—particularly the Internet—raise in client/server applications.)

Fundamentally, this boils down to a bachelor's degree in computer science, plus at least three to four years of development experience in a networked environment, involving relational database design and usage, and application architecture design, development, and deployment. Given the relative newness of the technologies involved, there are probably few certification candidates that meet these requirements. Particularly in the area of multitiered applications, most meet less than half of these requirements—at least, when they begin the certification process. But because those who have already achieved their MSCD certification have survived this ordeal, you can survive it too—especially if you heed what this Self-Assessment can tell you about what you already know and what you need to learn.

Put Yourself To The Test

The following series of questions and observations is designed to help you figure out how much work you must do to pursue Microsoft certification and what kinds of resources you may consult on your quest. Be absolutely honest in your answers, or you'll end up wasting money on exams you're not yet ready to take. There are no right or wrong answers, only steps along the path to certification. Only you can decide where you really belong in the broad spectrum of aspiring candidates.

Two things should be clear from the outset, however:

➤ Even a modest background in applications development will be helpful.

➤ Hands-on experience with Microsoft development products and technologies is an essential ingredient to certification success.

Educational Background

1. Have you ever taken any computer-programming classes? [Yes or No]

   If Yes, proceed to question 2; if No, proceed to question 5.

2. Have you taken any classes on applications design? [Yes or No]

   If Yes, you will probably be able to handle Microsoft's architecture and system component discussions. You will be expected, in most of the exams, to demonstrate core COM concepts. This will include an understanding of the implications of in-process and out-of-process components, cross-process procedure calls, and so on.

   If No, consider some basic reading in this area. The "Component Tools Guide" in the Visual Basic documentation is actually quite good and covers the core concepts. Third-party COM books can also be helpful.

3. Have you taken any classes oriented specifically toward Visual Basic, Visual FoxPro, or Visual C++? [Yes or No]

   If Yes, you will probably be able to handle the programming related concepts and terms in the "Desktop Applications" and "Distributed Applications" portions of the MCSD track. Each section allows you to choose between a Visual Basic, a Visual FoxPro, or a Visual C++ exam.

Assuming you have selected Visual C++ and you feel rusty, brush up on your Visual C++ terminology by going through the Glossary in this book and the product documentation.

If No, and if you don't have a good deal of on-the-job experience, you might want to take a training class or two, or read one or two books in this topic area. *Beginning Visual C++ 6*, by Ivor Horton, (Wrox Press Ltd., 1998, ISBN 1-861000-88-X) is really quite good and covers both C++ (the language) and MFC at an appropriate level.

4. Have you taken any database design classes? [Yes or No]

   If Yes, you will probably be able to handle questions related to general data access techniques. If you do not have experience specific to Microsoft Access or Microsoft SQL Server, you will want to touch up on concepts specific to either of those two products.

   If No, you will want to look over the exams that you can take from the "Elective Exams" portion of the MSCD. These exams cover a wide variety of topics, such as SQL Server and FrontPage. You may have expertise in one of these areas and should, therefore, aim to take one of those exams. All in all, whether you take the SQL Server (or Access) exam, you should consider reading a book or two on the subject. I like *Microsoft SQL Server 6.5 Unleashed*, by David Solomon, Ray Rankins, et al. (Sams Publishing, ISBN 0-672-39856-4), although some of the book covers concepts more appropriate to a DBA.

5. Have you done any reading on application design and development? [Yes or No]

   If Yes, go on to the next section, "Hands-On Experience."

   If No, be particularly alert to the questions asked in the next section. Frequently, a little experience goes a long way. For any areas where you may be weak, consider doing extra reading as outlined in questions 2, 3, and 4. Carefully review the Glossary in this book and take unfamiliar terms as cues to areas on which you need to brush up. Look at the "Terms you'll need to know" and "Techniques you'll need to master" lists at the beginning of each chapter. Again, for any terms or techniques that are unfamiliar, consider boning up in those areas.

Hands-On Experience

The most important key to success on all of the Microsoft tests is hands-on experience, especially with the core tool on which you are testing (Visual Basic, Visual FoxPro, or Visual C++), as well as an understanding of COM and

ADO. If I leave you with only one realization after taking this Self-Assessment, it should be that there's no substitute for time spent developing real-world applications. The development experience should include logical and physical design, the creation of remote COM services, and database programming. The recurring theme through nearly all of the tests will be COM and database techniques.

6. Have you created COM components?

    If Yes, you will probably be prepared for Exam 70-100, "Analyzing Requirements and Defining Solution Architectures." This satisfies the "Solution Architectures" section of the MCSD requirements. Go to question 7.

    If No, you need to bone up on COM concepts as outlined in question 2.

7. Have you done database programming?

    If Yes, go to question 8.

    If No, you will be in a weak position on all of the tests. You need to consult a book such as the one recommended in question 3.

8. Have you done ADO development?

    If Yes, go to question 9.

    If No, you need to consult an ADO reference. Use the MSDN library on your product's CD-ROM and review the ADO articles. Additionally, check out a book such as the one recommended in question 4.

9. Have you developed with Visual Basic?

    If Yes, you should be prepared to take Exam 70-176, "Designing and Implementing Desktop Applications with Microsoft Visual Basic 6.0." This will satisfy the Desktop Applications Development requirement. Go to question 10.

    If No, go to question 10.

10. Have you developed with Visual FoxPro?

    If Yes, you should be prepared to take Exam 70-156, "Designing and Implementing Desktop Applications with Microsoft Visual FoxPro 6.0." This will satisfy the Desktop Applications Development requirement. Go to question 11.

    If No, go to question 11.

11. Have you developed with Visual C++?

    If Yes, you should be prepared to take Exam 70-016, "Designing and Implementing Desktop Applications with Microsoft Visual C++ 6.0." If you also answered Yes to question 9 or 10, you can use Exam 70-016 or Exam 70-156 as your elective requirement. Go to question 12.

    If No and if you also answered No to questions 9 and 10, you probably should consider getting some real-world experience with Visual Basic, Visual FoxPro, or Visual C++.

12. Have you developed Distributed applications with Visual Basic, Visual FoxPro, or Visual C++?

    If Yes, you should be prepared to take Exam 70-175, "Designing and Implementing Distributed Applications with Microsoft Visual Basic 6.0," Exam 70-155, "Designing and Implementing Distributed Applications with Microsoft Visual FoxPro 6.0," or Exam 70-015, "Designing and Implementing Distributed Applications with Microsoft Visual C++ 6.0." Any one of these exams will satisfy the Distributed Applications requirement of the MSCD. Go to question 13.

    If No, consult the book recommended in question 3.

13. Have you used one of the products listed in the "Elective Exams" section of the MCSD?

    If Yes, go ahead and take that exam after consulting the Microsoft Web site for a list of the MCSD requirements. (MCSD requirements are also listed in the Introduction of this book.)

    If No, consider boning up on Microsoft Access or Microsoft SQL Server, as outlined in question 4, and taking one of those exams.

Testing Your Exam-Readiness

Whether you attend a formal class on a specific topic to get ready for an exam or use written materials to study on your own, some preparation for the Microsoft certification exams is essential. At $100 a try, pass or fail, you want to do everything you can to pass on your first try. That's where studying comes in.

I have included practice questions at the end of each chapter. If you answer them successfully, take the practice exam in Chapter 13 to see how you do.

For any given subject, consider taking a class if you've tackled self-study materials, taken the test, and failed anyway. The opportunity to interact with an instructor and fellow students can make all the difference in the world, if you can afford that privilege. For information about Microsoft classes, visit the

Training and Certification page at www.microsoft.com/train_cert/ (use the "Find a Course" link).

If you can't afford to take a class, visit the Training and Certification page anyway, because it also includes pointers to free practice exams. And even if you can't afford to spend much, you should still invest in some low-cost practice exams from commercial vendors because they can help you assess your readiness to pass a test better than any other tool. The following links may be of interest to you in locating practice exams:

➤ *SelfTest Software (www.stsware.com)*—At the time of this writing, the cost for the first test ordered was $79. There was no information available on Visual C++. The Visual Basic 6 exam included 300 questions.

➤ *MeasureUp (www.measureup.com)*—At the time of this writing, tests cost $99. The Visual C++ 6 exam was not yet ready. The Visual Basic 6 test included 206 practice questions.

14. Have you taken a practice exam on your chosen test subject? [Yes or No]

If Yes and you scored 70 percent or better, you're probably ready to tackle the real thing. If your score isn't above that threshold, keep at it until you break that barrier. (If you scored above 80, you should feel pretty confident.)

If No, obtain all the free and low-budget practice tests you can find and get to work. Keep at it until you can break the passing threshold comfortably.

 When it comes to assessing your test readiness, there is no better way than to take a good-quality practice exam and pass with a score of 70 percent or better. If you pass an exam at 80 percent or better, you're probably in great shape.

Assessing Readiness For Exam 70-015

In addition to the general exam-readiness information in the previous section, there are several things you can do to prepare for the Visual C++ 6 Distributed exam. As you're getting ready for Exam 70-015, you can cruise the Web looking for "braindumps" (recollections of test topics and experiences recorded by others) to help you anticipate topics you're likely to encounter on the test. A good place to start is Dunham Software's Web site (www.dunhamsoftware.com/cert.htm).

You can't be sure that a braindump's author can provide correct answers. Thus, use the questions to guide your studies, but don't rely on the answers in a braindump to lead you to the truth. Double-check everything you find in any braindump.

Microsoft exam mavens also recommend checking the Microsoft Knowledge Base (available on its own CD-ROM as part of the TechNet collection, or on the Microsoft Web site at **http://support.microsoft.com/support/**) for "meaningful technical support issues" that relate to your exam's topics. Although I'm not sure exactly what the quoted phrase means, I have also noticed some overlap between technical support questions on particular products and troubleshooting questions on the exams for those products.

A final note: As you review the material for that exam, you'll realize that real-world Visual C++ development experience will be invaluable. Although there will undoubtedly be some "paper MCSDs" emerging from the examination process, the exams are increasingly being designed to pose real-world problems. For these types of questions, book learning simply can't replace having actually "done it."

Onward, Through The Fog!

After you've assessed your readiness, undertaken the right background studies, obtained the hands-on experience that will help you understand the products and technologies at work, and reviewed the many sources of information to help you prepare for a test, you'll be ready to take a round of practice tests. When your scores come back positive enough to get you through the exam, you're ready to go after the real thing. If you follow this assessment regime, you'll not only know what you need to study, but when you're ready to make a test date at Sylvan or VUE. Good luck!

Microsoft
Certification Exams

Terms you'll need to understand:

√ Radio button

√ Checkbox

√ Exhibit

√ Multiple-choice question formats

√ Careful reading

√ Process of elimination

√ Adaptive tests

√ Fixed-length tests

√ Simulations

Techniques you'll need to master:

√ Assessing your exam-readiness

√ Preparing to take a certification exam

√ Practicing (to make perfect)

√ Making the best use of the testing software

√ Budgeting your time

√ Saving the hardest questions until last

√ Guessing (as a last resort)

Exam taking is not something that most people anticipate eagerly, no matter how well prepared they may be. In most cases, familiarity helps offset test anxiety. In plain English, this means you probably won't be as nervous when you take your fourth or fifth Microsoft certification exam as you'll be when you take your first one.

Whether it's your first exam or your tenth, understanding the details of exam taking (how much time to spend on questions, the environment you'll be in, and so on) and the exam software will help you concentrate on the material rather than on the setting. Likewise, mastering a few basic exam-taking skills should help you recognize—and perhaps even outfox—some of the tricks and snares you're bound to find in some of the exam questions.

This chapter, besides explaining the exam environment and software, describes some proven exam-taking strategies that you should be able to use to your advantage.

Assessing Exam-Readiness

Before you take any more Microsoft exams, I strongly recommend that you read through and take the Self-Assessment included with this book (it appears just before this chapter, in fact). This will help you compare your knowledge base to the requirements for obtaining an MCSD, and it will also help you identify parts of your background or experience that may be in need of improvement, enhancement, or further learning. If you get the right set of basics under your belt, obtaining Microsoft certification will be that much easier.

Once you've gone through the Self-Assessment, you can remedy those topical areas where your background or experience may not measure up to an ideal certification candidate. But you can also tackle subject matter for individual tests at the same time, so you can continue making progress while you're catching up in some areas.

Once you've worked through an *Exam Cram*, have read the supplementary materials, and have taken the practice test, you'll have a pretty clear idea of when you should be ready to take the real exam. I strongly recommend that you keep practicing until your scores top the 70 percent mark; 75 percent would be a good goal to give yourself some margin for error in a real exam situation (where stress will play more of a role than when you practice). Once you hit that point, you should be ready to go. But if you get through the practice exam in this book without attaining that score, you should keep taking practice tests and studying the materials until you get there. You'll find more information about other practice test vendors in the Self-Assessment, along with even more pointers on how to study and prepare. But now, on to the exam!

The Exam Situation

When you arrive at the testing center where you scheduled your exam, you'll need to sign in with an exam coordinator. He or she will ask you to show two forms of identification, one of which must be a photo ID. After you've signed in and your time slot arrives, you'll be asked to deposit any books, bags, or other items you brought with you. Then, you'll be escorted into a closed room. Typically, the room will be furnished with anywhere from one to half a dozen computers, and each workstation will be separated from the others by dividers designed to keep you from seeing what's happening on someone else's computer.

You'll be furnished with a pen or pencil and a blank sheet of paper, or, in some cases, an erasable plastic sheet and an erasable pen. You're allowed to write down anything you want on both sides of this sheet. Before the exam, you should memorize as much of the material that appears on The Cram Sheet (in the front of this book) as you can, so you can write that information on the blank sheet as soon as you are seated in front of the computer. You can refer to your rendition of The Cram Sheet anytime you like during the test, but you'll have to surrender the sheet when you leave the room.

Most test rooms feature a wall with a large picture window. This permits the exam coordinator to monitor the room, to prevent exam-takers from talking to one another, and to observe anything out of the ordinary that might go on. The exam coordinator will have preloaded the appropriate Microsoft certification exam—for this book, that's Exam 70-015—and you'll be permitted to start as soon as you're seated in front of the computer.

All Microsoft certification exams allow a certain maximum amount of time in which to complete your work (this time is indicated on the exam by an onscreen counter/clock, so you can check the time remaining whenever you like). The fixed-length Visual C++ Distributed exam consists of 50 randomly selected questions. You may take up to 90 minutes to complete the exam.

All Microsoft certification exams are computer generated and use a multiple-choice format. Although this may sound quite simple, the questions are constructed not only to check your mastery of basic facts and figures of Visual C++ and related tools and technologies, but they also require you to evaluate one or more sets of circumstances or requirements. Often, you'll be asked to give more than one answer to a question. Likewise, you might be asked to select the best or most effective solution to a problem from a range of choices, all of which technically are correct. Taking an exam is quite an adventure, and it involves real thinking. This book shows you what to expect and how to deal with the potential problems, puzzles, and predicaments.

Some Microsoft exams employ more advanced testing capabilities than might immediately meet the eye. Although the questions that appear are still multiple choice, the logic that drives them is more complex than older Microsoft tests, which use a fixed sequence of questions (called a *fixed-length* computerized exam). Other exams employ a sophisticated user interface (which Microsoft calls a *simulation*) to test your knowledge of the software and systems under consideration in a more or less "live" environment that behaves just like the original.

For some exams, Microsoft has turned to a well-known technique, called *adaptive testing*, to establish a test-taker's level of knowledge and product competence. These exams look the same as fixed-length exams, but an adaptive exam discovers the level of difficulty at and below which an individual test-taker can correctly answer questions. At the same time, Microsoft is in the process of converting some of its fixed-length exams into adaptive exams as well.

Test-takers with differing levels of knowledge or ability therefore see different sets of questions; individuals with high levels of knowledge or ability are presented with a smaller set of more difficult questions, whereas individuals with lower levels of knowledge are presented with a larger set of easier questions. Both individuals may answer the same percentage of questions correctly, but the test-taker with a higher knowledge or ability level will score higher because his or her questions are worth more.

Also, the lower-level test-taker will probably answer more questions than his or her more knowledgeable colleague. This explains why adaptive tests use ranges of values to define the number of questions and the amount of time it takes to complete the test.

Adaptive tests work by evaluating the test-taker's most recent answer. A correct answer leads to a more difficult question (and the test software's estimate of the test-taker's knowledge and ability level is raised). An incorrect answer leads to a less difficult question (and the test software's estimate of the test-taker's knowledge and ability level is lowered). This process continues until the test targets the test-taker's true ability level. The exam ends when the test-taker's level of accuracy meets a statistically acceptable value (in other words, when his or her performance demonstrates an acceptable level of knowledge and ability) or when the maximum number of items has been presented (in which case, the test-taker is almost certain to fail).

Microsoft tests come in one form or the other—either they're fixed-length or they're adaptive. Therefore, you must take the test in whichever form it appears—you can't choose one form over another. However, if anything, it pays off even more to prepare thoroughly for an adaptive exam than for a fixed-length one: The penalties for answering incorrectly are built into the test itself on an adaptive exam, whereas the layout remains the same for a fixed-length test, no matter how many questions you answer incorrectly.

> The biggest difference between an adaptive test and a fixed-length test is that, on a fixed-length test, you can revisit questions after you've read them over one or more times. On an adaptive test, you must answer the question when it's presented, and you'll have no opportunities to revisit that question thereafter. As of this writing, the Visual C++ Distributed exam is a fixed-length exam, but this can change at any time. Therefore, you must prepare as if it were an adaptive exam to ensure the best possible results.

In the section that follows, you'll learn more about what Microsoft test questions look like and how they must be answered.

Exam Layout And Design

Some exam questions require you to select a single answer, whereas others ask you to select one or more correct answers. The following multiple-choice question requires you to select a single correct answer. Following the question is a brief summary of each potential answer and why it is either right or wrong.

Question 1

Which debug feature activates the debugger when any program on your computer faults?

○ a. Edit and continue

○ b. Just-in-time debugging

○ c. COFF debug information

○ d. Any program compiled with the **_ACTIVEDEBUG** flag set

The correct answer is b. The just-in-time debugger can be enabled in the Debug tab of the Options dialog box, available from the Tools menu. Answer a is incorrect because the edit and continue feature allows you to modify code on the fly during a debug session. Answer c is incorrect because the COFF format is a different way of storing debug information. Answer d is incorrect because there is no _ACTIVEDEBUG flag.

This sample question format corresponds closely to the Microsoft certification exam format—the only difference on the exam is that questions are not followed by answer keys. To select an answer, position the cursor over the radio button next to the answer. Then, click the mouse button to select the answer.

Let's examine a question where one or more answers are possible. This type of question provides checkboxes rather than radio buttons for marking all appropriate selections.

Question 2

Which of these statements applies to stored procedures? [Check all correct answers]

❑ a. Stored procedures receive input parameters and return output parameters.

❑ b. Stored procedures cannot return more than one row of data.

❑ c. System stored procedures may only be invoked by a highly privileged database administrator.

❑ d. A stored procedure may not call a system stored procedure.

❑ e. Stored procedures improve application performance.

Answers a and e are correct. Answer b is incorrect because, unlike other RDBMS products, SQL Server can return as many rows within as many result sets as needed to a client. Answer c is incorrect because anybody can call any system stored procedure as long as they have the privilege to do so; for example, most sp_helpxxx procedures are callable by anyone. Likewise, answer d is incorrect because a stored procedure may call any other stored procedure regardless of whether it was supplied by the vendor or not.

For this type of question, more than one answer may be required. As far as can be determined (and Microsoft won't comment), such questions are scored as wrong unless all the required selections are chosen. In other words, a partially correct answer does not result in partial credit when the test is scored. For Question 2, you have to check the boxes next to items a and e to obtain credit for a correct answer. Notice that picking the right answers also means knowing why the other answers are wrong.

Although these two basic types of questions can appear in many forms, they constitute the foundation on which all the Microsoft certification exam questions rest. More complex questions include exhibits, which are usually screenshots of various Visual C++ tools or utilities. For some of these questions, you'll be asked to make a selection by clicking on a checkbox or radio button on the screenshot itself. For others, you'll be expected to use the information displayed therein to guide your answer to the question. Familiarity with the underlying tool or utility is your key to choosing the correct answer(s).

Other questions involving exhibits use charts or network diagrams to help document a workplace scenario that you'll be asked to troubleshoot or configure. Careful attention to such exhibits is the key to success. Be prepared to toggle frequently between the exhibit and the question as you work.

Recognizing Your Test Type: Fixed-Length Or Adaptive

When you begin your exam, the software will tell you the test is adaptive, if in fact the version you're taking is presented as an adaptive test. If your introductory materials fail to mention this, you're probably taking a fixed-length test. However, when you look at your first question, you'll be able to tell for sure: If it includes a checkbox that lets you mark the question (for later return and review) you'll know you're taking a fixed-length test, because adaptive test questions can only be visited (and answered) once, and they include no such checkbox.

The Fixed-Length Test-Taking Strategy

A well-known principle when taking fixed-length exams is to first read over the entire exam from start to finish while answering only those questions you feel absolutely sure of. On subsequent passes, you can dive into more complex questions more deeply, knowing how many such questions you have left. On adaptive tests, you get only one shot at the question, which is why preparation is so crucial for such tests.

Fortunately, the Microsoft exam software for fixed-length tests makes the multiple-visit approach easy to implement. At the top-left corner of each question is a checkbox that permits you to mark that question for a later visit. (Note that marking questions makes review easier, but you can return to any question if you're willing to click the Forward or Back buttons repeatedly.) As you read each question, if you answer only those you're sure of and mark for review those that you're not sure of, you can keep working through a decreasing list of questions as you answer the trickier ones in order.

There's at least one potential benefit to reading the exam over completely before answering the trickier questions: Sometimes, information supplied in later questions will shed more light on earlier questions. Other times, information you read in later questions might jog your memory about Visual C++ facts, figures, or behavior that also will help with earlier questions. Either way, you'll come out ahead if you defer those questions about which you're not absolutely sure.

Here are some question-handling strategies that apply only to fixed-length tests. Use them if you have the chance:

➤ When returning to a question after your initial read-through, read every word again—otherwise, your mind can fall quickly into a rut. Sometimes, revisiting a question after turning your attention elsewhere lets you see something you missed, but the strong tendency is to see what you've seen before. Try to avoid that tendency at all costs.

➤ If you return to a question more than twice, try to articulate to yourself what you don't understand about the question, why the answers don't appear to make sense, or what appears to be missing. If you chew on the subject for awhile, your subconscious might provide the details that are lacking, or you might notice a "trick" that will point to the right answer.

As you work your way through the exam, another counter that Microsoft thankfully provides will come in handy—the number of questions completed and questions outstanding. For fixed-length tests, it's wise to budget your time by making sure that you've completed one-quarter of the questions one-quarter of the way through the exam period (or the first 12 questions in the first 22 minutes) and three-quarters of the questions three-quarters of the way through (38 questions in the first 68 minutes).

If you're not finished when 85 minutes have elapsed, use the last 5 minutes to guess your way through the remaining questions. Remember, guessing is potentially more valuable than not answering, because blank answers are always wrong, but a guess may turn out to be right. If you don't have a clue about any of the remaining questions, pick answers at random, or choose all a's, b's, and so on. The important thing is to submit an exam for scoring that has an answer for every question.

At the very end of your exam period, you're better off guessing than leaving questions unanswered.

The Adaptive Test-Taking Strategy

If there's one principle that applies to taking an adaptive test, it could be summed up as "Get it right the first time." You cannot elect to skip a question and move on to the next one when taking an adaptive test, because the testing software uses your answer to the current question to select whatever question it plans to present to you next. Also, you cannot return to a question once you've moved on, because the software only gives you one chance to answer the question.

When you answer a question correctly, you are presented with a more difficult question next to help the software gauge your level of skill and ability. When you answer a question incorrectly, you are presented with a less difficult question, and the software lowers its current estimate of your skill and ability. This continues until the program settles into a reasonably accurate estimate of what you know and can do, and it takes you through somewhere between 25 and 35 questions, on average, as you complete the test.

The good news is that if you know your stuff, you'll probably finish most adaptive tests in 30 minutes or so. The bad news is that you must really, really know your stuff to do your best on an adaptive test. That's because some questions are so convoluted, complex, or hard to follow that you're bound to miss one or two, at a minimum, even if you do know your stuff. Therefore, the more you know, the better you'll do on an adaptive test, even accounting for the occasionally weird or unfathomable question that appears on these exams.

As of this writing, Microsoft has not advertised which tests are strictly adaptive. You'll be best served by preparing for the exam as if it were adaptive. That way, you should be prepared to pass no matter what kind of test you take (that is, fixed-length or adaptive). If you do end up taking a fixed-length test, remember the tips from the preceding section. They should help you improve on what you could do on an adaptive test.

If you encounter a question on an adaptive test that you can't answer, you must guess an answer. Because of the way the software works, you may have to suffer for your guess on the next question if you guess right, because you'll get a more difficult question next.

Exam-Taking Basics

The most important advice about taking any exam is this: Read each question carefully. Some questions are deliberately ambiguous, some use double negatives, and others use terminology in incredibly precise ways. I have taken numerous exams—both practice and live—and in nearly every one have missed at least one question because I didn't read it closely or carefully enough.

Here are some suggestions on how to deal with the tendency to jump to an answer too quickly:

➤ Make sure you read every word in the question. If you find yourself jumping ahead impatiently, go back and start over.

➤ As you read, try to restate the question in your own terms. If you can do this, you should be able to pick the correct answer(s) much more easily.

Above all, try to deal with each question by thinking through what you know about Visual C++ as well as the design and implementation of Win32 distributed applications—the characteristics, behaviors, facts, and figures involved. By reviewing what you know (and what you've written down on your information sheet), you'll often recall or understand things sufficiently to determine the answer to the question.

Question-Handling Strategies

Based on exams I have taken, some interesting trends have become apparent. For those questions that take only a single answer, usually two or three of the answers will be obviously incorrect, and two of the answers will be plausible—of course, only one can be correct. Unless the answer leaps out at you (if it does, reread the question to look for a trick; sometimes those are the ones you're most likely to get wrong), begin the process of answering by eliminating those answers that are most obviously wrong.

Things to look for in obviously wrong answers include spurious menu choices or utility names, nonexistent software options, and terminology you've never seen. If you've done your homework for an exam, no valid information should be completely new to you. In that case, unfamiliar or bizarre terminology probably indicates a totally bogus answer.

Numerous questions assume that the default behavior of a particular utility is in effect. If you know the defaults and understand what they mean, this knowledge will help you cut through many Gordian knots.

Mastering The Inner Game

In the final analysis, knowledge breeds confidence, and confidence breeds success. If you study the materials in this book carefully and review all the practice questions at the end of each chapter, you should become aware of those areas where additional learning and study are required.

Next, follow up by reading some or all of the materials recommended in the "Need To Know More?" section at the end of each chapter. The idea is to become familiar enough with the concepts and situations you find in the sample questions that you can reason your way through similar situations on a real exam. If you know the material, you have every right to be confident that you can pass the exam.

After you've worked your way through the book, take the practice exam in Chapter 13. This will provide a reality check and help you identify areas to study further. Make sure you follow up and review materials related to questions you miss on the practice exam before scheduling a real exam. Only when you've covered all the ground and feel comfortable with the whole scope of the practice exam should you take a real one.

 If you take the practice exam and don't score at least 75 percent correct, you'll want to practice further. Though one is not available for Visual C++ Distributed yet, Microsoft usually provides free Personal Exam Prep (PEP) exams and the self-assessment exams from the Microsoft Certified Professional Web site's download page (its location appears in the next section). If you're more ambitious or better funded, you might want to purchase a practice exam from a third-party vendor.

Armed with the information in this book and with the determination to augment your knowledge, you should be able to pass the certification exam. However, you need to work at it, or you'll spend the exam fee more than once before you finally pass. If you prepare seriously, you should do well. Good luck!

Additional Resources

A good source of information about Microsoft certification exams comes from Microsoft itself. Because its products and technologies—and the exams that go with them—change frequently, the best place to go for exam-related information is online.

If you haven't already visited the Microsoft Certified Professional site, do so right now. The MCP home page resides at **www.microsoft.com/mcp** (see Figure 1.1).

Note: This page might not be there by the time you read this, or it might have been replaced by something new and different, because things change regularly on the Microsoft site. Should this happen, please read the sidebar titled "Coping With Change On The Web."

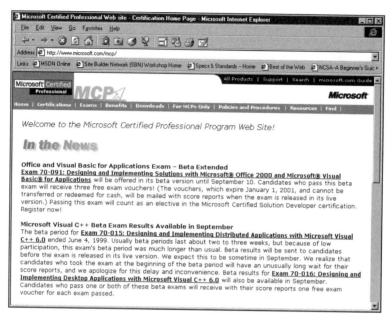

Figure 1.1 The Microsoft Certified Professional Program Web site.

The menu options on this site point to the most important sources of information in the MCP pages. Here's what to check out:

➤ *Certifications*—Use this menu entry to pick whichever certification program you want to read about.

➤ *Exams*—Use this menu entry to pull up a search tool that lets you list all Microsoft exams and locate all exams relevant to any Microsoft certification (MCP, MCP+SB, MCSD, and so on) or those exams that cover a particular product. This tool is quite useful not only to examine the options but also to obtain specific exam preparation information, because each exam has its own associated preparation guide.

➤ *Downloads*—Use this menu entry to find a list of the files and practice exams that Microsoft makes available to the public. These include several items worth downloading, especially the Certification Update, the Personal Exam Prep (PEP) exams, various assessment exams, and a general exam study guide. Try to make time to peruse these materials before taking your first exam.

These are just the high points of what's available in the Microsoft Certified Professional pages. As you browse through them—and I strongly recommend that you do—you'll probably find other informational tidbits mentioned that are every bit as interesting and compelling.

Coping With Change On The Web

Sooner or later, all the information I've shared with you about the Microsoft Certified Professional pages and the other Web-based resources mentioned throughout the rest of this book will go stale or be replaced by newer information. In some cases, the URLs you find here might lead you to their replacements; in other cases, the URLs will go nowhere, leaving you with the dreaded "404 File not found" error message. When that happens, don't give up.

You can always find what you want on the Web if you're willing to invest some time and energy. Most large or complex Web sites—and Microsoft's qualifies on both counts—offer a search engine. On all of Microsoft's Web pages, a Search button appears along the top edge of the page. As long as you can get to Microsoft's site (it should stay at **www.microsoft.com** for a long time), use this tool to help you find what you need.

The more focused you can make a search request, the more likely the results will include information you want. For example, search for the string "training and certification" to produce a lot of data about the subject in general, but if you're looking for a preparation guide for Exam 70-015, "Designing and Implementing Distributed Applications with Microsoft Visual C++ 6.0," you'll be more likely to get there quickly if you use a search string similar to the following:

```
"Exam 70-015" AND "preparation guide"
```

Likewise, if you want to find the Training and Certification downloads, try a search string such as this:

```
"training and certification" AND "download page"
```

Finally, feel free to use general search tools—such as **www.search.com**, **www.altavista.com**, and **www.excite.com**—to look for related information. Although Microsoft offers great information about its certification exams online, there are plenty of third-party sources of information and assistance that need not follow Microsoft's party line. Therefore, if you can't find something where the book says it lives, intensify your search.

The Development Environment

Terms you'll need to understand:

√ Integrated Development Environment (IDE)

√ Microsoft Data Access Components (MDAC)

√ Microsoft Management Console (MMC)

√ Microsoft Transaction Server (MTS)

√ Microsoft Message Queue Server (MSMQ)

√ Preprocessor definitions

√ Compiler switches

√ Libraries

√ Source management

√ Microsoft Distributed Transaction Coordinator (MS DTC)

Techniques you'll need to master:

√ Installing Visual C++ and supplemental products

√ Using AppWizard and ClassWizard

√ Modifying project settings

√ Installing SourceSafe, assigning permissions to users, and managing projects

√ Installing MTS, MSMQ, and SQL Server

√ Creating and deploying MTS application executables

Visual C++'s development environment is made up of many components: SourceSafe, SQL Server, Microsoft Transaction Server, and Microsoft Message Queue Server. After an overview of Visual C++ and its uses, I'll delve into an in-depth description of these components.

Overview Of Visual C++

Microsoft's Visual C++ product provides both a sophisticated programming editor—in the form of the Integrated Development Environment (IDE)—and powerful machine-code-generation tools, with an optimizing compiler and incremental linker. The IDE offers a number of *wizards* that can generate common template code for you. A drag-and-drop metaphor helps you construct user-interface components.

Editions And Features

Visual C++ is offered in the following three editions:

➤ *Standard*—The Standard Edition was formerly known as the *Learning Edition*. This edition allows only static linking to the MFC libraries.

➤ *Professional*—The Professional Edition supports the creation of applications, services, and controls for all of the Windows operating systems. This edition does not offer SQL debugging, Visual Modeler, or Internet Information Server (IIS).

➤ *Enterprise*—The Enterprise Edition supports all of the tools necessary to develop and debug n-tier architecture solutions. In addition, this product includes MTS and SQL Server.

Installation Issues

At the installation stage, you have two drawbacks to consider:

➤ Side-by-side installation is not supported.

➤ On a dual-boot computer, Visual C++ is installed in different locations.

NT Option Pack

The NT Option Pack is part of the distribution media that ships with Visual Studio Enterprise Edition, or it can be downloaded separately from Microsoft.

Installation

The NT Option Pack requires NT 4 (Server or Workstation) and Service Pack 3 to be installed. Alpha or beta versions of IIS must be uninstalled before Option Pack is installed.

Components

The following components are distributed in the NT Option Pack (the Custom Setup option allows you to install only those components you require):

➤ *Internet Information Server (IIS)*—Microsoft's Internet Information Server is a Web application server for Windows NT.

➤ *Microsoft Data Access Components (MDAC)*—The Option Pack supplies the most recent data-access components. These components provide access to a variety of data sources, including those that support the Open Database Connectivity (ODBC) and/or SQL standards, as well as nonrelational stores. The MDAC package provides support for ActiveX Data Objects (ADO), Object Linking and Embedding Database (OLE DB), and ODBC drivers and services.

➤ *Microsoft Management Console (MMC)*—The Microsoft Management Console offers single-point enterprise management that is both extensible and intelligible. The MMC offers an Explorer-like view of systems and services that are "snapped in." From a developer perspective, the Active Template Library (ATL) offers excellent support for the construction of MMC snap-in components.

➤ *Microsoft Transaction Server (MTS)*—Microsoft's transaction server is a component-based, scalable transaction engine.

➤ *Microsoft Message Queue (MSMQ) Server*—A message queue offers cost-based message routing and resilience to systems operating over unreliable communication links.

➤ *Systems Network Architecture (SNA) Server*—Microsoft's SNA Server implements an SNA-compatible data transport that connects the local Type 2.1 node to a remote host (PU4/5) and/or peer (PU2.1) system.

Server-Side Dependencies

The development of systems that make up an n-tier architecture requires both the major tier platform applications and the tools necessary to debug, deploy, and manage those systems. Following is a list of installation requirements for the Option Pack and its components:

➤ *Windows NT Option Pack 4*—Provides limited support on Windows 95 (that is, DCOM support).

➤ *SQL Server 7*—Developer Edition requires NT Workstation 4 or NT Server 4. Only some tools install on Windows 95.

➤ *SQL Server Debugging Service*—Requires SQL Server 6.5 (SP3) or better. Does not require Internet Explorer.

➤ *Visual SourceSafe Server Components*—Require Internet Explorer 4+ for HTML Help viewing.

➤ *Posting Acceptor 2*—Requires installation of NT Option Pack prior to installation of Posting Acceptor.

➤ *Remote Machine Debugging (Script Debugging)*—No special instructions.

➤ *Visual InterDev Server Components*—Install NT Option Pack, Microsoft Data Access Components, and FrontPage Extensions first.

➤ *FrontPage Server Extensions*—Install NT Option Pack and Microsoft Data Access Components before FrontPage Extensions.

➤ *Visual Studio Analyzer*—No special instructions.

➤ *Application Performance Explorer*—No special instructions.

➤ *MDAC 2 Update*—Install after NT Option Pack and before SNA Server.

➤ *SNA Server*—Install after Microsoft Data Access Components and Microsoft Transaction Server.

Unless otherwise specified, the following conditions apply for all component installations:

➤ Services run only under Windows NT.

➤ The Option Pack requires Internet Explorer 4+, unless otherwise specified.

➤ Internet Explorer 4+ supplies DCOM support for Windows 95 machines.

➤ All server components require NT Server 4 or NT Workstation 4 (unless specified).

Integrated Development Environment—Wizards

Visual C++ offers a number of code generators, in the guise of wizards, to help you during initialization and development of your software project. These include AppWizard, ClassWizard, and ATL Object Wizard.

➤ *AppWizard*—You can display the AppWizard selection list by selecting File|New from the menu and displaying the Projects tab. Important AppWizards include:

 ➤ Microsoft Foundation Class (MFC) AppWizard (DLL and EXE)

 ➤ MFC ActiveX ControlWizard

➤ ISAPI Extension Wizard

➤ ATL COM AppWizard

➤ Custom AppWizard

➤ *ClassWizard*—The most commonly used wizard when developing MFC- or ATL-based applications is the ClassWizard. It is almost essential when you want to define a message handler, create a class, respond to ActiveX events, and define an Automation interface.

➤ *ATL Object Wizard*—The ATL Object Wizard offers code generation support based on C++ templates, as opposed to ClassWizard's generation of classes, functions, and macros utilizing MFC's object hierarchy. ATL objects can be added to either ATL- or MFC-based projects. If you are using ATL in your MFC project, you must make sure that the project has been configured for ATL support.

Integrated Development Environment— Workspace

The *workspace* is a dockable window that provides three tabbed panes: ClassView, ResourceView, and FileView. Each pane contains a tree control whose root node is the Project Workspace, which may contain information for one or more projects.

 A project workspace may contain multiple projects. The default project's folder name is represented with bold type.

➤ *ClassView*—The first level of the tree includes the project's classes, interfaces, and globals. Globals and classes can be expanded to reveal their functions and variables. An interface can be expanded to reveal its methods and properties.

The context menu for classes offers access to many ClassWizard functions, including adding a member function or variable and adding a Windows message handler. The corresponding menu for interfaces allows the creation of methods and properties.

The context menus for functions and variables allow navigation to the corresponding definitions and/or declarations. The context menu for interface methods and properties simply offers to navigate to the declaration. ActiveX control interfaces allow the definition of new events.

➤ *ResourceView*—The ResourceView tree is arranged such that each resource category—such as Accelerator Table, Cursor, Dialog, and Menu—is given a top-level folder. Expansion of a resource folder displays the resources of that type.

The context menu for the resource view allows the import of resources contained within other files. Insert, Copy, and Export menus round out the powerful resource management functions offered by this view.

➤ *FileView*—The FileView displays a logical representation of the projects and files in the workspace. This logical view does not necessarily reflect their physical disk organization.

This tab also displays the source control management's state for each file, if you have SourceSafe installed on your computer and if the project(s) in your workspace have been introduced to source management.

Similar to the Workspace window, the Output window offers a number of tabs that aid in a program's creation and debugging. These tabs include Build, Find Results, Debug, Results, and SQL Debugging.

Using Visual C++

In Visual C++, the *project workspace* contains one or more projects. Each project may be created with a different AppWizard (MFC AppWizard, ISAPI Extension Wizard, ATL COM AppWizard, and so on). When you create a project workspace, a DSW file is created to store workspace-related information. The workspace also creates default DSP and OPT files for single projects. Table 2.1 contains more information regarding these files.

A Visual C++ project contains all of the files that are necessary to compile, link, and debug your application. When you start a project in Visual C++, AppWizard generates the files listed in Table 2.1.

Important Preprocessor Definitions

A number of preprocessor definitions are important to the Visual C++ developer, including:

➤ _WIN32—This symbol identifies the application as one that requires the Win32 runtime program to execute.

➤ _DEBUG/_NDEBUG—The compiler defines the _DEBUG symbol when you specify the /MTd or /Mdd option.

Table 2.1	Common working files needed to complete a Visual C++ application.
File/Extension	**Description**
DSW	The workspace file organizes all the projects in a single workspace.
OPT	The workspace options file contains individual user settings. Therefore, this file is generally not introduced into source management.
DSP	The project's makefile information is stored in this file. For previous releases of Visual C++, this information was stored in a MAK file.
CLW	The Visual C++ ClassWizard stores its information in this file.
ODL	The Object Description Language file contains OLE interface and type library definitions.
NCB	This extension, which stands for "No Compile Browser," contains information useful for the Component Gallery, ClassView, and the WizardBar.
README.TXT	Visual C++ generates a text file that describes each of the generated files and its purpose.

➤ _WINDOWS—Defines the _WINDOWS symbol for all source files in the project. This definition is not appropriate for console applications.

➤ _AFXDLL/_USRDLL—MFC offers support for two types of DLLs: those that contain a CWinApp object and those that share an existing CWinApp object. An _AFXDLL shares the MFC library with an application, therefore not requiring its own instance of CWinApp. Such a DLL requires a special version of DllMain()and a DLL initialization export.

➤ _MBCS/_UNICODE—The Visual C++ compiler supports three character-mapping modes: single-byte (default), multibyte (_MBCS), and Unicode (_UNICODE).

Important Compiler Switches

Before you can distribute release builds of your program, you need to be aware of Visual C++'s compiler switches and the importance they have for your programming needs. The following sections give details about these switches.

Calling Convention (/Gd, /Gr, /Gz)

Several compiler switches determine the order of stack construction for function call definitions. This information is used to determine who is responsible for removing arguments from the stack (the caller or the callee) and the name-decorating convention. The following list explains each of these calling switches:

➤ */Gd*—The /Gd option is the default compiler setting, utilizing the __cdecl naming convention, which specifies the C calling convention for all functions that are not members of a C++ class.

➤ */Gr*—Instructs the compiler to use the __fastcall specification, passing some arguments in the microprocessor's registers. This calling convention is specific to Intel platform builds only.

➤ */Gz*—The __stdcall convention pushes arguments on the stack from right to left and requires C prototype definitions for all functions.

Disable/Debug (/Od)

This option suppresses all code optimizations, speeding the compilation process. This option is available only in the Professional and Enterprise Editions (the Standard Edition does not support optimization switches). With the /Od switch, code movement is suppressed and the debugging process is simplified.

Runtime Library (/MD, /ML, /MT, /LD)

These compiler options identify the runtime library to be associated with the produced executable. The lowercase "d" at the end of a switch specifies the debug version of the library and defines the _DEBUG symbol:

➤ */MD, /MDd*—This switch indicates that the multithreaded DLL runtime libraries should be used. This switch also defines the _MT and _DLL symbols. The msvcrt.lib file is used to resolve externals and requires that the msvcrt.dll or msvcrtd.dll files be present at runtime.

➤ */ML, /MLd*—This switch indicates that the single-threaded libc.lib file will be used to resolve runtime externals.

➤ */MT, /MTd*—This switch selects the multithreaded versions of the statically linked runtimes. The _MT symbol is defined.

➤ */LD, /LDd*—This switch passes the /DLL option to the linker. This option is used to create a DLL.

Warning Level (/Wn)

The compiler defines warning levels from zero to four, where /W0 instructs the compiler not to issue warnings (even if they exist). The warning levels range from /W4 (lowest sensitivity) through /W1 (highest sensitivity).

Minimal Rebuild (/Gm)

This option speeds the build/debug cycle by allowing the compiler to maintain a database of C++ method signatures and to not recompile header (H) files if only the body of such functions changes.

Preprocessor Definition (/D)

This option defines symbol or constant preprocessor labels as command-line arguments to the compiler. This option affects code generation in a manner that is identical to #define statements contained in the actual code.

Precompiled Header (/Yc, /Fp, /Yu)

The first option—/Yc—instructs the compiler to generate a precompiled header (PCH) file. Without a file name provided, the compiler compiles code in the specified source file. If the /Yc option is followed by a file name, like /Yc "stdafx.h" (the default Visual C++ setting), the compiler compiles the code up to and including the specified header file.

The /Fp option allows you to specify the name and path for the precompiled header file. To instruct the compiler to use the existing precompiled header, specify /Yu.

Program Database (/Fd)

The /Fd compiler option requires a file name to follow, specifying the name for the PDB file (other than the default).

Catch Release-Build Errors In Debug Build (/GZ)

It is not uncommon to write code that works fine during development (in debug builds), but has problems (stack or otherwise) when built for release. This option changes code generation in the following two ways:

➤ Initializes all nonexplicitly set variables to a 0xCC value.

➤ Inserts code to verify that the stack pointer is not changed after a function call.

Debug Info (/Zd, /Z7, /Zi, /ZI)

The compiler offers a number of debug options that determine the type of debug information to be created and the location of the debug information. Debug information can be stored either in a program database (PDB) or in the compiled object (OBJ). The debug options are as follows:

➤ /Zd—By storing line numbers only, this option reduces the amount of debug information that is contained in the compiled object. This option does not include symbolic information, so the debugger's expression evaluator will not operate.

➤ /Z7—Use this option to produce object files that contain C 7-compatible debug information. This option includes line numbers and all symbolic debug information.

➤ /Zi—This option stores all debug information in a program database file, thus offering a small object file while still supporting debugging efforts.

➤ /ZI—New to Visual C++ 6, this option also stores debug information in a program database file, but it supports a format that allows operation of the Edit And Continue feature.

File Dependencies (/FD)

The Update Dependencies function is no longer available in the Visual C++ 6 compiler. Instead, the /FD switch ensures that the most reliable dependency information is used to build your project.

As a side note: Visual C++ 6 now supports dependency information placed in a separate, editable text file.

Libraries

A number of C runtime libraries form the foundation of Visual C++ applications. These libraries fall into two primary categories: debug and nondebug. In each of these categories are three libraries. In the nondebug category, the libraries are as follows:

➤ *libc.lib*—Supports single-threaded applications and is statically linked to the executable.

➤ *libcmt.lib*—Supports multithreaded applications and is statically linked to the executable.

➤ *msvcrt.lib*—Supports multithreaded applications that dynamically link the runtime libraries to the executable. This file contains the import library for the msvcrt.dll.

In the debug category, the libraries are the same in function, but each file name ends with a "d" before the .lib extension, so the libraries are libcd.lib, libcmtd.lib, and msvcrtd.lib.

Project Settings

Use the Project Settings dialog box to identify and configure compiler and linker settings. This dialog box is available either from the Project menu or by right-clicking on a file in the FileView tab of the Workspace window.

SourceSafe

Microsoft's SourceSafe software can be used to manage document changes produced by any application, language, or tool.

Purpose

One of the most important practices in software development is employing a source-control-management system. Source control is a critical tool for the release management process, and it ensures a level of safety and accountability in multiprogrammer development projects.

In more recent years, source control has become a highly popular method of maintaining Web site information. SourceSafe has always provided the ability to store files of any type. A Web site might use many different file types, including HTML, JPEG, and GIF. With the release of SourceSafe version 6, the product can verify hyperlinks and publish content to your Web server.

Platforms And Requirements

Microsoft recommends a Pentium-class computer for the client and server components of SourceSafe. Minimum operating-system requirements are either Windows 95/98 or Windows NT 4 with Service Pack 3. Both Unix and Macintosh variants are available through Microsoft partners. Additionally, a product named SourceOffSite offers an add-on product to SourceSafe that provides secure access to a SourceSafe database over the Internet.

Configuration Files

Two configuration files are important for SourceSafe operation. These configuration files are:

➤ *ss.ini*—This file contains information specific to an individual developer.

➤ *srcsafe.ini*—This file contains information for Visual SourceSafe's global variables.

Installation

SourceSafe is a typical client-server application. In a common configuration, the server-side installation is performed on a computer other than the computers on which the client software is installed. It is possible to install the client and server components on one computer, therefore making unnecessary a client installation on individual users' computers. (Of course, the proper licensing conditions must be met.)

Client

The client software can be installed from the SourceSafe distribution media or from a network drive. For a client installation from disk, you should select the Client option from the setup.exe program. You can also install the client software by double-clicking on the netsetup.exe program in the directory from which VSS is installed.

Server

A server installation of SourceSafe requires you to select the Server option from the setup.exe program that is part of the VSS distribution media.

The User Interface

SourceSafe offers two ways for creating projects and maintaining files. The first is a standalone utility, and the second involves integration with your Visual Studio environment.

Standalone File-Management Programs

SourceSafe offers a standalone file-management program named Microsoft Visual SourceSafe Explorer; see Figure 2.1. This client application can be deployed on every developer's desktop, allowing the rights assigned by an administrator to identify those projects or files that a user can view and change.

The Visual SourceSafe Administrator is another application, generally installed only on the computers of those in charge of configuration management. Configuration management allows the creation of source control databases, the

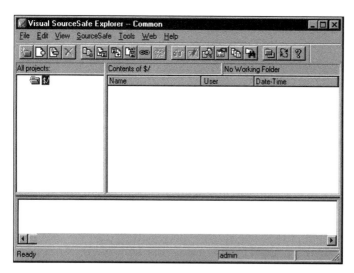

Figure 2.1 Microsoft Visual SourceSafe Explorer.

creation of user accounts, and privilege management for existing accounts. In addition, the Administrator program allows you to archive and restore source databases.

IDE Integration

SourceSafe can integrate directly into the Visual C++ environment. Additional toolbars and menus will be available in Developer Studio when both products are installed on the computer. You should not put workspace option files (OPT) into SourceSafe when you introduce the project to source control because these files contain information that is specific to each user's computer. The OPT file contains information regarding IDE window and toolbar layouts, which generally differ among developers.

Common Operations

Many of the source management functions you will perform on a daily basis using SourceSafe are intuitive and can be accomplished easily with the graphical tools. However, there are a few advanced functions, which you probably won't perform often, that require additional explanation.

Creating A Project

The SourceSafe hierarchy of file management places projects directly below the database. When logging into SourceSafe, you select the database to which you wish to connect. By default, the name given to this database is "Common," and its label designator is "$/". To create a project, simply use the Create Project option in the File menu. You must have the Add access privilege (on the parent object) to perform this operation.

You can also add projects to the SourceSafe database by displaying a project's context menu from the FileView tab of the Workspace window and selecting Add To Source Control.

Checking Files In And Out

Files under source control require a check-out process in order for changes to be made. Checking out a file places a writeable copy of the file on your computer.

Sharing

SourceSafe offers a powerful attribute to facilitate reuse with the **Share** command. This command allows a single instance of a component to be used with multiple projects in the SourceSafe environment. In this manner, changes made to the component from one project are immediately made available to other projects.

Branching

It is common in the software development process to take a file in two different directions, perhaps for a localization effort or for product stratification. Visual SourceSafe provides the **Branch** command for tracking the individual directions of the file as a project.

> *Note: The **Branch** command breaks any link that you established using the **Share** command.*

Multiple Checkouts And Merging Files

Visual SourceSafe can combine multiple changed copies of a file into a single file. The Multiple Checkout option allows more than one user at a time to check out a file for editing. When the files are checked back in, Visual Source-Safe automatically merges their contents. If the automatic merge detects conflicts, a visual merge tool is displayed. This tool identifies the differences between the files and allows you to identify what is to be placed in the master document file.

Binary Files

SourceSafe is capable of assigning version numbers to *binary* files—those that do not contain only character information, such as bitmaps or other resource formats. Visual SourceSafe, by default, assigns the binary file attribute to those files containing NULL characters. You may override this assignment if necessary.

Shadow Folders

A *shadow folder* is an optional view of the contents of a SourceSafe project; this folder contains the most recently checked-in version of each file in a project. A person with administrator privileges may initialize a centralized folder containing all of the files of a project. The shadow folder does not contain a master copy of the project files, nor should it be confused with a user's local working copy of the project files.

Cloaked Projects

A *cloaked* project is one in which the operations Get, Check In, Check Out, Undo Check Out, and Project Difference are not processed if they are attempted indirectly (i.e., as the result of a recursive operation). A cloaked project may have subprojects that are not cloaked. For these, a recursive **Get** command performed on the root project will result in the acquisition of files in only those subprojects that are not cloaked.

SQL Server

SQL Server 7 is the first in Microsoft's suite of next-generation back-office products. This release makes it easier to build, manage, and deploy database products with an emphasis on a reduction in total cost of ownership. This is accomplished by overhauling many of the management user interfaces, enhancing scalability and reliability, and supporting fast and simple programming models.

Platforms And Requirements

Microsoft SQL Server 7 is the first version that allows SQL Server to run on non-NT platforms—namely, Windows 95 and Windows 98. Microsoft provides two editions of SQL Server: Server and Desktop.

Server

With the release of SQL Server 7, Microsoft has introduced a number of new package options. The Server Edition is available for both Intel- and Alpha-based processor machines operating Windows NT 4 Server or NT Server 4 Enterprise Edition, both requiring Service Pack 4 (or later) installed. Internet Explorer 4.01 with Service Pack 1 (or later) is required. The Server Edition supports up to four processors, and the Enterprise Edition offers additional processor support.

Desktop

The Desktop Edition requirements are identical to those for the Server Edition, except that the Desktop Edition requires a per-seat client-access license for SQL Server 7. The Desktop Edition supports up to two processors.

Installation

The Installation Wizard for SQL Server 7 prompts you for information regarding the location of data files and an account from which you administer the process. By default, the SQL Server System Administrator Account, to which you assign a password, is "sa".

The SQL Server Settings dialog box, shown in Figure 2.2, allows you to configure properties, including the network protocol that is used to communicate between clients and the server. (The default protocol is Named Pipes.) In addition, a number of settings allow you to identify the default character set and sort order.

If you are upgrading from a version 6.x installation, you must choose the Unicode collation option. SQL Server 7's master database columns are Unicode versions of those contained in 6.x. Not choosing this option may result in the failure of user object conversions and the violation of uniqueness constraints.

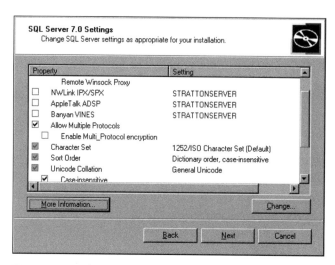

Figure 2.2   The SQL Server Settings dialog box.

Caveats

You should be aware of the following issues regarding the installation of SQL Server 7 and compatibility with previous versions and with other Microsoft products and components:

➤ SQL Server 7 is incompatible with Systems Management Server (SMS) 1.2. Installing SQL Server 7 without upgrading SMS will cause data to be lost. It is important that you upgrade to SMS 2—part of the BackOffice Server 4.5 distribution—before installing SQL Server 7.

➤ SQL Server 7 may reside on the same machine as version 6.5, but you should not install 7 in the directory that contains 6.5.

➤ The Microsoft Data Access Components (MDAC, version 2) are installed as part of the SQL Server 7 installation procedure. This package includes new ODBC components, requiring that applications using ODBC not be running.

Upgrading SQL Server 6.5 To 7

An Upgrade Wizard walks you through the migration process of transferring your server configuration and databases from a single 6.x SQL Server installation to SQL Server 7. The first step of the upgrade procedure offers options to define the data and object transfer. One of these options allows a tape device to serve as the transfer medium if disk space is at a premium. In addition, verification options allow you to specify the generation of a report comparing a list of objects, including schema and stored procedures. An exhaustive verification option performs a checksum for each column of each table before and after the upgrade. Further steps in the Upgrade Wizard involve selecting the code page (this might be important to international users) and selecting the databases to migrate.

There are three ways to create the SQL Server 7 version of your database and log files:

➤ The first is to use the default database configuration. The wizard performs all of the necessary database and log-file size calculations. Dump and mirror devices are not upgraded.

➤ The second option does not instruct the wizard to create any user databases. It is up to you to create the databases and logs in SQL Server 7 before starting the Upgrade Wizard.

➤ Finally, you can use an SQL script file that you provide. This option is recommended only for those intimately familiar with SQL Server 7's new **CREATE DATABASE** statement.

Executables

SQL Server includes a number of graphical tools for creating, upgrading, and maintaining the database system. These tools are:

➤ *Management Console*—This is the same utility used to administer various other Microsoft BackOffice products, including MTS and IIS.

➤ *Enterprise Manager*—The Enterprise Manager offers a way to administer an enterprise-wide distribution of SQL Server. Using this utility, you can manage user accounts and access, as well as databases, transaction logs, and backup devices.

➤ *Service Manager*—The Service Manager allows you to manage the system services that are part of the SQL Server runtime, including the SQL Server Agent and Distributed Transaction Coordinator processes.

Microsoft Transaction Server (MTS)

MTS is a middle-tier transaction engine that offers a scalable and resilient platform to host component-based systems.

Purpose

Microsoft's approach to software development revolves around a component-development strategy that is based on COM (Component Object Model). COM is the underlying technology of OLE (Object Linking and Embedding), whose origins are grounded in a document-centric approach for data containment. Microsoft's Windows and NT operating systems make extensive use of COM, both internally and in the form of an API that's accessible to third-party developers. Additionally, Microsoft's n-tier system-support products, IIS and SQL, also rely on and expose functionality via COM interfaces. It is therefore a natural evolution for this model to include products that aid in transaction scalability and increase fault tolerance. MTS offers a programming model that provides a mechanism to encapsulate business logic; this business logic leverages a component framework.

 MTS provides the following benefits to the application architecture:

➤ Distributed transactions

➤ Object and thread management

➤ Distributed security

Platforms And Requirements

MTS can operate on any NT, Windows 95, or Windows 98 system with the DCOM option support. MTS requires at least 32MB of memory and 30MB of disk space. This product is available in the NT 4 Option Pack.

Executables

This section describes two types of executables: those that manage the MTS environment and those that are created to run in the MTS environment.

MTS Explorer And Microsoft Management Console (MMC)

The MTS Explorer utility is a graphical user interface used to register and manage components that execute in the MTS environment. The MTS Explorer is a snap-in component to the Microsoft Management Console (MMC), an extensible management console for enterprise applications.

The MMC provides a root console object under which MMC-compliant utilities install. In addition to MTS, IIS is managed as an MMC snap-in.

Generating MTS Executables

MTS offers the tools to construct an application executable that installs and configures a user's computer to access an MTS-enabled application. Such a configuration requires the target computer to have nothing more than the application executable and an operating system that offers DCOM services.

Creating an application executable requires you to export the server application package. The Export option is available in the context menu that is displayed by right-clicking on the package in the MTS Explorer. The Export dialog box prompts for a package export path and file name. The MTS Explorer will create a "clients" subdirectory below the one that you specify. This subdirectory will contain the application executable with the name that you supplied, and it might also contain a clients.ini file. You can edit the initialization file to refer to other client installation executables and/or application-specific documentation.

You can distribute the application executable in one of the following ways:

➤ By placing the MTS-generated file into a directory that is shared on a network

➤ By attaching the executable to an email

➤ By incorporating the executable into a Web page (using the <Object> tag)

➤ By configuring SMS to "push" the application to target machines

The application executable performs the following packaging and distribution functions for your program:

➤ Extracts the necessary custom proxy-stub and type library files

➤ Transfers the files extracted above to a directory whose identifier is the GUID of the application, under the Program Files\Remote Applications directory

➤ Performs the necessary Registry-related operations to identify the program for use on the client machine and make it visible to the COM/OLE libraries

➤ Registers the application so that it is compatible with the Control Panel's Add/Remove Programs utility

➤ Deletes any temporary files used during installation

Installation

The MTS installation is part of the NT Option Pack.

Server

Installation of MTS is available from the NT Option Pack Setup utility. From the Custom Setup option, you should deselect all of the Option Pack components. Display the subcomponents dialog box for the Transaction Server option and select the Transaction Server Core Components option. This selection will cause the installation of the Microsoft Management Console (MMC)—

a necessary component for MTS operations—as well as causing the installation of the Microsoft Data Access Components (MDAC).

Client

In addition to running an MTS-generated application executable (described in the "Generating MTS Executables" section), a client computer may also run the MTS services, thus allowing the server and client to distribute MTS packages among two or more machines. The product's installation is no different from that of the server installation.

Object Model

Programming for MTS requires an understanding of components that constitute the runtime environment.

Application Component

Components that you create for MTS that contain "business logic" or "business rules" are called *application components*. MTS objects are in-process server components that reside in DLLs and are designed to operate in the MTS runtime environment. Transactional operations that occur within MTS pass the so-called ACID test (i.e., they are Atomic, Consistent, Isolated, and Durable).

Resource Manager

A *resource manager* is a system service that is responsible for a persistent data store. The MTS resource manager supports the following stores:

➤ Relational databases

➤ File systems

➤ Document storage systems

Resource Dispenser

A *resource dispenser* is similar to a resource manager, but whereas resource managers guarantee durability, resource dispensers don't. MTS offers two resource dispensers: an ODBC resource dispenser and a Shared Property Manager. The ODBC resource dispenser is really just the ODBC 3 Driver Manager (installed with MTS). The Shared Property Manager provides an easy way to share state in a multiuser environment.

Distributed Transaction Coordinator

The Microsoft Distributed Transaction Coordinator (MS DTC) is fundamental to MTS operation, exposing interfaces to which applications and resource managers bind. From the developer's perspective, MS DTC—built on a COM framework—offers the ability to create, destroy, manage, and monitor transactions. Originally offered as part of SQL Server 6.5, MS DTC implements a two-phase commit protocol, ensuring transaction atomicity regardless of failures.

Microsoft Message Queue (MSMQ) Server

MSMQ is a middle-tier component employing messages and queues in the transfer of application data.

Purpose

A message queue enhances the reliability of a distributed system, especially if components of the system are separated by slow, nonpersistent, or unreliable connections. Additionally, MSMQ product offers support for communication across heterogeneous networks.

Message Delivery

Among the most important benefits of constructing an application to use MSMQ is the ability of the system to guarantee message delivery.

Message Routing

The message queue can be instructed, via the graphical management tools, to identify and select the most "cost-effective" route for messages to take from source to destination.

Platforms And Requirements

MSMQ 2 can be deployed on Windows 2000, Windows NT 4, Windows 95, and Windows 98. Optional bridge software called the MSMQ-MQSeries—available to work with Microsoft System Network Architecture (SNA) Server—can be used to communicate with IBM MQSeries systems.

Executables And Components

The message queue software is used to create and manage queues and messages and to establish communication routes between sites.

MSMQ Explorer

One of the most common management metaphors within Windows has become the Explorer-style application, with a tree control in a left-hand pane and a ListView to the right. MSMQ Explorer displays only those computers running the MSMQ service, including dependent clients, MSMQ routing servers, Backup Site Controllers (BSCs), Primary Site Controllers (PSCs), and the Primary Enterprise Controller (PEC). MSMQ remote dependent clients are not displayed.

Replication delays may result in information that is not current.

Installation

The MSMQ product consists of installations for both the client and server computers, where a computer traditionally identified as a server is identified as a "Controller."

Client

There are two client configurations:

➤ *Dependent client*—Requires a connection to a network and its supporting message store for the purpose of sending and receiving messages.

➤ *Independent client*—Contains its own message store and may send and receive messages without a network connection.

The final client component that MSMQ offers is the RAS Connectivity Service, which is best identified as a proxy or forwarding service. This product allows independent clients to send and receive messages from computers other than the RAS server.

Controller (Server)

Message queue terminology defines a *controller* as a durable store to which MSMQ clients communicate. The MSMQ Setup dialog box, shown in Figure 2.3, allows you to choose which type of controller you want to install. There are three types of controllers:

➤ *Primary Enterprise Controller (PEC)*—For MSMQ to function, you must install one Primary Enterprise Controller on your enterprise network to act as the master repository for data.

➤ *Primary Site Controller (PSC)*—A Primary Site Controller must exist at each location where communication among client computers is fast and reliable, such as those computers connected by a LAN. A PEC performs the functions of a PSC for its location.

➤ *Backup Site Controller (BSC)*—The Backup Site Controller is an optional MSMQ component. You can install BSCs at locations that contain PSCs to enhance reliability and to perform load balancing.

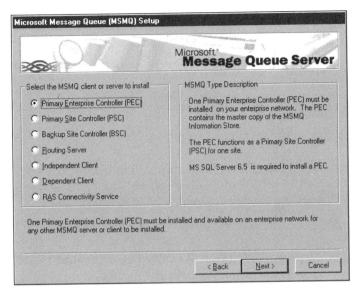

Figure 2.3   The MSMQ Setup dialog box.

Another type of server component that MSMQ offers is a routing server. A routing server's purpose is to identify paths that messages can travel to reach their destinations. Such paths are delimited by attributes that identify the "cost" (in terms of speed) that the link poses to delivery.

The final MSMQ server component is the Connector. This product bridges MSMQ with non-Microsoft message queuing systems.

Object Model

Programming for MSMQ requires an understanding of components that constitute the runtime environment.

Queues

Queues are containers that maintain messages. Message sources include applications that you write (application queues) or messages from MSMQ itself (system queues). Application queues can be further divided into four categories: message, administration, response, and report. System queues consist of journal and dead-letter categories. Applications may give read-only access to system queues.

Messages

MSMQ maintains information in the form of messages. Messages, as with queues, may be created either by an application or by the MSMQ system.

Messages that originate in MSMQ are called *system messages*, of which acknowledgment and report are examples.

An important characteristic of a message is a unique message identifier. This key is a combination of the machine GUID of the originating computer and a machine-specific sequence number. Such an identifier is useful for MSMQ to send an acknowledgment or report message to the original application message.

Properties

Information specific to computers, queues, and messages are identified as *properties*. Properties may be defined as either private or public and may be stored in the object they define, on a single computer, or in an Active Directory.

Computers

Computers that participate within an MSMQ enterprise are defined as machine objects. The MSMQ administrator creates and modifies these profiles, using the MSMQ Explorer utility.

Security

Information contained within messages poses a potential security lapse. Such concerns are addressed by MSMQ in a variety of ways. Certificates can be employed to certify a sender or receiver, and encryption further secures the exchange of message data. MSMQ supports one-way authentication, in which the message recipient must identify the message's origin.

Connectors

The concept of a message queue is not something that Microsoft invented. Message queues are common in large transaction-oriented systems. The connector server is a component that Microsoft provides to attach MSMQ to foreign messaging systems. In this manner, contents of foreign message queues—such as those found on IBM AS/400 or 3090 machines—can be introduced to MSMQ through a computer executing the MSMQ Connector server.

Practice Questions

Question 1

ActiveX class member functions can be easily added from the context menu of which window?

○ a. The ClassView pane of the Workspace window

○ b. The FileView pane of the Workspace window

○ c. The ResourceView pane of the Workspace window

○ d. The Build pane of the Output window

Answer a is correct. Only the ClassView pane allows you to add functions and variables to a class, as well as respond to ActiveX events. Answers b and c are incorrect because FileView and ResourceView are also panes of the Workspace window, but they don't offer object manipulation menus. Answer d is incorrect because the Build pane contains output from the compiler and linker.

Question 2

The Visual C++ compiler allows the specification of various calling conventions using command-line switches. Which switch is not architecture dependent and specifies the C calling convention for only those functions that are not members of a C++ class?

○ a. /Gd

○ b. /Gr

○ c. /Od

○ d. /Zi

Answer a is correct. The /Gd option, which is the default compiler setting, specifies the "C" calling convention for nonmember functions. Answer b is incorrect because the /Gr option employs register passing for Intel platforms. Answer c is incorrect because /Od allows you to disable optimization. Answer d is incorrect because /Zi allows you to produce a program database. Neither /Od nor /Zi is involved with processor architecture or calling convention.

Question 3

> Which compiler switch disables code optimizations for the Visual C++ Standard Edition?
>
> ○ a. /GZ
>
> ○ b. /Fd
>
> ○ c. /Od
>
> ○ d. None of the above.

Answer d is correct. The Standard Edition does not allow you to disable optimizations. Otherwise, /Od (answer c) would be correct because it is the compiler switch that performs this function for Professional and Enterprise Editions. Answer a is incorrect because /GZ is designed to help you identify errors that may occur in a release build. Answer b is incorrect because /Fd can be followed by a name for the program database (PDB) file.

Question 4

> Which library supports multithreaded debug applications, dynamically linked to an executable?
>
> ○ a. libc.lib
>
> ○ b. msvcrt.lib
>
> ○ c. libcd.lib
>
> ○ d. msvcrtd.lib

Answer d is correct. The msvcrtd.lib file resolves runtime externals for a dynamically linked debug library named msvcrt.dll. Answers a and c are incorrect because libc.lib and libcd.lib are the single-threaded and the single-threaded debug libraries, respectively. Answer b is incorrect because msvcrt.lib is the nondebug version of the msvcrt.dll library.

Question 5

Identify three benefits of the MTS architecture.

- ❏ a. Distributed transactions
- ❏ b. Object and thread management
- ❏ c. Distributed security
- ❏ d. Guaranteed fault tolerance

Answers a, b, and c are correct. The first three choices are all valid statements about MTS. Answer d is incorrect because MTS application construction does not guarantee that your objects will not fault

Question 6

Which SourceSafe operation allows you to take a software project in multiple directions for the sake of product stratification?

- ○ a. Branching
- ○ b. Sharing
- ○ c. Cloaking
- ○ d. Checking in

Answer a is correct. The branching operation allows you to track the individual directions of a file under source management. Answer b is incorrect because sharing allows a file to be used across multiple projects. Answer c is incorrect because cloaking allows recursive operations to be ignored. Answer d is incorrect because checking in is the command that moves a file back into source management, creating a new version.

Question 7

Providing your own script file when updating a SQL Server database from 6.x to 7 is recommended only if you are intimately familiar with what command?

○ a. **CREATE**

○ b. **CREATE DATABASE**

○ c. **CREATE TABLE**

○ d. **UPGRADE**

Answer b is correct. The **CREATE DATABASE** command has been expanded to include new options for SQL Server 7. Answers a and c are incorrect because the **CREATE** command has numerous modifiers used in initializing databases, including **CREATE TABLE, CREATE QUERY,** and **CREATE REPORT**. Answer d is incorrect because **UPGRADE** is not a valid SQL Server command.

Question 8

Which is not a true statement regarding a client computer that wants to activate an application executable that is exported from MTS?

○ a. The client machine can access the application executable from an HTML page.

○ b. The client machine can access the application executable from a shared drive.

○ c. The client machine must support the DCOM protocol.

○ d. The client machine needs access to an SMS server.

Answer d is correct. The client machine does not need to communicate with an SMS server to acquire the MTS application executable. DCOM is required for an application executable to function, and the application can be acquired via a browser or Explorer.

Question 9

> A system that employs MSMQ as part of its architecture must have at least one:
>
> ○ a. PPC
>
> ○ b. PSC
>
> ○ c. BSC
>
> ○ d. PEC

Answer d is correct. At least one Primary Enterprise Controller (PEC) must be present in any system that employs MSMQ. A Primary Site Controller (PSC) should be located at any site where communication between machines is cheap and reliable (i.e., on a LAN).

Question 10

> What form of security does MSMQ not employ?
>
> ○ a. One-way authentication
>
> ○ b. Two-way authentication
>
> ○ c. Certificates
>
> ○ d. Encryption

Answer b is correct. Microsoft Message Queue does not support two-way. Answers a, c, and d are incorrect because MSMQ does support one-way authentication, certificates, and encryption.

Need To Know More?

 Homer, Alex and David Sussman. *MTS MSMQ with VB and ASP*: Wrox Press, 1998. ISBN 1-861001-46-0. This text describes many of Microsoft's Distributed Network Architecture (DNA) components, including installation, configuration, and development.

 Kruglinski, David J., George Shepherd, and Scott Wingo. *Programming Microsoft Visual C++*. 5th ed. Redmond, WA: Microsoft Press, 1998. ISBN 1-57231-857-0. This book strikes a good balance between theory and practical application. It is divided into six parts and covers nearly every aspect of MFC programming, from the basics to database management and the Internet.

MFC Architecture

Terms you'll need to understand:

- √ Document object
- √ View object
- √ Frame window object
- √ Document template object
- √ **CRuntimeClass** object
- √ **RUNTIME_CLASS** macro
- √ **CSingleDocTemplate** class
- √ **CMultiDocTemplate** class

- √ Multitasking
- √ Thread
- √ Multithreading
- √ User interface (UI) thread
- √ Worker thread
- √ Primary thread
- √ Regular MFC DLL
- √ MFC extension DLL

Techniques you'll need to master:

- √ Understanding the purpose of documents, views, frames, and templates within the document/ view architecture, and explaining how they interact
- √ Creating SDI and MDI applications that employee multiple views
- √ Implementing serialization in an application
- √ Describing how printing works with MFC
- √ Correctly identifying which type of thread—UI or worker—to implement

- √ Choosing the most appropriate method to communicate between threads in your application
- √ Selecting the best synchronization object to use in your application
- √ Choosing the most appropriate type of DLL to build
- √ Building a regular DLL that links to MFC
- √ Building an MFC extension DLL

This chapter covers the Microsoft Foundation Classes (MFC) library. First, I explain each of the objects that make up the document/view architecture and how they interact. Next, I describe how printing works with MFC and how serialization works. The last two sections cover multithreading and dynamic link libraries.

Document/View Architecture

This section begins with an overview of various components of the document/view architecture and how they fit together. In turn, each of the two categories of document/view applications—single-document interface (SDI) and multiple-document interface (MDI)—is presented. SDI applications support just one open document at a time. MDI applications allow the user to have two or more documents open concurrently.

Document/View Components

The document/view architecture is one of the cornerstones of the MFC library. Central to this architecture is the concept of a document object and a corresponding view window. The document object is responsible for storing, loading, and saving the data associated with the application, whereas the view object renders the data on screen and provides a user interface for manipulating the data. This separation of the data from the user interface supports and encourages the use of modular and object-oriented development techniques, thus allowing you to produce applications that are easier to enhance and maintain.

There are four main components of the MFC document/view architecture: documents, views, document/view frames, and document templates. The following sections address each component.

The Document Object

The *document object* conceptually holds the data used by the application. Usually, the data is stored by the program itself, but this does not need to be the case. The data could be in a database or some other remote data source. The important thing is that the document object serves as a data source and provides data management for the application. When you implement a document within your application, you will usually add data members to hold the data and the public member functions that other objects can use to query and edit the document's data. How the data storage is implemented in the document is your responsibility. The document object is constructed from a class derived from **CDocument**. A document object can have any number of views associated with it and maintains a list of the views. The **AddView()** function, as its name implies, adds a view to the list. The **UpdateAllViews()** function calls each view's **OnUpdate()**

function to tell all the views attached to the document to update themselves. In an SDI application with just one view, **UpdateAllViews()** usually isn't used because the single view often updates itself in response to user input either before or after updating the document's data. But in multiple-view applications, whenever the document is modified, **UpdateAllViews()** is called to keep all the other views in sync.

The **CDocument** class also has a number of virtual functions that can be overridden to customize a document's behavior. Four of these virtual functions are almost always overridden in a derived document class:

➤ **OnNewDocument**—This function is called by the framework when the document object is being created. The default implementation of this function calls **DeleteContents()** to tidy up any existing document data and then sets the document's modified state to **FALSE**. Override this function to initialize the data object before a new document is created.

➤ **OnOpenDocument**—This function is called by the framework when an existing file is being opened. The default implementation of this function calls **DeleteContents()** to delete any data in the document, opens and reads the file, and then sets the document's modified state to **FALSE**. Override this function if the default implementation (which calls **Serialize()**) is not adequate for your application.

➤ **DeleteContents**—This function deletes the document's contents without actually destroying the document object itself. You need to override this function to free any memory or resources you allocated for the document.

➤ **Serialize**—This function is called by the framework to both load the document and store the document to disk. You need to override this function to serialize each of your application's objects.

In an SDI application, the document object is constructed just once and is reused each time a document is created or opened. Therefore, one-time initialization code should be put in **OnNewDocument()** and **OnOpenDocument()**, rather than in the document object's constructor.

The View Object

The *view object* keeps a pointer to the document object, which it uses to access the document's member variables in order to display and modify them. This pointer is exposed through the view's **GetDocument()** member function. When AppWizard generates the source code for a view class, it hides the **CView::GetDocument()** function with one that casts the pointer to the appropriate document type and returns the result.

CView is an abstract class that defines the basic properties of a view. You will normally derive your view class from **CView**. MFC provides a number of view classes derived from **CView**. Some of these classes are used directly. Others, like **CView**, are abstract base classes used for deriving view classes of your own.

CView and its derivatives include several virtual member functions that can be overridden to customize a view's operation. **OnDraw()**, which is the most important, is called by the framework whenever the view needs to be updated. **OnDraw()** can be used to render to the screen or to a printer.

The Frame Window Object

The *frame window object* defines the application's physical workspace on the screen and serves as a container for a view. SDI applications use just one frame window— a **CFrameWnd** that serves as the application's top-level window and frames the view of the document. MDI applications use several frame windows—a **CMDIFrameWnd** that acts as a top-level window and a **CMDIChildWnd** child window that frames views of the application's documents. A frame window orchestrates much of what goes on behind the scenes in a document/view application. A frame window's main role is to host one or more views as well as user-interface elements such as toolbars and status bars.

The Document Template

The *document template* ties the other three components together. Your application has one document template for each type of document that it supports. The document template is responsible for creating and managing all the documents of its type.

The document template object provides the means whereby MFC can dynamically create instances of the document, view, and frame window classes that you define in your code. The document template object can do this because it stores pointers to the **CRuntimeClass** objects associated with each of your document, view, and frame window classes. Using the RUNTIME_CLASS() macro, you specify these **CRuntimeClass** objects when constructing a document template.

MFC defines two document template classes that can be used in your application: **CSingleDocTemplate** and **CMultiDocTemplate**. Both of these classes are derived from **CDocTemplate**, which is an abstract base class that defines the basic functionality for document templates. You usually create one or more document templates in the implementation of your application's **InitInstance()** function. After creating a document template, you call **CWinApp::Add-DocTemplate()** to add it to the list of available document templates that the application maintains.

Be sure you understand and can explain the document/view architecture. You should know the objects that make up the architecture, the purpose of each object, and how the objects relate to each other.

Multiple Views

As you already know, a view can be attached to only one document, but a document can have multiple views attached to it at the same time, such as when the contents of a document are displayed in a splitter window or in multiple child windows in an MDI application. To help you implement multiple views, a document object keeps a list of its views, provides member functions for adding and removing views, and supplies the **UpdateAllViews()** member function, which sends a message to the views when the user changes the data in a document.

 Command routing is one of the noteworthy features of the document/view architecture. Command messages can be handled almost anywhere. Be sure you understand and can explain the routing of command messages from the user interface through the various document/view objects.

Splitter Windows

Splitter windows are one way of providing multiple views of the same data. A *splitter window* is nothing more than a window that can be divided into two or more panes vertically or horizontally, or both vertically and horizontally, by movable splitter bars. Each pane is a child of the splitter window, and the splitter window itself is a child of the frame window. MFC provides a class, **CSplitterWnd**, that does most of the work.

Multiple-Document Interface

The major difference between single- and multiple-document interfaces is that MDI applications allow you to have more than one document open at the same time. In fact, subject to limits on memory and resources, you can open as many documents as you want. Some applications handle only one type of document, whereas others support multiple document types.

Both SDI and MDI applications store their data in a document object derived from **CDocument** and present views derived from **CView** or one of its many derived classes. SDI applications use just one frame window—a **CFrameWnd** that serves as the application's top-level window and frames the view of the document. However, in MDI applications, the main window is derived from **CMDIFrameWnd** instead of from **CFrameWnd**. The client area of the frame window contains a special client window created by the frame window. View windows are wrapped with "document frames" that are derived from **CMDIChildWnd**. These **CMDIChildWnd**-derived windows float within the workspace defined by the client area.

In an MDI application, the client window is a child of the top-level frame window. Moving on down the hierarchy, the **CMDIChildWnd**-derived windows are children of the MDI client window, and views are children of the document frames. Document objects, of course, contain the data displayed in the views.

Combinations Of Documents And Views MDI Supports

Think about the various relationships between document objects and view objects that you might want to implement in an application. Simply saying "multiple views and multiple documents" isn't quite specific enough. More specifically, the relationships are as follows:

➤ Single view on a single document type

➤ Multiple views on a single document type

➤ Single views on multiple document types

➤ Multiple views on multiple document types

Keeping each of the views current as the content of the document changes is an important matter. Two functions, **CDocument::UpdateAllViews()** and **CView::OnUpdate()**, are key in providing the necessary functionality. You should know when and by whom these functions are called.

View Classes

MFC provides a number of classes, derived directly or indirectly from **CView**, that provide unique functionality. Some of these classes are used directly. Others, like **CView**, are abstract base classes used for deriving view classes of your own. Table 3.1 provides a summary description of each of these classes.

CCtrlView and its derivatives adjust the document/view architecture to the new common controls supported by Windows 95 and Windows NT versions 3.51 and later. **CFormView** and its derivatives support Dialog Data Exchange and can be used as you would a **CDialog**-derived class. **CDialog** is covered in a later section.

Table 3.1 MFC CView-derived classes.

Class	Description
CCtrlView	Derived from **CView**, this is the base class for the specialized view classes that apply the document/view architecture to the 32-bit Windows common controls.
CEditView	Derived from **CCtrlView**, this class provides a simple view based on the Windows edit box control. Because **CEditView** allows text to be entered and edited, it can be used as the foundation for a simple text-editor application. See also **CRichEditView**.
CRichEditView	Derived from **CCtrlView**, this view contains a **CRichEditCtrl** object. This class is like **CEditView**, but better. **CRichEditView** handles formatted text, fonts, colors, and embedded OLE objects.
CListView	Derived from **CCtrlView**, this view contains a **CListCtrl** object. Displays icons and strings in a manner similar to the right-hand pane of the Windows 95 Explorer.
CTreeView	Derived from **CCtrlView**, this view contains a **CTreeCtrl** object. Displays icons and strings arranged in a hierarchy in a manner similar to the left-hand pane of the Windows 95 Explorer.
CScrollView	Derived from **CView**, this class provides basic scrolling capabilities.
CFormView	A form view—that is, a view that contains controls. Derived from **CScrollView**, it is the base class for more specialized views containing controls. The form layout is based on a dialog box resource.
CHtmlView	A Web-browser view with which the application's user can browse sites on the World Wide Web, as well as folders in the local file system and on a network. The Web-browser view can also work as an active document container. This class is derived from **CFormView**.
CRecordView	Derived from **CFormView**, this view displays ODBC database records in controls. If you select ODBC support in your project, the view's base class is **CRecordView**. The view is connected to a **CRecordset** object.

(continued)

Table 3.1 MFC CView-derived classes (continued).	
Class	**Description**
CDaoRecordView	Derived from **CFormView**, this view displays DAO database records in controls. If you select DAO support in your project, the view's base class is **CDaoRecordView**. The view is connected to a **CDaoRecordset** object.
COleDBRecordView	Derived from **CFormView**, this view displays OLE DB records in controls. If you select OLE DB support in your project, the view's base class is **COleDBRecordView**. The view is connected to a **CRowset** object.

Each **CCtrlView**-derived class has its own set of style bits. Some of these style bits need to be set before the Windows window is created; others can be set after the Windows window is created but before it is visible; and still others can be set after the window is visible. Depending on when the style bits need to be set, you can specify them in the **Create** function, in the override of **PreCreateWindow()**, **OnCreate()** or **OnInitialUpdate()**, or in some other manner, such as in a menu.

 You should never use **CCtrlView** directly in your code. Instead, use one of the derivatives: **CEditView**, **CListView**, **CRichEditView**, and **CTreeView**.

Printing With MFC

Handling printing is one of the harder parts of writing a Windows program. MFC, with its document/view architecture, makes this task easier, but there are still a lot of details that need to be attended to. An item of major importance is correctly setting the size of the document and figuring out where the page breaks go.

MFC provides a set of wrappers that take care of most of the details of printing. And when you add printing capabilities to a document/view application, things become even simpler. Printing from a document/view application, like drawing on the screen, is managed by a **CView**-derived class.

Roles And Responsibilities—Yours And MFC's

The MFC wrapper classes take on much of the responsibilities that otherwise would be yours. Nevertheless, it is still your responsibility to ensure that your view class performs the following tasks:

➤ Inform the framework of the number of pages.

➤ Print each page as required, including headers and footers.

➤ Allocate and deallocate the necessary resources.

It is the framework's responsibility to:

➤ Display the Print dialog box.

➤ Create a CDC object.

➤ Inform the printer driver when a new print job is to start or end.

➤ Inform the printer driver when a new page is to be started, inform the view class which page should be printed, and inform the printer driver when the page is finished. This step is repeated for each page.

➤ Call the view-overrideable functions at the appropriate times.

Understanding The Printing Sequence

Key to printing from a document/view application is a set of virtual functions of the view class. The framework calls these functions at various stages of the printing process. By overriding these functions, you can tailor the printing process as you see fit. Which of these functions you override and what you do in the override depends on the type of document you are printing. The beauty of these functions is that you can put most, if not all, of your printing code in them. These functions are listed in Table 3.2.

Many applications draw on the printer just as they draw on the screen—in **OnDraw()**. However, trying to manage both drawing on the screen and drawing on the printer in **OnDraw()** can become quite complicated. Even when you can manage drawing on both from **OnDraw()**, more times than not, you will need to override **OnPrint()** to handle such things as page numbers, headers, and footers. Therefore, it is sometimes more practical to just go ahead and put the entire printer-output logic in **OnPrint()**.

Table 3.2	Key CView overrideable printing functions.
Function	**Description**
OnBeginPrinting	Override to allocate fonts and other resources needed for the print job. You can also set the maximum page count here. This function is called just before printing starts.
OnEndPrinting	Override to deallocate resources allocated in **OnBeginPrinting**. This function is called when printing ends.
OnPrepareDC	Override to modify the device context. This function is called before each page is printed.
OnPreparePrinting	Override to call **DoPreparePrinting()**, which is responsible for displaying the Print dialog box and creating the printer DC. This function is called at the beginning of the print job.
OnPrint	Override to print headers, footers, and other page elements that are not drawn by **OnDraw** or to do all printing here instead of in **OnDraw**. This function is called to print (or preview) one page.

When printing a document, MFC calls the functions in Table 3.2 in a specific order. The functions are presented below in the sequence in which MFC calls them:

1. OnPreparePrinting()

```
BOOL CExampleView::OnPreparePrinting(CPrintInfo* pInfo)
  {
    // default preparation
    return DoPreparePrinting(pInfo);
  }
```

This is how AppWizard implements **OnPreparePrinting()**. As you can see, **OnPreparePrinting()** receives a pointer to a **CPrintInfo** object and then calls **DoPreparePrinting()**, passing it the **CPrintInfo** object. **DoPreparePrinting()** presents the Print dialog box and creates a printer device context. The **CPrintInfo** object has a number of functions that allow you to perform tasks such as setting the document's minimum and maximum page numbers and finding out the number of the last page the user selected for printing. **CPrintInfo**'s data members also provide information, including the current number of the page being printed and whether the document is in print preview.

If you know the maximum number of pages in your document, you should call **CPrintInfo::SetMaxPage()** before calling **DoPreparePrinting()**. This will allow the Print dialog box to present the page count to the user.

2. **OnBeginPrinting()**

   This function receives two parameters: a pointer to a device context and a pointer to the same **CPrintInfo** object that was passed to OnPreparePrinting(). Here is where you allocate fonts and other resources needed for the print job. You might also perform calculations to determine the line width, the position of the left margin, the number of lines per page, and the maximum number of pages to print. If the maximum number of pages is known, call **CPrintInfo::SetMaxPage()** to set the number of the last page of the document.

3. **OnPrepareDC()**

   This function is called once for each page of the document. Here is where you should control print-time pagination and set the document's viewpoint origin.

4. **OnPrint()**

   MFC calls **OnPrint()** to print the actual page. If you are using OnDraw() to do printing, then after printing the header and footer, you would call the base class's **OnPrint()**, which, in turn, would call OnDraw().

5. As long as there are more lines to print, MFC continues to call **OnPrepareDC()** and **OnPrint()** for each page in the document. After the last page has been printed, MFC calls **OnEndPrinting()**. OnEndPrinting() is used to destroy any resources that were created in OnBeginPrinting().

Serialization

The MFC framework provides the means whereby an application's objects can persist on disk after the application is exited. Then, when it's restarted, the application's objects can be restored. This process of writing and reading an object to and from persistent storage used by MFC is known as *serialization*. Two classes, a **CObject** virtual function, and a couple of macros are the key ingredients of the framework's built-in support for serialization.

A **CFile** object is created and used to encapsulate a binary file handle. This provides unbuffered binary disk input/output operations. The **CFile** object is then attached to a **CArchive** object, which is used to serialize the data to and from a file.

The **CArchive** object directs the serialization process. It provides the mechanism for streaming the objects to and from disk. The **CArchive** object maintains a flag that indicates whether it is writing to disk or reading from disk. **CArchive::IsStoring()** and **CArchive::IsLoading()** are used to test this flag.

Writing A Serializable Class

For a class to be serializable, you must follow these steps:

1. Derive your class from **CObject** or from a **CObject**-derived class.

2. Provide a default constructor.

3. Include the **DECLARE_SERIAL()** macro in the class declaration, using the name of your class as its one argument.

4. Include the **IMPLEMENT_SERIAL()** macro in the class implementation file. This macro takes three parameters: the name of your class, its base class, and a schema (version) number.

5. Override the base class's **Serialize()** function. Your serialization function will almost always call the **Serialize()** function of its base class before it archives its own data members.

Serializing An Object

If your application employs the document/view architecture, everything is keyed to the document. When the user chooses Save or Open from the File menu, the framework creates a **CFile** object. It then creates a **CArchive** object, passing it the **CFile** object. Next, it calls your document class's **Serialize()** function, passing a reference to the **CArchive** object. Your document's **Serialize()** function then serializes each of its data members.

Outside the document/view architecture, you will need to provide the code to do what the framework does when using the document/view architecture. Follow this process to serialize your objects:

1. Create a **CFile** object and open the file.

2. Create a **CArchive** object, passing it the **CFile** object.

3. Call the object's **Serialize()** function and pass it a reference to the **CArchive** object.

4. After you have serialized all of your objects, you can close the archive file by calling **CArchive::Close()** and **CFile::Close()**. Or you can let the **CArchive** and **CFile** destructors close the archive and file when the objects go out of scope.

CFile And Its Derivatives

All programs maintain and manipulate data in one way or another. Many programs also store and retrieve their data to and from a disk or other medium. MFC makes this task easier for the programmer by providing a family of classes that abstract the medium being used. All of these classes are derived directly or indirectly from **CFile**. Figure 3.1 shows the hierarchy of these classes.

The **CFile** Class

CFile doesn't have to be used with **CArchive**. You can use it by itself to perform basic disk I/O in an object-oriented manner. **CFile** has more than 25 functions that allow you to do such things as read, write, position, and extract status. Many of these functions throw a **CFileException** object when an error occurs.

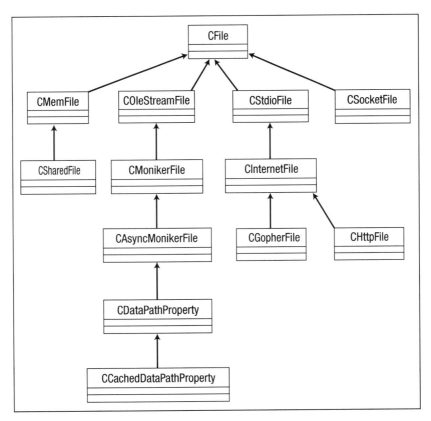

Figure 3.1   CFile and its derivatives.

CFile Derivatives

As shown previously in Figure 3.1, **CFile** is the root class for a number of MFC classes. Table 3.3 provides a short description for each of the classes derived from **CFile**.

As you can see from the descriptions, some of these classes provide file-like interfaces to nonfile media. Others provide wrappers around OLE interfaces, and still others simplify the reading of files over the Internet.

Because **CFile** reads and writes binary files, extra steps are required if you want to read or write text files. **CStdioFile,** however, has two functions that make this task much simpler: **ReadString()** and **WriteString()**.

Table 3.3 Classes derived from CFile.	
Class Name	**Description**
CMemFile	A **CMemFile** object behaves like a **CFile** object, except that the file is stored in RAM rather than on disk. **CMemFile** allocates, reallocates, and deallocates memory, using the runtime library functions malloc, realloc, and free.
CSharedFile	The class is like **CMemFile**, except that **GlobalAlloc** is used to allocate memory, which returns an **HGLOBAL** handle instead of a pointer.
COleStreamFile	This class represents an **IStream** in a compound file as part of OLE Structured Storage.
CMonikerFile	This class binds a moniker to a stream, giving you **CFile** functionality. By using **CMonikerFile**, you do not have to bind to a stream yourself.
CAsyncMonikerFile	This class allows you to Internet-enable your application and ActiveX controls. It uses the **IMoniker** interface to access a data stream asynchronously.
CDataPathProperty	Implements an OLE control property that can be loaded asynchronously.
CCachedDataPathProperty	Like **CDataPathProperty**, but cached in a memory file.
CSocketFile	Used for sending and receiving data across a network via Windows Sockets.
CStdioFile	Represents a C runtime stream file.
CGopherFile	Used to find and read files on a Gopher server.
CHttpFile	Used to find and read files on an HTTP server.
CInternetFile	Base class for **CGopherFile** and **CHttpFile**.

Multithreading

Most modern operating systems allow you to run several programs at the same time. This capability is called *multitasking*. Each running task, in the Win32 environment, constitutes a *process*, and each process consists of one or more threads. A *thread*, simply stated, is a path or flow of execution through a process's code. Threads give you the ability to execute different parts of your program at the same time. In essence, they allow you to have multitasking within multitasking.

All of the 32-bit Windows operating systems are *preemptive*. This means that they control how long a thread executes. At the end of its allocated time, the executing thread is stopped and a different thread starts executing. The amount of time a thread is allowed to execute is very small, so, to a human, all of the threads appear to be executing at the same time. If you are running Windows NT on a system with more than one processor, it may indeed mean that multiple threads are executing at the same time. Windows NT is a *symmetric multiprocessing*, or *SMP*, operating system, which means that it can assign different threads—including threads belonging to the operating system—to different processors.

The CPU knows nothing about threads; it simply executes one instruction after another. As each instruction executes, it changes one or more of the CPU registers, or some part of memory, or maybe the instruction counter. It is the operating system that switches the flow of execution from one thread to another. To do this, the operating system maintains information about each thread. This information is collected into a thread context, or *context record*. This collection of data is used to restore the CPU so that a thread can pick up execution in the same state it was in before losing control. Switching from one thread to another is done in such a manner that a thread never knows about it.

Thread Priorities

The *scheduler* is the component of the operating system that decides which threads run when and for how long. The scheduler uses a variety of techniques to improve multitasking performance and to try to ensure that each thread in the system gets an adequate amount of CPU time. The amount of time a thread gets is based on its own needs and the needs of the process it serves. Ultimately, the decision about which thread should execute next boils down to the thread with the highest current priority value. At any given moment, each thread is assigned a value from 1 to 31, which is a combination of the process's priority class, the thread's priority level, and the dynamic boost currently being applied by the operating system. The higher the number, the higher the base priority level.

The operating system uses the current priority value of all executable threads to determine which thread gets the next slice of CPU time. Threads are scheduled in a round-robin fashion at each priority level, and only when there are no executable threads at a higher level does scheduling of threads at a lower level take place.

The priority level is used to adjust the priority class of the process. Without knowing the importance of the process, you can change the relative importance of a thread. Once started, if it needs to, a process can call **::SetPriorityClass()** to change its priority class.

All threads are created with the thread priority set the same as the process priority class. After a thread is created **::SetThreadPriority()** or **CWinThread:: SetThreadPriority()** can be used to adjust the thread's priority relative to other threads in the process.

Thread Types

All threads are the same as far as Windows is concerned. However, MFC distinguishes between *user interface (UI) threads*, which have a message pump and typically perform user interface tasks, and *worker threads*, which do not. Creating a UI thread is particularly appropriate when you need to have a thread running to service a particular window and the processing associated with it. On the other hand, you normally create a worker thread when you need to perform background tasks that receive no direct input from the user.

Every process has at least one thread: the *primary thread*, sometimes called the *main thread*. This thread is created by the system when the process is loaded into memory; the thread begins executing and runs as long as the program is active. For an MFC program, the **CWinThread** portion of your **CWinApp** object represents the primary thread. It, like any thread, can dynamically create and destroy other threads. It is also possible for a thread to decide for itself to terminate.

There are two ways to create threads in MFC applications. The first method is very much the same as creating any other Windows object: Create an instance of the **CWinThread** class, and then call that object's **CreateThread()** function to create the thread. The second method is to call the **AfxBeginThread()** function. MFC defines two versions of this function: one for UI threads and another for worker threads.

Both **AfxBeginThread()** overloads do more than simply create a thread. They also initialize internal variables used by the framework, perform sanity checks at various points during the creation process, establish the thread's priority, and take measures to ensure that the runtime library is accessed in a thread-safe manner.

Don't use the Win32 API functions in an MFC application. When using the Win32 API, you should always link with the multithreaded C runtime library, use **_beginthreadex()** to create a thread, and use **_endthreadex()** to terminate a thread.

Creating A Worker Thread

To create a worker thread by using MFC, all you need to do is write a function that you want to run parallel with the rest of your application. Then, call **AfxBeginThread()** to start a thread that will execute your function. The thread remains active as long as the thread's function is executing; when the thread function exits, the thread is destroyed. There are two ways that a worker thread can safely terminate: executing a **return** statement or calling **AfxEndThread()**.

Creating A User Interface Thread

Creating a user interface thread is entirely different from creating a worker thread. You must derive a class from **CWinThread** and override some functions to make sure you gain the functionality you need. **CWinThread::InitInstance()** is similar to **CWinApp::InitInstance()** in that it is called each time you create the thread that is wrapped by the instance of the thread. You must override **InitInstance()**. This is where you should perform any initialization your thread needs. **CWinThread** has a corresponding **ExitInstance()** function that is called when your thread terminates. This is where you would place any destruction code required by your thread.

Thread Communication And Synchronization

The primary advantage of multithreading programming is that you can design your application so that different parts of it are executing concurrently. However, doing this introduces the potential problems of race conditions and data corruption. To avoid these problems, you need a way for threads to communicate with one another and synchronize their actions. Some common situations that can occur are:

➤ The main thread needs to communicate with one or more worker threads.

➤ A worker thread needs to communicate with the main thread.

➤ Two threads require access to the same resource.

In the following sections, you'll look at how these situations, as well as others, can be managed.

User-Defined Windows Messages

Using user-defined Windows messages is probably the easiest method for a worker thread to communicate with a user interface thread. The first step is to define a user message:

```
const int WM_THREADEND = WM_APP + 100;
```

After defining the message, you can call ::**PostMessage()** from the worker thread to post the message in the message queue connected with the user interface thread. A typical call to ::**PostMessage()** might look like this:

```
::PostMessage((HWND)param, WM_THREADEND, 0, 0);
```

The **param** parameter is the window's handle, which is passed to the worker thread through the second parameter of the **AfxBeginThread()** function:

```
AfxBeginThread(ThreadProc, m_hWnd);
```

::**PostThreadMessage()** can be used to post messages to a thread. ::**PostThreadMessage()** takes a thread ID instead of a window handle. The receiving thread must have a message queue.

Events

A somewhat more sophisticated method of signaling between threads is to use *event objects*. An event object can be in one of two states: *signaled* or *unsignaled*. You can create an event and leave it in its unsignaled state. Then, when the condition you wish to signal occurs, you can signal the event. Any other thread watching will know the event is signaled and then perform the appropriate action.

Creating an event object is as easy as declaring a global variable and is done as follows:

```
CEvent g_PrintingDone;
```

The **CEvent** constructor has four optional arguments, but you can normally take the defaults as shown in the previous line of code. When created, the event is in the unsignaled state. To signal the event, you call the object's **SetEvent()** member function:

```
g_PrintingDone.SetEvent();
```

Any thread watching for the signal might do so by calling ::**WaitForSingleObject**(). Here's its prototype:

```
DWORD WaitForSingleObject(
    HANDLE hHandle,          // Handle to the object.
    DWORD dwMilliseconds );  // Time-out interval, in milliseconds
```

The function returns if the interval elapses, even if the object's state is unsigned. If **dwMilliseconds** is zero, the function tests the object's state and returns immediately. If **dwMilliseconds** is **INFINITE**, the function's time-out interval never elapses. The return value can be tested for **WAIT_OBJECT_0** or **WAIT_TIMEOUT**. **WAIT_OBJECT_0** indicates that the state of the specified object is signaled. **WAIT_TIMEOUT** means that the time-out interval elapsed and the object's state is unsignaled.

Critical Sections

Critical sections provide an easy way to ensure that only one thread at a time can access a resource. When you use a critical section, you give your threads a **CCriticalSection** object that they share. When each thread requires exclusive access to the resource, it locks the critical section before accessing the resource. If another thread, running in the same process, tries to lock the same critical section while it's locked by the first thread, the second thread blocks until the first thread unlocks the critical section.

Mutexes

Critical sections are almost all you need to write good multithreaded applications. Critical sections are easy to use and impose little overhead. However, they are visible in only one process, and there are occasions when you might need to protect data accessed by two different threads in two different processes. To address this situation, Windows implements a larger variety of critical sections called *mutexes*. "Mutex" is a combination of the words "mutually" and "exclusive." The **CMutex** class wraps access to mutexes for MFC applications. Here's the **CMutex** constructor:

```
CMutex::CMutex(BOOL bInitiallyOwn = FALSE,
               LPCTSTR lpszName = NULL,
               LPSECURITY_ATTRIBUTES lpsaAttribute = NULL );
```

When you create a **CMutex** object, you can request immediate ownership of the object, and you can specify a name for the object. If you create a mutex with the default constructor, you will create a new mutex object that cannot be shared across processes. If you create a mutex and use a name that doesn't exist anywhere on the system, you'll get a new, unique handle. Threads in other processes can open the same mutex by creating a **CMutex** object using the same name that the creating thread used.

MFC provides a couple of classes—**CSingleLock** and **CMultiLock**—that supply an access-control mechanism that can be used to wrap **CMutex, CEvent,** and **CSemaphore.**

CSingleLock lets you gain access to a single object at a time. In situations where you need to acquire more than one resource, you can use **CMultiLock. CMultiLock** requires an array of **CSyncObject** pointers and a count of them.

The **CMultiLock::Lock()** function takes three optional parameters. Here's its prototype:

```
DWORD Lock( DWORD dwTimeOut   = INFINITE,
            BOOL  bWaitForAll = TRUE,
            DWORD dwWakeMask  = 0 );
```

The first parameter is the time-out in milliseconds. Like **CSingleLock,** this value can be the constant **INFINITE.** The second parameter specifies whether or not you wish to wait for all of the objects to signal. The third parameter, **dwWakeMask,** is a flag that specifies other conditions that will wake up the thread. Descriptions of the various conditions are provided in the documentation for ::**WaitForMultipleObjects().**

The return value from **CMultiLock::Lock()** indicates what situation caused the function to return. If **Lock** fails, it returns –1. If **Lock** succeeds, it returns a value that must be compared against **WAIT_OBJECT_0, WAIT_ ABANDONED_0,** and **WAIT_TIMEOUT.** Consult the documentation for **CMultiLock::Lock()** to see how these comparisons should be done.

Semaphores
Events, critical sections, and mutexes are binary in the sense that **Lock()** blocks on them if any other thread has them locked. Semaphores are different. They maintain a resource count. The *semaphore* decreases its count whenever **CSemaphore::Lock()** is called. When the resource count goes to zero, any future calls to **CSemaphore::Lock()** will block the thread making the call. This thread will remain blocked until another thread unlocks the semaphore and thereby raises the resource count, or until a specified time-out period has elapsed. A semaphore's count never goes negative.

The maximum number of users who can access the controlled resource at one time is specified during construction of the **CSemaphore** object. To use a **CSemaphore** object, you construct the **CSemaphore** object when it is needed. Specify the name of the semaphore you wish to create and specify that your application should initially own it. You can then access the semaphore when the constructor returns.

Dynamic Link Libraries

A *dynamic link library (DLL)* is a binary file that contains functions and, sometimes, data and resources that can be used by an application (or by another DLL). Before a process can use a DLL, the DLL's file image must first be loaded into memory and mapped to the process's address space. This can be done in one of two ways: *implicit load-time linking* or *explicit runtime linking*. DLLs are used for a number of reasons, primarily for one of these two reasons:

➤ Modularizing an application so that functionality can be updated and reused more easily

➤ Sharing common functionality across a number of executing applications at the same time

Visual C++ has two categories of DLLs—those that use MFC and those that don't. Each category has its own AppWizard. The support provided by AppWizard and MFC in Visual C++ 6 has made the development of DLLs much easier than it was in the past.

Basic DLL Theory

Before you look at MFC's support for DLLs, you need to understand how Win32 integrates DLLs into a process. As I stated earlier, in order for a process to call a function contained within a DLL, the DLL must be mapped to the virtual address space of the process. The DLL's functions are then available to all the threads running within the process. To the threads in the process, the DLL functions simply look like any other function in the process's address space. Whenever a thread calls a DLL function, the thread's stack is used for passing parameters and local variables. Also, the calling thread or process owns any objects created by the DLL function.

The DllMain() Function

When a DLL loads, it will usually need to do some initialization. By default, the linker assigns the main entry point _DllMainCRTStartup() to your DLL. When Windows loads the DLL, it calls this function, which does several things, including initializing the C/C++ runtime library and invoking C++ constructors on static, nonlocal variables. In addition to initializing the C/C++ runtime library, _DllMainCRTStartup() calls a function called DllMain(). Depending on the type of DLL, Visual C++ provides DllMain(), and it gets linked in so that **_DllMainCRTStartup()** has something to call. Here's one example of code provided by AppWizard:

```
BOOL APIENTRY DllMain( HANDLE hModule,
                       DWORD  ul_reason_for_call,
                       LPVOID lpReserved )
{
  switch (ul_reason_for_call)
  {
    case DLL_PROCESS_ATTACH:
    case DLL_THREAD_ATTACH:
    case DLL_THREAD_DETACH:
    case DLL_PROCESS_DETACH:
            break;
  }
  return TRUE;
}
```

The first parameter, **hModule**, is a module handle for the DLL instance that is just being loaded. Because the DLL is a separate module, it can have its own resources. If this is the case, **hModule**'s value should be saved in nonvolatile memory for later use.

The second parameter, **ul_reason_for_call**, indicates why **DllMain()** is being called. In addition to being the entry point during loading, **DllMain()** is also called when the DLL is terminating. During loading, **ul_reason_for_call** is set to **DLL_PROCESS_ATTACH**, and during termination, it is set to **DLL_PROCESS_ DETACH**. You should also be aware that **DllMain()** is called when a thread in the process creates or destroys a secondary thread. For the creation of a thread, **ul_reason_for_call** will be set to **DLL_THREAD_ ATTACH**, and when a thread terminates, it will be set to **DLL_THREAD_ DETACH**.

The third parameter, **lpReserved**, provides additional information concerning initialization and cleanup.

Exporting And Importing Functions

Dynamic linking provides a way for a process to call a function that is not part of its executable code. The executable code for the function, located in a DLL, is linked to the process in one of two ways: implicitly at load-time or explicitly at runtime. Dynamic linking depends on a table contained in the DLL. This table, commonly referred to as the *exports table* or the ***name table***, holds the symbolic names and ordinal numbers of every function and global data variable the DLL exposes to the outside world. The address for each exposed function is also in the **name** table. When the process first loads the DLL, it doesn't know the address of the functions it needs to call, but it does know the symbols or ordinals. The dynamic linking process connects the client's calls to the function addresses in the DLL.

There are two ways of letting the linker know which symbols (functions and variables) to put in the **exports** table. One way is to list the exported symbols in a module-definition (DEF) file. A *module-definition file* is a text file that contains statements for defining an EXE file or DLL. The descriptions of the module-definition statements provided in the MSDN *Visual C++ Programmer's Guide* give the command-line equivalent for each statement. The second way to let the linker know which symbols to include is to declare explicitly in the DLL code each function that should be exported. Here's an example:

```
__declspec(dllexport) int DoSomething(int n);
```

In the client code, you need to declare explicitly each of the functions that need to be imported, as follows:

```
__declspec(dllimport) int DoSomething(int n);
```

By convention, a header file and a preprocessor macro are used to make the inclusion of DLL declarations much simpler. The technique might look like this:

```
// MYDLL.H
#if !defined(_MYDLL_H_)
#define _MYDLL_H_

#if !defined(_MYDLL_)
#define MYDLL_LIB  __declspec(dllimport)
#else
#define MYDLL_LIB  __declspec(dllexport)
#endif // !defined(_MYDLL_)

MYDLL_LIB int DoSomething(int n);

#endif // !defined(_MYDLL_H_)
```

By including the header file, you let the preprocessor decide whether to export or import the **DoSomething()** function. Now you can share the header file between the DLL developer and the DLL user. The only difference is that the DLL developer needs to define **_MYDLL_H_** in the implementation file prior to the **#include** statement:

```
// MYDLL.CPP
#define _MYDLL_H_
#include "mydll.h"
```

 Many shops are finding that without a DEF file, there's no centralized interface definition, so they lose control of the interface. DEF files can help you keep your interfaces concise and cohesive and can help you control dependencies.

While building the DLL, the linker produces a companion import (LIB) file, which contains the symbolic name and ordinal value of all of the exported symbols. The LIB file is a surrogate for the DLL that must be added to the client program's project to enable implicit linking.

Implicit Linking

As you learned earlier, there are two ways to link to a DLL: implicitly and explicitly. Implicitly linking your application to a dynamic link library is by far the most common method for the simple reason that it requires little extra work. The application programmer simply includes the necessary header file, makes the desired function calls, and links with the DLL's static LIB file. During linking, the imported symbols (or ordinals) are matched to the exported symbols in the LIB file, and those symbols are bound into the EXE file.

Now everything is in place so that when the application gets loaded, Windows finds and loads the DLL and then dynamically links it by symbol or by ordinal. When attempting to load a DLL, Windows looks in the following places, in the following order:

1. The directory containing the EXE
2. The current directory for the process
3. The Windows system directory
4. The Windows directory
5. The directories in the system **PATH** environment variable

Clearly, implicit linking usually is the way to go. However, you should be aware of two drawbacks:

➤ Load time will be increased if a lot of dynamic link libraries are being used.

➤ A dynamic link library will be loaded even if no function in the DLL is ever called.

To use an extension other than .dll with implicit linking, you must override the default output file name passed to the linker (/OUT). This option allows you to change the location and file name of your DLL. It also puts the file name in the LIB file.

Explicit Linking

Explicit linking involves specifically telling Windows which file to load and when to load it. For an application programmer, using explicit linking requires more work than using implicit linking. Here's the process:

1. The client calls ::**LoadLibrary**(), passing it the name of the DLL to load. If the function succeeds, the specified DLL is mapped into the address space of the calling process, and a handle to the DLL is returned to the client. **LoadLibrary**() attempts to locate the DLL, using the same search sequence used for implicit linking. If the function fails, it returns **NULL**.

2. The client calls ::**GetProcAddress**(), passing it both the handle returned by ::**LoadLibrary**() and the symbolic name or ordinal value of the desired function. If the function succeeds, it returns the address of the DLL's exported function. This address can be used like a normal function pointer. If ::**GetProcAddress**() fails, it returns **NULL**. To get extended error information, call ::**GetLastError**().

3. Step 2 must be repeated for each function the client wishes to use.

4. When the client is finished with the DLL, it should call ::**FreeLibrary**() to unload the library.

These steps are tedious and prone to error, but they allow the application programmer to avoid the drawbacks intrinsic to implicit linking.

MFC DLLs

When you build a DLL with MFC, you must first decide if you want a regular DLL or an extension DLL. This decision can be made, in part, by answering the following questions:

➤ Will the DLL use MFC but not expose MFC-derived classes to applications that use the DLL?

➤ Will the DLL let applications referring to the DLL use MFC-derived classes from the DLL?

➤ Will the DLL be called from other front-end development tools, such as Visual Basic or PowerBuilder?

➤ Should the DLL statically or dynamically link to the MFC library?

Regular MFC DLLs

A *regular MFC DLL* is a DLL that uses MFC internally and can export C-style functions. This, of course, means that you need to be mindful of name mangling and use **extern "C"** appropriately. If you need to write a DLL that can be used by Visual Basic, Delphi, or another language that can call C-style functions, then this is the DLL to build.

When you build a regular MFC DLL, you can choose whether to link it statically or dynamically to MFC. The method you choose will determine whether you will need to distribute the MFC DLLs with your application.

 The easiest method of creating a regular MFC DLL is with the aid of AppWizard. After invoking AppWizard, simply choose the MFC AppWizard (DLL) project type. The first dialog box is where you specify the type of DLL and, for a regular DLL, specify whether you want it linked statically or dynamically. The Standard Edition of Visual C++ allows only dynamic linking to the MFC libraries.

If you look at the code AppWizard generates, you won't find **DllMain()**. You know that the function must be there, so where is it? Well, as it turns out, it's inside the framework, and you end up with a class derived from **CWinApp** (and a global object of that class), just as you would with an EXE program. The advantage of having a **CWinApp** class is that you can program your DLL as you would any other **CWinApp**-derived class. For example, you can override **CWinApp::InitInstance()** and **CWinApp::ExitInstance()** to initialize and deinitialize your DLL. **DllMain()** calls **InitInstance()** whenever a process attaches to the DLL, and calls **ExitInstance()** whenever a process detaches from the DLL.

Once loaded, any C or C++ program that doesn't use MFC can call your DLL. No extra initialization or protection is needed. If your program does, however, use MFC and you want to pass MFC objects between the program and the DLL, some extra work is required in coding the DLL.

MFC keeps some internal global state information regarding the application or DLL. So, if your DLL dynamically links to MFC, you must use the

AFX_MANAGE_STATE() macro to maintain the proper global state. Here's an example:

```
extern "C" int ShowDlg(HWND hwParent)
{
  AFX_MANAGE_STATE(AfxGetStaticModuleState());
  CWnd * pParent = CWnd::FromHandle(hwParent);
  CDialog dlg(IDD_DIALOG1, pParent);
  return dlg.DoModal();
}
```

By default, MFC uses the resource handle of the main application to load the resource template. Because the exported function, **ShowDlg()**, launches a dialog box using a template that is actually stored in the DLL module, the module state must be switched for the correct handle to be used.

MFC Extension DLLs

Whereas regular MFC DLLs are typically used by non-MFC clients, *MFC extension DLLs* are used to export functions and classes that enhance MFC. For example, let's say you have created a class called **CEmployee** that is derived from the MFC class **CObject**. To export this class, you would place it in an extension DLL. Like a regular MFC DLL, an MFC extension DLL can be created with AppWizard. However, there are a number of fundamental differences between the two types of DLLs. To understand these differences, start by looking at the code AppWizard generates.

Unlike a regular MFC DLL, an MFC extension DLL does not have a **CWinApp**-derived object. It does, however, have a **DllMain()** function.

The **DllMain()** Function

The **DllMain()** function is called whenever a process is attaching to or detaching from the DLL. When a process is attaching, the DLL module state needs to be initialized. That is what **AfxInitExtensionModule()** does for you. **AfxInitExtensionModule()** takes two parameters: a reference to an **AFX_EXTENSION_MODULE** structure and a handle to the instance of the DLL. After initialization, the **AFX_EXTENSION_MODULE** structure contains the state of the DLL, which allows the DLL to work with MFC properly. If **AfxInitExtensionModule()** returns **FALSE**, something is terribly wrong, so **0** is returned from **DllMain()**. If **AfxInitExtensionModule()** returns **TRUE**, a **CDynLinkLibrary** object is created. **CDynLinkLibrary** allows the extension DLL to export **CRuntimeClass** objects or resources to the client application. The framework maintains a linked list of **CDynLinkLibrary** objects.

The last thing to look at is the situation in which the process is detaching from the DLL. Here, the only thing to be done is to delete any local storage attached to the module and remove any entries from the message map cache, which is exactly what **AfxTermExtensionModule()** does.

Of course, you might need to do some other work in **DllMain()**. While attaching to the DLL, be sure to do that work after your call to **AfxInitExtension-Module()**, and while detaching, do it before your call to **AfxTerm-ExtensionModule()**.

Exporting Classes And Functions

You normally implement an MFC extension DLL when you need to export classes that are based on MFC. To expose a class, you simply add the C++ class to your project and add the **AFX_EXT_CLASS** macro to the class declaration, as shown here:

```
class AFX_EXT_CLASS CEmployee : public CObject
```

This modification goes into the H file for the class. Both the DLL project and any client project then use this same H file. **The AFX_EXT_CLASS** macro generates different code depending on the situation—it exports the class in the DLL and imports the class in the client.

On occasion, you might not need to export an entire class. In these situations, you still use **AFX_EXT_CLASS**, but instead of placing it in front of the class name, you simply place it in front of the function you wish to export.

Resources

As mentioned previously, resources can be stored in DLLs. Retrieving these resources is easy if you have the handle to the module that contains the resource. MFC makes things even easier by providing the **AfxGetResourceHandle()** function. This function returns the handle that should be used to retrieve resources. If you're executing in the context of your DLL, MFC will return the handle of your DLL's module; otherwise, it will return the handle of the executing application. Once obtained, the handle can be used as a parameter for the **LoadResource()** and **FindResource()** functions.

Another situation in which you might use the **AfxGetResourceHandle()** function is when you need to set the default module that MFC uses to first locate requested resources. This might be the case in two circumstances: faster resource availability and two similar resources in different modules with the same ID.

If your application code requests that MFC load a resource, MFC first attempts to load the requested resource from the current module. If the requested resource cannot be located in the current module, MFC "walks" the application's linked list of **CDynLinkLibrary** objects in an attempt to locate the resource. Walking the list means that resources at the beginning will be found faster than those at the end. It also means that resources that have the same ID as those earlier will be hidden. Fortunately, you can change the search sequence. Suppose you want your application to search the MFC extension DLL first. Here's how you might do it:

```
// get the EXE's resource handle
HINSTANCE hInstance = AfxGetResourceHandle();

// use the Dll's handle instead
AfxSetResourceHandle(::GetModuleHandle("Employee.dll"));
CString strRes;
strRes.LoadString(IDS_NAME);

// restore EXE's resource handle
AfxSetResourceHandle(::GetModuleHandle(hInstance));
```

Be sure to keep in mind that an MFC extension DLL can move pointers to MFC-based objects across the DLL-application boundary. A regular MFC DLL can't.

Practice Questions

Question 1

> When printing a document, the framework calls a number of **CView** virtual functions. Which of the following lists the correct sequence?
>
> ○ a. **OnPrepareDC(), OnPreparePrinting(), OnBeginPrinting(), OnPrint(), OnEndPrinting()**
>
> ○ b. **OnBeginPrinting(), OnPrepareDC(), OnPreparePrinting(), OnPrint(), OnEndPrinting()**
>
> ○ c. **OnBeginPrinting(), OnPreparePrinting(), OnPrepareDC(), OnPrint(), OnEndPrinting()**
>
> ○ d. **OnPreparePrinting(), OnBeginPrinting(), OnPrepareDC(), OnPrint(), OnEndPrinting()**

Answer d is correct. **OnPreparePrinting()** is called at the beginning of the print job. This function should set the maximum number of pages by calling **CPrintInfo::SetMaxPage()** and then calling **DoPreparePrinting()**. **DoPreparePrinting()** displays the Print dialog box and creates the printer device context. After calling **OnPreparePrinting()**, the framework calls **OnBeginPrinting()**. It's the responsibility of **OnBeginPrinting()** to allocate all of the needed resources. **OnPrepareDC()** is then called to adjust print-time pagination. The **OnPrint()** function is then called to print or preview a page. **OnPrepareDC()** and **OnPrint()** are called for each page being printed. After the document has been printed, the framework calls **OnEndPrinting()** so that the allocated resources can be freed.

Question 2

> Concerning regular MFC DLLs, which statements are true? [Check all correct answers]
>
> ❏ a. Regular MFC DLLs use MFC internally and can export C-style functions.
>
> ❏ b. When regular MFC DLLs are statically linked to the MFC library, the preprocessor symbol **_AFXDLL** must be defined.
>
> ❏ c. When regular MFC DLLs are dynamically linked to the MFC library, the **AFX_MANAGE_STATE()** macro is used to maintain the proper global state.
>
> ❏ d. The **AFX_MANAGE_STATE()** macro must be placed at the beginning of all the exported functions.

Answers a and c are correct. A regular MFC DLL can be either statically or dynamically linked to MFC. One of its key features is that the client can be written in any language that supports the use of DLLs and can make C-compatible function calls. Therefore, answer a is correct.

When a regular MFC DLL is dynamically linked to MFC, all exported functions that use MFC resources must switch the module's state so that the correct resource handle is used. You can do this by placing the **AFX_MANAGE_STATE()** macro at the beginning of a function. The **AFX_MANAGE_STATE()** macro contains the module's state information that is pushed onto the stack. Therefore, answer c is correct and answers b and d are incorrect. Answer b is incorrect because of the phrase "statically linked," and answer d is incorrect because of the phrase "all the exported functions." Functions that don't use the DLL's resource don't require the **AFX_MANAGE_STATE()** macro.

Question 3

> Concerning **CFormView**, which of the following statements are true? [Check all correct answers]
>
> ❏ a. It's derived from **CDialog**.
>
> ❏ b. Its constructors must identify a dialog resource either by name or by its ID.
>
> ❏ c. You must provide an override from **OnDraw()**.
>
> ❏ d. It can use DDX and DDV.
>
> ❏ e. It will automatically support scrolling.

Answers b, d, and e are correct. Because **CFormView** uses a dialog resource, its constructors must identify a dialog resource. Therefore, answer b is correct. Although you must call **UpdateData()** yourself at the appropriate times, **CFormView** can use **DDX** and **DDV**. Therefore, answer d is correct. Because **CFormView** is derived from **CScrollView**, it inherits **CScrollView** scrolling capabilities. Therefore, answer e is correct. Answer a is incorrect because **CFormView** is derived from **CScrollView**, not from **CDialog**. Answer c is incorrect because **CScrollView** provides an **OnDraw** override, which **CFormView** inherits.

Question 4

Concerning the document/view architecture, which of the following statements are true? [Check all correct answers]

❏ a. An MDI application can handle only one type of document.

❏ b. An MDI application can have two documents of dissimilar types open at the same time.

❏ c. An SDI application can handle only one type of document.

❏ d. An MDI application can have two documents of the same type open at the same time.

Answers b and d are correct. MDI applications can have multiple documents open at the same time. The open documents can be of the same type or of different types. Therefore, answers b and d are correct. Although AppWizard provides support for only a single document type, you can add support for additional document types by creating a **CDocument**-derived class and a **CView**-derived class for each document type that you want your application to support. Depending on the application, it might support one, two, or more document types. Therefore, answers a and c are incorrect.

Question 5

Which statement is true?

○ a. MFC always provides version-checking on embedded objects derived from **CObject**.

○ b. A **CFile** object provides an actual connection to a physical file.

○ c. MFC provides the **CFile** class to facilitate transferring a document's data to a storage medium.

○ d. **CFile** provides buffered file I/O.

Answer b is correct. **CFile** and **CArchive** objects work together to provide serialization of MFC objects. The **CFile** object provides unbuffered, binary disk I/O to and from a physical file. The **CArchive** object provides a type-safe buffering mechanism for writing or reading serializable objects to or from a **CFile** object. The insertion and extraction operators are overloaded both as member functions of **CArchive** and as global functions for a number of different data types. These overloads provide version-checking. However, MFC does not provide an overload for **CObject** embedded objects.

Question 6

What is the function of the following code?

```
pDocTemplate = new CMultiDocTemplate(
                IDR_DRAW,
                RUNTIME_CLASS(CMyDoc),
                RUNTIME_CLASS(CChildFrame),
                RUNTIME_CLASS(CDrawView));
    AddDocTemplate(pDocTemplate);
pDocTemplate = new CMultiDocTemplate(
                IDR_FORM,
                RUNTIME_CLASS(CMyDoc),
                RUNTIME_CLASS(CChildFrame),
                RUNTIME_CLASS(CFormView));
    AddDocTemplate(pDocTemplate);
```

○ a. Attach two views to the same document object.

○ b. Register two different views on the same document type.

○ c. Register two different views on two different document types.

○ d. Insufficient information is provided.

Answer d is correct. Either b or c could be correct if you knew the value of the *filterExt* substring of the string resource. But because the string resource is not provided, you do not know the value of the *filterExt* substring. Not knowing the value of *filterExt* means that you cannot determine whether you are dealing with one or two document types. Answer a is incorrect because the question is dealing with document types, not document objects. Answer b is a trick; both function calls are using the same document object class, **CMyDoc**, to trick you. Remember that it is the contents of the *filterName* substring—not the document class—that determines the document type.

Question 7

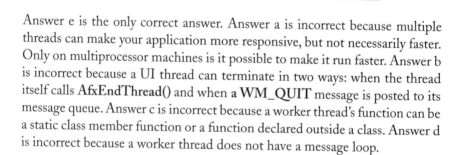

Which of the following statements are true? [Check all correct answers]

- ❑ a. Using multiple threads in your application will always make it run faster.
- ❑ b. A user interface thread can be terminated only by calling **AfxEndThread()**.
- ❑ c. A worker thread's function must be a global function.
- ❑ d. An easy way for the main thread to communicate with a worker thread is to use **PostMessage()**.
- ❑ e. A thread can call **SuspendThread()** on itself.

Answer e is the only correct answer. Answer a is incorrect because multiple threads can make your application more responsive, but not necessarily faster. Only on multiprocessor machines is it possible to make it run faster. Answer b is incorrect because a UI thread can terminate in two ways: when the thread itself calls AfxEndThread() and when a WM_QUIT message is posted to its message queue. Answer c is incorrect because a worker thread's function can be a static class member function or a function declared outside a class. Answer d is incorrect because a worker thread does not have a message loop.

Question 8

To adjust the viewport origin for the scrolling window, **CScrollView** overrides which function?

- ○ a. **CView::OnPrepareDC()**.
- ○ b. **CView::OnDraw()**.
- ○ c. **CView::OnPrepareDraw()**.
- ○ d. **CView::OnUpdate()**.

Answer a is correct. CView::OnPrepareDC() is called by the framework before the OnDraw() member function is called. Classes derived from CView override CView::OnPrepareDC() to adjust attributes of the device context. CScrollView overrides CView::OnPrepareDC() to adjust the viewport origin for the scrolling window. Answer b is incorrect because **CView::OnDraw()** is called to render an image of the document after the DC has been prepared. Answer c is incorrect because **CView::OnPrepareDraw()** is not a valid function. Answer d is incorrect because **CView::OnUpdate()** is called to notify a view that its document has been modified. This function has nothing to do with adjusting the device context's attributes.

Need To Know More?

 Bates, Jon and Tim Tompkins. *Using Visual C++ 6*. Indianapolis: Que Corporation, 1998. ISBN 0-7897-1635-6. This book is aimed at the beginning to intermediate programmer. In typical Que style, its focus is on "how to." Chapters 18 and 19 provide examples, one each, for **CScrollView, CListView, CTreeView,** and **CRichEditView.**

 Kruglinski, David J., George Shepherd, and Scot Wingo. *Programming Microsoft Visual C++*. 5th ed. Redmond, WA: Microsoft Press, 1998. ISBN 1-57231-857-0. This book strikes a good balance between theory and practical application. It covers nearly every aspect of MFC programming, from the basics to database management and the Internet. Chapters 17 and 18 include information on serialization. Chapter 19 covers printing and print previewing. Chapter 22 covers dynamic link libraries.

 Lacey, James M. *MCSD Visual C++ 6 Desktop Exam Cram*. Scottsdale, AZ: The Coriolis Group, 2000. ISBN 1-57610-373-0. This book provides more detailed coveragdeclare e of the topics covered in this chapter. Chapters 6 and 7 cover the document/view architecture, Chapter 11 covers printing and serialization, Chapter 12 covers multithreading, and Chapter 13 covers dynamic link libraries.

 Prosise, Jeff. *Programming Windows with MFC*. Redmond, WA: Microsoft Press, 1999. ISBN 1-57231-695-0. This is the updated version of the author's popular book, *Programming Windows 95 with MFC*. The author's approach is first to present a number of fundamental concepts, using snippets of code where appropriate, and then present a completed program that employs the concepts, followed by an explanation of the code. After you have worked through the book, not only will you know how to use MFC to write 32-bit applications, but you will also understand the code that AppWizard, ClassWizard, and other code generators produce. This is absolutely my favorite MFC book.

 Shepherd, George and Scot Wingo. *MFC Internals: Inside the Microsoft Foundation Class Architecture*. Reading, MA: Addison-Wesley, 1996. ISBN 0-201-40721-3. This book's focus is on how MFC works. Chapters 7 and 8 cover the document/view architecture. Chapter 7 alone probably provides more about the

workings of the document/view architecture than most programmers care to know. Chapter 9 includes a very detailed section on
splitters. The authors really know MFC and present it well.

 Sphar, Chuck. *Learn Microsoft Visual C++ 6.0 Now.* Redmond,
WA: Microsoft Press, 1999. ISBN 1-57231-965-8. Chapter 16
covers serialization, and Chapter 17 covers printing. This is a
basic Visual C++ book, but it provides a thorough and clear description of both serialization and printing.

Creating User Services

Terms you'll need to understand:

√ **ON_COMMAND_RANGE** macro

√ **ON_COMMAND_UI_RANGE** macro

√ **ON_COMMAND_EX** macro

√ **LoadToolBar** function

√ **EnableDocking** function

√ **DockControlBar** function

√ **FloatControlBar** function

√ **DoDataExchange** function

√ **UpdateData** function

√ Notification messages and notification codes

√ **WM_NOTIFY** message

√ **NMHDR**

√ **coclass**

Techniques you'll need to master:

√ Writing code that creates and docks a toolbar

√ Writing code that creates a status bar, adds panes, and keeps the status bar updated

√ Understanding how to write custom DDX and DDV functions

√ Writing code that properly instantiates, manipulates, and destroys a modeless dialog box

√ Writing code that employs both modal and modeless property sheets

√ Creating controls dynamically

√ Implementing an MFC ActiveX control container

√ Adding an ActiveX control to your application

√ Accessing the control's methods and properties

√ Adding event handlers for the control

√ Dynamically creating an ActiveX control

√ Adding help to your application

User services fall into two broad categories. The first category consists of *input mechanisms* that allow the user to direct the application to take some action or to operate in a certain manner. Examples are menus and toolbars. The second category of user services provides information to the user. This category can be divided into two subcategories. One is dynamic and provides immediate feed-back to the user; this subcategory includes status bars and ToolTips. The other subcategory, online help, is static in nature and can be browsed as the user desires. This chapter covers menus, toolbars, status bars, dialog boxes and con-trols, and online help.

Menus are an important part of most Windows applications and are probably the most widely recognized component of user interfaces. Well-designed menus allow users to move quickly and easily through the high-level structure of the user interface. Because menus are such an important element of the user inter-face, both Windows and Microsoft Foundation Classes (MFC) provide a lot of support to applications that use them.

Toolbars provide one of the basic parts of the Windows user interface. A *toolbar* is a child window with buttons and sometimes other types of controls. These controls allow the user to issue commands with a simple mouse click.

Status bars, like toolbars, are a basic part of the Windows user interface. A *status bar* is a child window positioned at the bottom of the main window. It is used to display context-sensitive help messages for menu items and toolbar buttons. It also displays text messages, such as "NUM" to tell the user that Num Lock is on.

Dialog boxes are one of the primary methods Windows programs use to dis-play information and receive input from users. Dialog boxes promote good user-interface design by providing a standard way for the application program-mer to put controls up for the user. Because dialog boxes work in essentially the same way in all Windows programs, users know how to navigate the con-trols. This uniformity among Windows programs means that users—whether they are new, infrequent, or regular users—will be more productive in both speed of action and speed of thought.

Most commercial applications provide some form of online help. Most appli-cations today use Rich Text Format (RTF), but the trend is moving toward the Hypertext Markup Language (HTML) format. The first format is commonly known as WinHelp, and the latter format is known as HTML Help. This chapter covers both formats.

Menus

Most of the time, you will use the Resource Editor to create menus. However, what if you need to change a menu at runtime? You cannot use the Resource Editor then. Instead, you need to add the required code to your application.

The terminology used to describe menus can be confusing. At the top level of the hierarchy is the *menu bar*—menus drop down from the menu bar—and at the lower levels are *sub-menus*. A menu bar is sometimes called a *top-level menu*. The menu that appears when a top-level menu item is clicked is a *drop-down menu*, and items in that menu are referred to as *menu items*. Because the Resource Editor uses **POPUP** statements to define top-level menu items and the associated submenus, drop-down menus are also known as *pop-up menus*.

Windows also provides *shortcut menus*. A shortcut menu is not attached to the menu bar; it can pop up anywhere on the screen. Because of this feature, they are also known as *pop-up menus*. A shortcut menu is typically associated with a portion of a window, such as the client area, or with a specific object, such as an icon. For this reason, these menus are also called *context menus*.

Many applications will use the same **POPUP** menu as both a drop-down menu and a context menu.

As it does in other areas, MFC provides macros that make the task of implementing menus a little easier. Often, a menu allows the user to change a specific attribute of the application by selecting one item from a list. Examples include menus for selecting colors, zoom levels, and dimensions. Because there are many menu items, there are also many command handlers that are nearly identical in their functionality. To provide a more maintainable and elegant solution, you can use the **ON_COMMAND_RANGE** macro to map all the messages with similar functionality to a single handler. There is also an **ON_UPDATE_COMMAND_UI_RANGE** macro that allows you to map a contiguous range of command IDs to a single update message handler. Update message handlers update the state of menu items and toolbar buttons associated with the command.

ClassWizard doesn't support message-map ranges, so you must place these macros yourself. Be sure to put them outside the ClassWizard's comments. You must also add the function prototype entry to the class's header file in the **DECLARE_MESSAGE_MAP** section.

ClassWizard cannot add the **ON_COMMAND_RANGE** or **ON_COMMAND_UI_RANGE** macros to the message map. You must type them in yourself.

 MFC also provides the **ON_COMMAND_EX(ID, FUNC)** macro. Like the **ON_COMMAND_RANGE** macro, the **ON_COMMAND_EX** macro allows several menu commands to be mapped to the same handler. However, because a distinct **ON_COMMAND_EX** macro must be provided for each menu item, nonsequential IDs can be used.

This section describes three ways that a menu might be changed at runtime:

➤ *Dynamic menus*—Dynamic menus allow you to present the user with a different set of choices, depending on the context.

➤ *Cascading menus*—Cascading menus enable you to provide the user with a level of depth that is easy to follow and understand.

➤ *Owner-drawn menus*—Owner-drawn menus enable you to display graphical items, instead of just text, in a menu. For example, you can create an owner-drawn menu to display color palettes and drawing objects in menus.

Dynamic Menus

Normally, you use the Resource Editor at design time to define the menus for your application. Menus defined at design time are static. But what about the times that you would like to provide menu options based on system, user, or data settings? To do this, you need to add and delete menu items at runtime. These kinds of menus are known as *dynamic menus*.

You add and delete menus at runtime by using the **CMenu** member functions: **GetMenu()**, **GetSubMenu()**, **AppendMenu()**, and **RemoveMenu()**. Use **GetMenu()** to retrieve a pointer to the top-level menu. Then, use the pointer to call **GetSubMenu()** to retrieve a pointer-desired submenu. Next, either add items to or remove items from the submenu by using **AppendMenu()** or **RemoveMenu()**, respectively.

Cascading Menus

Cascading menus allow you to display your menu items in a multitier arrangement. This technique can be very useful when you have a lot of menu items and you want to reduce clutter. Cascading menus also can be used to organize your menus as submenus that contain related selections, such as colors, pen widths, or fonts.

Although there is no practical limit to the number of menus that you can nest by cascading, keep in mind that additional levels mean additional complexity. For this reason, Microsoft's user interface guidelines suggest that no more than four levels of nesting be used. The guidelines also recommend that cascading menus be avoided for frequent, repetitive commands. However, that being said, such menus can be beneficial when applied judiciously.

Creating a cascading menu is not that much different from creating a dynamic menu. Rather than attaching a number of individual menu items, you instead attach a **CMenu** object. Start by instantiating a **CMenu** object. Next, call its member function **CreatePopupMenu()** to create a pop-up menu. After that, append the menu items to the pop-up menu and then use the **AppendMenu()** member function to append the **CMenu** object to the appropriate submenu. Normally, you'll create the **CMenu** object on the stack and **Detach()** it when you **AppendMenu()** it. Use **DeleteMenu()** to remove the pop-up menu.

Owner-Drawn Menus

All of the previous menu items have been presented to the user in the form of text. This is fine for most applications, but sometimes something more is needed. At these times, a picture really can be worth a thousand words. Depicting menu items with bitmap images is easy and straightforward. You simply create a **CBitmap** object for each of the menu items and then call **CMenu::AppendMenu()** to append the object to the menu. Windows then displays the bitmap when the menu is displayed. Unfortunately, bitmaps are fixed in size and not easy to adapt to changes in screen metrics.

Fortunately, however, Windows provides a more flexible way to replace the text with graphics: It allows you to draw your own menu items. This kind of menu is called an *owner-drawn menu*. Because it is more flexible, it requires a little more work on your part. Here are the steps that you must follow when implementing an owner-drawn menu:

1. Label each menu item as owner-drawn with the **MF_OWNERDRAW** flag. This must be done at runtime using **AppendMenu()**, **InsertMenu()**, or **ModifyMenu()**.

2. Provide an **OnMeasureItem** handler and associated message-map entry. The **OnMeasureItem** handler is passed a control ID and a **MEASUREITEMSTRUCT** command. In **OnMeasureItem()**, set the *itemWidth* and *itemHeight* fields of **MEASUREITEMSTRUCT** with the menu item's width and height in pixels.

3. Provide an **OnDrawItem** handler and associated message-map entry. The **OnDrawItem** handler's job is to draw the menu item on the screen.

 Windows sends the **WM_MEASUREITEM** message only once for each owner-drawn menu before it's displayed the first time. The **WM_DRAWITEM** message is sent to the owner of the menu every time a menu item should be drawn.

 It is the job of the window that owns the menu to handle the **WM_MEASUREITEM** and **WM_DRAWITEM** messages. However, a more elegant and object-oriented method for implementing owner-drawn menus is to derive a class from **CMenu** and override the **MeasureItem()** and **DrawItem()** virtual functions.

Toolbars

The basic MFC class for toolbars is **CToolBar**, which is derived from **CControlBar**. **CControlBar** is derived from **CWnd**. **CControlBar** windows are positioned inside frame windows and can resize and reposition themselves as the parent window's size and position changes.

Most applications use toolbars to provide instant access to commonly used commands. Toolbars normally consist of a number of buttons, where each button serves as a shortcut to a menu item. Then, rather than navigating through menus or needing to remember keystrokes, the user can simply click on a toolbar button. As with a menu item, when a toolbar button is clicked, a **WM_COMMAND** message is created. When the same command ID is assigned to a menu item and a toolbar button, the same command and update handlers will serve both the menu item and the toolbar button. Although this use is not nearly as frequent, toolbars can also operate as standalone objects.

If you create an SDI or MDI application using the AppWizard and you accept the default toolbar setting in Step 4, the code to create the standard toolbar window, load the button images, and attach it to the main frame window will be generated. This standard toolbar provides buttons for the commonly used File and Edit menu commands, as well as a button for the About dialog box. This is a good start, but as your application design evolves, you will quickly discover that the standard toolbar does not satisfy the unique requirements of your application.

Understanding The Standard Toolbar

When AppWizard generates your skeleton MFC application, it adds a **CToolBar** object, **m_wndToolBar**, to the **CMainFrame** class definition. AppWizard also adds code to **CMainFrame::OnCreate()** that creates the toolbar as a child window of the frame window and loads the associated resource:

```
if(!m_wndToolBar.CreateEx(this, TBSTYLE_FLAT,
          WS_CHILD | WS_VISIBLE
          | CBRS_TOP | CBRS_GRIPPER | CBRS_TOOLTIPS | CBRS_FLYBY
          | CBRS_SIZE_DYNAMIC) ||
             !m_wndToolBar.LoadToolBar(IDR_MAINFRAME))
{
  TRACE0("Failed to create toolbar\n");
  return -1;      // fail to create
}
```

The function used to create the toolbar's window is **CreateEx()**. This function is new to Visual C++ 6. The function's second parameter allows you to set the new toolbar style flags. Here, **TBSTYLE_FLAT** is used to create a flat toolbar in which both the toolbar and the buttons are transparent. **TBSTYLE_FLAT** is one of three styles that affect the 3D aspect of the toolbar buttons. If you want to create a toolbar that resembles the Internet Explorer 4 toolbars, use **TBSTYLE_FLAT|TBSTYLE_TRANSPARENT**. Use 0 to create the old-look "raised buttons" style. Here is a description of all three 3D toolbar styles:

> ► **TBSTYLE_FLAT**—Creates a flat toolbar where both the toolbar and the buttons are transparent, and the button text appears under the button bitmap. The button underneath the cursor is automatically highlighted.

> ► **TBSTYLE_TRANSPARENT**—Like **TBSTYLE_FLAT**, except that only the toolbar is transparent. Buttons appear raised.

> ► **TBSTYLE_LIST**—Like **TBSTYLE_TRANSPARENT**, except that text is to the right of the button bitmap.

The third parameter specifies the control-bar style. This parameter can be a combination of the appropriate standard window styles, such as **WS_CHILD** and **WS_VISIBLE**, and any of the **CControlBar** styles.

After you create the toolbar window, you load the toolbar resource by calling **LoadToolBar()** and passing the ID of the toolbar to be loaded. For the default toolbar, use **IDR_MAINFRAME**.

After you create and load the toolbar, three additional actions are necessary to place a dockable toolbar in your application:

1. Enable docking for the toolbar.

2. Enable docking for the frame window.

3. Dock the toolbar to the frame window.

Here is the code that AppWizard generates for the standard toolbar:

```
m_wndToolBar.EnableDocking(CBRS_ALIGN_ANY);
EnableDocking(CBRS_ALIGN_ANY);
DockControlBar(&m_wndToolBar);
```

The first line enables the toolbar to dock to any edge of the frame window. By combining the flags listed in Table 4.1, you can specify that the toolbar can dock only to specific edges. Alternately, if you want the toolbar to float, pass a 0. For example, to allow the standard toolbar to dock on the top and left edges, you would change the line of code to the following:

```
m_wndToolBar.EnableDocking(CBRS_ALIGN_TOP | CBRS_ALIGN_LEFT);
```

The next line of code calls **EnableDocking**, a member function of the frame window. This function specifies which edges of the frame window will allow docking. You pass this function the same combination of flags shown in Table 4.1.

The **DockControlBar** function is then called to specify the initial edge of the frame window where the toolbar will be docked. The prototype for the function is as follows:

```
void DockControlBar( CControlBar * pBar,
                     UINT nDockBarID = 0,
                     LPCRECT lpRect = NULL );
```

The first parameter points to the toolbar to be docked. The second parameter, *nDockBarID*, specifies which sides of the frame window to consider for docking.

Table 4.1 Docking styles.

Docking Style	Description
CBRS_ALIGN_TOP	Allows docking at the top of the client area.
CBRS_ALIGN_LEFT	Allows docking at the left of the client area.
CBRS_ALIGN_RIGHT	Allows docking at the right of the client area.
CBRS_ALIGN_BOTTOM	Allows docking at the bottom of the client area.
CBRS_ALIGN_ANY	Allows docking on any side of the client area.

The value of this parameter can be 0 or one or more of the values shown in Table 4.2. If it's 0, the control bar can be docked to any side enabled for docking in the destination frame window. The third parameter determines, in screen coordinates, where the toolbar will be docked in the nonclient area of the destination frame window. If you replace **DockControlBar()** with **FloatControlBar()**, the toolbar will initially not be docked to the frame window.

Use only **nDockBarID** values that are allowed by **EnableDocking()**.

Adding Your Own Toolbar

Now that you understand the standard toolbar, let's look at what it takes to add one of your own design. The steps are as follows:

1. Make certain that there is a command ID and a handler for every control that you place on your toolbar. Normally, you will use the same IDs and handlers that you use for your menu items.

2. Use the Resource Editor to create your toolbar resource. Associate each toolbar button with the appropriate command ID.

Notice that the Toolbar Button Properties dialog box has a Prompt property. This property allows you to enter text that will appear in the status line when the cursor passes over the toolbar button or when the menu item with the matching ID is selected. You can also add a ToolTip by adding the ToolTip string after a **\n** separator code.

3. Add a menu item that will allow the user to make the toolbar visible and invisible.

Table 4.2 Values of the nDockBarID parameter.	
Value	**Description**
AFX_IDW_DOCKBAR_TOP	Docks to the top side of the frame window.
AFX_IDW_DOCKBAR_BOTTOM	Docks to the bottom side of the frame window.
AFX_IDW_DOCKBAR_LEFT	Docks to the left side of the frame window.
AFX_IDW_DOCKBAR_RIGHT	Docks to the right side of the frame window.

4. Add a **CToolBar** variable to the appropriate header file. Normally, this will be your **CMainFrame** class header file. This variable can be an object or a pointer; it's your choice. If you do make it a pointer, ensure that it is initialized to 0 in the **CMainFrame** constructor.

5. If you haven't already done so, provide the implementation code to support each of the toolbar buttons.

6. Write the code for the menu item specified in Step 3. Here, you need to provide code that will make the toolbar visible and invisible. Additionally, if in Step 4 you chose to use a pointer, you must create the toolbar before you use it. And don't forget to add a **WM_DESTROY** message handler so that you can delete it. If in Step 4 you decided to use an object, then provide code for your frame window's **OnCreate** function to create your toolbar.

7. Add a UI handler to the frame window.

Don't confuse **CToolBar** with **CToolBarCtrl**. **CToolBar**, inherited from **CControlBar**, is a control bar that has a row of bitmapped buttons and optional separators. **CToolBarCtrl**, inherited from **CWnd**, provides the internal control of the **CToolBar** object. **CToolBarCtrl** is available only for programs running under Windows 95 and Windows NT version 3.51 and later. **CToolBar::GetToolBarCtrl** allows you to obtain a reference to the **CToolBarCtrl** object.

Be sure you understand the difference between these two toolbar classes, and which controls are specific to or different in various operating systems.

Status Bars

Most modern Windows programs include a status bar that displays—without interrupting the user's work—various kinds of status information. Typically displayed at the bottom of a parent window, the status bar is a horizontal window that can be divided into one or more areas. These areas are commonly referred to as *panes*, *panels*, or *indicators*. Each pane is a rectangular area that can be set individually, so one pane might be used to display context-sensitive help for a menu item or toolbar, whereas another displays the current line and column number in a document.

The default MFC status bar, created by the AppWizard, displays the state of the Caps Lock, Num Lock, and Scroll Lock keys in the rightmost panes and displays the currently selected menu item or toolbar button in the leftmost pane (pane 0), commonly referred to as the *message pane*.

In this section, the default status bar will first be examined. Then you will look at how you can add a new pane to a status bar and keep it updated.

Understanding The Standard Status Bar

The basic MFC class for status bars is **CStatusBar**. Like **CToolBar**, **CStatusBar** is derived from **CControlBar**. When AppWizard generates your skeleton MFC application, it adds a **CStatusBar** object, **m_wndStatusBar**, to the **CMainFrame** class definition. It also adds code to **CMainFrame::OnCreate()** that creates the status bar as a child window of the frame window and sets the indicators or panes:

```
if (!m_wndStatusBar.Create(this) ||
    !m_wndStatusBar.SetIndicators(indicators,
      sizeof(indicators)/sizeof(UINT)))
  {
    TRACE0("Failed to create status bar\n");
    return -1;        // fail to create
  }
```

The default AppWizard-generated indicators array is defined at the top of **MainFrm.cpp**:

```
static UINT indicators[] =
{
  ID_SEPARATOR,           // status line indicator
  ID_INDICATOR_CAPS,
  ID_INDICATOR_NUM,
  ID_INDICATOR_SCRL,
};
```

Except for the first, each entry specifies a string resource that is to be displayed when the pane is enabled. The first entry, **ID_SEPARATOR**, is a special ID value, meaning that there is no string resource associated with it. The framework will display the menu item and toolbar button prompts in this area. The other three entries are IDs that are handled by the framework to display the current status of the Caps Lock, Num Lock, and Scroll Lock keys:

```
STRINGTABLE DISCARDABLE
BEGIN
    ID_INDICATOR_EXT        "EXT"
    ID_INDICATOR_CAPS       "CAP"
    ID_INDICATOR_NUM        "NUM"
    ID_INDICATOR_SCRL       "SCRL"
    ID_INDICATOR_OVR        "OVR"
    ID_INDICATOR_REC        "REC"
END
```

The framework positions all panes after the first to the far right of the status bar. It sizes the width of each of these panes for the text string assigned to them and draws them "indented," so that they are visible even when they are blank. The first pane is stretched to fill the remaining space.

Adding A New Pane

Now that you understand the standard status bar that AppWizard provides, adding a new pane to the standard status bar is not very difficult. The process entails only three steps:

1. Define the pane's command ID.

2. Create a new string resource to be displayed in the pane.

3. Add the pane to the indicators array.

Dialog Boxes

Dialog boxes come in two basic varieties: modal and modeless. *Modal dialog boxes* require the user to respond before the application continues. These dialog boxes can be stacked so that one dialog box starts another, thus forcing control to the most recent dialog box and returning to the calling dialog box when closed. *Modeless dialog boxes*, on the other hand, behave much more like normal windows, allowing the user to do other work within the application. A user might open a modeless dialog box and carry out some action; then, for convenience, rather than closing it, the user might just move it out of the way and continue working with the application.

Modal dialog boxes are the most common and easiest to program, but they are also the most restrictive for the user. For your application, the choice of modal or modeless dialog box will depend on a number of factors. In general, however, modal dialog boxes are usually employed for detail windows required to complete a command: which file to save to, how to format the selected text, and so on. These boxes are used to ask questions of the user, to collect details, and to confirm actions. By contrast, modeless dialog boxes are generally used to implement "tools" that may be used alongside documents.

Creating A Modal Dialog Class

Developing a dialog box, whether modal or modeless, entails two basic steps: creating a dialog template using the Resource Editor and then using ClassWizard to create a **CDialog**-derived class to handle the dialog box's functionality. Your new class, as created by ClassWizard, will know what template is associated with it and may have member variables that reflect the state of the controls in the template. By using ClassWizard and hand-coding, you can add specialized code to initialize, reset, validate, or process information, and you can add a message map and message handlers so that your dialog box can react to the user.

Modal dialog boxes are constructed by using one of these two constructors:

```
CDialog(LPCTSTR lpszTemplateName, CWnd* pParentWnd = NULL);

CDialog(UINT nIDTemplate, CWnd* pParentWnd = NULL);
```

With both of these constructors, the first argument specifies the template resource and the second specifies the parent window. If you do not specify a parent window, MFC automatically uses the application's top-level window as the dialog box's parent.

ClassWizard provides a default constructor for your **CDialog**-derived dialog box that initializes the base class using the second of the two constructors. If you look at the constructor that ClassWizard provides, you will see code similar to this:

```
CMyDialog::CMyDialog(CWnd* pParent /*=NULL*/)
     : CDialog(CMyDialog::IDD, pParent)
```

After constructing the **CDialog**-derived object, you then call **CDialog::DoModal()** to display the dialog box. **DoModal()** blocks the calling function until the dialog box is closed, normally by the user clicking on the OK or Cancel button. Both **CDialog::OnOK()** and **CDialog::OnCancel()** call **CDialog::EndDialog()**, which terminates the dialog box. When **EndDialog()** is called, it is passed one argument, which is the value returned to the caller of **DoModal()**. The value passed to **EndDialog()** by **OnOK()** is **IDOK**, and the value passed by **OnCancel()** is **IDCANCEL**. You can override this behavior by calling **CDialog::EndDialog()** and specifying the value that should be returned.

Dialog Data Exchange (DDX)

DDX is an easy way to move data to and from a dialog-box control. Once you have everything in place, the framework transfers the initial value to the control when the dialog box is created and transfers the contents of the control back when the dialog box is dismissed.

When using ClassWizard to create a data member that is associated with the control on the dialog template, ClassWizard also adds a **DDX_** function call between the // **AFX_DATA_MAP** lines inside the dialog box's **DoDataExchange()** function. Several of these **DDX_** functions handle the various types of controls and data types. You can also add your own entries manually at the end of the **DoDataExchange()** function after the ClassWizard map.

DoDataExchange() is called by the framework to exchange and validate dialog data. It is passed a pointer to a **CDataExchange** object that holds context information needed for DDX to take place. **CDataExchange** contains two data members:

➤ **m_bSaveAndValidate** indicates the direction of a DDX operation.

➤ **m_pDlgWnd** is a pointer to the **CWnd** object for which DDX is taking place.

DoDataExchange() is never called directly. Instead, **CWnd::UpdateData()** is called. **CWnd::UpdateData()** creates a **CDataExchange** object and calls **DoDataExchange()**. **UpdateData()** takes one parameter.

If the value of the parameter is **TRUE**, then the DDX value member variable associated with the control is updated with the data that is in the control on the dialog box. However, if the value of the parameter is **FALSE**, then the control will be updated with the value of the member variable.

UpdateData() is automatically called twice by the framework. The first time, it is called by **CDialog::OnInitDialog()**. **CDialog::OnInitDialog()** is a virtual function that is invoked when the dialog box is initialized and before it is displayed. **CDialog::OnInitDialog()** calls **UpdateData(FALSE)**, so as long as your derived class calls (or fails to override) **CDialog::OnInitDialog()**, the controls on your dialog box will be initialized. The second time **UpdateData()** is automatically called by the framework is in **CDialog::OnOK()**, but here the argument passed is **TRUE**.

Dialog Data Validation (DDV)

DDV is an easy way to validate dialog-box information entered by the user. Typically, this means checking for boundaries, such as the maximum length for string values in an edit-box control or the minimum or maximum values when you expect a number to be entered. As with DDX, the easy way to set this up is with ClassWizard. As you add some types of variables to a dialog box, you can also supply validation parameters. When you specify a validation parameter, ClassWizard will place, in the **DoDataExchange()** function, a **DDV_** function call directly after the corresponding **DDX_** function call.

You can also add your own validation code immediately after //}}AFX_DATA_ MAP to check for conditions not covered by the **DDV_** functions. This code can, of course, be in line statements or function calls. Either way, if the validation fails, you need to inform the user, call **CDataExchange::PrepareCtrl()** or

CDataExchange::PrepareEditCtrl() so that the focus can return to the correct control, and then call **CDataExchange::Fail()** to fail the validation.

 By making special entries in ddx.clw or in your project's .clw file, you can integrate your own **DDX_** and **DDV_** routines into the ClassWizard user interface. The instructions for doing this are specified in MFC Technical Note 26.

 Validating and processing user input are important elements of well-designed user interfaces. Be sure you understand the flow of control and the functions involved in the movement of data to and from a dialog-box control.

Using A Modeless Dialog Box

Unlike a modal dialog box, a modeless dialog box is asynchronous. It doesn't take over the application's input and output. Instead, it is usually displayed to complement the normal running of the application by passing information back to the client window.

Creating And Destroying A Modeless Dialog Box

When creating modeless dialog boxes, you use **CDialog** as the base class, just as you do for modal dialog boxes. However, because **CDialog** assumes it will be modal, you will need to override the default behavior if you want your dialog box to be modeless.

This means that the **DoModal()** function is not used to create, display, and terminate the dialog box. Instead, three functions must be called: **CDialog::Create()** to create the dialog box, **CWnd::ShowWindow()** to display it, and **CWnd::DestroyWindow()** for termination. It's possible to eliminate calling ShowWindow(). If you set the dialog template's **Visible** property to **TRUE**, the dialog box will be displayed by **Create()**. Much of the time, the calls to **Create()** and **ShowWindow()** are added to the **CDialog**-derived class constructor.

Because modeless dialog boxes have a longer life than modal dialog boxes, you will normally instantiate the object on the heap and maintain a pointer to it as a protected or private data member. This does, however, present a problem. A dialog box does not automatically free its memory. This problem is usually solved in one of two ways: The client uses the **delete** operator to delete the object, or the object deletes itself.

Data Exchange Between A Modeless Dialog Box And Its Client

Through its access pointer, the client can set values and call member functions of the modeless dialog box at any time during its lifetime. The client can also call **UpdateData(FALSE)** to transfer the contents of the member variables to the controls.

The dialog box needs to inform the client about user input. One way it might do this is to post or send messages to the client. This means the dialog box needs a pointer to the client, and the client and the dialog box must share one or more user-defined messages. Additionally, the dialog box's **OnClose()** and **OnOK()** functions need to be changed. Actually, because this is a modeless dialog box, you probably want to replace the OK button with an Apply button. Or you can leave the OK button and add an Apply button.

Dialog Bars

Dialog bars, a close relative to dialog boxes, are like toolbars. Instead of having an array of bitmap buttons like a toolbar, a dialog bar uses a dialog template, which allows you to use all of the controls that you can use with a dialog box. MFC's **CDialogBar** class implements the dialog bar. The dialog-bar component declares a member variable of type **CDialogBar** in your frame window class. The dialog bar is initialized during the creation of the frame window. All you then need to do is add a menu item for displaying the dialog bar, add controls to the template, and add the necessary handlers.

Customizing Common Dialog Boxes

Windows provides a number of standard dialog boxes to gather information from the user. These common dialog boxes provide advantages for both the programmer and the user. For you, the programmer, they allow you to easily incorporate into your program dialog boxes that you often need, and they are easy to use. Users like them because, from one program to the next, they carry out the same common tasks in the same way. All of these common dialog box classes are derived from a common base, **CCommonDialog**. A list of these classes is shown in Table 4.3.

Usually, you can use these common dialog box classes directly. Sometimes, however, you will need to make minor behavior changes. To change only the behavior of a common dialog box, first consult the Windows Software Development Kit (SDK). You can customize each common dialog box class to perform in different ways, depending on flags or settings in the construction of the object. For example, you can customize the File Open dialog box to hide the

Table 4.3 Common dialog box classes.	
Class	Purpose
CColorDialog	Allows the user to select or create a color.
CFileDialog	Allows the user to open or save a file.
CFindReplaceDialog	Allows the user to substitute one string for another.
CPageSetupDialog	Allows the user to input page measurement parameters.
CFontDialog	Allows the user to select a font.
CPrintDialog	Allows the user to set up the printer and to print documents.
COleDialog	Provides common functionality for a number of **COleDialog**-derived classes.

Read-Only checkbox that appears by default. However, on rare occasions, you might need to make more drastic changes. If major changes are needed, consider starting with the dialog box template and making whatever changes you need—adding controls, deleting controls, and deriving a unique class from **CDialog**. You can make these changes in the template, but the resulting dialog box will not be a common dialog box.

Between the two extremes is another method whereby you "nest" one dialog box inside of another so that multiple dialog boxes appear as one. Refer to Chapter 5 of *MCSD Visual C++ 6 Desktop Exam Cram* for an example of how to do this.

Property Sheets

Dialog boxes are useful for displaying and receiving small amounts of information. Users can quickly become frustrated, however, when they are required to navigate through many dialog boxes to accomplish what is a single logical task. A better way to handle this situation is to use a dialog box that contains tabs. Each tab corresponds to a related page of controls. In MFC terminology, this type of dialog box is known as a *property sheet*, with *property pages*. Property sheets represent the actual dialog box, and property pages represent the tabs. Users can flip from one property page to another by clicking on the tab control that is hosted by the property sheet.

MFC supports property sheets and property pages through the **CPropertySheet** and **CPropertyPage** classes. Surprisingly, **CPropertySheet** is derived from **CWnd**, not from **CDialog**. However, after a little thought, this makes sense.

CDialog provides a programmatic interface to a Windows dialog box, and Windows dialog boxes are closely tied to a dialog template resource that specifies the dialog box's controls and their placement. **CPropertySheet** has nothing to do with dialog templates; instead, the controls on a property sheet are maintained in one or more overlapping property pages, with each one containing controls for setting a group of related properties. Because the property pages maintain the controls and are intimately related to dialog template resources, it is the **CPropertyPage** class that is derived from **CDialog**.

Creating Property Page Resources

You create property-page resource templates in the Resource Editor in nearly the same way that you create dialog-bar resource templates. The only difference is that instead of selecting **IDD_DIALOGBAR**, you need to select **IDD_PROPPAGE_SMALL, IDD_PROPPAGE_MEDIUM,** or **IDD_PROPPAGE_LARGE.** The only difference between the three is the initial size of the property sheet. If you have different-size property pages, the largest one will determine the size of the property sheet.

Creating A **CPropertyPage**-Derived Class

After designing a property page template, you can use ClassWizard to create a CPropertyPage-derived class. You do this in very much the same way that you create a **CDialog**-derived class. Be careful, though. ClassWizard will default the base class to **CDialog**, so you will need to change this.

Creating And Displaying A Modal **CPropertySheet**

Although **CPropertySheet** objects are not derived from **CDialog**, they are constructed and displayed in the same way that **CDialog** objects are constructed and displayed. For example, to create and display a modal property sheet, you would normally declare a **CPropertySheet** object and call **DoModal()**. However, you also need to make an instance of each **CPropertyPage**-derived class and attach these instances to the property sheet by using **CPropertySheet::AddPage()**. You can use ordinary DDX calls on the **CPropertyPage** objects to initialize and retrieve control data.

Creating And Displaying A Modeless **CPropertySheet**

The major difference between displaying a modeless property sheet and a modal property sheet is what you might suspect. Instead of using the **DoModal()** function to display the property sheet, you use the **CPropertySheet::Create()**

function. When using modeless property sheets, you must exercise the same care as when you're using modeless dialog boxes. Avoid constructing the property sheet and property pages on the stack.

Common Controls

Since the first version of Windows, there have been push buttons, checkboxes, and edit boxes that developers could use in their applications. Some programmers found the standard controls limiting, however, so they implemented their own controls. Microsoft noticed this and decided to include the more popular ones as part of the operating environment of Windows 95. Collectively known as the *common controls*, these controls range from a simple slider to an edit control that provides character and paragraph formatting. Most of these controls belong to a window class implemented in comctl32.dll. The window class and the corresponding window procedure define the properties, appearance, and behavior of the control.

Since the release of Windows 95, additional common controls have been added to the list, resulting in new versions of comctl32.dll. Table 4.4 outlines the different DLL versions. MSDN online help covers all versions, marking elements above version 4 with a version number.

 MFC provides classes to wrap nearly all of the common controls. You should be familiar with all of the common controls and their wrapper classes. The MSDN library contains a wealth of information and provides a number of sample programs that demonstrate how to use most of the common controls.

For an MFC programmer, there are two ways that you normally create a common control. First, you can add a control to a dialog template and let the Visual C++ Dialog Editor write a **CONTROL** statement for you. Or, you can instantiate

Table 4.4   Comctl32.dll versions.

Version	Distribution Platform
4.00	Windows 95 and Windows NT 4
4.70	Internet Explorer 3.x
4.71	Internet Explorer 4
4.72	Internet Explorer 4.01 and Windows 98
5.80	Internet Explorer 5
5.81	Windows 2000

the MFC class and then call **Create()**. The following statements create an IP address control by using the second method:

```
/ / . . .
CIPAddressCtrl ipAddress;
ipAddress.Create(WS_CHILD | WS_VISIBLE | WS_BORDER,
    CRect(x1, y1, x2, y2), this, IDC_IPADDRESS);
// . . .
```

The **Create()** function's four arguments are the control's style flags, the control's position and size (as a **CRect** object), a pointer to the control's parent window, and the control's ID. The style flags must include **WS_CHILD** because common controls, like other controls, are child windows used in conjunction with other windows to provide user interaction. In addition to the standard window styles, each type of common control has a set of control styles that can be used to vary the appearance and behavior of the control. There is also a set of styles that are common to two or more types of common controls.

Common controls also share the means by which they send notifications to their parents. Unlike the standard controls, which send notifications to their parents by using **WM_COMMAND** messages, most common controls enclose their notifications in **WM_NOTIFY** messages. A **WM_NOTIFY** message's **wParam** holds the child window ID of the control that sent the message, and **lParam** holds a pointer to either an **NMHDR** structure or a structure that's a superset of **NMHDR**. **NMHDR** is defined as:

```
typedef struct tagNMHDR {
  HWND hwndFrom;
  UINT idFrom;
  UINT code;
} NMHDR;
```

hwndFrom holds the window handle to the control sending the message. **idFrom** is the identifier to the control, and **code** is the notification code. The notification code can be control-specific, or it can be any one of a number of common notification codes.

A number of the common notifications define a structure that starts with a **NMHDR**-type variable. For instance, **NM_CHAR** passes the address of a **NMCHAR** structure that contains additional information about the character that caused the notification message. **NMCHAR** is defined as:

```
typedef struct tagNMCHAR {
  NMHDR hdr;
  UINT ch;
```

```
  DWORD dwItemPrev;
  DWORD dwItemNext;
} NMCHAR ;
```

The **ch** member contains the character being processed. The **dwItemPrev** and **dwItemNext** members are specific to the control that is sending the notification.

In addition to the preceding notification codes, many of the common controls define their own unique codes to signify control-specific events. For example, the parent of an up-down control is notified when the position of the control is about to change. The parent is sent a **WM_NOTIFY** message with a code of **UDN_DELTAPOS**. **lParam** points to an **NMUPDOWN** structure that contains information about the position change. **NMUPDOWN** is defined as:

```
typedef struct _NM_UPDOWN {
    NMHDR hdr;
    int    iPos;
    int    iDelta;
} NMUPDOWN;
```

The **iPos** member represents the up-down control's current position, and **iDelta** represents the proposed change in the up-down control's position.

Although they are similar in many ways, each common control is unique in some way. They can differ in how they are created, in the unique window styles and notification codes they support, and in how they are used. Jeff Prosise's book, *Programming Windows with MFC*, provides excellent coverage of the common controls.

ActiveX Controls

ActiveX controls are designed for use both in ordinary ActiveX control containers and on the Internet, in World Wide Web pages. ActiveX controls, unlike Java applets and Netscape plug-ins, are language-neutral and can be used in applications written in programming languages different from the one used to create the ActiveX control.

ActiveX controls are 32-bit controls that can be used in any container that can support the control's interfaces. This interface provides a collection of related attributes (called *properties*) and functions (called *methods*). This interface is the mechanism through which the control exposes its functionality.

Properties are values that are maintained by the control and that change the appearance or behavior of the control. Properties have symbolic names that are matched to integer indexes. Each property has a name, such as **BackColor** or **TitleFont**, and a type, such as **int** or **BSTR**. A typical ActiveX control consists of a user-interface representation both at design time and at runtime. The design-time interface allows the application developer to specify a property's initial value. The runtime interface allows a client program to change a property at runtime. A client program retrieves and sets a control's property by specifying the property's index.

Methods define the actions that the control is capable of performing. A method has a symbolic name, a set of parameters, and a return value. You call a method by calling a C++ member function of the class representing the control.

When an ActiveX control is used within an ActiveX *control container*, the container communicates with the control through the control's properties and methods. However, for the control to communicate with the container, a second mechanism is used. When the control needs to notify the container that something has happened to the control, the control "fires" an *event*. Common examples of events include clicks on the control, data entered using the keyboard, and changes in the control's state. When these actions occur, the control fires an event to alert the container. An event has a symbolic name and can have an arbitrary sequence of parameters.

ActiveX controls are implemented as in-process servers and are essentially simple COM objects that support the **IUnknown** interface. However, if **IUnknown** were the only interface supported, the control wouldn't do much more than take up disk space. It therefore usually supports many more interfaces in order to offer functionality. Because all additional interfaces can be viewed as optional, a container should not rely on any additional interfaces being supported. By not specifying additional interfaces that a control must support, a control can efficiently target a particular area of functionality without having to support particular interfaces to qualify as a control. As always with COM, whether in a control or a container, it should never be assumed that an interface is available, and standard return-checking conventions should always be followed. It is important for a control or container to degrade gracefully and to offer alternative functionality if a required interface is not available.

As COM servers, ActiveX controls have *type libraries*. A type library contains information about the control's properties, methods, and events. Type libraries can exist as separate files (usually with a .tlb extension, but occasionally .olb is used) or can be included in the same file as the control. Type libraries also contain the control's **coclass** (COM class) information. A **coclass** contains one or more interfaces defined by the control.

Selecting And Adding ActiveX Controls To Your Project

Literally thousands of ActiveX controls are available today, with functionality ranging from a timer control (which simply notifies its container at a particular time) to full-featured spreadsheets and word processors. Very sophisticated third-party ActiveX controls are readily available that quickly and easily integrate into your application. Using these controls can save you hours, weeks, or even months of programming effort. ActiveX controls are freely distributed or available as shareware on the Internet. Keep in mind, however, that you usually get what you pay for, and with shareware controls, the documentation is often poor or nonexistent.

Let's assume you have found a neat ActiveX control that you want to use. The first thing you need to do is copy it to your hard disk. You probably want to put it in the \Windows\System or \Winnt\System32 directory. If there are accompanying help (HLP) files and license (LIC) files, copy them into the same directory.

Next, you need to register the control in the Windows Registry. Because all ActiveX Controls must support self-registration by implementing **DllRegisterServer()** and **DllUnregisterServer()**, this step is quite simple. You merely run the Windows utility RegSvr32, passing it the control's file name on the command line. After you register your ActiveX control, you need to add it to your project by using the Components And Controls Gallery. Files will be added to your project that implement the interface classes (also known as *dispatch classes*) needed for the control.

Whenever you insert an ActiveX control, ClassWizard uses the information in the control's type library to generate a wrapper class for each of the control's internal **coclasses**. These wrapper classes provide an easy programmatic interface for a control. Each class has member functions for all properties and methods, and each class has constructors that you can use to dynamically create an instance of the control. The functions are known as *dispatch functions*. Each dispatch function calls the **CWnd::InvokeHelper()** function. Properties always have separate **Set** and **Get** functions. To call a method, you simply call the corresponding function.

InvokeHelper() converts the parameters to **VARIANTARG** values and then invokes the **IDispatch::Invoke()** method. The first parameter passed to **InvokeHelper()** specifies the dispatch ID for the corresponding property or method in the control. The second parameter is a flag describing the context of the **Invoke** call. These two parameters provide the needed information to determine the specific implementation code. The fourth parameter is the address of the variable that will receive the property value or return value. It must match the type specified by the third parameter.

Adding An ActiveX Control To A Dialog Box

Not only have the wrapper classes for the new control been added to your project, but a new icon representing the ActiveX control has also been added to the Resource Editor's Control toolbar. You place this control on the dialog box just like any other control.

After the control has been added to the dialog box, you can change the properties. As with regular controls, you can set several properties for the ActiveX controls, arranged as pages in a property sheet. Property sheets for ActiveX controls have one General tab, which, as with normal controls, allows you to assign an ID and set the standard enabling and visible flags. The other property pages are specific to the control itself.

Using ClassWizard, you can add a member variable for the ActiveX control. However, you can map an ActiveX control against only its dispatch or interface class. Therefore, the Category combo box allows only the Control category, and the Variable Type can be only the wrapper class. After the control variable is defined, you can invoke methods and get and set properties by calling the appropriate wrapper-class member functions.

You can add event handlers for ActiveX controls in the normal fashion by adding an event handler with ClassWizard or by using the New Windows Messages And Event Handlers dialog box. The first time you add an event handler, an event sink map is declared and defined in your project. For each handler, an event map entry (**ON_EVENT**) is added to the event sink map, and an event handler function is added to the container's CPP file.

Creating ActiveX Controls At Runtime

When you create an ActiveX control at runtime without a resource entry, here are the programming steps to follow:

1. Insert the component into the project.

2. Add an embedded ActiveX-control wrapper-class member to the appropriate window class.

3. Add an ID for the control.

4. Add code to call the control's **Create()** function.

5. Add the event sink declaration and definition macros.

6. Add the necessary event message handlers and prototypes.

At AppWizard Step 2, be sure the ActiveX control option is selected (this is the default). When the AppWizard ActiveX control option is checked, AppWizard inserts the following line of code to **InitInstance()** of your application class:

```
AfxEnableControlContainer();
```

It also inserts the following to the project's stdafx.h file:

```
#include <afxdisp.h>
```

If you build an application without this option checked and you later decide you want to use ActiveX controls, you can simply add these lines of code.

WinHelp

The Microsoft Help Workshop allows you to create HLP files that can be attached to your application. After an HLP file is in place, it is a simple matter of calling **WinHelp()** or **CWinApp::WinHelp()** to invoke the WinHelp application. The MFC AppWizard can also add code that makes it easy for you to provide context-sensitive help.

The WinHelp application provides a consistent interface that allows the user to select an item from the help contents and then view, search, and navigate the various help screens by jumping from one topic to another.

 The Microsoft Help Workshop's online help, usually referred to as the Help Author's Guide, is a graphical help file (hcw.hlp) that is an excellent source of information. It will provide much of the information you need to develop and create a robust help system.

Building Simple Help Files

The process of building your own help files consists of four distinct steps:

1. Create the help text or topic file, using Microsoft Word or another RTF-compatible word processor.

2. Create the help project file, using Visual C++ or another text editor.

3. Compile the help file, using the Help Compiler and project file.

4. Attach the help file to your application.

The help text or topic file contains topics that are linked via hypertext or hypergraphics. *Hypertext* is text composed of blocks of words that contain links to other text. *Hypergraphics* are images with hot spots that, like hypertext, link to text. This linking is what enables a user to move from one topic to another or to display a pop-up window.

 Refer to Microsoft Help Workshop's online help for detailed information on how to format the help text file.

The help project file is a simple ASCII text file that you create with your favorite text editor. It is formatted like an INI file. The most commonly used sections are presented in Table 4.5. Refer to Microsoft Help Workshop's online help for detailed information about the help project file.

 You can also use Microsoft Help Workshop to create and maintain your HPJ (help project) file.

After you've prepared your help text file and help project file, you should compile and view the help file. First, from Windows, run the Microsoft Help Workshop utility. Open the HPJ file, and then click on the Save And Compile button. Then, from Windows Explorer, double-click on the newly created HLP file.

If you want, you can add the tree-view table of contents. You do this by placing the table-of-contents information in a text file that has a CNT extension. After

Table 4.5 Frequently used sections of the help project file.	
Section	**Description**
OPTIONS	Specifies how the help file is to be compiled.
FILES	Specifies the RTF files to be used to create the HLP file.
WINDOWS	Defines the primary help window and any secondary windows.
MAP	Maps help context IDs to numbers. Required when context-sensitive help is implemented.
ALIAS	Equates one context ID with another.

creating and saving your contents file, when you run WinHelp with the HLP file, you'll see a new contents screen.

> Refer to Microsoft Help Workshop's online help for detailed information about the contents (CNT) file.

CWinApp::WinHelp() is used to invoke the WinHelp application from within an MFC program. Here is its prototype:

```
virtual void WinHelp(DWORD dwData, UINT nCmd = HELP_CONTEXT);
```

The *nCmd* argument specifies the type of request, and *dwData* provides additional information for *nCmd*. Refer to Visual C++ online help for a complete list of the possible values for *nCmd* and the corresponding values for *dwData*.

The name of the help file used matches the name of the application. Assuming that the name of your application is myapp.exe and the help file is myapp.hlp, you would invoke the WinHelp application and display the contents screen by using one of the following:

```
AfxGetApp->WinHelp(0, HELP_INDEX); // old style
```

```
AfxGetApp->WinHelp(0, HELP_FINDER); // new style, .CNT required
```

> You can use a name different from the name of the application by setting **CWinApp::m_pszHelpFilePath**.

Creating Context-Sensitive Help

Most Windows applications allow the user to press F1 to get information related to the current task. When the user presses F1, the application is smart enough to determine which object (window, control, menu item, etc.) has the focus, read the object's context reference, and send it to WinHelp, which in turn displays the appropriate help topic. The [MAP] section of your HPJ file is where you define your context reference IDs. You can use #define, #include, and assignment statements in the [MAP] section. It's often convenient to use your program's resource IDs as the context reference IDs, so that you can simply place a single #include statement in the [MAP] section. The problem with this approach is that the jump tag names in your RTF file must be the same as your resource ID names. Another approach is to use the **[ALIAS]** section to associate your program resource IDs with the jump tags used in the RTF file.

You can add help to an MFC application by hand if you so desire. However, it is much simpler to have AppWizard add the basic support when you initially create your project. You do this by selecting the Context-Sensitive Help option at MFC AppWizard Step 4 of 6 for MDI and SDI projects, and at MFC AppWizard Step 2 of 4 for dialog-based projects.

For SDI and MDI projects, AppWizard adds the necessary message-map entries, adds a menu item to the Help menu, and adds a button to the toolbar. For dialog projects, AppWizard adds a message-map entry and a Help button.

AppWizard also provides you with a Help starter kit. It creates an HPJ file, a help contents (CNT) file, a number of bitmap (BMP) files, and, depending on the type of project, one or more starter topic (RTF) files. All of these files are placed in an HLP directory that AppWizard creates in your project directory. The HPJ file is added to your project so that you can build the HLP file for the Build menu.

As you add new resources to your project, you should add topic information to your RTF file. Visual C++ automatically provides you with context reference IDs to use as your jump tags. The context reference ID names are simply the resource ID names with an H added as the first letter. Each value assigned is the sum of a resource ID value and a base value. Each resource type has its own base value. These base values are defined in afxpriv.h and explained in the online help article "TN028: Context-Sensitive Help Support." The context reference IDs are kept in a help mapping (HM) file that is maintained by Visual C++. When you do a build and your resource.h file has changed, Visual C++ runs the MakeHm application. MakeHm reads your resource.h file and creates an HM file, which is included in the **[MAP]** section of the HPJ file.

Using Graphics And Hypergraphics

When adding a graphic or hypergraphic image to the RTF file, you can either paste it directly into the file or include it by reference. Placing the bitmap image directly into the help file is the easiest method, but it is very restrictive. Inserting the bitmap image by reference provides many advantages and is not all that difficult to do. You simply place special "embraced" text in the file. Then, when you compile the help file, the compiler will include the image as part of the HLP file.

You create hypergraphics with the Hotspot Editor (shed.exe), normally located in C:\Program Files\Microsoft Visual Studio\Common\Tools. You can use the Hotspot Editor to open a BMP, a DIB, or a WMF file, and add hot spots to the existing graphic image. You then save the file as a hypergraphic (SHG) file. After you have defined the hot spots, the file can be included by reference into your RTF file and then compiled into your help (HLP) file.

A hot spot can be any rectangular area within the image. After drawing a hot spot, you will need to specify its context ID and its type. Its type can be a jump, pop-up, or macro.

Using Help Macros

Help macros are routines built into the WinHelp application that allow you to further customize your help system. There are more than 50 macros that you can use to customize the way WinHelp works with your help files. These macros can be grouped into four major categories:

➤ Button manipulation

➤ Menu manipulation

➤ Hypertext link

➤ WinHelp auxiliary

Macros can be placed in the HPJ file, the RTF file, or your application. If you place a macro in the [CONFIG] section, the macro will run when WinHelp first opens your help file. If you place a macro in a topic footnote, the macro will run whenever the user jumps to the topic. When you place a macro in a topic footnote, be sure to use the special footnote symbol, an exclamation mark (!). You can also use macros, instead of jump tags, with hypertext and hypergraphics.

 Be sure you know the various file types and the purpose of each type. Remember, there are some help-related files generated by AppWizard and Visual C++ that you don't directly maintain.

HTML Help

By using HTML-based Help, you will be able to provide a wide range of new types of help. HTML Help can include such features as hyperlinks, ActiveX controls, scripting, and Dynamic HTML (DHTML). Microsoft touts HTML Help as its next-generation online authoring system. Like WinHelp, HTML Help uses a project file to combine topic, content, index, and other source files into one compiled help file. Which types of files you use in your help project will depend on your design and on how you plan to distribute it. After you have your HTML Help system complete, you can mount it on disk, on the Internet, or on an intranet. Table 4.6 lists some of the most commonly used files.

 If HTML Help is not installed on your system, refer to the online help article "Installing HTML Help."

Creating Help

As with WinHelp, HTML Help uses a project file to bring all of the various help components together. You use the HTML Help Workshop to create your project file and most other files as well. One very useful feature of the HTML Help Workshop is the ability to convert existing WinHelp projects. You simply choose File|New, choose Project, click on OK, and select the Convert WinHelp Project checkbox. The wizard does the rest.

After converting a WinHelp project or when creating a new HTML Help project, you can add or remove HTML topic files and specify the location of

Table 4.6 Commonly used HTML Help files.

Name	Type	Description
Project	HHP	Manages your topics, art, contents, index, and other source files. Also defines the on-screen appearance of your help system.
Topic	HTM, HTML	Contains the text that appears on the screen and contains formatting codes (tags) that tell a browser how to display each page.
Image	JPEG, GIF, PNG	HTML image files.
Contents	HHC	Contains the topic titles for your table of contents.
Index	HHK	Contains the index entries (keywords) for your index.
Alias	ALI	Maps IDs to help topics. Used for context-sensitive help support.
Compiled	CHM	A single file that contains all the elements of your help system. This file is distributed with your application and can be viewed using Internet Explorer.

index, contents, image, and multimedia files. When you're creating a new HTML topic file, the HTML Help Workshop provides a skeleton to which you add text; pointers to graphics, sounds, and animated images; and links or jumps within the same file, to another file or to a Web site.

Each topic requires its own HTM file. You can design your table of contents so that the user will be able to click on a topic to open the corresponding HTML topic file. The topic file itself can be part of the CHM file stored locally or be a file located on some remote system or Web site.

The index file behaves in the same manner as the topic file, but it uses key-words rather than topics. The two types of indexes you can use, depending on your requirements, are:

➤ *Binary index*—Used with a CHM file.

➤ *Site map index*—Works on a Web site.

Compiling Help Using Visual C++

By adding your HTML Help project file to your Visual C++ project, you en-sure that any time any of your help source files change, a new version of your CHM file will be built. For this to occur, you must use the Visual C++ custom build rules. After you add your HHP file to your project, in the Workspace pane, select the HHP file; then, choose Project|Settings|Custom Build and make the necessary entries. The Command entry is as follows:

```
pathname\hhc.exe $(InputDir)\$(InputName).hhp
@echo off
```

The Output entry is as follows:

```
$(InputDir)\$(InputName).chm
```

Calling HTML Help From Your Application

As in WinHelp, only one API is used with HTML Help. This function is HtmlHelp(), which is prototyped as follows:

```
HWND HtmlHelp( HWND hwndCaller,
               LPCSTR pszFile,
               UINT uCommand,
               DWORD_PTR dwData
             );
```

As you can see, this function is modeled after **WinHelp()**. This makes it simple to update existing programs from WinHelp to HTML Help. Be aware, however, that the command names and parameters are different.

To use **HtmlHelp()** in your program, you need to modify your project settings to include the paths to the HTML Help support files:

➤ Use Project|Settings|Link|Category: Input|Additional Library Path to specify the directory location of HtmlHelp.lib.

➤ Use Project|Settings|Link|Category: Input|Object/Library Modules to specify HtmlHelp.lib.

➤ Use Project|Settings|C/C++|Category: Preprocessor|Additional Include Directories to specify the directory location of HtmlHelp.h.

➤ Place **#include <HtmlHelp.h>** in your stdafx.h file.

 HTML Help comes with an authoring guide with sections on how to design a help system and how to use the HTML Help Workshop. This is currently the best source of information.

Practice Questions

Question 1

In the **OnInitDialog** function, you want to dynamically add a static control to the dialog box. Which of the following would you use?

○ a. `m_pName = new CStatic;`
   `m_pName->Insert(_T("Employee Name"),`
   `                WS_CHILD|WS_VISIBLE|SS_LEFT,`
   `                CRect(10,10,150,50), this);`

○ b. `m_pName = new CStatic;`
   `m_pName->Create(_T("Employee Name"),`
   `                WS_CHILD|WS_VISIBLE|SS_LEFT,`
   `                CRect(10,10,150,50), this);`

○ c. `m_pName = new CStatic;`
   `m_pName->Add(_T("Employee Name"),`
   `                WS_CHILD|WS_VISIBLE|SS_LEFT,`
   `                CRect(10,10,150,50), this);`

○ d. `m_pName = new CStatic;`
   `m_pName->Show(_T("Employee Name"),`
   `                WS_CHILD|WS_VISIBLE|SS_LEFT,`
   `                CRect(10,10,150,50), this);`

Answer b is correct. **Create()** is a member of the **CStatic** class. Answers a, c, and d are incorrect because **Insert()**, **Add()**, and **Show()** are not members of the **CStatic** class.

Question 2

> Which statements are true? [Check all correct answers]
>
> ❑ a. A **coclass** can expose one or more interfaces.
>
> ❑ b. Type libraries always exist as separate TLB files.
>
> ❑ c. Type libraries contain information about a control's properties, methods, and events.
>
> ❑ d. Type libraries contain **coclass** information.

Answers a, c, and d are correct. Answer a is correct because most controls will support a number of interfaces, and the control's **coclass** will expose each of these interfaces for use by the control container. Answer c is correct because a control container uses the type information to learn about a control's methods, properties, and events. Answer d is correct because a type library also contains a control's **coclass** information. Answer b is incorrect because a type library can be a separate file or a component within another file.

Question 3

> Which statements are true? [Check all correct answers]
>
> ❑ a. Modal dialog boxes are invoked with **CDialog::Create()**, and modeless dialog boxes are invoked with **CDialog::Create()**.
>
> ❑ b. Modal dialog boxes are invoked with **CDialog::Create()**, and modeless dialog boxes are invoked with **CDialog::DoModeless()**.
>
> ❑ c. Modal dialog boxes are invoked with **CDialog::DoModal()**, and modeless dialog boxes are invoked with **CDialog::Create()**.
>
> ❑ d. Modal dialog boxes are invoked with **CDialog::DoModal()**, and modeless dialog boxes are invoked with **CDialog::DoModeless()**.

Trick! question

Answer c is correct. This is a trick because there is only one correct answer. After you construct a **CDialog** object, **CDialog::DoModal()** is called to display a modal dialog box. **DoModal()** blocks the calling function until the dialog box is closed, normally by the user clicking on the OK or Cancel button. However, the purpose of a modeless dialog box is to complement the normal running of the application, which means that it cannot block the calling function. Instead, a modeless dialog box must operate like a normal window might. As with most windows, three functions are used to create, display, and terminate the modeless dialog box. These functions are **CDialog::Create()** to create the dialog box, **CWnd::ShowWindow()** to display it, and **CWnd::DestroyWindow()** to terminate it.

Question 4

Which of the following statements regarding data exchange is true?

○ a. The **DoDataExchange()** function is called by the framework to exchange data between a parent window and a dialog box.

○ b. The **DoDataExchange()** function is called by the framework to exchange data between a dialog box and a dialog box's controls.

○ c. The **DoDataExchange()** function is called by the framework to exchange data between a frame window and a dialog box's control.

○ d. The **DoDataExchange()** function is not called by the framework; instead, it must be called directly.

Answer b is correct. **DoDataExchange()** is called by the framework to exchange and validate dialog data. It is never called directly; instead, **CWnd::UpdateData()** is called. **CWnd::UpdateData()** creates a **CDataExchange** object and calls **DoDataExchange()**. **UpdateData()** is automatically called twice by the framework. The first time, it's called by **CDialog::OnInitDialog()**. **CDialog::OnInitDialog()** is a virtual function that is invoked when the dialog box is initialized and before it is displayed. **CDialog::OnInitDialog()** calls **UpdateData(FALSE)**, so as long as your derived class calls (or fails to override) **CDialog::OnInitDialog()**, the controls on your dialog box will be initialized. The second time **UpdateData()** is automatically called by the framework is in **CDialog::OnOK()**, but here the argument passed is **TRUE**, causing the data in the controls to be transferred to the dialog box's data members.

Question 5

Which of the following statements regarding toolbars and status bars is true?

○ a. **CToolBar** is derived directly from **CWnd**, and **CStatusBar** is derived directly from **CControlBar**.

○ b. **CToolBarCtrl** is derived directly from **CWnd**, and **CToolBar** is derived directly from **CWnd**.

○ c. **CToolBar** is derived directly from **CWnd**, and **CToolBarCtrl** is derived directly from **CControlBar**.

○ d. **CStatusBar** is derived directly from **CControlBar**, and **CStatusBarCtrl** is derived directly from **CWnd**.

Answer d is correct. **CToolBar** and **CStatusBar** inherit directly from **CControlBar**. **CToolBarCtrl** and **CStatusBarCtrl** inherit directly from **CWnd**.

Question 6

When you initially created your application at AppWizard Step 4 of 6, you deselected the Initial Status Bar option. Now you have decided that you would like your application to have a status bar. Where do you need to add code to create and display the status bar?

○ a. In **InitInstance()** of your application class

○ b. In **OnCreate()** of **CMainFrame**

○ c. In **PreCreateWindow()** of **CMainFrame**

○ d. In **OnDraw** of your view class

Answer b is correct. When the frame window is created, **CMainFrame::OnCreate()** is called. In **CMainFrame::OnCreate()** is where the status bar needs to be created and attached to the frame. Answer a is incorrect because **InitInstance()** of the application class instantiates a document template, adds the template to the list of document templates, and processes the command-line parameters. Answer c is incorrect because **PreCreateWindow()** is called prior to the creation of the Windows window, which is too early to create and display the status bar. Answer d is incorrect because the status bar belongs to the frame, not the view.

Question 7

You used AppWizard to generate an MDI application, and in Step 4 of 6, you selected Context-Sensitive Help. The user will be able to access context-sensitive help with which of the following methods?

○ a. By pressing F1 only

○ b. By pressing F1 or by pressing Shift+F1

○ c. By pressing F1 or by clicking on the Context Help toolbar button

○ d. By pressing F1, by pressing Shift+F1, or by clicking on the Context Help toolbar button

Answer d is correct. Context-sensitive help can be accessed by pressing F1, by pressing Shift+F1, or by clicking on the Context Help toolbar button. When the user presses F1, the program makes a best guess about the help context and calls WinHelp. In this mode, help is invoked for the currently active GUI object. Shift+F1 is more powerful than F1. When the user presses Shift+F1, the cursor changes to an arrow with a question box. In this mode, the program can identify help context for a selected menu item, a toolbar button, a window, the status bar, and other client and nonclient elements. When the user clicks on the Context Help toolbar button, it is the same as pressing Shift+F1.

Question 8

Which macros are used to map a range of command IDs to a single message-handler function? [Check all correct answers]

❏ a. **ON_UPDATE_COMMAND_UI_RANGE**

❏ b. **ON_COMMAND_RANGE**

❏ c. **ON_CONTROL_RANGE**

❏ d. **ON_COMMAND_EX**

Answers b and d are correct. Answer b is correct because **ON_COMMAND_RANGE** maps a contiguous range of command IDs to a single message handler. Answer d is correct because **ON_COMMAND_EX** is used to map several distinct menu commands to the same handler without constraining their respective IDs. Answer a is incorrect because **ON_UPDATE_COMMAND_UI_RANGE** is used to map a contiguous range of command IDs to a single update-message-handler function. Answer c is incorrect because ON_CONTROL_RANGE is used to map a contiguous range of control IDs to a single message-handler function for a specified Windows notification message, such as BN_CLICKED.

Need To Know More?

 Bates, Jon and Tim Tompkins. *Using Visual C++ 6*. Indianapolis: Que Corporation, 1998. ISBN 0-7897-1635-6. This book is aimed at the beginning-to-intermediate programmer, and in typical Que style, its focus is on "how to." Chapter 6 covers **CListCtrl** and **CTreeCtrl**. Chapter 7 covers **CProgressCtrl**, **CScrollBar**, **CSliderCtrl**, **CDateTimeCtrl**, and **CMonthCalCtrl**. Chapter 9 covers the use of ActiveX controls. This book provides a good introduction to the controls it covers.

 Kruglinski, David J., George Shepherd, and Scot Wingo. *Programming Microsoft Visual C++, Fifth Edition*. Redmond, WA: Microsoft Press, 1998. ISBN 1-57231-857-0. This book strikes a good balance between theory and practical application. It is divided into six parts and covers nearly every aspect of MFC programming, from the basics to database management and the Internet. Chapter 6 provides a good example on customizing the File Open and Save As dialog boxes. Chapter 8 is all about using ActiveX controls. One of the examples shows how to use the WebBrowser ActiveX control. Chapter 13 covers menus. Chapter 14 covers toolbars and status bars. Chapter 21 covers MFC and the WinHelp system of context-sensitive help.

 Lacey, James M. *MCSD Visual C++ 6 Desktop Exam Cram*. Scottsdale, AZ: The Coriolis Group, 2000. ISBN 1-57610-373-0. This book provides more detailed coverage of the topics covered in this chapter. Chapter 3 covers menus. Chapter 4 covers toolbars and status bars. Chapter 5 covers dialog boxes and property sheets. Chapter 8 covers common controls. Chapter 9 covers ActiveX controls. Chapter 10 covers WinHelp and HTML Help.

 Prosise, Jeff. *Programming Windows with MFC*. Redmond, WA: Microsoft Press, 2000 ISBN 1-57231-695-0. This is an updated version of the author's popular *Programming Windows 95 with MFC* book. After you have worked through the book, not only will you know how to use MFC to write 32-bit applications, but you will also understand the code that AppWizard, ClassWizard, and other code generators produce. Chapter 4 provides a good description of menus and contains two example programs. Chapter 8 covers dialog boxes, property sheets, and common dialog boxes. Chapter 12 covers **CToolBar** and **CStatusBar**. Chapter 16 provides an excellent overview of common controls, followed by detailed descriptions for many of them. Chapter 16 provides two example programs. The first is a demonstration of how slider controls, spin button controls, and ToolTip controls can be put to work in a dialog box. The second is a dialog-based application that uses the **CComboBoxEx** control.

 Williams, Al. *MFC Black Book.* Scottsdale, AZ: The Coriolis Group, 1998. ISBN 1-57610-185-1. Chapter 5 provides practical cookbook-style solutions to problems programmers will encounter when implementing modeless dialog boxes and when using DDX and DDV.

 MFC Technical Note 26 describes the DDX and DDV architecture. It also describes how to write a **DDX_** or **DDV_** procedure and how to extend ClassWizard to use the routines.

 MFC Technical Note 28 describes Context-Sensitive Help Support.

 MSDN Library, Visual Studio 6.0 Documentation\Visual C++ Documentation\Using Visual C++\Visual C++ Programmer's Guide\Adding User Interface Features\Details\Help Topics (WinHelp): Context-Sensitive Help for Your Programs.

 MSDN Library, Visual Studio 6.0 Documentation\Visual C++ Documentation\Using Visual C++\Visual C++ Programmer's Guide\Adding User Interface Features\Details\Help Topics (HTML Help): Context-Sensitive Help for Your Programs.

Component Object Model

. . . .

Terms you'll need to understand:

√ Standard interface, custom interface, Automation interface

√ **IUnknown**, **IDispatch**, **IClassFactory**, and **IClassFactory2** interfaces

√ Reference counting

√ Containment, aggregation

√ Apartment

√ Single-threaded apartment (STA) model

√ Multithreaded apartment (MTA) model

√ Main, or primary, STA

√ Marshaling, proxy, stub

√ Type library marshaling

√ Universal Marshaler

√ Standard marshaling, custom marshaling

√ **COM_SMARTPTR_TYPEDEF()**

Techniques you'll need to master:

√ Writing code that implements the **IUnknown** interface

√ Writing code that implements the **IClassFactory** interface

√ Correctly determining which type of COM threading model to implement

√ Explaining the difference between aggregation and containment

√ Creating a COM component by using the SDK (Software Development Kit), MFC (Microsoft Foundation Class), and ATL (Active Template Library)

√ Creating a COM component that reuses existing components

√ Creating an ActiveX control

COM (Component Object Model) is the foundation on which ActiveX, OLE (Object Linking and Embedding), OLE DB, ADO (ActiveX Data Objects), and DirectX are built. COM is a language- and platform-independent standard that defines how different objects can communicate with each other using a common protocol. It provides a way in which large and small applications can be divided into a number of small standalone components. Because COM is language-neutral, developers can write these components in the language of their choice. However, some languages are better than others. Languages that support arrays of function pointers and can call functions through those pointers can be used directly. These languages include C, C++, and Pascal. Languages that do not support arrays of functions can be extended so that they can create and call COM objects. The most obvious example of such a language is Visual Basic.

DCOM (Distributed Component Object Model) extends COM to support distributed objects. In simple terms, DCOM is a software layer that manages the network protocol and takes care of data marshaling. *Marshaling* is the process of packaging and sending data across process and machine boundaries. Because COM has always been a distributed technology, from the application developer's point of view there is really no difference between COM and DCOM—a few enhancements were made to the COM API to provide improved security and performance. As with COM, DCOM allows developers to focus their efforts on the functionality of their applications. But now, instead of all of their application objects being located on a single machine, these objects can be easily distributed in global cyberspace.

The Basics

COM is all about designing and building reusable software components. It was designed with the C++ programmer in mind and supports encapsulation, polymorphism, and reuse. COM enforces encapsulation by separating an object's interface from its implementation. In addition to providing the customary method-level polymorphism, COM also supports polymorphism at the interface level.

The third pillar of object-oriented programming (OOP) is inheritance. Most OOP languages support simple inheritance, which provides both interface and implementation reuse at the source code level. Instead of providing reuse through inheritance, COM provides reuse at the binary level. Therefore, COM avoids the potential problems that can arise with implementation inheritance and, at the same time, allows greater interoperability among heterogeneous components.

Clients And Servers

COM objects are packaged as software components—*servers*—that provide services to some other entity. Software entities that use a component's services are called *clients*. There are two general categories of servers in the COM world: in-process servers and out-of-process servers. *In-process servers* are housed in Windows DLLs and reside in the same process and address space as their client. For this reason, in-process servers provide the best performance. However, this advantage comes with a risk. If an error occurs in an in-process server, the error could potentially crash the client.

There are two types of *out-of-process* servers. One resides and executes on a client's machine. This type of out-of-process server is called a *local server*. The other out-of-process server executes on a remote machine and is called a *remote server*. Local servers are housed in EXE files, run in their own address space, and have their own execution context. An *execution context* is an encapsulated execution scope that can be a single thread or a collection of threads. In the world of COM, an execution context is known as an *apartment*. Whenever COM calls span apartment or process boundaries, parameters must be marshaled between the processes.

Because the housing for a local server is constructed and registered differently than the housing for an in-process server, the development of local servers, when compared to in-process servers, requires some additional effort. Fortunately, all of the extra work is concerned with the housing itself and doesn't affect the code used to implement a component's functionality, which can be placed in either an in-process server or a local server.

Local servers provide a couple of benefits that are not available with in-process servers. First, local servers offer more protection to the client application. Because a local server is loaded into its own address space, a fatal error in the server will not crash the client application. Instead, an error will be returned. Second, local servers have more control over their threading model, which allows them to build in their own scalability features.

If an in-process server is a DLL and a local server is an EXE, then what is a remote server? Well, a DCOM remote server can exist as either a DLL or an EXE. Remote servers that are EXEs can simply be launched and run when needed. However, a remote server that is a DLL requires some help—an EXE must act as a surrogate. DCOM provides a default surrogate (dllhost.exe) that can be used to load and host a DLL. This doesn't just happen automatically, however. In order for an in-process component to be activated in the context of a DLL surrogate, the proper entries must be made in the Registry. The Distributed COM Configuration Utility (dcomcnfg.exe) can be used to DCOM-enable older components.

Whether a server is in-process, local, or remote is usually not important and is unknown to the client. This feature is called *location transparency*. When a client asks COM to load a component, COM looks in the Registry for the component's location and activation information.

Interfaces

Key to COM is the idea of interfaces. An *interface* is a logical grouping of behaviors. It consists of function prototypes and a protocol for their use. Each interface is a contract between the client program and the COM object; this contract specifies the passing of parameters and return values. Microsoft has defined a number of *standard interfaces* that any COM object can support. Interfaces that are user-defined are called *custom interfaces*.

Every COM object supports one or more interfaces. There is, however, one interface that every COM object must support: the **IUnknown** interface. All COM interfaces are derived, directly or indirectly, from **IUnknown**. In C++, the **IUnknown** interface is an abstract class that has three pure virtual functions: **QueryInterface()**, **AddRef()**, and **Release()**.

 Don't confuse COM inheritance with C++ inheritance. Although you can model COM inheritance using C++ inheritance, doing so isn't a requirement. Lots of COM objects have been written in C.

It is important to realize that the definition of an interface does not include the implementation. The component has the responsibility of providing the implementation that is appropriate for that component. Realize also that an interface can be reused in different situations. One component can be swapped with another component that supports the same set of interfaces.

Pure abstract base classes provide little more than a table of function entry points, and the entry points are allocated by the compiler. This table is commonly known as a *vtable*. Any language or tool that can use pointers or references can construct this table. However, C++ compilers use vtables, so using the vtable as the standard COM interface structure was a logical choice. This standard also makes defining and implementing COM interfaces easy for C++ programmers.

QueryInterface()

As mentioned previously, the **IUnknown** interface declares three pure virtual functions, and the component provides the implementation. The first of these functions, **QueryInterface()**, is used by the client to request an interface of the component. If the request is successful, the client can then, through indirection, call the functions of the interface. Here's the prototype for **QueryInterface()**:

```
HRESULT QueryInterface(REFIID iid, void ** ppvObject);
```

As you can see, **QueryInterface()** has two parameters. The first is an *interface identifier*, which will be discussed in detail later. The second is a pointer to an interface pointer. The return value is of type **HRESULT**, which is the COM return type. **HRESULT** is simply a 32-bit number containing an error code. **HRESULT** consists of four parts: severity (bit 31), reserved (bits 29 and 30), facility code (bits 16 to 28), and return code (bits 0 to 15). The predefined severity constants are **SEVERITY_SUCCESS** (zero) and **SEVERITY_ERROR** (one). You should use the **SUCCEEDED()** or **FAILED()** macros to test an **HRESULT** value for simple success or failure. Use **if(SUCCEEDED(hr))** or **if(FAILED(hr))**; don't use **if(S_OK == hr)**. Many of the predefined **HRESULT** codes can be found in winerror.h.

You can use the **MAKE_HRESULT(sev, fac, code)** macro to construct an **HRESULT**.

Every implementation of **QueryInterface()** must follow five rules:

➤ *Identity*—Comparing **IUnknown** pointers is the only way to determine object identity. If the **IUnknown** pointers match, the interfaces are from the same component.

➤ *Predictability*—If a call to **QueryInterface()** for a pointer to a specified interface succeeds the first time, it must succeed again; if it fails the first time, it must fail on all subsequent queries.

➤ *Reflexivity*—Querying an interface for itself always succeeds.

➤ *Symmetry*—If you can successfully query an interface for a second interface, you can also successfully query for the first interface from the second interface.

➤ *Transitivity*—If you can query an interface for a second interface and you can successfully query the second interface for a third interface, then you can successfully query the first interface for the third interface.

Reference Counting

COM interfaces do not have virtual destructors; instead, COM has a strict protocol that is followed for deleting objects. All objects that implement **IUnknown,** or any interface based on it, must maintain an internal reference count on that interface. When a client gains a pointer to an interface, the internal reference count must be incremented. When a client releases a pointer to an interface, the internal reference count is decremented. If the internal reference count goes to zero, the object destroys itself. **AddRef()** and **Release()** are the functions used to increment and decrement the reference count.

To ensure that reference counts are maintained correctly, you must remember the following:

➤ If the call to **QueryInterface()** is successful, the reference count will be incremented.

➤ If you make a copy of an interface pointer, you must call **AddRef()**.

➤ If you are finished with an interface, you must call **Release()**.

Identifiers And The Registry

In the prototype shown earlier, you saw that **QueryInterface()**'s first parameter is of type **REFIID**, which is a reference to an **IID** (interface identifier). **IID**s are just **GUID**s used to identify interfaces. **GUID** stands for Globally Unique Identifier. A **GUID** is a 128-bit number created mainly from a combination of the Ethernet card in the machine it's generated on and the current time in 100-nanosecond intervals since 1582.

You can generate your own **GUID**s by using the **GUID** generator (guidgen.exe) supplied with Visual C++. If you should ever need to generate a **GUID** programmatically, you can call **CoCreateGuid()**.

Every interface must be identified by an **IID** so that there is a unique way of referring to it with no possibility of name clashes between it and all the other interfaces in the world. Using **QueryInterface()**, the client asks an activated object if it supports a particular interface by passing it an **IID**. But how does the client locate the component? Well, it simply asks COM, and COM looks in the Registry. Each COM object class is identified by a **CLSID**, which, like an **IID**, is a **GUID**. All the COM classes registered on your system have entries under **HKEY_CLASS_ROOT\CLSID**{*clsid*}, where {*clsid*} represents the 128-bit number. Under the **CLSID\\{*clsid*}** is a key that associates the CLSID GUID with a server that will create and manage the COM object when requested. These keys are usually **InprocServer32** or **LocalServer32**. Under each of these keys is the path and file name of the DLL or EXE that creates and manages the COM object.

Class Factory

When a client requests an object, a specific type of COM entity, known as a *class factory object*, is used to create the requested object. A class factory object is responsible for instantiating other components.

Class factory objects implement **IClassFactory**, which is derived from **IUnknown**. In addition to the functions inherited from **IUnknown**, class factory objects must implement the two functions declared in **IClassFactory**: the **CreateInstance()** function and the **LockServer()** function. To create a class factory object, you call **CoGetClassObject()**. You can then use the returned **IClassFactory** pointer to call **CreateInstance()** to create one or more instances of the requested object.

If you need to create only one instance of an object, you can use **CoCreate-Instance()**. It combines the two steps of obtaining a class factory and then calling **CreateInstance()**. **CoCreateInstance()** creates a single object of the class associated with a specified **CLSID**. If you call **CoCreateInstance()** several times, the class factory might be created and destroyed between each call.

To support DCOM, one of **CoGetClassObject()**'s parameters is a pointer to a remote machine. However, because **CoCreateInstance()** has no such pointer, a new method, **CoCreateInstanceEx()**, was added to the COM API to support remote activation. Like **CoGetClassObject()**, one of **CoCreateInstanceEx()**'s parameters is a pointer to a remote machine. **CoCreateInstanceEx()** also has a parameter that allows clients to query for multiple interfaces in one call, thus reducing the number of round trips between machines.

Be sure you understand the difference between **CoGetClass-Object()**, **CoCreateInstance()**, and **CoCreateInstanceEx()**. Also, be careful that you don't confuse **CreateInstance()** with **CoCreateInstance()**.

Reusing Existing COM Components

Central to COM is the idea of code reuse. The ability to use and reuse components dynamically allows developers to build robust, reliable applications. Using an existing, proven component that encapsulates a business rule, a logic entity, or a concept means less time spent coding, debugging, and testing. It can also mean greater functionality. Leveraging the work of others—especially those with more expertise—allows developers to focus on the problem at hand rather than retracing the steps of a hundred programmers before them. Given that code reuse works so well for application development, why not apply this same technique when implementing your own COM classes?

The idea of code reuse has been around for quite some time. Languages such as C++ rely on implementation inheritance as a primary mechanism for reusing existing code. Because COM objects are language-neutral, however, implementation inheritance is not a viable approach. Instead, COM provides reuse through two other mechanisms: *containment* and *aggregation*.

The concepts behind both containment and aggregation are quite simple. Both rely on a relationship between objects where one object, known as the *outer object*, uses the services of another object, known at the *inner object*.

Containment

With containment, the outer object acts as a client of the inner (or contained) object. The outer object simply creates the inner object and then calls the inner object's functions to carry out its own. The outer object can provide simple wrappers that merely pass method calls to the inner object. This action is called *delegation* because the work is being delegated by the outer object to the inner object.

Containment can be more involved than simply wrapping the inner object's methods. The outer object might want to inspect and appropriately modify method parameters before passing them to the inner object. The outer object also might modify the inner object's return value. Additionally, the outer object might provide a higher-level set of methods than that provided by the inner object. Each outer object method would invoke some number of inner object methods in order to carry out its function.

Containment is relatively easy to implement. The inner object doesn't require any special functionality to support containment; in fact, it can't differentiate between containment and direct use by a client. Any object that can stand alone can be used as an inner object.

To create the inner object, the outer object can apply one of two basic strategies. As the outer object is being constructed, it can create the inner object via **CoCreateInstance()**. Alternately, the outer object can wait and create the inner object on demand. The outer object releases the inner object in its destructor.

Aggregation

Aggregation differs from containment in two ways. First, the outer object exposes the inner object's interface directly to the client as its own. Second, if an object is to be used via aggregation, the object must be written to support it.

Here's a short description of how aggregation works. When the client queries the outer object for an interface that belongs to the inner object, the outer object simply queries the inner object and returns the interface pointer back to the client. From then on, the outer object is out of the picture. The client uses the interface to directly call methods implemented by the inner object.

Writing an object that can be aggregated is more difficult than writing one that isn't. The two big issues that must be managed are getting reference counts right and making sure that **QueryInterface()** works correctly. You do this by implementing two sets of **IUnknown** functions: delegating and nondelegating.

To make aggregation work, you must follow these rules:

➤ When the outer object is creating the inner object, the outer object must pass its own **IUnknown** to the inner object through the **pUnkOuter** parameter of **IClassFactory::CreateInstance()**.

➤ In **CreateInstance()**, the inner object must check the **pUnkOuter** parameter. If it is non-**NULL** and the inner object supports aggregation, **pUnkOuter** is stored for later use. **AddRef()** is not called. If the inner object does not support aggregation, it must fail with **CLASS_E_NOAGGREGATION**.

➤ If the **pUnkOuter** parameter in **CreateInstance()** is non-**NULL**, the inner object returns its nondelegating **IUnknown**.

➤ When the client queries for the interface that is supported by the inner object, the outer object delegates that call to the inner object.

➤ When **QueryInterface()**, **AddRef()**, or **Release()** is called on any inner object interface (except for **IUnknown**), the inner object must delegate to **pUnkOuter**.

Automation

Recall that a custom interface is the standard vtable interface. One of the features of a custom interface is that it requires some form of compile-time binding with the client. In other words, the client must have compile-time knowledge of the interface methods. As you know, this form of binding uses the virtual table of function pointers and is known as *vtable binding*. This is fine for C/C++ clients that can include files that contain interface descriptions, **CLSID**s, and so on. But what about clients that don't have access to the included files or can't use them—for example, Visual Basic?

One technique is to use the type library, which contains binary information about a component. By referring to the type library, Visual Basic can statically bind to the methods and properties. However, scripting languages, such as VBScript and JScript, need to be able to bind to methods and properties dynamically at runtime. For this type of client, COM supports the **IDispatch** interface. Each method and property supported by the **IDispatch** interface is assigned a unique ID, known as a *dispid* (dispatch ID). To access a method or property, the client must call **IDispatch::Invoke()**, passing a dispid identifying a given method or property. This type of user-defined interface is commonly referred to as an *Automation interface*.

 You can declare an Automation interface by deriving your interface from **IDispatch**. Alternately, you can use the keyword **dispinterface**, which automatically implies that the actual implementation will be an implementation of the **IDispatch** interface.

The **IDispatch** interface consists of the four methods shown in Table 5.1.

 Interfaces derived from **IDispatch** are restricted to the Automation-compatible types—that is, types listed in the **VARIANT** union. You should be familiar with these types.

Threading Models

Prior to the release of Windows NT 3.51, COM didn't support multithreading, and calls were made only to in-process DLLs. Concurrency and thread safety were not issues that developers needed to worry about. Each process had only

Table 5.1 IDispatch methods.	
Method	Description
GetTypeInfoCount	Gets the number of type information interfaces. It will return a 1 or a 0.
GetTypeInfo	Gets the type information for an object.
GetIDsOfNames	Gets a list of dispids, given a list of method names.
Invoke	Invokes the target method or property using a dispid.

one thread of execution, and all component access occurred on this thread. This is now commonly referred to as the *single threading model.*

With the introduction of Windows NT 3.51 and Windows 95, developers can take advantage of multithreading. It's now possible for an application to have a number of threads of execution occurring at the same time. To take advantage of multithreading, COM introduced a conceptual entity known as the *single-threaded apartment* (STA) model, sometimes referred to as the *apartment threading model* and occasionally as a *user-interface-style thread.* This model allows multiple threads to be created, where each thread will belong to only one apartment. When instantiated, the COM object is placed in its own apartment and will automatically be thread-safe because the same thread is always used to call its methods.

With the release of Windows NT 4 and the Windows 95 DCOM upgrade, the *multithreaded apartment* (MTA) model was introduced. This model is sometimes referred to as the *free threading model* and occasionally as a *worker thread.* The MTA model allows multiple threads to operate within the same thread-safe "box." However, because objects in different threads can access one another directly, to maintain thread safety within the box, objects must implement their synchronization.

 Probably the hardest thing to keep straight concerning the COM threading models is the terminology. It is important that you understand each of the models and the different terms used to refer to each of them.

The Single-Threaded Apartment Model

This model allows you to avoid the complexity of interthread communication and synchronization. A single process can have any number of STAs. The first STA created in a process is special and is known as the *main STA* or *primary STA.* All other STAs are referred to simply as STAs.

At the heart of each STA is a Windows message pump. A thread enters an STA by calling **CoInitialize(NULL)** or **CoInitializeEx(NULL, COINIT_ APARTMENTTHREADED)**, at which point COM creates an invisible window and hooks it to the thread's message queue. Only one thread can ever execute within a particular STA, and it is this thread that pumps the message queue. Whenever a method is called, a request is posted to the message queue, where it stays until it is retrieved and dispatched. If the client and object reside in different apartments, interface pointers and method parameters must be marshaled. Because messages are retrieved and dispatched in order by the apartment thread, the component doesn't need to be thread-safe—that is, global and static data are automatically protected from concurrent access because the same thread can't be doing two things at the same time. There is, however, one issue that should be considered: *reentrancy*. One example of reentrancy occurs when an object inside an STA calls a method in another STA and that method calls back to the first STA. COM also supports reentrancy in STAs by processing certain window messages, such as **WM_PAINT**, while a call is block-waiting for the return of a method invocation.

 The **CoInitialize()** function has been deprecated and should no longer be used. All new applications should use **CoInitializeEx()**.

You can also implement an **IMessageFilter** interface to selectively manage outgoing and incoming method calls during the block-wait of an out-of-apartment method call. This interface lets you add code to improve performance and help prevent deadlocks. The **IMessageFilter** interface has three methods that are called by COM at the appropriate time. The **CoRegisterMessageFilter()** API function must be used to register this interface with COM.

One advantage of using the STA model is that it allows you to develop multithreaded COM applications with minimum effort. Recall that only one thread can enter and thus reside in an STA. So for each additional thread, there must be an additional STA. For example, if the main STA spawns a thread and that thread requests to enter an STA, it will enter into a brand-new STA.

Although the STA model is simple and easy to use, it doesn't scale very well. For example, if you have a large number of objects and you create an STA for each one, you will end up with a separate apartment and thread for each object. As the number of apartments and threads increases, so will resource consumption. On the other hand, if you place all of the objects in the same STA, your component can become very sluggish because all the objects will be serialized through the same message queue.

 Components written prior to the introduction of the COM threading model are run in the main STA.

Crossing Apartment Boundaries

Recall that when an interface pointer is passed across an apartment boundary, it must be marshaled. This usually occurs implicitly as part of the normal operation of COM. However, occasionally it is necessary to explicitly marshal an interface from one apartment to another. COM provides two API functions that allow the marshaling and unmarshaling of an interface pointer: **CoMarshalInterface()** and **CoUnmarshalInterface()**. There is nothing especially difficult about these two functions, but they are somewhat low level and require some amount of supporting code.

To make things simpler, COM provides two wrapper functions that implement the required support code around **CoMarshalInterface()** and **CoUnmarshalInterface()**. The first wrapper function, **CoMarshalInterThreadInterfaceInStream()**, creates a marshaling packet and marshals the given interface. However, unlike **CoMarshalInterface()**—which allows you to marshal an interface pointer from one process to another—**CoMarshalInterThreadInterfaceInStream()** allows you to marshal an interface pointer only from one apartment to another within the same process. **CoMarshalInterThreadInterfaceInStream()** takes an **IID**—a pointer to the interface to be marshaled—and returns a pointer to an **IStream** interface that contains the necessary information for the marshaling and unmarshaling.

In the other apartment, **CoGetInterfaceAndReleaseStream()** unmarshals the interface pointer and releases the stream. This function takes a pointer to the **IStream** containing the buffer to be unmarshaled, an **IID**, and returns a pointer to a local interface proxy. Because **CoGetInterfaceAndReleaseStream()** releases the stream, the pointer can be used only once. Another technique, which uses the *Global Interface Table* (GIT), allows you to write the interface pointer once and read it many times. COM provides one GIT per process. This GIT can be accessed by all apartments in a process and can be used with both objects and proxies.

The Multithreaded Apartment Model

Unlike the STA model, the MTA model doesn't have a hidden window, and a message pump is not required. Furthermore, although many STAs can be used, only one MTA per process can be used. However, a single MTA can support any number of threads, each with a number of objects. High performance and flexibility are what the MTA model is all about. When you need a component that is I/O-intensive or highly computational, the MTA model is ideal.

A thread enters the only MTA in the process by calling **CoInitializeEx(NULL, COINIT_MULTITHREADED)**. Upon entering an MTA, the thread can directly access any COM object that lives in the MTA and can pass direct pointers to other threads. Thus, all MTA-compatible objects must be thread-safe in every way. This requirement puts the burden on you, the developer, to ensure that all global, static, and instance data and all resources are protected against concurrent access. This means that all class factories and object members must be synchronized using system primitives. For example, you need to implement **AddRef()** and **Release()**, like so:

```
STDMETHODIMP_(LONG) AddRef()
{
  return InterlockedIncrement(&m_lRef);
}

STDMETHODIMP_(LONG) Release()
{
  long ref = InterlockedDecrement(&m_lRef);
  if(!ref)
    delete this;
  return ref;
}
```

You will also need to use mutexes, semaphores, critical sections, or events for interthread coordination and communications.

In the MTA model, there is no correlation between objects and threads. That is, each call to a given object can be handled by a different thread. This means that you must not save any kind of object-related state in thread-local storage. Thread-local storage, or TLS, is a mechanism whereby each thread has its own unique copy of a local variable.

The Mixed Model

It's possible for a process to use what is sometimes referred to as the *mixed model*. In this model, one MTA and one or more STAs are supported by the same process. This process has multiple threads. Many threads can enter the MTA, but each STA can host only one thread. The threads within the MTA can use direct interface pointers, but interface pointers that cross apartment boundaries must be marshaled.

Out-Of-Process Server Considerations

When you're developing an out-of-process server, you must consider the possibility of race conditions. There are two times in the life of an out-of-process server when a race condition is most likely to occur. The first is during activation, and the other is at shutdown.

Activation

Suppose that you have an MTA server that registers two or more class factories. After the server registers the first factory, COM will allow it to immediately start servicing incoming activation requests. Before the second factory is registered, a client can request an object, use it, and request the server to shut down, thereby causing possible access violations to future calls to use the second factory. To prevent this situation, you need to register all of your factories by using the **REGCLS_SUSPENDED** flag. After all of your factories are registered, you can then call **CoResumeClassObjects()**, telling COM to activate the factories.

Shutdown

Suppose that a local server is running an MTA or has multiple STAs registered. There is a small window of opportunity when a new activation request can arrive while the server is shutting down. This race condition would mean that a client would be holding a nonvalid interface pointer. The **CoAddRefServerProcess()** and **CoReleaseServerProcess()** functions can be used to prevent this potential race condition from occurring.

The **CoReleaseServerProcess()** function has a built-in feature whereby it automatically calls **CoSuspendClassObjects()** when the reference count goes to zero. The **CoSuspendClassObjects()** function ensures that any incoming activation requests are refused, so that the component need not worry about a simultaneous activation while unregistering its class factories. An activation request received during shutdown of a component is redirected to the COM Service Control Manager so that a new instance of the component is created.

The routine that calls **CoReleaseServerProcess()** must test its return value and take the appropriate action. When the main thread is executing in an MTA, the most logical action is for the routine to set an exit event. If the main thread is executing in an STA, a message pump waits for the **WM_QUIT** window message. Therefore, rather than setting an exit event, the routine needs to post the **WM_QUIT** window message to the main thread, causing the component to shut down.

In-Process Server Considerations

In-process components use the Registry to tell COM their concurrency constraints. One of four threading model types is placed under the **HKEY_CLASS_ROOT\CLSID\{*clsid*}\InprocServer32** key. A **Threading-Model** value specifies one of four variations of concurrency. The variations are

ThreadingModel=, ThreadingModel=Apartment, ThreadingModel=Free, and ThreadingModel=Both.

ThreadingModel=

COM regards in-process components that do not have a **ThreadingModel** value as legacy components. A legacy component and its instantiated objects can live and execute only in the client's main STA. COM assumes that this type of component is totally thread-ignorant and prevents any occurrence of multiple access to the object. Therefore, when you're implementing a component that doesn't support a threading model, you need not worry about protecting data or resources. These types of objects are the easiest to write, but because there is only one thread of execution, they don't scale at all.

In-process objects that don't support any **ThreadingModel** are best used with single-threaded clients with only one STA. This is the only case where direct interface pointers will be used. Calls from all other apartments, whether STA or MTA, won't be able to use direct interface pointers. When the client activates an object from an apartment other than the main STA, the apartment will acquire a pointer to an interface proxy.

ThreadingModel=Apartment

In-process objects that support **ThreadingModel=Apartment** can live and execute in any client STA. Unlike objects of a legacy component, which can be created only in the main STA, these objects can be created in multiple STAs of the client process. COM assumes that this type of object isn't thread-safe but that the DLL is. Therefore, you need to protect all global and static data. You also need to ensure that **DllGetClassObject()** and **DllCanUnloadNow()** are thread-safe.

In-process objects that support **ThreadingModel=Apartment** are ideal candidates for use with multithreaded clients with multiple STAs. All STAs that activate an object will receive a direct pointer. However, because the object must be instantiated within an STA, the client MTA will still obtain a pointer to an interface proxy.

ThreadingModel=Free

In-process objects that support **ThreadingModel=Free** live and execute in the client's one and only MTA. Client STAs that wish to access this kind of object must go through a proxy. Recall that COM provides no synchronization whatsoever for this kind of object. Because COM assumes that both the component's objects and the DLL are thread-safe, you must protect all data and resources against concurrent access.

In-process objects that support **ThreadingModel=Free** perform best with clients that have an MTA with many busy worker threads. MTA client threads that activate this type of object will use direct interface pointers. However, when a client STA activates this type of object, the object will be instantiated in the MTA, and calls will be marshaled into and out of it.

ThreadingModel=Both

In-process objects that support **ThreadingModel=Both** can live and execute in any STA or MTA. When an STA thread activates this object, it is created in the STA. Likewise, when an MTA thread activates this object, it is created in the MTA.

In-process objects that support **ThreadingModel=Both** provide the best performance. When the client activates this type of object, the object will be instantiated in the same apartment that the client thread is running in, and the client will receive a direct pointer to the interface.

Because this kind of object can be created inside an STA or an MTA, it has two special requirements that must be taken into consideration. First, when making a callback, it must use the same thread that passed the callback interface pointer to it. Second, interface pointers must be marshaled between threads.

Interaction Among In-Process Objects

COM allows interoperability using any combination of threading models between clients and components. However, when the threading models do not match, there will be a performance penalty. Often, through a combination of investigation, creative thinking, and careful design, you will be able to avoid this type of problem.

Free-Threaded Marshaler

Recall that in-process components that support **ThreadingModel=Both** must always marshal interface pointers between threads. Because marshaling is slow, COM provides an object known as the *Free-Threaded Marshaler (FTM)*, which can be used to significantly improve performance. When the FTM is aggregated by an object with **ThreadingModel=Both**, threads in different apartments but in the same process can access the object without going through a proxy. The FTM implements the **IMarshal** interface and performs custom marshaling to marshal 32 bits (a **DWORD**). This **DWORD**, which represents a raw interface pointer, can be passed from one apartment to another. The importing apartment can unmarshal the **DWORD** and convert the 32 bits into a direct interface pointer.

The **CoCreateFreeThreadedMarshaler()** API function allows objects that support **ThreadingModel=Both** to aggregate the FTM. **CoCreate-FreeThreadedMarshaler()** takes two parameters. The first parameter is a pointer to the **IUnknown** interface of the aggregating object. The second parameter returns a pointer to the **IUnknown** interface of the FTM.

If your object aggregates the FTM, it shouldn't cache raw interface pointers as member variables. See Microsoft Knowledge Base article Q150777 for specific details.

Marshaling

When a client holds a pointer to an in-process server interface, the pointer points directly to the object's interface. However, when the object is a out-of-process server, the pointer will point to a *proxy* object within the client's address space. Then, when the client invokes a method using the interface pointer, the proxy takes the parameters passed by the client, packages them for transfer, and sends an interprocess request to the server transferring the package of parameters.

When the request arrives at the local server, another piece of special code known as a *stub* unpackages the parameters and invokes the appropriate server method. The method executes, and any results are packaged by the stub and sent back to the proxy. The proxy unpackages the results and returns to the client.

Recall that the process of packaging and sending data across process and machine boundaries is known as marshaling. As you might well imagine, the marshaling code can be rather involved. Luckily, COM hides all the details of marshaling from both the client and the server.

You don't need to know a lot about marshaling to use it. For standard COM interfaces, such as **IUnknown** and **IClassFactory**, Microsoft provides proxy and stub implementations that COM uses automatically. However, for custom interfaces (those that you develop), you must also provide the necessary proxies and stubs.

You can code the proxy and stub code manually, but a much easier way is to write and compile an IDL file. IDL stands for *Interface Description Language*. The IDL file defines, in a language-independent way, a component's interface, which can then be used by clients of the component.

You compile your IDL file by using the MIDL (Microsoft Interface Description Language) tool. The MIDL tool creates a series of files that will produce a standard proxy-stub DLL. Although the MIDL tool produces all the necessary C++ files, it's up to you to actually build the proxy-stub DLL. To build the proxy-stub DLL, you simply compile and link the files produced by the MIDL tool. By building and then registering the proxy-stub DLL, you provide standard marshaling for your component.

If you don't want to ship a proxy-stub DLL for each of your components, you can instead use *type library marshaling*. COM provides a proxy-stub DLL called the *Universal Marshaler*, which is implemented in oleaut32.dll. The marshaler can be used to marshal any interface described in a type library. When using the Universal Marshaler, you must be sure that you use only automation types and add the **oleautomation** attribute to your interface declaration.

Both MIDL-produced marshaling and type-library marshaling are forms of what is known as *standard marshaling*. Occasionally, standard marshaling might not meet your needs. In this case, you can use your own *custom marshaling*. Custom marshaling requires that your component implement the **IMarshal** interface. You'll still need to provide a proxy object to enable a client to communicate with your component.

Don't make the mistake of thinking that your custom interfaces require custom marshaling. Typically, you will choose to implement custom marshaling only when COM does not support the desired behavior or when you have detailed knowledge that can be used to increase performance.

Using MIDL

MIDL is IDL-extended to support COM. You don't need to specify your interfaces in MIDL, but doing so can make life easier. The MIDL compiler will generate the files that can be used in the building and distribution of your objects. The MIDL syntax is C-like. The only real difference is that attributes are specified for all data, methods, interfaces, classes, and libraries. Attributes always prefix what they modify and are enclosed in brackets.

Make sure you are familiar with the keywords and basic structure IDL files.

Microsoft Foundation Class And COM

As it does for the Win32 API, Microsoft Foundation Class (MFC) abstracts much of COM to allow developers to concentrate on the business problem they are solving. This section provides a cursory look at the support that MFC provides for the development of COM components.

COM Components

Within the MFC framework, **CCmdTarget** provides the implementation for the **IUnknown** interface. The three **IUnknown** methods—**QueryInterface()**, **AddRef()**, and **Release()**—are implemented in two sets. The first set— **ExternalQueryInterface()**, **ExternalAddRef()**, and **ExternalRelease()**—is used the most. The other set has an **Internal** prefix.

MFC COM interfaces are implemented as nested classes. To simplify the coding required, MFC includes an implementation of *interface maps* and a number of macros similar to MFC's implementation of message maps and dispatch maps. The surrounding class is the component, which is derived from **CCmdTarget**. The nested classes form the interfaces. Used within the interface methods, the macro **METHOD_PROLOGUE()** creates access to the outer class by defining a variable **pThis**. With this variable, access is granted to the **IUnknown** methods and data members of the component. The **METHOD_PROLOGUE()** macro uses the C runtime function **offsetof()** to calculate a back pointer.

METHOD_PROLOGUE() takes two parameters: The first is the component class name, and the second is the current interface. The naming convention for interfaces used by the MFC COM macros is **m_xInterfaceName**, where InterfaceName is the second parameter and **m_x** is a prefix attached by the macro.

 See "TN038: MFC/OLE IUnknown Implementation" in the MFC technical notes for a detailed description of MFC's implementation of **IUnknown**.

The Interface Maps

The following macros declare and define the interface maps.

The header file uses these macros:

➤ DECLARE_INTERFACE_MAP()

➤ BEGIN_INTERFACE_PART()

➤ END_INTERFACE_PART()

The implementation file uses these macros:

➤ BEGIN_INTERFACE_MAP()

➤ END_INTERFACE_MAP()

➤ INTERFACE_PART()

 All of these macros can be confusing. Be sure that you know which ones go in the header file and which ones go in the implementation file. Also, be sure that you know the purpose of each one and which ones work together.

The MFC COleObjectFactory Class

The **COleObjectFactory** class is used to create objects at runtime. This class is a wrapper around **IClassFactory2**. All you need to do is use macros like these in the class declaration:

```
DECLARE_DYNCREATE(CShipping)
DECLARE_OLECREATE(CShipping)
```

Use macros like these in the implementation file:

```
IMPLEMENT_DYNCREATE(CShipping, CCmdTarget)
// {FF62987B-AA1B-11d2-A46A-00C04F688CFA}
IMPLEMENT_OLECREATE(CShipping, "CShipping", 0xff62987b, 0xaa1b,
    0x11d2, 0xa4, 0x6a, 0x0, 0xc0, 0x4f, 0x68, 0x8c, 0xfa);
```

The **DECLARE_DYNCREATE()** and **IMPLEMENT_DYNCREATE()** macros enable **CShipping** to be created dynamically at runtime. The **DECLARE_OLECREATE()** and **IMPLEMENT_OLECREATE()** macros declare and define a global object of class **COleObjectFactory** with the specified **CLSID**.

 IClassFactory2 is an extension of **IClassFactory**. **IClassFactory2** enables a class factory executing on a licensed machine to provide a license key that can be used later to create an object instance on an unlicensed machine. The license key gives only one client application the right to instantiate objects through **IClassFactory2** when a full machine license does not exist.

Containment And Aggregation With MFC

As with the SDK, MFC doesn't provide any direct support for containment. You simply create other COM objects during your own operations, use them as needed, and release them when you are finished with them.

The support that MFC provides makes aggregation almost as simple as containment. To allow your component to be part of an aggregate, you simply call **CCmdTarget::EnableAggregation()** in your object's constructor. That's all there is to it. This one line replaces all the steps listed above for the SDK. Because this is so trivial and adds very little overhead, it's probably a good idea to always add this method call to your class's constructor.

Creating a component that is an outer object requires more effort, but it's pretty straightforward and isn't much different than what is needed for containment.

The Active Template Library

The Active Template Library (ATL) makes it easy to develop small, fast, and efficient COM objects. These objects can be implemented so that they do not depend on secondary DLLs, including the standard C runtime DLL. Unlike MFC, where the library is included at link time, ATL works at compile time to configure and control code generation. ATL is basically a set of C++ templates and other kinds of support for writing COM classes. To get at ATL's built-in functionality, you simply **#include** the necessary header and CPP files; then, at compile time, the ATL code is included directly into your project.

Basic ATL Features

ATL allows you to easily create COM objects, Automation servers, and ActiveX controls. It handles many of the tedious implementation details that a developer must deal with when using the SDK. Here's a partial list of benefits you gain by using ATL:

➤ Built-in support for **IUnknown, IClassFactory, IClassFactory2,** and **IDispatch**

➤ Support for the Interface Definition Language (IDL)

➤ Support for dual interfaces and standard COM enumerator interfaces, connection points, tear-off interfaces, and ActiveX controls

➤ Support for OLE DB

➤ Support for Microsoft Management Console Snap-in Objects

➤ Support for dynamic HTML-based Web control

➤ AppWizard, which creates the initial ATL project

➤ Object Wizard, which generates code for basic COM components

➤ Smart pointers for interface pointers and wrappers for **BSTR** and **VARIANT**

ATL Project Structure

The ATL AppWizard creates the initial housing code for your component. After the project is created, you then use the ATL Object Wizard to add objects to your component. For each object you add with the Object Wizard, a number of files are added to your project. Additionally, the wizard adds code to some of the other project files. The actual code generated depends on the category and type of object you select and the attributes you assign. For a simple object, the Object Wizard lets you specify the threading model to use, whether you want to implement a custom or a dual interface, and whether you want your object to support aggregation. You can also choose to support **ISupportErrorInfo** and connection points, and choose whether to use the Free-Threaded Marshaler. A *dual interface* supports both vtable binding and **IDispatch**.

If you look at the initial header file that the Object Wizard generates for a simple dual interface object, you'll see that the component is derived from three template classes. Here's a snippet of code that illustrates this point:

```
class ATL_NO_VTABLE CObjectName :
  public CComObjectRootEx<CComSingleThreadModel>,
  public CComCoClass<CObjectName, &CLSID_ObjectName>,
  public IDispatchImpl<IObjectName, &IID_IObjectName,
                      &LIBID_PROJECTNAMELib>
{
```

CComObjectRootEx takes care of reference counting. **CComCoClass** provides class factory support and basic methods to retrieve its **CLSID**. **IDispatchImpl** provides the implementation of the **IDispatch** portion of the dual interface.

It's possible to implement a COM object with only an **IDispatch** interface, but the Object Wizard doesn't present this as an option. Remember that it allows you to choose either a custom interface or a dual interface. Either way, you have to implement the methods of your interface only once—for the custom interface. The ATL **IDispatch** implementation will **Invoke()** the corresponding vtable interface method.

The **ATL_NO_VTABLE** macro expands to **__declspec(novtable)**, which is a special compiler optimization introduced for Visual C++ 5. When **__declspec(novtable)** is used in a class declaration, it prevents the vtable pointer from being initialized in the class's constructor and destructor. The linker can thus eliminate the vtable and all the functions pointed to by the vtable, reducing the size of your code.

Farther down in the file, you'll see the following macros:

```
DECLARE_REGISTRY_RESOURCEID(IDR_OBJECTNAME)
DECLARE_PROTECT_FINAL_CONSTRUCT()

BEGIN_COM_MAP(CObjectName)
  COM_INTERFACE_ENTRY(IObjectName)
  COM_INTERFACE_ENTRY(IDispatch)
END_COM_MAP()
```

The **DECLARE_REGISTRY_RESOURCEID()** macro implements script-based Registry support and provides the resource ID for the Registry script information. The **DECLARE_PROTECT_FINAL_CONSTRUCT()** macro guards the object against deletions if an inner object increments the reference count and then decrements the count to zero during the final phase of component creation. The **COM_INTERFACE_ENTRY()** macro adds an entry to a table that provides the interface information ATL needs when performing **QueryInterface()**. When a request for an interface is received, ATL searches the table by executing the code created by the **BEGIN_COM_MAP()** and **END_COM_MAP()** macros.

The Object Wizard also places three macros in the project CPP. These macros are **BEGIN_OBJECT_MAP()**, **OBJECT_ENTRY()**, and **END_OBJECT_MAP()**. They set up a table of **CLSID**s and their associated ATL implementation classes. ATL uses this table to update the Registry with information for each object within the housing and to create instances of an object.

Last, the IDL file is updated with declarations for the ObjectName **coclass** and its **IObjectName** interface.

ATL Architecture

The ATL AppWizard provides the basic housing support that COM components need. After creating the housing, you use the Object Wizard to add basic objects to the housing. All COM objects have several things in common. Each COM object must support the **IUnknown** interface, along with others, such as **IDispatch,** that expose specific functionality. Each COM object must also provide a class factory so that it can be created by client applications. ATL provides built-in support for each of these requirements. This section examines the ATL architecture to determine how the framework satisfies these requirements.

Implementing **IUnknown**

The implementation and control for **IUnknown** is distributed among several ATL classes to allow for maximum flexibility. This makes it rather difficult to understand, but the most important point to remember is that the implementation of the three **IUnknown** methods isn't determined until your component class is created. Because your class is an abstract class, it can't be instantiated directly. Instead, another class is always derived from your class. This class is always the most-derived in the inheritance chain. It provides the vtable and basic implementation of the three **IUnknown** methods. Figure 5.1 shows the class hierarchy of the COM object based on **CObjectName**.

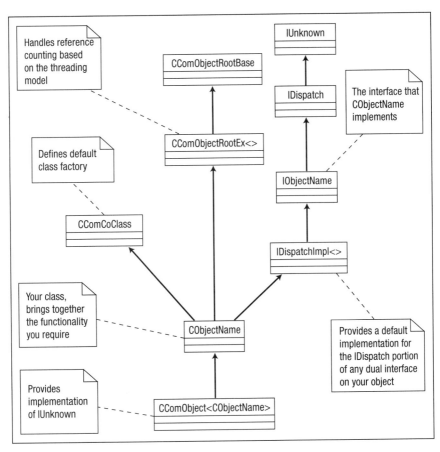

Figure 5.1 Class hierarchy of **CObjectName**.

CComObject<>

This class is one of a number of classes that provide the implementation of the **IUnknown** methods. All of these classes work in a similar manner. They are all template classes that require a **CComObjectRoot**-derived class (your ATL class) parameter. The new class derives from the parameter and is the final destination in ATL's inheritance chain. This new class will contain the implementation of the three **IUnknown** methods and use code in your class to get access to the interface map.

Why doesn't ATL instantiate your class directly? Depending on circumstances, the class at the bottom of the hierarchy will need to exhibit different behaviors. Rather than requiring your class to account for these various circumstances, ATL provides a set of template classes from which the most efficient one can be chosen for a specific situation. There are 10 of these **CComObject**-like classes.

CComObjectRootBase And CComObjectRootEx<>

These two classes indirectly provide implementation of the **IUnknown** methods for your class. Although they don't provide the methods themselves, they do provide much of the code used in the implementation. **CComObjectRootBase** provides reference counting for aggregate components, and **CComObjectRootEx<>** provides reference counting for nonaggregate components. The **CComObject**-like class simply calls the appropriate routine: **CComObjectRootEx<yourclass>::InternalAddRef()** or **CComObjectRootBase::OuterAddRef()** to increment the count, or **CComObjectRootEx<yourclass>::InternalRelease()** or **CComObjectRootBase::OuterRelease()** to decrement the count.

CComCoClass<>

This class provides class factory support, along with basic methods to retrieve the **CLSID** and component-specific error information. It contains very little code and provides most of its support through two macros: **DECLARE_CLASSFACTORY()** and **DECLARE_AGGREGATABLE(*yourclass*)**. The **DECLARE_CLASSFACTORY()** macro provides the actual class factory, and the **DECLARE_AGGREGATABLE(*yourclass*)** macro indirectly calls CreateInstance(). If you select No or Only as the aggregation attribute in the Object Wizard, one of these two macros will be applied to your class:

```
DECLARE_NOT_AGGREGATABLE(yourclass)

DECLARE_ONLY_AGGREGATABLE(yourclass)
```

Each of these macros will cause a different version of **CreateInstance()** to be used to create your object.

Adding A Property Or Method

Properties are attributes of the component that the component user can change, although some may be read-only, hidden, or both. Because COM interfaces follow the object-oriented principle of encapsulation and data hiding, only functions are exported. To allow the client access to a property, the component will provide functions with access to the data member—one to "get" its value and one to "set" its value.

To add a property to your interface, select the ClassView tab in the Project Workspace window, right-click on an interface name, and choose Add Property from the context menu.

Adding a method to your interface isn't much different than adding a property. Select the ClassView tab in the Project Workspace window. Then, right-click on an interface name and choose Add Method from the context menu.

Creating Clients

An object with a dual interface can be accessed by using vtable binding or through the **IDispatch** interface. Three approaches can be used. With the first approach, you simply use the MIDL-generated files: ProjectName.h and ProjectName_i.c. The ProjectName.h file contains the interface declarations for the components housing. The ProjectName_i.c file contains all the **CLSID**s and **IID**s defined for the server.

For the second approach, rather than using the ProjectName.h and ProjectName_i.c files, you can import the type library by using the **#import** directive, like so:

```
#import "..\ProjectName.tlb"
using namespace PROJECTNAMELib;
```

The **#import** preprocessor reads the type library and creates two files that it **#include**s in your compilation. These files are stored in your output directory and have the same base name as the type library, with the extensions .tlh and .tli. These files will provide a number of advantages over the MIDL-generated files:

➤ A number of smart pointers are provided, some of which hide the details of reference counting.

➤ Function return values are specified by [retval] instead of **HRESULT**.

➤ Exception handling can be used instead of **HRESULT** testing.

➤ Property methods can be accessed like data members.

The TLH file contains a smart pointer definition for each of your interface pointers, using the **COM_SMARTPTR_TYPEDEF()** macro. For example, in ProjectName.tlh, the **#import** preprocessor has created a smart pointer for the **IObjectName** interface using the following code:

```
_COM_SMARTPTR_TYPEDEF(IObjectName, __uuidof(IObjectName));
```

This macro takes the same parameters as **__com_ptr_t<>**: the interface of the object that the pointer refers to and the **IID** of the interface. Here you see the use of the **__uuidof()** operator to obtain the **IID**. After execution of **_COM_SMARTPTR_TYPEDEF()**, there will be a **typedef** of a specialization of **__com_ptr_t<>** with the name of the interface pointer plus a suffix of **Ptr**. When you instantiate this class, it will obtain your class factory, call the class factory to create an object, call **IUnknown::QueryInterface()** to obtain the interface, and create a **__com_ptr_t<>** smart pointer object around this pointer. You then use the indirect member selection operator (->) to access its functionality. A major benefit of this smart pointer is that you don't need to worry about reference counting because the smart pointer will call **AddRef()** and **Release()** automatically.

Following are two examples of how the property methods can be accessed like data members. The first one retrieves the value, and the second one changes the value:

```
prop = pObject->AProperty;
pObject->AProperty = prop;
```

TLH files consist of sections:

➤ The **#include** statement for COMDEF.H, which defines the macros used in the header

➤ Forward references and **typedefs**, structure declarations for interface IDs, and class names

➤ Smart pointer **typedef** declarations, using the **_COM_SMARTPTR_TYPEDEF** macro to create **typedefs** of specialized **_com_ptr_t** template classes

➤ Type library items, class definitions, and other items generated from the specified type library

➤ Named **GUID** constants' initializations, if the **named_guids** attribute was specified

➤ An **#include** statement for the type library implementation (TLI) file

Most of a TLH file is enclosed in a namespace, with its name specified by the **library** statement in the original IDL file. A number of attributes can be applied to the **#import** directive; two of these affect the namespace. One attribute, **no_namespace,** suppresses the namespace altogether; the other, **rename_ namespace,** changes the name of the namespace.

The TLI file implements *inline* wrappers for the direct COM interface calls. These wrapper functions will *throw* an exception via the **_com_issue_errorex()** call. It throws a **_com_error** object, which your client code is prepared to **catch()**.

The last approach uses the Automation or **IDispatch** interface. Using an Automation interface involves an extensive lookup to resolve dispids from given method names, resulting in performance problems. For that reason, C/C++ clients seldom use this approach. However, for clients such as VBScript, where dynamic invocation is needed, this approach is great.

Here is some pseudo code that uses **IDispatch** to call the Display method:

```
... initialize COM

OLECHAR *method = L"Display";
DISPPARAMS parms = {NULL, NULL, 0, 0};
DISPID dispid;
pDisp->GetIDsOfNames(IID_NULL, &method, 1,
                  LOCALE_SYSTEM_DEFAULT, &dispid);
pDisp->Invoke(dispid, IID_NULL, LOCALE_SYSTEM_DEFAULT,
           DISPATCH_METHOD, &parms, NULL, NULL, NULL);

... release the object and uninitialize COM
```

IDispatch::GetIDsOfNames() is used to obtain the **dispid** of the **Display()** method. Then **IDispatch::Invoke()** is called, and the **dispid** specifies the method to dynamically invoke.

Building ActiveX Controls

Technically, an ActiveX control is any COM object that exposes the **IUnknown** interface and is self-registering. If **IUnknown** were the only interface supported, however, the control wouldn't do much more than take up disk space. Therefore, it usually supports many more interfaces in order to offer functionality, but all additional interfaces can be viewed as optional, and as such, a container should not rely on any additional interfaces being supported. Because the **IUnknown** interface is the only interface that the ActiveX Control Specification (OC96) requires to be implemented, a control can efficiently target a particular area of functionality without having to support specific interfaces to qualify as a control. As always with COM, whether in a control or a container, you should never assume that an interface is available, and you should always follow standard return-checking conventions. It is important for a control or container to degrade gracefully and to offer alternative functionality if a required interface is not available.

This section covers the basic aspects of ActiveX controls, examines the support that ATL provides, examines the support that MFC provides, and looks at ActiveX control containers. MFC support is touched on, but the primary focus is on the various ways in which a container can be implemented using ATL.

ActiveX Controls

ActiveX controls live inside an in-process component (DLL or OCX) that can be dynamically loaded by a hosting process. This type of server is commonly referred to as an *ActiveX container* or simply as a *container*. Examples of available containers are Visual Basic (VB), MFC dialog boxes, and Internet Explorer (IE). Both the control and the container implement a number of standard, but different, COM interfaces. The control and the container establish and maintain a peer-to-peer relationship by exchanging interface pointers.

Some ActiveX controls are designed to be used with IE. These controls are lightweight components that can readily be downloaded over the Internet and installed on the user's computer automatically by IE. ActiveX controls that are used exclusively by IE are usually referred to as *lite controls*. ActiveX controls that work equally well with VB, MFC dialog boxes, and IE are known as *full-blown controls*.

Interfaces

Recall that an ActiveX control is a COM object and therefore must support, at a minimum, the **IUnknown** interface. To do any meaningful work, however, an ActiveX control must support a number of interfaces. When building an ActiveX control, you can choose many standard interfaces to implement. Refer to the "Platform SDK: COM" online document for a list of interfaces that you might implement.

A number of the interfaces that a control might support have a related interface that the container implements. The container supplies the interface to the control so that the control can call the container's methods. For example, the container uses the **IPersistPropertyBag** interface to supply the control with an **IPropertyBag** interface that the control can use to load or save its properties.

Events

Events always involve two or more COM objects. A COM object that fires an event is called an *event source* or a *connectable object*, and a COM object that receives the event notification is called an *event sink*. It's possible for more than one event sink to receive the same event from an event source. ActiveX controls (event sources) use this mechanism to make requests and provide notifications to their containers (event sinks). The control must provide an *outgoing* (or source) interface for its events, and the container must provide a *sink* for that interface. The container reads the control's type library to discover the events that the control expects to send. The container then dynamically creates an implementation of **IDispatch::Invoke()** that supports those methods. The ActiveX control standard describes a set of standard events that a control can implement. The events are primarily for user interaction involving the keyboard and mouse.

To make events work, the event source must implement the **IConnectionPointContainer**, **IConnectionPoint**, **IEnumConnectionPoints**, and **IEnumConnections** interfaces. On the opposite end, the event sink needs to notify the event source that it wants to receive events. It typically does so by requesting the **IConnectionPointContainer** interface and then calling **FindConnectionPoint()** for a specific **IConnectionPoint** interface. If the specific interface exists, the event sink then uses the **IConnectionPoint** interface to call **Advise()**, passing a pointer to its own callback interface. **Advise()** returns a cookie that the sink will pass back to the source when it calls **UnAdvise()**. **UnAdvise()** terminates the flow of events from a specific connection point.

You can define the callback interface as a custom interface, but if you want scripting environments to receive callbacks, make the callback interface a **dispinterface** and implement the methods of **IDispatch**.

Properties

ActiveX control properties come in two flavors: stock and custom. *Stock properties* are properties that use names and dispatch IDs specified in the ActiveX control specification. Stock properties are defined in olectl.h. Examples of stock properties are background color (**BackColor**), border style (**BorderStyle**), and text to be displayed (**Caption**). *Custom properties* are properties that you, the developer, create.

The control container can also have properties. These properties are known as *ambient properties* and are exposed to the control through the default **IDispatch** interface. By reading the ambient properties and taking the appropriate action, a control can smoothly fit into the container's environment. For example, the control might read the container's background color (**AmbientBackColor**) and adjust its own background color to match the container's. An interesting ambient property is **UserMode**. The control can examine this ambient property to determine if the container is in design mode or run mode. Often, a control will need to behave differently in design mode than it behaves in run mode.

Design Time User Interface

Some control containers, such as Visual Basic, provide a Properties window, which gives the developer a direct way to examine and change a control's properties. Other control containers, such as Visual C++, do not provide such a mechanism. Therefore, a control must provide another way for the design-time developer to examine and change the control's properties.

Property pages are used to implement this design-time interface mechanism. Each property page is a COM object that interacts with the container by exposing an **IPropertyPage** interface or an **IPropertyPage2** interface. To learn about the property pages that a control supports, the container calls **ISpecifyPropertyPages::GetPages()**. GetPages() fills a **CAUUID** structure with a pointer to an array of property page **CLSID**s and a count indicating the number of items in the array. The container can then create a property frame, which instantiates each property page object.

Each property frame exposes the **IPropertyPageSite** interface, and its respective property page; then, they communicate with each other. The property page notifies the property frame of value changes by calling **IPropertyPageSite::OnStatusChange()**.

All of this requires a lot of code. Fortunately, COM provides functions—**OleCreatePropertyFrame()** and **OleCreatePropertyFrameIndirect()**—that greatly simplify things. These functions create a Property Sheet dialog box that holds all the property pages that are passed during the call. These functions also create all necessary property frame-site objects and manage interaction between the property pages and the frame.

Property Persistence

A key feature of most ActiveX controls is *persistence*, the capability to save the property state between instantiations. An example of persistence occurs when a control is used in a Visual Basic program. During design time, each control embedded in a form is an instance of that control, and each instance has its own set of property values that make it unique. The developer modifies these values through the Visual Basic Properties window or through the control's property pages. Then, when told to do so by the container (form), the control saves and restores these values. The container, not the control, determines where the control's property values are stored.

Persistence is not restricted to design time. For example, a control that can be hosted in a Word document or a Web page might display different information based on user input. In this case, the control might need to save and reload the user's input.

All this is accomplished through a set of COM interfaces. The three most important are **IPersistStreamInit, IPersistStorage**, and **IPersistPropertyBag**. **IPersistStreamInit** lets the container ask the control to load its persistent data from—and save to—a stream. A *stream* is a simple file structure that provides a stream-oriented structure (a stream of bytes) to the control. By calling **IPersistStreamInit::InitNew()**, the container can inform the control that it's being initialized for the first time. **IPersistStorage** lets the container ask the control to load its persistent data from and save it to a storage. A *storage* is an object capable of creating and managing streams and other storages. **IPersistPropertyBag** allows a container to ask the control to load and save its persistence data as text-based properties. This form of persistence is useful in a Web-based environment.

Component Categories

By assigning category identifiers (**CATID**, a **GUID**) to your components, you can group your components into logically related groups or *component categories*. The purpose of component categories is to allow components to specify their capabilities and requirements. The **ICatRegister** and **ICatInformation** interfaces provide methods that can be used to write component category information to the Registry, as well as remove and retrieve component category information from it. The defined **CATID**s on individual components are stored under the **HKEY_CLASSES_ROOT\Component Categories** Registry key. Each category has its own unique subkey named by its **CATID**. Beneath its subkey, each category has one or more named values that contain the human-readable description of the category. These named values are coded by locale ID; for example, 409 is English.

Under its **CLSID**, each component can have two subkeys that store **CATIDs**: Implemented Categories and Required Categories. The Implemented Categories entry lists the category capabilities that the component provides, and the Required Categories entry lists the categories that require a client or container to implement.

Licensing

One of the greatest advantages of ActiveX controls is the ease with which they can be moved from one system to another and reused. However, this wide distribution presents a potential problem—unauthorized use.

Licensing is the feature that allows the author of an ActiveX control to determine how others use the control. There are two types of license verification. The first type occurs at design time. First, a license file (LIC) must be present in the same directory as the development tool or the control (DLL or OCX). Without this file, the development tool cannot create the control as part of the design-time environment. The second type of license verification occurs at runtime, when the application must present the license key when it attempts to instantiate the control.

Licensing relies on the **IClassFactory2** interface. An extension of the **IClassFactory** interface, **IClassFactory2**, adds three methods: **CreateInstanceLic()**, **GetLicInfo()**, and **RequestLicKey()**. **CreateInstanceLic()** is used to create an instance of a control. This method is like **IClassFactory::CreateInstance()**, but it also requires its caller to pass in a license key. **GetLicInfo()** is called to learn whether a design-time license exists on this machine for a control. **RequestLicKey()** is called by obtaining a copy of the license key.

ATL Support

The ATL Object Wizard provides six controls:

➤ *Full control*—Supports the interfaces for all control containers. It implements complete OLE Embedding protocol and complete OLE Control protocol. It can be queried for property pages and persist to streams and storage. Finally, it can provide type information to the client.

➤ *Lite control*—Supports only the subset of interfaces necessary to host the control needed by Internet Explorer. It supports the OLE Control protocol, but not all of the OLE Embedding protocol.

➤ *Composite control*—A dialog resource that can host several controls internally.

➤ *Lite composite control*—A composite control that supports only the interfaces that Internet Explorer needs.

➤ *HTML control*—A full control that contains DHTML functionality and can show Web pages within its frame.

➤ *Lite HTML control*—Like an HTML control, but it supports only the Internet Explorer interfaces.

When you create a control with the ATL Object Wizard, ATL provides the code needed to implement the basic control. Your control is derived from either **CComControl** or **CComCompositeControl**. You, of course, need to add the necessary code to provide your control's unique functionality.

The full control is derived from the **CComControl** template class to provide most of its functionality. **CComControl** supports a number of COM interfaces, stock properties, property persistence, and basic windowing functionality. It is derived from **CComControlBase** and **CWindowImpl**.

The composite control implements the same interfaces as the full control. However, rather than managing a single control, the composite manages a group of other controls. It uses a standard dialog box to host these controls. Instead of being derived from **CComControl**, the composite control is derived from **CComCompositeControl**. **CComCompositeControl** is derived from **CComControl** and manages the dialog box.

Like the full control, the HTML control is derived from **CComControl**. This control is like the **CComCompositeControl** in that it provides a resource for the layout of its user interface elements. However, rather than using a dialog resource, it uses an HTML resource. That is, the HTML control specifies its user interface by using HTML. The HTML control programmatically accesses the browser by using **IWebBrowser2**.

The lite versions of the controls are derived from the same base class as their full-form counterparts. However, they are slimmer because they do not support as many interfaces.

ATL, by default, doesn't support connection points or error reporting. However, this support is easy to add; simply select the appropriate checkbox on the Attributes tab of the ATL Object Wizard Properties dialog box. Connection points are needed for the control to report events to the container. To handle COM error handling, the **ISupportErrorInfo** interface must be supported.

MFC Support

Visual C++ includes an MFC ActiveX ControlWizard that generates a full ActiveX control. Step 1 of the ControlWizard lets you add from 1 to 99 controls in the OCX. Step 2 provides several selections that can modify the control's behavior. For each control that the ControlWizard generates, you get a class derived from **COleControl** and a default property page. **COleControl** is a large and complex class that implements basically the same set of interfaces that the ATL full control does. **COleControl** also handles a large number of Windows messages, implements stock methods, properties, and events, and provides a huge number of virtual functions you can override.

Creating an ActiveX control with MFC is as easy as it gets. Unfortunately, you can create only a full control, and you are dependent on the MFC library, which can be limiting. Another downside to using MFC is that it doesn't support dual interfaces. MFC uses the Automation (**IDispatch**) interface, and to support a dual interface, you'll need to add a lot of extra code.

ActiveX Control Containers

Recall that an ActiveX control container is just a program that can host an ActiveX control. Unlike a control, a container is required to support certain interfaces. All ActiveX control containers must support the **IDispatch** interface. This interface is how the container makes ambient properties available to the control. A container also needs to support another **IDispatch** if it traps events fired by the control. For every control that is plugged into a container, the container must provide a control site object that supports the **IOleControlSite** interface. However, not all of its methods are mandatory. Nonmandatory methods simply return **E_NOTIMPL, S_FALSE**, or **S_OK** as appropriate.

IOleContainer is a required interface—although, like **IOleControlSite**, not every method is mandatory. **IOleContainer** provides the capability to enumerate objects, thus allowing controls to navigate to other controls in the same document or form. For every compound document object that a container contains, it must provide one instance of **IOleClientSite**. **IOleClientSite** allows objects to request services from the container. **IOleInPlaceSite** allows the container to participate in in-place activation. This interface allows a control to obtain information about placement-related issues and to send placement notifications to the container. A couple of **IOleInPlaceSite**'s methods are not required.

Like **IOleInPlaceSite, IOleInPlaceFrame** is involved with in-place activation. This interface allows an object to merge its top-level user interface (such as menu items and toolbars) with the container's. Nearly all of **IOleInPlace-Frame**'s methods are nonmandatory. **IErrorInfo** is required, however, if the container supports dual interfaces.

Using MFC To Host ActiveX Controls

MFC makes it easy to use ActiveX controls in an application. When you select a checkbox in AppWizard, MFC provides the interfaces needed to host an ActiveX control. When AppWizard is done, you can use the Components and Controls Gallery to insert an ActiveX control into your project. Then, with the assistance of the MFC ClassWizard, you can add the desired functionality.

Using ATL To Host ActiveX Controls

ATL provides four ways in which you can host ActiveX controls: windows, dialog boxes, composite controls, and HTML controls. **CAxHostWindow**, found in atlhost.h, implements the required container interfaces. It is both a window and a COM object. You don't create a **CAxHostWindow** directly. Rather, you call **AtlAxWinInit()** to register a Win32 window class named **AtlAxWin**. Next, you create an **AtlAxWin** window instance by using the standard Win32 **CreateWindow()** function. Then, you use the **IAxWinHostWindow** interface to create or load an ActiveX control in the window.

ATL also provides **CAxWindow**, a **typedef** of **CAxWindowT<CWindow>**. **CAxWindow** is easier to use than **CAxHostWindow**; you don't have to deal with **CreateWindow()** or **IAxWinHostWindow**. **CAxWindow** provides methods that allow you to create a window, create and host a control in the window, and attach an existing control to the host.

The ATL Object Wizard can add a dialog resource to your project and generate an associated class, derived from **CAxDialogImpl**. Both Windows controls and ActiveX controls can be added to this **CAxDialogImpl**-derived class.

Hosting ActiveX controls in a composite control is similar to using a dialog box. The ATL composite control uses a dialog resource to lay out its user-interface elements, which can be Windows controls or ActiveX controls.

The way that the ATL Object Wizard provides a resource for an HTML control is similar to the way it provides a resource for a composite control, except that instead of using a dialog resource, an HTML control uses an HTML resource. The WebBrowser control used by IE4 will parse the HTML resource at runtime. The following code demonstrates an HTML control hosting the Calendar control.

```
<HTML>
<BODY>
<OBJECT
  CLASSID="CLSID:8E27C92B-1264-101C-8A2F-040224009C02"
  WIDTH=400
  HEIGHT=300
  ID="Calendar"
>
<PARAM NAME="BackColor" VALUE=1262256>
</OBJECT>
<BODY>
<SCRIPT LANGUAGE=VBScript>
Sub Calendar_Click()
  dt = Calendar.Day
  mon = Calendar.Month
  yr = Calendar.Year
  MsgBox(CStr (mon) + "/" + CStr(dt) + "/" + CStr(yr))
End Sub
</SCRIPT>
</HTML>
```

Practice Questions

Question 1

> You are implementing a local COM server that has a **ProgID** of **SalesServer**. In which subkey of **HKEY_CLASSES_ROOT** is the fully qualified path and EXE name of your server located?
>
> ○ a. **CLSID\LocalServer32**
>
> ○ c. **LocalServer32**
>
> ○ b. **CLSID\{***clsid***}\LocalServer32**
>
> ○ d. **ProgID\LocalServer32**

Answer c is correct. COM classes are registered beneath the HKEY_ CLASSES_ROOT\CLSID key. Each class is a subkey of HKEY_CLASSES_ROOT\CLSID, where the name of the class subkey corresponds to the class GUID. The class subkey has several critical subkeys hanging off it, which will vary depending on the type of server. In this case, the COM component is a local server, so the path and EXE name are located in the LocalServer32 subkey. The complete entry would look like: HKEY_ CLASSES_ROOT\CLSID\{*clsid*}\LocalServer32 = "C:\MyComponents\SalesServer.exe".

Question 2

> When you register the proxy-stub DLL, which subkeys of **HKEY_ CLASSES_ROOT\Interface\{iid}** are stored in the Registry? [Check all correct answers]
>
> ❑ a. **NumMethods**
>
> ❑ b. **ProgID**
>
> ❑ c. **ProxyStubClsid32**
>
> ❑ d. **LocalServer32**

Answers a and c are correct. Answer a is correct because the value entry for NumMethods specifies the number of methods that the proxy-stub DLL implements. Answer c is correct because the value entry for ProxyStubClsid32 maps the interface's IID to the CLSID of its proxy and stub objects. Answers b and d are both incorrect because these subkeys are not subkeys of **HKEY_ CLASSES_ROOT\Interface\{iid}** but are subkeys created by the server's own registration. The value entry for **ProgID** is the human-readable name of the application, and it allows a client to obtain the **CLSID** by calling **CLSIDFromProgID()**. The value entry for **LocalServer32** is the full path to the local server.

Question 3

You are using the Object Wizard to generate a simple object. If you choose the dual option on the Object Wizard's Attribute tab, your ATL class will be derived from which of the following templates? [Check all correct answers]

❑ a. **CComCoClass<>**

❑ b. **CComCoGlobal<>**

❑ c. **IDispatchImp<>**

❑ d. **CComCoDual<>**

Answers a and c are correct. Answer a is correct because **CComCoClass<>** is the template that provides class factory support. Answer c is correct because **IDispatchImpl<>** is the implementation for **IDispatch**. Answers b and d are incorrect because both are nonexistent templates.

Question 4

Which two of the following statements are always true?

❑ a. Given a class that can be aggregated, when created as a nonaggregated component, the constructor ensures that the **IUnknown *** member variable is **NULL**.

❑ b. When the outer object queries an interface belonging to the inner object, the reference count belonging to the outer object is incremented.

❑ c. One of the advantages of containment over aggregation is that when you're using containment, you can extend the interface by adding code to an existing interface.

❑ d. A client can determine if a component is using aggregation.

Answers b and c are correct. Answer b is correct because, when queried, the inner object delegates the **AddRef()** call to the outer unknown. The result is that the outer object component's reference count is incremented (not the inner object component's reference count). Answer c is correct because one of the major uses of containment is to extend an interface by adding your own code, which you can't do when you use aggregation. Answer a is incorrect because the inner object's **IUnknown** * member variable must be initialized to point to the outer unknown or the inner unknown. Answer d is incorrect because the inner component's **IUnknown** is hidden from the client. When the client queries for **IUnknown**, it is always presented with the outer component's **IUnknown**.

Question 5

You are implementing a COM local server using the SDK. Which function would you use to register your class factory?

○ a. **DllGetClassObject()**

○ b. **CoRegisterClassObject()**

○ c. **IClassFactory::CreateInstance()**

○ d. **CoRegisterClassFactory()**

Answer b is correct. You would use **CoRegisterClassObject** to register your class factory. Answer a is incorrect because **DllGetClassObject()** is a function that returns a class factory object from an in-process server. Answer c is incorrect because **IClassFactory::CreateInstance()** is used to create an object of the class identified with the specified **CLSID**. Answer d is incorrect because **CoRegisterClassFactory()** is not a valid function.

Question 6

Which of the following statements are correct? [Check all correct answers]

❑ a. The **END_INTERFACE_PART** macro creates a stack variable named **pThis**.

❑ b. Both **BEGIN_INTERFACE_PART** and **BEGIN_INTERFACE_MAP** prepend an X to the nested class name.

❑ c. The **BEGIN_INTERFACE_PART** macro defines a nested class that implements one COM interface.

❑ d. The **END_INTERFACE_PART** macro declares a member variable that's an instance of the nested class.

Answers c and d are correct. The **BEGIN_INTERFACE_PART** and **END_INTERFACE_PART** macros are placed in the header file. **BEGIN_INTERFACE_PART** defines the nested class and prepends an X to the class name. It also declares **QueryInterface()**, **AddRef()**, and **Release()**, which you must implement. **END_INTERFACE_PART** ends the class definition and declares a member variable of the nested class. It names the variable **m_x** plus the class name. Each nested class requires its own pair of **BEGIN_INTERFACE_PART** and **END_INTERFACE_PART** macros. Answer a is incorrect because **METHOD_PROLOGUE()** defines **pThis**. Answer b is incorrect because only **BEGIN_INTERFACE_PART** prepends an X to the nested class name.

Question 7

Which of the following statements are correct? [Check all correct answers]

❑ a. A process can have no STAs and no MTAs.

❑ b. A process can have more than one STA.

❑ c. A process can have no STAs and one MTA.

❑ d. A process can have one MTA and more than one STA.

❑ e. A process can have one STA and no MTAs.

Answers a, b, c, d, and e are correct. This is a tricky question because all answers are correct. Answer a tries to confuse you into thinking about only COM objects. Answer a is correct because it describes a process that isn't using COM. Answer b is correct because it describes a process that has multiple threads.

One thread is the main STA, and each of the other threads are associated with one and only one apartment. Answer c is correct because it describes a process that can have any number of threads using COM. All of the threads will belong to the same MTA. Answer d is correct because it describes a combination of b and c. This model is commonly referred to as the *mixed model*. Answer e is correct because its process has only one thread using COM. This STA is called the *main STA*. COM uses this model to support legacy code.

Question 8

Which of the following statements can be used to specify that your **ISpell** interface supports dynamic invocation? [Check all correct answers]

❑ a. **interface ISpell : IAutomation**

❑ b. **dispinterface ISpell**

❑ c. **interface ISpell : IDispatch**

❑ d. **interface ISpell : IDynamic**

Answers b and c are correct. To specify that an interface supports dynamic invocation, you either derive it from **IDispatch** or use the **dispinterface** keyword. Answers a and d are incorrect because **ISpell** is being derived from a nonexistent interface.

Question 9

Which of the following actions must you take to make an MFC class aggregatable?

○ a. Include an **INTERFACE_AGGREGATE()** macro entry in your interface map.

○ b. Declare an **IUnknown *** member variable and initialize it during **OnCreateAggregates()**.

○ c. In the object's constructor, call **EnableAggregation()**.

○ d. Declare an **IUnknown *** member variable and initialize it by calling **GetControllingUnknown()**.

Answer c is correct. This question tries to trick you by providing two answers, a and b, that would be correct if you were implementing an MFC class that employed aggregation. Enabling an MFC component to be aggregated is trivial.

By calling **EnableAggregation()** in your component's constructor, MFC initializes the object's inner unknown pointer with an **IUnknown** vtable. This is all you need to do to enable your component to operate smoothly as an inner object.

Question 10

Which of the following statements is correct?

○ a. **CoMarshalInterThreadInterfaceInStream()** allows you to marshal a raw interface pointer from one process to another process.

○ b. By repeatedly calling **CoGetInterfaceAndReleaseStream()**, you can unmarshal multiple copies of the same interface pointer.

○ c. Threads that execute within an MTA must marshal interface pointers from one thread to another thread.

○ d. Objects that live in an MTA must support both concurrency and reentrancy.

Answer d is correct. COM does not synchronize method invocations to objects in an MTA. Therefore, the objects must support concurrency. When a thread makes an outgoing method invocation to another apartment, the thread is then blocked until the method invocation returns. During this time, it is possible for a second apartment to make a callback or for a different thread to call a method on the same object. For this reason, objects in an MTA must support reentrancy.

Answer a is incorrect because **CoMarshalInterThreadInterfaceInStream()** only marshals interface pointers from one thread to another thread in the same process. Answer b is incorrect because you can call **CoGetInterface-AndReleaseStream()** to unmarshal an interface pointer only one time. **CoGetInterfaceAndReleaseStream()** releases the stream, making it impossible to be called more than one time on the same stream. Answer c is incorrect because threads that execute within an MTA can all access a raw interface pointer belonging to the MTA. Marshaling is not required within a single MTA.

Need To Know More?

 Li, Sing and Panos Economopoulos. *Professional COM Application with ATL*. Wrox Press Ltd., Birmingham, UK, 1998. ISBN 1-861001-70-3. If you have a good COM/ATL foundation, this is the book for you. It starts by having you build an ActiveX control from scratch. Then you use ATL to develop a distributed calendar system. This is a real-world three-tier application that uses flexible, browser-based controls for the client UI, business objects on both the client and server, and UDA to perform queries and updates. One feature I especially like about this book is the authors' use of UML and design patterns.

 Major, Dr. Al. *COM IDL and Interface Design*. Wrox Press Ltd, Acock's Green, Birmingham, UK, 1999. ISBN 1-861002-25-4. At the time of writing, this is the only book on the market that is devoted to IDL. This book explains the syntax and usage of IDL in a clear and concise manner.

 Prosise, Jeff. *Programming Windows with MFC*. Microsoft Press, Redmond, WA, 1999. ISBN 1-57231-695-0. This is an updated version of the author's popular book. The book has four parts: "Fundamentals of Windows and MFC"; "The Document/View Architecture"; "Beyond the Basics"; and "COM, OLE and ActiveX." Chapter 18 covers MFC and the Component Object Model. Chapter 21 first covers ActiveX controls in general and then covers the specific support MFC provides.

 Rector, Brent, and Chris Sells. *ATL Internals*. Addison-Wesley, Reading, MA, 1998. ISBN 0-201-69589-8. This book focuses on the usage of ATL as a tool, so you should know COM before reading this book. The authors cover ATL in a very skillful and insightful manner. They dissect the ATL architecture and explain how all the pieces fit together.

 Shepherd, George and Scott Wingo. *MFC Internals, Inside the Microsoft Foundation Class Architecture*. Addison-Wesley, Reading, MA, 1996. ISBN 0-201-40721-3. If you want to learn how MFC does its magic when it comes to COM, this is the book for you. The authors have done an admirable job of taking a complex topic and presenting it in a straightforward and understandable manner. To aid comprehension, they show what the code looks like after all of the macros are expanded. Despite the fact that this book is more than three years old, which is a lifetime in the computer field, it is still the best source of information about the inner workings of MFC.

 Thai, Thuan L. *Learning DCOM*. O'Reilly & Associates, Inc. Sebastopol, CA, 1999. ISBN 1-56592-581-5. This is an excellent book that is aimed at experienced C++ programmers. It is well written, clear, and to the point. The first four chapters cover the basics—but are well worth reading even by experienced COM programmers—and lay a solid foundation for what's to come. The remainder of the book then provides the details on how to build and use distributed components. I have a number of books on COM and DCOM, but this is without a doubt my favorite. I recommend it very highly. If I could own only one COM/DCOM book, this would be it.

 Zaratian, Beck. *Visual C++ 6.0 Programmer's Guide*. Microsoft Press, Redmond, WA, 1998. ISBN 1-57231-866-X. This updated version of the author's previous book, *Visual C++ Owners Manual*, focuses on how to use the Visual C++ tool. The section on ActiveX controls has the best explanation that I have seen of licensing, what it is, and how it works.

 MSDN Library\Visual Studio 6.0 Documentation\Visual C++ Documentation\Reference\Microsoft Foundation Class Library and Templates\Active Template Library

 MSDN Library\Platform SDK\Component Services

 MSDN Library\Technical Articles\Component Object Model

 www.microsoft.com/com—Microsoft places the most current information online. This Web page contains articles, white papers, presentations, downloadable code, and much more.

 www.worldofatl.com—Alex Stockton maintains The World of ATL Web page. This Web page provides a lot of useful information and links to a number of other Web pages.

Component Distribution And Scalability

Terms you'll need to understand:

- √ Digital certificate
- √ COM (Component Object Model) objects
- √ Connection pooling
- √ Transaction
- √ Package
- √ ACID
- √ Locking
- √ Commit/abort
- √ Resource

Techniques you'll need to master:

- √ Implementing basic security functions
- √ Identifying the benefits offered to COM objects by MTS (Microsoft Transaction Server)
- √ Understanding the role of Microsoft Distributed Transaction Coordinator (MS DTC) in MTS
- √ Changing a COM object to make it MTS-ready
- √ Creating MTS packages
- √ Adding MTS-compliant COM objects to packages

The increasing popularity of the Internet has placed a strong demand on developers to construct systems that can scale appropriately. In the recent past, systems that served hundreds or a thousand users were considered to be large scale. Today, it is not inconceivable for a handful of developers to be responsible for designing and coding systems that permit tens of thousands of connections, processing hundreds of thousands of transactions a week. This chapter introduces Microsoft's Transaction Server and its place in aiding the construction of such scalable applications.

Security

One of the most important areas of concern when you're building a distributed application is making sure that it is secure. That is, the system can connect to privileged data sources and deliver highly confidential information to those who present the necessary credentials while denying access to everyone else. Such concerns are magnified many times over when such systems can be accessed from the public Internet.

Security Concepts

To construct secure systems, you need to understand three concepts: auditing, authentication, and encryption.

Auditing

Maintaining an audit log of user activity is important in identifying typical user access, thus providing a reference when you're attempting to locate abuses and/or other unauthorized activity.

> *Note: An audit system can be connected to software that can notify you via email or pager when a defined number of error entries appear or when an entry that should never be made is triggered.*

Authentication

Authentication is all about identification and is usually grounded in a system that uses a password or a challenge and response. Authentication allows the software administrator to map resource rights and restrictions to the user, process, or component.

Encryption

Encryption masks information in a way that makes it unintelligible to anyone other than its intended recipient when it's intercepted. Numerous forms of encryption are available. Most experts agree that algorithms that are available for public scrutiny are among the safest to use; because they can be easily challenged, it's also easy to identify and compensate for their weaknesses. Among the most popular encryption algorithms are those developed by RSA Data Security, Inc.

NT Security

Microsoft's Windows NT operating system and Distributed Network Architecture (DNA) middleware components employ the security concepts discussed previously, integrating them into a comprehensive security model. NT favors a centralized user-management scheme using domains and groups, but NT can also be used in peer-to-peer, trust-based workgroups.

> *Note: NT offers several file systems when you install the operating system. The NT File System (NTFS) is the most secure, offering permissioning options down to the individual file.*

Internet Issues

Entire books, conferences, and trade shows are dedicated to discussing the risks of building software for use on the Internet and connecting corporate LANs to the Internet. With that being said, there are some fundamental devices used to secure a distributed system, such as firewalls and digital certificates.

> *Note: It's important to monitor the Microsoft Web site for updates for the operating system and other middleware products that your applications rely upon.*

Firewalls

A *firewall* is a device that isolates a corporate LAN from the Internet or other potentially malicious networks. A firewall can block connections to certain ports on computers behind it. *Ports* are connections that are made by sockets using the TCP/IP protocol.

Some ports are generally made available to anonymous users; for example, port 80 is the default for HTTP traffic, your everyday Web pages. FTP and Telnet have their own ports, which, for security reasons, you may or may not want available. Other ports are identified with the configuration consoles of computers running middleware modules or other network devices. These ports you certainly wouldn't want available for hacking. A firewall usually offers a plethora of logging and auditing options and sometimes supports additional levels of user authentication.

Digital Certificates

Digital certificates are rooted in the concept of encryption security. A *digital certificate* identifies the user or organization from which a program or data file originated. A certificate contains the organization's name, country, and address, an activation date, an expiration date, and encryption-algorithm data.

Certificates that are used on the Internet are based on *asymmetric* encryption. Such a system has two keys: a private key and a public key. The private key is held closely by the developer and is generally used to *sign* ActiveX controls that end users download and install on a computer. The public key can be freely circulated, allowing end users to decode the contents of a signed file. However, it is important for users to verify that the code they are about to install originated from the software company they trust and isn't a Trojan horse program. It is at this point that Certificate Authorities (CAs) are important.

A CA acts as a trusted intermediary between two parties. End users trust a well-known CA, such as Verisign, and you provide the necessary documentation to unequivocally identify yourself or your company to Verisign. Verisign issues you a certificate and a private key, while retaining a copy of the certificate and the public key. End users specify Verisign as a trusted CA who can vouch for the authenticity of software signed with one of their issued certificates. (In this example, users specify acceptable CAs in their browsers.) Upon encountering such a certificate, associated with an ActiveX control, users can rest assured that the code is from the stated source and hasn't been modified since it was issued.

> *Note: Digital certificates may also be incorporated into the process of securing a system based on Microsoft's Distributed Network Architecture components. Using Microsoft's certificate server, you can create and issue your own certificates and use Internet Information Server to map certificates and user/directory access.*

Microsoft Transaction Server (MTS)

The Microsoft Transaction Server (MTS) is the keystone for Microsoft's Distributed Network Architecture (DNA). Although the moniker *transaction server* may sound intimidating to developers whose forte is not database design or development, the product is very powerful middleware that offers much to systems whose primary purpose doesn't revolve around data storage and retrieval. MTS is equally beneficial for applications that require a number of component activations and for systems that perform multiple database transactions. Under MTS, execution of object methods occurs in a transactional context. Using MTS, you can create applications that will scale in a manner that remains useful to a larger number of concurrent users.

System Requirements

The MTS components are part of NT Option Pack 4 (or later) and are also packaged with the Enterprise Edition of Windows. MTS requires Internet Explorer 4.01+ to be present on the target computer as well.

Client Options

MTS supports two client options: Win32 and browser:

➤ A Win32 client can be installed and executed from any Windows operating system that supports the DCOM extensions.

➤ The browser client must be able to communicate with Microsoft Internet Information Server (IIS) and be capable of invoking ActiveX components.

Benefits Of MTS

There are a number of reasons that you should design your enterprise or Internet applications using MTS. One reason is developing systems using a component architecture, such as COM.

 Although there are other component standards, such as JavaBeans for the Java language, Microsoft's software development approach favors COM, which is both platform and language independent. The component-based software approach aids in the development of large and/or complex software by dividing the problem into well-defined and isolated units.

Out-Of-Process Protection

All COM servers that will participate in MTS transactions must be implemented as DLLs. Developers often prefer an in-process server over an out-of-process (EXE) server as a vehicle for object creation because there is a speed advantage in bringing the server into your application's process space. The downside of in-process servers is that, if they are improperly coded, a fault in the server will bring your application down along with the server.

MTS offers the best of both worlds...almost. Because all COM servers in MTS are in-process, there is an advantage in execution time. Second, because the server resides in a surrogate server process, your MTS application is protected from faults caused by COM servers.

> *Note: Components that occupy the same MTS package default to sharing the same process space. Therefore, the package may experience the same fault-tolerance issues that any in-process client faces. You can achieve greater fault tolerance by placing unproven COM objects in their own packages.*

Persistent Context

MTS objects are provided a context that is similar to the context given to a process or application by an operating system. The context retains information that is important to the object, such as its creator and transaction status.

Connection Pooling

Creating and destroying resources, especially database connections, can be a costly operation. Therefore, MTS maintains a cache of idle database connections. MTS borrows a connection from the cache when creating a transactional context and releases the connection when the transaction finishes.

Just-In-Time Activation

When you get right down to the mechanics of programming even the simplest of COM servers, you will immediately recognize the amount of code (and therefore processor time) it takes for a component client to acquire an instance of an object. A number of OLE libraries intervene on behalf of the COM client to locate and start the necessary server from which the object is instantiated. A similar analysis of the destruction of a component tells you that time is spent returning resources to the operating system.

MTS maintains a *pool* of objects that can be shared among component clients. Within this pool, objects that hold valuable system resources can be temporarily deactivated, while a client reference is used to fulfill a different client's requests. This activation scheme is helpful in offsetting the additional overhead that the Microsoft Distributed Transaction Coordinator (MS DTC) may place on MTS operations.

Distributed Transactions

A powerful aspect of MTS is its ability to provide a developer with transactional facilities in a heterogeneous environment using a common management console and a unified API. The primary components of MTS include the following:

➤ *Resource manager*—Resource managers are fundamental to the MTS architecture. They are system services that manage data storage, interfacing with durable stores. Microsoft's SQL Server is a resource manager. Resource managers are typically associated with databases. To qualify as a resource manager, the service must work with the Microsoft Distributed Transaction Coordinator (DTC) and provide isolation and atomicity.

➤ *Microsoft Distributed Transaction Coordinator (MS DTC)*—The Microsoft Distributed Transaction Coordinator provides the ability to manage transactions across multiple resource managers. This service allows a transaction to be committed or rolled back even if it spans multiple resource managers on multiple computers. MS DTC employs a two-phase commit protocol when executing transactions.

➤ *Resource dispenser*—A resource dispenser is a service that manages access to nondurable resources, such as database connections, within a process. Resource dispensers exist for ODBC access to databases, CICS and IMS transaction monitors, and Microsoft Message Queue (MSMQ) Server.

Component Design

When you're designing a COM object that participates in an MTS-based system, you have several things to consider. These include the transaction attribute, the **IObjectContext** methods, and the retaining state.

Transaction Attribute

The transaction attribute can be set for any component under MTS management and is stored in the MTS catalog. This setting identifies how the object behaves when it is activated by MTS. There are four options:

➤ *Requires a transaction*—If a transaction already exists, the component will run; otherwise, a new transaction will be started before the component begins executing.

➤ *Requires a new transaction*—A new transaction will be initiated by MTS each time an instance of this component activates.

➤ *Supports transactions*—The component is indifferent to transactions. The component will execute in a transactional context if one exists and will operate equally well outside of a transaction.

➤ *Does not support transactions*—The component operates only when it's outside any existing transactions.

IObjectContext Methods

There are four **IObjectContext** methods that allow a COM object to participate in a transaction and determine its outcome. These methods work in conjunction with the transaction attribute that is associated with the component. A component that wishes to participate in MTS must implement the four methods of this interface:

➤ **SetComplete**—Indicates a successful completion of the object's participation in a transaction.

➤ **SetAbort**—Indicates that the component has completed its participation in the transaction; however, the work it performed is not to be committed.

➤ **EnableCommit**—Allows the work that was performed to be committed. That is, the operation's current result will leave the system in a consistent state, but the component is not necessarily done.

➤ **DisableCommit**—Indicates that the work currently performed by the component is not in a state that can be committed.

Note: The SetComplete and SetAbort methods cause MTS to deactivate the object on return to the calling function. The object is then reactivated on the next method call.

Retaining State

One of the advantages that MTS offers is quick activation of administered components. MTS can almost be thought of as a Web server where each method call to a COM object that it supports is a page request by a browser. Just as the communication between a browser and a Web server is stateless under the HTTP protocol, an analogy may be made to your client application and an instance of a component in MTS. In order for MTS to support large numbers of connections, it shares COM objects among its clients. Therefore, the object that you used for your first method call may not be the same object instance that you use for subsequent method invocations.

Objects can preserve their states across multiple calls. You may use the **DisableCommit** and **EnableCommit** commands to *bracket* the operations necessary for a transaction to complete (either successfully or aborted). Such an approach requires the object to call the **DisableCommit** command before returning to the calling function. This does not mean that the component is out of circulation for use by other clients; it just means that the specific state of the object must be reconstructed between similar client invocations. When the object completes the work that is necessary for it to be committed, it calls the **EnableCommit** command.

The following rules can be applied to your component design to help your object scale well:

➤ A component should call the **SetComplete** method as soon as possible and as often as possible, allowing MTS to free its managed state of the object.

➤ Database resources should be acquired as late in the execution process as possible and should free them as soon as they're no longer needed.

➤ The acquisitions of object handles are maintained by MTS, and there is little processor overhead. Therefore, client processes should acquire these handles early. The process can hold these handles for as long as necessary without penalty.

The MTS Explorer

The MTS Explorer is the graphical management tool from which you package, deploy, and manage MTS applications. The MTS Explorer is constructed as a plug-in to the Microsoft Management Console (MMC). The tree-view pane to the left of the MMC allows you to manipulate the application hierarchy from the package level through the component, interface, and method levels. Administrative functions include new package creation, inspection, and destruction. Additionally, you can annotate your component methods for administrative reference.

The MTS Catalog

MTS maintains package and component configuration information in a data store known as the *MTS Catalog*. The MTS Explorer provides a graphical user interface for initializing and administering this information.

Security

Using the MTS Explorer, you can define your package and component security roles. The security role model allows you to interface with NT's user and group domain definitions and map them to the MTS role scheme. Thus, a user's group affiliations are checked against the MTS role declaration when the application starts and when a call is made across package boundaries.

> *Note: Security checking is not performed between components occupying the same package because components within the same package share a process space.*

Package Management

Packages are collections of components that together perform a task or a set of related tasks. This grouping allows an administrator to manage the properties and permission set as a whole. Packages are installed and maintained with the MTS Explorer. To create a new package, you identify the computer that you want to host the package (My Computer), and you use the context menu of the

Packages Installed folder to select New Package (some of these locations may change in Windows 2000). This command invokes a three-step wizard:

1. Choose one of the two package-creation options. You may either use a prebuilt package (software components that you purchased or that exist on a different machine), or you may create a new, empty package.

   Note: MTS applications can execute in one of two clients: either through a Web browser or as a Win32 client.

2. Name the package.

3. In the Set Package Identity dialog box, do one of two things: either assign an NT account, through which the package components access system services; or select the Interactive User option, which uses the account of the user who is logged on. For browser-based clients, the Interactive User setting is appropriate because the current user will be identified as IIS.

After you create the package, a package icon is displayed in the Packages Installed folder. Each package is associated with a number of properties, accessed from the object's Properties menu. Two of the property tabs involve activation issues. In the first tab, you choose where the package activation takes place. In the second, you choose when to terminate a package's executing state.

You can specify that package activation occur either in a dedicated server process (the default) or in the creator's process space. Choosing the creator's process space offers higher performance at the risk of crashing all components in a package if a component faults. The Package Timeout option allows you to either keep the package running when idle or shut down the package after a specified number of minutes.

Component Management

Adding components is an even simpler process. You simply drag them from an Explorer window and drop them in the Components folder of the desired package.

Note: The MTS Explorer is not limited to package management for the machine on which it is running. Through the magic of DCOM, you can load packages on other machines on the network and administer them accordingly.

Transactions

Transactional support is necessary to retain the integrity of any distributed system. Encapsulating operations into transactional *blocks* offers you a way to deal with the countless failure modes that are inherent in any complex system. Operating in a transactional system, a program may elect not to commit changes that have been specified. This can occur because of a lack of resources, because of an inability to obtain a record lock, or as a result of a user abort operation. A *rollback* is usually performed to bring the system back to its previous state.

ACID

Four laws identify transactional systems. These rules, commonly referred to as the *ACID rules* because they form the acronym ACID, are described here:

➤ *Atomic*—A transaction is something in a binary operation. It has two states: either the transaction completes successfully, updating the system, or the transaction does not complete and the system remains in its original state. The transaction is an all-or-nothing proposition. MTS supports atomic operations with the **SetComplete** and **SetAbort** methods.

➤ *Consistent*—Many operations may occur inside a transactional context. These suboperations may produce inconsistent system states. However, the result of the entire transaction must produce a valid state. All operations within MTS, by default, occur within a transactional context that MTS creates and maintains.

➤ *Isolated*—The possible inconsistent states that may occur within a transactional context must never be visible to other transaction operations. The transaction context offers a safe and private haven for the operations to take place in, and it provides a way for rollback operations to take place. Only when the transaction is finally committed is the consistent result applied to the transaction system. Isolation is generally provided by a lock manager system, acting to properly block and serialize operations through the system. The MS DTC is the lock manager that MTS uses to ensure isolation.

➤ *Durable*—Durability refers to physical protection that is given to transactional data. Often this refers to storage on a hard disk or other physical media. Such fault-tolerant measures are important for failover or recovery purposes. Transactional logging features of the durable stores generally allow you to recover state even if the hardware fails. A number of durable stores are supported by MTS, including Message Queue Server and SQL Server.

Locking

Lock management was briefly mentioned as a component of transactional iso-lation. The concept of *obtaining* a lock is something that database-oriented developers deal with on a daily basis. For database operations, it is important to place write locks on those records that are being updated for a transaction. Placing locks on only those records that are involved in a transaction offers more system concurrency than does placing locks on entire tables or indices.

> *Note: The locking mechanisms that are necessary for transactional isolation can affect concurrency and increase operation latency.*

MTS uses the Microsoft Distributed Transaction Coordinator (MS DTC) to coordinate transactions and access to resources. MS DTC runs as a system service and can span multiple resource managers across one or more machines. Resource managers exist for SQL Server; some resource managers also sup-port OLE transactions, X/Open XA protocols, and LU 6.2 Sync Level 2 operations.

> *Note: The MS DTC can be started and stopped from the MTS Explorer. The context menu for each computer in the Microsoft Transaction Server hierarchy offers an option to control the running state of the MS DTC.*

The IIS-MTS Connection

Two technologies that Microsoft introduced to Web developers with the launch-ing of IIS were Internet Server API (ISAPI) and Active Server Pages (ASP). The first, ISAPI, allows a developer to write code that hooks into the request and response actions of the Web server. Although the purpose of ASP is to introduce powerful component-based programming to Web-page-content gen-eration, both of these server extensions are related because ASP support exists in the form of an ISAPI DLL. These powerful extensions are welcomed by developers, but they share a weakness by loading into the IIS process space. Thus, a fault in any of this code results in crashing the Web server.

With the release of IIS 4, Microsoft introduced Web Application Manager (WAM), a way to encapsulate ISAPI in a COM wrapper. Furthermore, this COM object is implemented as an MTS-compliant component, allowing you to marry MTS process protection with IIS.

Practice Questions

Question 1

> Which three concepts are central to securing a single computer or an entire computer network? [Check all correct answers]
>
> ❑ a. Auditing
>
> ❑ b. Recovery
>
> ❑ c. Authentication
>
> ❑ d. Encryption

Answers a, c, and d are correct. Answer b is incorrect because recovery may be part of the fault tolerance that a system needs to achieve, but it is not central to securing a system.

Question 2

> Which statement about Microsoft's NT operating system and certificates is not true?
>
> ○ a. You can map certificates to directory access.
>
> ○ b. You can map certificates to user rights.
>
> ○ c. Certificates carry an expiration date.
>
> ○ d. Certificates created by Microsoft's Certificate Server guarantee the identity of the issuer.

Answer d is correct. The statement is false because just creating a certificate from the Microsoft Certificate Server does not validate the contents of the certificate. If this were true, then anyone could purchase Certificate Server and configure it to offer certificates from an entity known as Microsoft. A trusted intermediary, a Certificate Authority, is used to guarantee the identity of the issuer.

Question 3

> MTS supports which types of clients? [Check all correct answers]
>
> ❑ a. Browsers
>
> ❑ b. Applets
>
> ❑ c. Win32
>
> ❑ d. ActiveX

Answers a and c are correct. Support is available for HTML/DHTML browser-based clients and for heavyweight (traditional) Win32 clients.

Question 4

> Which of the following are benefits of using MTS? [Check all correct answers]
>
> ❑ a. In-process protection
>
> ❑ b. Connection pooling
>
> ❑ c. Just-in-time activation
>
> ❑ d. Distributed transactions

Answers b, c, and d are correct. Connection pooling, just-in-time activation, and distributed transactions are benefits of using MTS. Answer a is incorrect because there is no inherent protection in creating COM objects from in-process servers. Although their response time is generally faster than out-of-process servers, they are inherently more prone to failure.

Question 5

> Which is not an MTS transaction attribute?
>
> ○ a. Requires a transaction
>
> ○ b. Supports transactions
>
> ○ c. Requires a new transaction
>
> ○ d. Supports nested transactions

Answer d is correct. "Supports nested transactions" is not an MTS transaction attribute. Transaction nesting is not a concern in MTS because MTS creates and maintains the transaction context.

Question 6

Which is not an **IObjectContext** method?

- ○ a. **EnableCommit**
- ○ b. **DisableCommit**
- ○ c. **SetRollback**
- ○ d. **SetComplete**

Answer c is correct. Rolling back may be a result of the **SetAbort** method, but there is no method named **SetRollback**.

Question 7

What is the significance of locking during a transaction? [Check all correct answers]

- ❑ a. Ensure consistency during the transaction.
- ❑ b. Aid a transaction in being an atomic operation.
- ❑ c. Enable durability for transactions that rely on durable stores.
- ❑ d. Help isolate transactions from each other.

Answers a, b, c, and d are all correct. Locking is a fundamental component of the ACID rules for transactional systems.

Need To Know More?

 Box, Don, Keith Brown, Tim Ewald, and Chris Sells. *Effective COM—50 Ways to Improve your COM and MTS-based Applications*. Addison-Wesley, 1999. ISBN 0-201-37968-6. A book by Don Box and others at Developmentor. The Transaction chapter alone makes this an important addition to any professional COM developer's library.

 Dickman, Alan. *Designing Applications with MSMQ*. Addison-Wesley, 1998. ISBN 0-201-32581-0. Offering a solid overview of one of MTS's most popular durable stores (Microsoft Message Queue Server), this book also contains sections on authentication and on the underpinnings of transactional systems.

 Grimes, Richard. *Professional DCOM Programming*. Wrox Press, 1997. ISBN 1-861000-60-X. This book provides in-depth coverage regarding all aspects of DCOM programming and component deployment.

 Homer, Alex and David Sussman. *Professional MTS and MSMQ with VB and ASP*. Wrox Press, 1998. ISBN 1-861001-6-0. This book includes a very good overview of MTS installation and package management, as well as the basics of NT security in a distributed system.

Writing SQL

Terms you'll need to understand:

- √ Relational database
- √ SQL
- √ Data Manipulation Language (DML)
- √ **USE**
- √ Projection
- √ **SELECT**
- √ **FROM**
- √ Aggregates
- √ **NULL**
- √ **GROUP BY**
- √ **COMPUTE BY**
- √ **ORDER BY**
- √ Restriction
- √ **WHERE**

- √ **HAVING**
- √ Join
- √ Self-join query
- √ Outer join
- √ Set operations
- √ **UNION**
- √ Intersection
- √ Difference
- √ Subquery
- √ View
- √ Index
- √ **INSERT**
- √ **UPDATE**
- √ **DELETE**

Techniques you'll need to master:

- √ Retrieving data by using **SELECT**
- √ Joining multiple tables by using **SELECT**
- √ Modifying data by using **INSERT**, **UPDATE**, and **DELETE**

Most applications need to access data in a remote database. Indeed, corporate data critical to the business will reside in a database. It is important for the application developer to understand how databases work and how to retrieve and modify data.

Relational Database Fundamentals

The predominant database model today is called the *relational database*. A relational database organizes its information in collections of tables. Think of a table as being like a two-dimensional spreadsheet. Each table has an arbitrary number of rows, but all rows have the same sequence of columns. A later chapter will discuss the options available for defining a table.

A *table* stores data about a specific business *entity*: person, place, or thing. The techniques for identifying entities are *logical data modeling* and *data normalization*. The resulting database model is called an *Entity Relationship Diagram (ERD)*.

Consider an **EMPLOYEE** table. Each *row* represents a different occurrence of an employee. Each row is described using the same *attributes*, or *columns*. In this case, the columns are **EMP_ID, DEPT_ID, FIRST_NAME, LAST_NAME, PHONE, MANAGER_ID**, and **SALARY**.

Every employee can be uniquely identified by a column or a combination of columns called *candidate keys*. No two values of a candidate key in a table may be the same. In this case, there are two candidate keys:

➤ EMP_ID

➤ FIRST_NAME, LAST_NAME, PHONE

One of the candidate keys is chosen as the definitive *primary key* to uniquely identify any given employee. Ideally, the value of the primary key should never change. **EMP_ID** seems like our best choice for primary key.

DEPARTMENT would be a separate table, and it could be described by the columns **DEPT_ID, DEPT_NAME**, and **COST_CENTER**. The **DEPT_ID** column is the primary key in **DEPARTMENT**.

Because one department has many employees working in it, the *relationship* between **DEPARTMENT** and **EMPLOYEE** is one-to-many. **DEPARTMENT** is referred to as the parent entity and **EMPLOYEE** as the child entity. The department an employee works in is indicated by redundantly storing its **DEPT_ID** primary key in the **EMPLOYEE** table.

Note that **DEPT_ID** is a fact about a department, not about an employee. The **DEPT_ID** in the **EMPLOYEE** table is said to be a *foreign key* of **EMPLOYEE**.

Every one-to-many relationship will have the parent's primary key stored as a foreign key in its child. Tables 7.1 and 7.2 show the **DEPARTMENT** and **EMPLOYEE** tables with some sample data.

SQL Server allows you to define many named databases that contain a collection of tables. To tell SQL Server which database to access, we use the **USE** command as shown below:

```
USE database_name
```

Retrieving Data

Structured Query Language (SQL) has become the industry-standard language for relational database manipulation. SQL has three components:

➤ Data Manipulation Language (DML), for data manipulation

Table 7.1	DEPARTMENT table.	
DEPT_ID	DEPT_NAME	COST_CENTER
100	Finance	F3W
200	Marketing	H1Q
300	Sales	S8G
400	R&D	R4U

EMP_ID	DEPT_ID	FIRST_NAME	LAST_NAME	PHONE	MANAGER_ID	SALARY
Table 7.2	EMPLOYEE table.					
1234	200	James	Jones	617-555-1015	6789	$65,000
2345	300	Eric	Sanderson	617-555-1018	6789	$120,000
3456	100	Rosa	Marinaro	617-555-1011	NULL	$65,000
4567	300	Jessica	Jones	617-555-1014	6789	$70,000
5678	100	Christopher	Phillips	617-555-1017	3456	$55,000
6789	200	Gail	LaVila	617-555-1012	NULL	NULL

➤ Data Definition Language (DDL), for database definition

➤ Data Control Language (DCL), for security

DML's **SELECT** statement is used for retrieving data. Retrieving data involves relational operations called *projection* and *restriction*.

> SQL statements are not case sensitive, so **SELECT** is the same as select or Select. Many developers use uppercase for all SQL keywords and lowercase for column and table names. This makes code easier to read and debug.

Projection

A projection displays all or some of the columns of the tables being accessed. The statement below is a full projection of the **DEPARTMENT** table:

```
SELECT dept_id, dept_name, cost_center
FROM department
```

When we select, we create a *result set*. The set looks just like another table containing rows and columns. Later we'll see how to input a result set into another query. Here is the result set for the previous query:

DEPT_ID	DEPT_NAME	COST_CENTER
100	Finance	F3W
200	Marketing	H1Q
300	Sales	S8G
400	R&D	R4U

The syntax for projection is shown below. We will be expanding on this syntax:

```
SELECT [ DISTINCT ]
    { * | column [[AS] heading] [ , ...column_list ] }
FROM table
```

The parameters are:

➤ **SELECT * FROM table**—Selects all the columns in the table.

➤ **SELECT DISTINCT column_list**—Removes result rows that repeat a value.

➤ The **column_list** can contain function calls and expressions.

➤ The column heading can be changed with the **AS** keyword.

Aggregate Functions

Each of the following functions—called *aggregate functions*—operates on a set of rows to calculate and return a single value:

➤ COUNT(*)—Counts the number of rows.

➤ COUNT(column)—Counts the number of non-null values in the column.

➤ COUNT(DISTINCT column)—Counts the number of unique values in the column.

➤ SUM(column)—Totals the values in the column.

➤ MIN(column)—Returns the smallest value in the column.

➤ MAX(column)—Returns the largest value in the column.

➤ AVG(column)—Returns the average of all the values in the column.

For example:

```
SELECT COUNT(dept_id),SUM(salary), MIN(last_name),
  MAX(last_name), AVG(salary)
FROM employee
```

| -- | ------ | ----- | --------- | ----- |
| 6 | 375000 | Jones | Sanderson | 75000 |

It is illegal to mix aggregate functions with nonaggregate columns in the **SELECT** list. The aggregate wants to return one value, whereas the nonaggregate column wants to return multiple values. The **SELECT** statement can do only one or the other. The query below will return an error:

```
SELECT emp_id, AVG(salary)    /* generates an error */
FROM employee
```

NULL Values

It is possible for a field to have no value. When a value is unknown, it is said to be **NULL**. **NULL** is a keyword that can be assigned to a column. **NULL** is not the same as a zero-length string. A zero-length string *is* a value; **NULL** is not.

NULL fields are not included in the calculation of aggregate functions. Using the data from Table 7.2, the **COUNT(salary)** is 5. The **AVG(salary)** uses five rows in the divisor of the average, not six.

Grouping Results

It is common to examine an aggregate function by some grouping of data—for example, salary averages by department or employee count in each department. The syntax for grouping is shown below:

```
SELECT group_by_column_list, aggregate_function_list
FROM table
GROUP BY group_by_column_list
```

For example:

```
SELECT dept_id, COUNT(*), AVG(salary)
FROM employee
GROUP BY dept_id
```

```
DEPT_ID
-------        ---        -----
100             2                 60000
200             2                 65000
300             2                 95000
```

One row is displayed for each distinct value of the column(s) being grouped. The result of a **GROUP BY** is called an *aggregate result set*.

Creating A Summary Data Report With **COMPUTE [BY]**

COMPUTE [BY] is a SQL Server enhancement that allows the display of summary data to be intermingled with grand totals. **BY** is an optional keyword used for subgrouping. In essence, multiple result sets are being presented from one **SELECT** statement. **COMPUTE BY** is a little odd, so an **ORDER BY** clause is used to arrange the listing so the location of the **COMPUTE BY** makes sense. For example:

```
SELECT emp_id, dept_id, salary
FROM employee
ORDER BY dept_id
COMPUTE AVG(salary) BY dept_id
COMPUTE SUM(salary)
```

```
EMP_ID        DEPT_ID         SALARY
------        -------         -------
3456          100             65000
5678          100             55000
                              AVERAGE
                              -------
                              60000
EMP_ID        DEPT_ID         SALARY
------        -------         -------
1234          200             65000
6780          200             null
                              AVERAGE
                              -------
                              65000
EMP_ID        DEPT_ID         SALARY
------        -------         -------
2345          300             120000
4567          300             70000
                              AVERAGE
                              -------
                              95000
                              SUM
                              -------
                              375000
```

Restriction

So far, we have run queries that look at every row in a table. Restriction is a relational operation that allows us to select the specific rows in the table to be considered in the query. The syntax is:

```
SELECT [ DISTINCT ]
    { * | column [[AS] heading] [ , ...column_list ] }
FROM table
WHERE boolean_expr | boolean_expr conjunctive_optor boolean_expr
```

For example:

```
SELECT first_name, last_name, salary
FROM employee
WHERE last_name = 'Jones'
```

```
FIRST_NAME    LAST_NAME       SALARY
----------    ---------       ------
James         Jones           65000
Jessica       Jones           70000
```

Character strings are surrounded by single quotes and are case sensitive.

The **WHERE** clause is used to specify criteria that rows must meet to be returned. The keyword is followed by one or more expressions. Operators used in the expression include those listed in Table 7.3. The expression can be preceded with **NOT**, which negates the value of the expression.

Following is an example of a **WHERE** expression and its result set.

```
SELECT first_name, last_name, salary
FROM employee
WHERE NOT last_name = 'Jones'
```

FIRST_NAME	LAST_NAME	SALARY
Eric	Sanderson	120000
Rosa	Marinaro	65000
Christopher	Phillips	55000
Gail	LaVila	NULL

NULLs

A **NULL**—when compared in any manner to another **NULL**—is always false. The query below never returns any rows:

```
SELECT first_name, last_name, salary
FROM employee
WHERE salary = NULL   /* This is always false */
```

> *Note: This statement works correctly with SQL Server 7. However, with SQL Server 6.5, it returns the one row.*

Table 7.3 Operators used in WHERE expressions.	
Operator	**Meaning**
=	Equal to
>	Greater than
<	Less than
>=	Greater than or equal to
<=	Less than or equal to
<> or !=	Not equal to

Instead, we use the keyword **IS NULL** or **IS NOT NULL** to test for **NULL** values:

```
SELECT first_name, last_name, salary
FROM employee
WHERE salary IS NULL
```

LIKE

The **LIKE** operator is used for pattern matching in character strings. Table 7.4 shows the symbols used for pattern matching with the **LIKE** operator. Here is an example using **LIKE**:

```
SELECT first_name, last_name, salary
FROM employee
WHERE first_name LIKE '%a'
```

```
FIRST_NAME      LAST_NAME       SALARY
----------      ----------      ------
Rosa            Marinaro        65000
Jessica         Jones           70000
```

LIKE can be preceded with **NOT**.

 Beginning a **LIKE** pattern with a wildcard character—as in the example above—can slow down performance significantly. If there were millions of **first_name**s, it would take a long time to look at every single **first_name** value.

BETWEEN

The **WHERE** clause can combine many Boolean expressions using **AND** and **OR** operators (called *conjunctive* or *Boolean operators*). For example:

Table 7.4 Symbols used for pattern matching with LIKE.	
Symbol	**Description**
%	Any string of any number of characters
_ (underscore)	Any single character
[ ]	Any character matching the characters or range of characters in [ ]; for example, [L-Q]
^	Not what follows; for example, [^L-Q] means A through K and R through Z

```
SELECT first_name, last_name, salary
FROM employee
WHERE last_name = 'Jones' AND first_name = 'Jessica'
```

```
FIRST_NAME      LAST_NAME       SALARY
----------      ----------      ------
Jessica         Jones           70000
```

Note that without qualifying parentheses around expressions, all **AND**s are evaluated first, and then all **OR**s. Consider the query below:

```
SELECT first_name, last_name, salary
FROM employee
WHERE salary >= 60000 AND salary <= 70000
```

The **BETWEEN** clause can be used as shorthand for this type of range search:

```
SELECT first_name, last_name, salary
FROM employee
WHERE salary BETWEEN 60000 AND 70000
```

BETWEEN can be preceded by **NOT**.

IN

The **IN** clause is used to abbreviate a sequence of **OR** clauses. The query:

```
SELECT first_name, last_name, salary
FROM employee
WHERE dept_id = 100 OR dept_id = 200 OR dept_id = 300
```

is the same as:

```
SELECT first_name, last_name, salary
FROM employee
WHERE dept_id IN (100, 200, 300)
```

 If one of the values in the list is **NULL**, no rows will be returned for the **NULL**. This is because the expression is equivalent to **dept_id = NULL**, rather than **dept_id IS NULL**.

IN can be preceded with **NOT**.

If we say **dept_id NOT IN (100, 200, NULL)**, the query will never return any rows. The expression is equivalent to **dept_id <> 100 AND dept_id <> 200 AND dept_id <> NULL**. The last expression will always be false, so the whole thing will always be false, so no rows will ever be returned.

Restricting A **GROUP BY** With **HAVING**

Just as the **WHERE** clause restricts a result set, the **HAVING** clause restricts an aggregate result set from a **GROUP BY** clause. The **HAVING** clause selects which rows of an aggregate result set should be considered. Recall the query:

```
SELECT dept_id, COUNT(*), AVG(salary)
FROM employee
GROUP BY dept_id
```

```
DEPT_ID
-------     ---       -----
100          2        60000
200          2        65000
300          2        95000
```

If we want to see only aggregate rows whose average is less than $70,000, the query becomes:

```
SELECT dept_id, COUNT(*), AVG(salary)
FROM employee
GROUP BY dept_id
HAVING AVG(salary) < 70000
```

```
DEPT_ID
-------     ---       -----
100          2        60000
200          2        65000
```

Creating Sorted Reports With **ORDER BY**

You can sort a result set for display purposes by using **ORDER BY**. Any number of columns can be sorted in ascending order (the default) or descending order. Here is an example of sorting by descending order:

```
SELECT *
FROM employee
ORDER BY dept_id DESC , last_name
```

Putting It All Together

The major clauses of a **SELECT** statement must be in a specific order. Below is the syntax for what you've seen so far:

```
SELECT
FROM
WHERE
GROUP BY
HAVING
ORDER BY
COMPUTE BY
```

Using Joins To Retrieve Data

As in the **DEPARTMENT-EMPLOYEE** example, it"s often useful to examine parent-child relationships. Often, we'd like to ask questions about both entities together. For example:

➤ What is the name of the department that Jessica Jones works in?

➤ Who works in Finance?

➤ What is the average salary for the Finance people?

Each of these queries accesses nonkey attributes in both the **DEPARTMENT** and **EMPLOYEE** tables. The tables must be considered together in the same query. This type of query—one accessing two tables—is called a *relational join*. Examine Table 7.5. The questions just posed can be answered by following the **DEPARTMENT** table's primary key **DEPT_ID** to and from the associated foreign key in the **EMPLOYEE** table. Matching the primary and foreign keys between parent-child relationships is the essence of joining.

Referring to multiple tables in the **FROM** clause causes the DBMS (database management system) to internally execute what's called a *Cartesian product*. The DBMS internally takes every row from one table and merges it with every row from the other table(s). In particular, it internally creates a large row that contains all the columns of all the tables in the **FROM** clause. Joining a table containing M rows and X columns with a table containing N rows and Y columns results in an internal table having M*N rows with X+Y merged columns. Though this is logically what occurs, a DBMS will find shortcuts to ensure that join processing is efficient.

Each of the previous questions is coded later in this section as a join. Note that in each case, the parent's primary key is joined with the child's foreign key. Each join uses an equality (=) when comparing the keys; such joins are called *equi-joins*.

Table 7.5   DEPARTMENT and EMPLOYEE tables can be joined by their DEPT_IDs.

DEPARTMENT Table

DEPT_ID	DEPT_NAME	COST_CENTER
100	Finance	F3W
200	Marketing	H1Q
300	Sales	S8G
400	R&D	R4U

EMPLOYEE Table

EMP_ID	DEPT_ID	FIRST_NAME	LAST_NAME	PHONE	MANAGER_ID	SALARY
1234	200	James	Jones	617-555-1015	6789	$65,000
2345	300	Eric	Sanderson	617-555-1018	6789	$120,000
3456	100	Rosa	Marinaro	617-555-1011	NULL	$65,000
4567	300	Jessica	Jones	617-555-1014	6789	$70,000
5678	100	Christopher	Phillips	617-555-1017	3456	$55,000
6789	200	Gail	LaVila	617-555-1012	NULL	NULL

Often the join columns have the same name. Therefore, SQL needs to distinguish which table a column belongs to. The full syntax for a column is shown below (when **database_name** and **owner_name** are not specified, they are assumed to be the current database and user):

```
database_name.owner_name.table_name.column_name
```

What is the name of the department that Jessica Jones works in?

```
SELECT department.dept_name
FROM employee , department
WHERE employee.dept_id = department.dept_id AND
    employee.first_name = 'Jessica' AND
    employee.last_name = 'Jones'
```

Who works in Finance?

```
SELECT employee.first_name , employee.last_name
FROM department , employee
WHERE department.dept_id = employee.dept_id AND
    department.dept_name = 'Finance'
```

What is the average salary for the Finance people?

```
SELECT AVG(employee.salary)
FROM department , employee
WHERE department.dept_id = employee.dept_id AND
    department.dept_name = 'Finance'
```

Joins that don't use equality are called *theta joins*. Joins based on columns that are not primary or foreign keys are called *natural joins*. For example, finding employees working in the same state as a given customer would involve a natural join between the employee's and the customer's state columns.

SQL lets us abbreviate the table names using table *aliases*. When a column name appears in more than one table in the **FROM** clause, the column name must be preceded by either the table name or the table alias. For example:

Who works in Finance? (The department ID is also shown for the sake of example.)

```
SELECT e.first_name , e.last_name , d.dept_id
FROM department AS d , employee AS e
WHERE d.dept_id = e.dept_id
AND d.dept_name = 'Finance'
```

Aliases are assigned with the **AS** keyword. However, it doesn't make any difference whether you include the word **AS**—if omitted, it is implied.

Please note a few rules about joins:

➤ Tables can be in any order in the **FROM** clause.

➤ Any number of tables can be in the **FROM** clause.

➤ There's a practical limit to the number of tables. After six to eight tables, the DBMS query optimizer (which decides how best to access the tables) becomes ineffective.

➤ Boolean expressions can be in any order in the **WHERE** clause.

➤ Columns being joined do not need to have the same name.

➤ Only column names that are present in more than one table must be preceded by a table name or alias. In our example, only **dept_id** must be qualified by the table name or alias.

SQL Server provides an alternative syntax for joins, as shown here:

```
SELECT e.first_name , e.last_name , d.dept_id
FROM department d JOIN employee e
ON d.dept_id = e.dept_id
WHERE d.dept_name = 'Finance'
```

Self-Join Queries

Sometimes it is necessary for a table to be joined to itself. Consider the question:

Who manages Christopher Phillips? Observe the data from the **EMPLOYEE** table that appears in Table 7.6.

First, we must access Christopher Phillips's record. Chris's manager is employee #3456. Using this value, we go back into the **EMPLOYEE** table a second time and get employee #3456, who happens to be Rosa Marinaro. The code looks like this:

```
SELECT mgr.first_name , mgr.last_name
FROM employee chris , employee mgr
WHERE chris.first_name = 'Christopher'
AND chris.last_name = 'Phillips'
AND chris.manager_id = mgr.emp_id
```

The "chris" alias refers to Christopher's record, where chris's **manager_id** = 3456. In the expression, **mgr** re-accesses the **EMPLOYEE** table to retrieve Chris's manager, where **mgr.emp_id** will be the same as chris's **manager_id**.

Table 7.6   Who manages Christopher Phillips?

EMP_ ID	DEPT_ ID	FIRST_ NAME	LAST_ NAME	PHONE	MANAGER_ ID	SALARY
3456	100	Rosa	Marinaro	617-555-1011	**NULL**	$65,000
5678	100	Christopher	Phillips	617-555-1017	3456	$55,000

Who does Gail LaVila manage? Observe the **EMPLOYEE** data found in Table 7.7.

Now we're going the other way in the self-relationship. Gail is **emp_id** 6789. Let's see whom she manages:

```
SELECT emps.first_name , emps.last_name
FROM employee gail , employee emps
WHERE gail.first_name = 'Gail' AND gail.last_name = 'LaVila'
AND gail.emp_id = emps.manager_id
```

```
FIRST_NAME     LAST_NAME
----------     ----------
James          Jones
Eric           Sanderson
Jessica        Jones
```

Outer Joins

All the joins discussed so far are called *inner joins*. Inner joins have the disadvantage of displaying only parents that have a child, and vice versa. If a parent does not have a child, the parent will not be considered by the query.

In the **FROM** clause, assume that the parent table is on the left, and the child table is on the right. A **LEFT OUTER JOIN** chooses parents that have no child. A **RIGHT OUTER JOIN** chooses children that have no parent. A **FULL OUTER JOIN** does both.

Consider **DEPARTMENT** and **EMPLOYEE** (in that order). In the case of a **LEFT OUTER JOIN**, every row of **DEPARTMENT** will be considered, whether or not it has an **EMPLOYEE** row. Recall that a join operation merges all columns from one table with all columns from the other table. In this case,

Table 7.7 Who does Gail LaVila manage?						
EMP_ ID	DEPT_ ID	FIRST_ NAME	LAST_ NAME	PHONE	MANAGER_ ID	SALARY
1234	200	James	Jones	617-555-1015	6789	$65,000
2345	300	Eric	Sanderson	617-555-1018	6789	$120,000
4567	300	Jessica	Jones	617-555-1014	6789	$70,000
6789	200	Gail	LaVila	617-555-1012	NULL	NULL

any department that does not have an employee will assign the associated empty **EMPLOYEE** columns a **NULL** value. This query performs a **LEFT OUTER JOIN** between **DEPARTMENT** and **EMPLOYEE**:

Which departments have no employees?

```
SELECT d.dept_id, dept_name, cost_center
FROM department d   LEFT OUTER JOIN  employee e
ON d.dept_id = e.dept_id
WHERE e.last_name  IS NULL
```

DEPT_ID	DEPT_NAME	COST_CENTER
400	R&D	R4U

Set Operations

The behavior of relational databases is based on a mathematical set theory. A *set operation* manipulates two sets in some manner that results in a new, third set. Relational databases support several set operations—namely, Union, Intersection, and Difference:

➤ *Union*—Adds all the elements of the second set to the first set.

➤ *Intersection*—Presents the elements that are common to the two sets.

➤ *Difference*—Removes the common elements of the two sets from the first set.

Union

Union combines lists of values. Suppose we also have a **CUSTOMER** table with **CUST_LNAME** and **CUST_FNAME** columns. We can get a list of all employees *and* customers with the query:

```
SELECT last_name, first_name
FROM employee
UNION
SELECT cust_lname, cust_fname
FROM customer
```

The **UNION** statement removes duplicate values that are present in each result set and displays the value only once.

Now that we've seen an example of a set operation, there are some rules to follow:

➤ Any number of columns can be selected.

➤ Each **SELECT** statement can be as complicated as necessary.

➤ The **SELECT** statements must have the same number of columns.

➤ The column lists are matched up one to one. The first column of the first **SELECT** is matched with the first column from the second **SELECT**, etc. Therefore, their data types must match.

➤ The column names do not need to be the same in the two different **SELECT** statements.

Intersect

Intersect shows what two sets have in common. Each value is displayed only once. In SQL Server, intersection is written as a join. Some texts may suggest writing intersection using **EXISTS** syntax, but this is not recommended due to its poor performance characteristics. To exemplify intersection, we'll show the department IDs that employees have in common with the departments:

```
SELECT DISTINCT d.dept_id
FROM department d , employee e
WHERE d.dept_id = e.dept_id
```

Difference

Difference has some very interesting practical applications. Difference can identify what's in one set that's not in the other set. Recall the question, "What departments have no employees?" We know (1) all the departments, and (2) the departments that employees are in. When we subtract (2) from (1), we are left with the departments with no employees. SQL Server uses an outer join to implement a difference. Some texts may suggest writing difference using **EXISTS** syntax, but this is not recommended due to its poor performance characteristics. To find the departments that have no employees:

```
SELECT dept_id
FROM department d  LEFT OUTER JOIN  employee e
ON d.dept_id = e.dept_id
WHERE e.last_name  IS NULL
```

A second technique used to find a difference involves a construct called a subquery.

Subqueries

Recall that the result of every query can be regarded as a table. It is possible to pass the results (output table) of one query into another query (input table).

Consider the question, "Who has the largest salary?" We'd like to write the query like this:

```
SELECT last_name, first_name
FROM employee
WHERE salary = MAX(salary)
```

However, the **WHERE** clause does not allow aggregates. Instead, find the maximum salary in one query and pass that result as an input into a second query with the following code:

```
SELECT last_name, first_name
FROM employee
WHERE salary = ( SELECT MAX(salary) FROM employee )
```

This is the only way to write this example. The query in parentheses is the *subquery*, and the first **SELECT** is the *outer query*.

As this example demonstrates, not all subqueries can be written as joins. However, every join can be written using subqueries. It's really a matter of personal preference. The following code presents the original join followed by a example using a subquery that returns the same result set:

Who works in Finance?

```
SELECT e.first_name , e.last_name   /* Original Join */
FROM department d, employee e
WHERE d.dept_id = e.dept_id
AND d.dept_name = 'Finance'

SELECT first_name , last_name    /* As a subquery */
FROM employee
WHERE dept_id IN
    ( SELECT dept_id
      FROM department
      WHERE dept_name = 'Finance' )
```

Recall that the **IN** keyword in a **WHERE** clause allows us to ask if a column is equal to a list of possible values. For example:

```
WHERE dept_id IN (100, 200, 300)
```

For subqueries, **IN** is used to indicate that the subquery may return one *or more* rows. Alternatively, an equal sign indicates that only one row is allowed to be returned; a runtime error will occur if more than one row is returned.

The **IN** clause can be preceded by a **NOT** operator. If we say **dept_id NOT IN (SELECT...)** and the subquery returns a **NULL** in its list, the query will never return any rows. The expression evaluates to **dept_id <> 100 AND dept_id <> 200... AND dept_id <> NULL**. The last expression will always be false, so the whole thing will always be false, so no rows will ever be returned.

As mentioned in earlier in this chapter, subqueries provide another way of coding a difference where one set is subtracted from another set. The previous difference example—"What departments have no employees?"—can be written as:

```
SELECT dept_name
FROM department
WHERE dept_id NOT IN
    ( SELECT dept_id
      FROM employee )
```

Modifying Data

Three DML commands modify data: **INSERT, UPDATE,** and **DELETE.** Each command can affect only one table at a time.

INSERT

There are two forms of the **INSERT** statement: single row and multirow. Single-row **INSERT** takes the form:

```
INSERT INTO department (dept_id, dept_name, cost_center)
VALUES (500, 'Customer Service', 'C6S')
```

The **VALUES** list contains constants or expressions. Columns cannot be referred to. The values in the list are placed into the columns in the optional column list. A column for which no value is provided must allow a **NULL** value or have a default value specified.

 Although the column list is optional, including it is a good habit to get into. Listing the columns increases the probability that your **INSERT** will continue to operate correctly in the event that table changes occur.

A multirow **INSERT** uses a **SELECT** subquery to define the values list. Suppose we have a **TERMINATED_EMPLOYEE** table. To copy all sales employees into the **TERMINATED_EMPLOYEE** table:

```
INSERT INTO terminated_employee
   (emp_id, dept_id, first_name, last_name,
    phone, manager_id, salary)
SELECT emp_id, e.dept_id, first_name, last_name,
   phone, manager_id, salary
FROM employee e , department d
WHERE e.dept_id = d.dept_id
AND dept_name = 'Sales'
```

DELETE

DELETE removes existing rows from a table. To remove all rows from the **EMPLOYEE** table:

```
DELETE FROM employee
```

To remove only employees in department 300:

```
DELETE FROM employee
WHERE dept_id = 300
```

To remove employees from the sales department, you need to use a subquery:

```
DELETE FROM employee
WHERE dept_id IN
   ( SELECT dept_id
     FROM department
     WHERE dept_name = 'Sales' )
```

UPDATE

UPDATE changes column values in existing rows. To increase the salary of all employees by 5 percent:

```
UPDATE employee
SET salary = salary * 1.05
```

To increase the salary of all employees in department 300:

```
UPDATE employee
SET salary = salary * 1.05
WHERE dept_id = 300
```

To increase the salary of all employees in department 300 and have them report to employee 9000:

```
UPDATE employee
SET salary = salary * 1.05 ,
    manager_id = 9000
WHERE dept_id = 300
```

To increase the salary of all employees in department 300 and have them report to Gail LaVila, you use a subquery in the **SET** clause:

```
UPDATE employee
SET salary = salary * 1.05 ,
    manager_id = ( SELECT emp_id
                   FROM employee
                   WHERE first_name = 'Gail' AND
                         last_name = 'LaVila' )
WHERE dept_id = 300
```

And, last, to increase the salary of all sales employees and have them report to Gail LaVila, use a subquery in the **WHERE** clause:

```
UPDATE employee
SET salary = salary * 1.05,
    manager_id = ( SELECT emp_id
                   FROM employee
                   WHERE first_name = 'Gail' AND
                         last_name = 'LaVila')
WHERE dept_id IN
   ( SELECT dept_id
     FROM department
     WHERE dept_name = 'Sales' )
```

Creating Views

Thus far, this chapter has examined many of the techniques that SQL provides to access data directly in actual database tables. *Views* let you present alternative logical representations of data. For example, to create a view to see only salespeople, use the following code:

```
CREATE VIEW sales_people
AS
SELECT d.dept_id, dept_name, emp_id, last_name, phone, salary
FROM employee e, department d
WHERE e.dept_id = d.dept_id
AND dept_name = 'Sales'
```

To find the employees who are not salespeople, we can use the view:

```
SELECT * FROM employee
WHERE emp_id NOT IN
        ( SELECT emp_id FROM sales_people )
```

The view is merely a **SELECT** statement that presents data in a different manner—the data in the base tables is not being copied into new tables. Views can be referred to—just like any other table—within **SELECT, INSERT, UPDATE,** and **DELETE** commands. Views have several uses:

➤ *Manifesting subtypes or supertypes*—During database design, you could subdivide the **EMPLOYEE** entity into "subtypes" called **SALES_PEOPLE** and **NON_SALES_PEOPLE.** Because these subtype entities are described similarly and behave similarly, you can combine them into an **EMPLOYEE** supertype. Views can be defined to allow us to see the two subtypes lost during database design.

➤ *Security*—In the previous example, the sales manager can be granted all access privileges to the **SALES_PEOPLE** view, whereas all other users are granted only **SELECT** access.

➤ *Client/server mappings*—One view can be defined for each screen interface that maps screen entry fields to database columns. This hides the complexity of the data mapping from the client developer.

There are severe restrictions on inserting, updating, and deleting rows in views that are defined for more than one table. Generally, most development organizations will grant **SELECT** access to such views and will revoke **INSERT/ UPDATE/DELETE.**

 INSERT, **UPDATE**, and **DELETE** operations can only be permitted if the changes that must be made to the underlying table (note singular) are unambiguous. Columns not exposed in the view must be nullable or have default values.

The Importance Of Indexes

If you don't give the RDBMS specific instructions, it examines all the rows in a table to answer a query. This is inefficient and can severely impact performance. RDBMSs provide a fast access mechanism called an *index*. An index works much like looking up a word in a dictionary. You begin by opening the book to the vicinity of the word in question and then narrow your search many pages at a time. The DBMS performs all the search logic for you.

Indexes are placed on a column or combination of columns in one table. The index sorts (in ascending or descending order) the values found in each row for the column(s) and places them into a special disk-based structure. So, although there is a disk space overhead with an index, access time is often instantaneous. It makes sense to place indexes on columns that are frequently present in **WHERE, GROUP BY,** and **HAVING** clauses, as well as on primary and foreign keys.

A table can have many indexes defined. Each time a row is inserted or deleted, each index in the table must be modified. There is a notable overhead associated with modifying each index. On-Line Transaction Processing (OLTP) applications that are characterized by modification-intensive operations should carefully define indexes. Decision Support Systems—such as data warehouses that are predominantly read-only applications—can define indexes more liberally.

Practice Questions

All of the practice questions are based on the following scenario:

An order contains a customer ID, order date, and order total. (Order total would not normally be stored in a table—it's here strictly for the questions.) A product contains a name, quantity on hand (in stock), description, and price. A line item is for a given order and a given product. The line item contains the number of items ordered for the product on that order, and the date the item shipped. Line items implement a many-to-many relationship between orders and products. One order can have any number of line items. One product may be on any number of order line items. Each line item must be associated with one order and with one product. The table definitions are as follows:

```
CREATE TABLE orders
( order_id INTEGER NOT NULL ,
  customer_id INTEGER NOT NULL ,
  order_date DATETIME NOT NULL ,
  order_total MONEY NULL )

CREATE TABLE products
( product_id INTEGER NOT NULL ,
  prod_name VARCHAR(20) NOT NULL ,
  qty_on_hand INTEGER NOT NULL ,
  description VARCHAR(100) NULL ,
  price MONEY NOT NULL )

CREATE TABLE line_items
( order_id INTEGER NOT NULL ,
  product_id INTEGER NOT NULL ,
  line_num INTEGER NOT NULL ,
  quantity INTEGER NOT NULL ,
  ship_date DATETIME NOT NULL )
```

Question 1

Which query implements the following business request?

"What product names have been ordered by customer 1234?"

a. ```
SELECT prod_name
    FROM orders o , line_items li , products p
    AND   o.customer_id = 1234
```

b. ```
SELECT prod_name
    FROM orders o , line_items li , products p
    WHERE o.order_id = p.product_id
    AND   o.customer_id = 1234
```

c. ```
SELECT prod_name
    FROM orders o , line_items li , products p
    WHERE o.order_id = li.order_id
    AND   li.product_id = p.product_id
    AND   o.customer_id = 1234
```

Answer c is correct. One order has many line items, and one line item has one product. It is necessary to join the tables through their respective primary and foreign keys.
```

Question 2

> Which query implements the following business request? [Check all correct answers]
>
> "How many different products has customer 1234 ordered?"
>
> ❑ a. `SELECT COUNT(*)`
> `FROM orders o , line_items li`
> `WHERE o.order_id = li.order_id`
> `AND   o.customer_id = 1234`
>
> ❑ b. `SELECT COUNT(DISTINCT prod_name)`
> `FROM orders o , line_items li, products p`
> `WHERE o.order_id = li.order_id`
> `AND    li.product_id = p.product_id`
> `AND    o.customer_id = 1234`
>
> ❑ c. `SELECT COUNT(*)`
> `FROM orders o , line_items li, products p`
> `WHERE o.order_id = li.order_id`
> `AND    li.product_id = p.product_id`
> `AND    o.customer_id = 1234`
>
> ❑ d. `SELECT COUNT(DISTINCT product_id)`
> `FROM orders o , line_items li`
> `WHERE o.order_id = li.order_id`
> `AND    o.customer_id = 1234`

Answers b and d are correct. A customer may have placed many orders, where each order may have several line items, each with a respective product. So a given product will appear more than once across many orders for a given customer. It is necessary to count each product only once. The **COUNT DISTINCT** clause counts the number of different values in the given column. Counting the distinct **prod_id**s or the distinct **prod_name**s provides the desired answer. Answers a and c are incorrect because they count the number of line items for customer 1234, but do not distinguish them from one another.

Question 3

Which query implements the following business request?

"How many line items are on each order for customer 1234?"

○ a.
```
SELECT COUNT(DISTINCT line_num)
    FROM orders o , line_items li
    WHERE o.order_id = li.order_id
    AND   o.customer_id = 1234
```

○ b.
```
SELECT o.order_id, COUNT(*)
    FROM orders o , line_items li
    WHERE o.order_id = li.order_id
    AND   o.customer_id = 1234
    GROUP BY o.order_id
```

○ c.
```
SELECT line_num, COUNT(*)
    FROM orders o , line_items li
    WHERE o.order_id = li.order_id
    AND   o.customer_id = 1234
    GROUP BY line_num
```

Answer b is correct. The key here is the phrase "on each order." We want one row displayed for each **order_id**, so we use **GROUP BY order_id**. The first query displays the number of different **line_num** values there are, and the last query displays the number of orders for each **line_num**.

Question 4

Which query implements the following business request?

"How many units of each product name has customer 1234 ordered?"

a.
```
SELECT p.prod_name, SUM(quantity)
FROM orders o , line_items li , products p
WHERE o.order_id = li.order_id
AND    li.product_id = p.product_id
AND    o.customer_id = 1234
GROUP BY prod_name
```

b.
```
SELECT p.prod_name, COUNT(quantity)
FROM orders o , line_items li , products p
WHERE o.order_id = li.order_id
AND    li.product_id = p.product_id
AND    o.customer_id = 1234
GROUP BY prod_name
```

c.
```
SELECT p.prod_name, COUNT(*)
FROM orders o , line_items li , products p
WHERE o.order_id = li.order_id
AND    li.product_id = p.product_id
AND    o.customer_id = 1234
GROUP BY prod_name
```

Answer a is correct. The number of units ordered for a given product on a given order is the quantity column in **line_items**. Answer b is incorrect because it counts the number of times a product was ordered (if the quantity has a value in it, count it—add one to a counter). Answer c is incorrect because it counts the number of rows, whether the columns contain values or **NULL**s.

Question 5

Which query implements the following business request?

"We think the **order_total** column in orders has invalid values in it. Without using the **order_total** column, display the order number and order value of all orders, by customer 1234, worth more than $500."

○ a. SELECT o.order_id, quantity*price
     FROM orders o , line_items li , products p
     WHERE o.order_id = li.order_id
     AND   li.product_id = p.product_id
     AND   o.customer_id = 1234
     AND   quantity*price > 500

○ b. SELECT o.order_id, SUM(quantity*price)
     FROM orders o , line_items li , products p
     WHERE o.order_id = li.order_id
     AND   li.product_id = p.product_id
     AND   o.customer_id = 1234
     AND   SUM(quantity*price) > 500
     GROUP BY o.order_id

○ c. SELECT o.order_id, SUM(quantity*price)
     FROM orders o , line_items li , products p
     WHERE o.order_id = li.order_id
     AND   li.product_id = p.product_id
     AND   o.customer_id = 1234
     GROUP BY o.order_id
     HAVING SUM(quantity*price) > 500

Answer c is correct. You need to understand how an order total is calculated. For each line item for the order, the line item's value is calculated as **quantity*price**, and then all the values are added up for all the line items for each order. Note the last part of that sentence—"for each order." So we must do a **GROUP BY order_id**. We want only order values greater than $500. We're not allowed to put aggregates in a **WHERE** clause, so answer b is incorrect. Aggregate result sets are restricted to using a **HAVING** clause, so answer c is correct.

Question 6

Which query implements the following business request?

"Which product names have not been ordered?"

○ a. `SELECT prod_name`
       `FROM products p , line_items li`
       `WHERE p.product_id <> li.product_id`

○ b. `SELECT prod_name`
       `FROM products`
       `WHERE product_id IN`
           `( SELECT product_id`
             `FROM line_items )`

○ c. `SELECT prod_name`
       `FROM products p LEFT OUTER JOIN line_items li`
       `ON p.product_id = li.product_id`
       `WHERE li.order_id IS NULL`

Answer c is correct. This is a difference query. The database tells us what products are ordered and what all the products are, but not what's *not* ordered. Difference can be implemented two ways: one with a **NOT IN** subquery construct (answer b uses **IN**), and the other with a **LEFT OUTER JOIN** where the rows with **NULL** children are selected.

Question 7

Which query implements the following business request?

"Which order numbers have an order total larger than the average order total?"

- a.
```
SELECT order_id
FROM orders
WHERE order_total >
    ( SELECT AVG(order_total)
      FROM orders )
```

- b.
```
SELECT o2.order_id
FROM orders o1 , orders o2
WHERE o1.order_total = o2.order_total
AND    o1.order_id <> o2.order_id
AND    o1.order_total > AVG(order_total)
```

- c.
```
SELECT order_id
FROM orders
GROUP BY order_id
HAVING order_total > AVG(order_total)
```

Answer a is correct. This question requires a subquery construct. Answer a's query is like a self-join query in that orders are being compared to other orders, and the subquery allows us to do the comparison. Answer b is incorrect because the **AVG()** function is in the **WHERE** clause. Answer c's **HAVING** clause would fail because the first **order_total** is not being aggregated in the **GROUP BY** clause.

Question 8

Which query implements the following business request?

"Increase the price of popular products that are on 1,000 or more orders by 25 percent."

○ a.
```
INSERT INTO products (product_id, prod_name,
                            description, price)
    WHERE price = price * 1.25
    AND product_id IN
        ( SELECT product_id
          FROM line_items li
          GROUP BY product_id
          HAVING COUNT(*) >= 1000 )
```

○ b.
```
UPDATE products
    SET price = price * 1.25
    WHERE product_id IN
        ( SELECT product_id
          FROM line_items li
          GROUP BY product_id
          HAVING COUNT(*) >= 1000 )
```

○ c.
```
UPDATE products
    WHERE price = price * 1.25
    AND product_id IN
        ( SELECT product_id
          FROM line_items li
          GROUP BY product_id
          HAVING COUNT(*) >= 1000 )
```

Answer b is correct. The subquery correctly gathers the products on 1,000 or more orders, and for those **product_id**s, the price is increased. Answer a is very syntactically incorrect for an **INSERT**. Answer c needs some kind of **SET** clause.

Question 9

Which query implements the following business request?

"Remove products that are on no orders."

○ a. ```
DELETE FROM products
    WHERE product_id IN
        (SELECT product_id
            FROM products p LEFT OUTER JOIN
                line_items li
            ON p.product_id = li.product_id
            GROUP BY li.product_id
            HAVING COUNT(line_num) = 0)
```

○ b. ```
DELETE FROM products
    WHERE product_id IN
        ( SELECT product_id
            FROM products p LEFT OUTER JOIN
                line_items li
            ON p.product_id = li.product_id
            WHERE line_num IS NOT NULL )
```

○ c. ```
DELETE FROM products
    WHERE product_id IN
        (SELECT product_id
            FROM line_items
            WHERE product_id NOT IN
                (SELECT product_id
                    FROM products))
```

Answer a is correct. This is a tricky question because the correct answer is unlike any of the code presented in the text. The products being removed are those that result from a difference query of all products less the products that are on an order. In the outer join, recall that child columns might be null. A column with a null value will not be counted. So counting a product with a null **line_num** child will yield a count of zero. The subquery returns the products that have zero orders. Answer b is incorrect because the **WHERE** clause should check for **IS NULL line_nums**. Answer c is incorrect because the two subqueries are reversed; the innermost subquery should select from **line_items**. This would then be subtracted from the outer subquery, which should select from products.
```

Question 10

> What business request does the SQL query implement?
>
> ```
> SELECT DISTINCT order_date
> FROM products p , line_items li , orders o
> WHERE p.product_id = li.product_id
> AND    li.order_id = o.order_id
> AND    o.order_date = li.ship_date
> AND    prod_name = 'Widget'
> ```
>
> ○ a. On what dates have Widgets been shipped?
>
> ○ b. On what dates have Widgets been ordered?
>
> ○ c. On what dates have Widgets been shipped on the same day they
>   were ordered?
>
> ○ d. What are the unique dates Widgets were ordered and shipped?

Answer c is correct. The first join clause is examining **order_dates** that are the same as **ship_dates**. The **SELECT** line is displaying **order_dates** and making sure the values don't repeat in the listing; it may be possible for more than one order to have the same order date.

Question 11

What business request does the following SQL query implement?

```
SELECT customer_id, SUM(quantity)
FROM products p , line_items li , orders o
WHERE p.product_id = li.product_id
AND    li.order_id = o.order_id
AND    prod_name = 'Widget'
GROUP BY customer_id
```

○ a. How many orders have there been for Widgets for each customer?

○ b. How many Widgets have been ordered by each customer?

○ c. How many different customers have ordered Widgets?

○ d. For each customer order, show the number of Widgets that were
ordered.

Answer b is correct. The **GROUP BY** will display one row for each customer
ID. The join clauses gather all Widget orders, and the **GROUP BY** therefore
considers all Widget orders for each customer. The **SELECT** line then displays the customer ID as well as the number of Widgets they ordered across all
orders.

Question 12

What business request does the following SQL query implement?

```
SELECT DISTINCT p.product_id, prod_name
FROM products p LEFT OUTER JOIN line_items li
ON p.product_id = li.product_id
WHERE quantity IS NULL
```

○ a. Show the products that have orders with no line items.

○ b. Show the products that have line items with no orders.

○ c. Show the products that have orders with zero quantity line items.

○ d. Show the products that are not on an order.

Answer d is correct. To answer this question, you must know that, when a parent has no children, the outer join will place nulls into the child of the childless parent as a placeholder. In this case, for products that have no line items, if the product is not on a line item, then it can't be on an order either.

Question 13

What business request does the following SQL query implement?

```
SELECT DISTINCT p1.product_id , p1.price
FROM   orders o , line_items li , products p1
WHERE o.order_id = li.order_id
AND    li.product_id = p1.product_id
AND    customer_id = 1234
AND    p1.price = ( SELECT MAX(price)
FROM products p2 )
```

○ a. Which products were on the order with the largest order value for customer 1234?

○ b. What was the largest price of any product customer 1234 has every purchased?

○ c. Which highest-priced products has customer 1234 purchased?

○ d. Which products have the same price as the most expensive product customer 1234 purchased?

Answer c is correct. All the orders for customer 1234 are found. Separately, the highest price of any product (not just 1234's) is found. This price is compared to the products customer 1234 has purchased, and any price matches are considered. All the products customer 1234 has purchased having the same price as the most expensive product are displayed.

Question 14

What business request does the following SQL query implement?

```
SELECT order_id , product_id
FROM   line_items li
WHERE order_id = 9876
AND quantity >
   ( SELECT qty_on_hand
     FROM products p
     WHERE p.product_id = li.product_id )
```

○ a. Which products on order 9876 don't have enough in stock?

○ b. Which products on order 9876 have enough in stock?

○ c. Display the order and products only if all the products on the order have enough in stock.

○ d. Display the order and products only if none of the products on the order have enough in stock.

Answer a is correct. This is a tricky question because the text didn't specifically review this kind of query, but you should be able to put the pieces together. This is called a correlated subquery. For each **product_id** in the outer query, the **product_id** is passed to the inner query, which is then executed. So the query is asking, "For each product quantity ordered on order 9876, is this quantity more than the product's quantity on hand?" If so, there's not enough in stock. Note that correlated subqueries are very slow performers.

Need To Know More?

 Forta, Ben. *SAMS Teach Yourself SQL in 10 Minutes*. SAMS Publishing, Indianapolis, IN, 1999. ISBN: 0-672-31664-1. This book is easy to read and provides the right level of detail for an application developer.

 McEwan, Bennett William, and David Solomon. *Transact–SQL in 21 Days*. SAMS Publishing, Indianapolis, IN 1997. ISBN: 0-672-31045-7. A good introduction at the right level of detail.

 Taylor, Allen G. *SQL For Dummies*. IDG Books Worldwide, Foster City, CA, 1998. ISBN: 0-7645-0415-0. A good introduction with a very good treatment of joins.

 www.microsoft.com/backoffice/sql lets you download Microsoft SQL Server 7 evaluation software and peruse SQL Server books online.

Advanced Data Manipulation

Terms you'll need to understand:

✓ Trigger

✓ Stored procedure

✓ Cursor

✓ Pessimistic locking

✓ Optimistic locking

Techniques you'll need to master:

✓ Controlling locking strategies

✓ Writing SQL programs

✓ Implementing business rules

✓ Using system stored procedures

You can create two kinds of database-resident SQL-based program objects: business rules, which are automatically enforced through *triggers*; and business transactions, which are maintained in *stored procedures*. This chapter covers these programmable, executable SQL objects. After triggers and stored procedures is the section on cursors. Cursors allow an application to browse through the data rows in a result set one row at a time. The last section ("Locking Strategies") looks at the way in which a database management system (DBMS) ensures data integrity while users are simultaneously accessing the same relational data tables.

Triggers

Triggers are an integral part of the DBMS. They are used to enforce application-independent business rules. Examples of business rules are:

➤ Report any cash transaction over $10,000.

➤ Reorder parts that drop below an inventory threshold.

➤ Don't allow a product to be ordered more than once on a given order.

➤ Modify the account balance when a transaction is processed for the account.

Each of these rules must be enforced no matter which application causes the data to change.

A trigger is an event-driven SQL program. When data changes, the trigger fires. Triggers are attached to a specific table for a specific operation: insert, update, or delete.

Creating Triggers

Let's look at two common examples of triggers that enforce parent-child referential integrity between two tables. Referential integrity guarantees that every child record will have a parent—e.g., every employee must be associated with an existing department. In this example, you can get "orphans" in two ways: by deleting a department that has employees, or by inserting an employee who works in a nonexistent department. You'll continue using the **EMPLOYEE** table defined in the previous chapter. The **DEPARTMENT** table will also be used, but it will include an additional column. The **DEPARTMENT** table's columns are: **DEPT_ID, DEPT_NAME, COST_CENTER,** and **DEPT_HEAD_ID.** The first trigger will delete employee records when the employee's department is deleted:

```
CREATE TRIGGER del_depts
ON department
FOR DELETE
AS
BEGIN
DELETE FROM employee
WHERE dept_id IN
    ( SELECT dept_id
      FROM deleted )
END
```

This trigger fires whenever a department record is deleted. When a **DELETE** trigger fires, a temporary table called **DELETED** is automatically created, containing the row(s) being deleted. The row(s) in this table can be joined with any table in the database, including the table on which the trigger is defined. In this case, you remove any employee record that has the deleted department's **dept_id**.

The next trigger prevents an employee record from being inserted if the employee's department does not exist:

```
CREATE TRIGGER ins_emp
ON employee
FOR INSERT
AS
BEGIN
IF NOT EXISTS
   ( SELECT *
     FROM department d , inserted new_emp
     WHERE d.dept_id = new_emp.dept_id )
   BEGIN
     RAISERROR('Department is not valid for this employee', 16, 1)
     ROLLBACK
   END
END
```

When an **INSERT** trigger fires, a temporary table called **INSERTED** is automatically created, containing the row(s) being inserted. This trigger checks for the existence of a department that has the **dept_id** of the new employee record being inserted. If the department does not exist, then an error is flagged (at SQL Server priority 16, state 1), and the transaction is rolled back (undone).

Triggers are also used to enforce application-independent business rules. For example, the following trigger would be used to enforce a business rule dictating that department heads must work in the same department they head:

```
CREATE TRIGGER valid_head_dept
ON department
FOR INSERT, UPDATE
AS
DECLARE @emp_dept_id INTEGER
BEGIN

/*  Get this dept_head's dept_id from EMPLOYEE */
SELECT @emp_dept_id = e.dept_id
FROM employee e , inserted new_head
WHERE e.emp_id = new_head.dept_head_id

IF @emp_dept_id IS NULL
   BEGIN
      RAISERROR('This department head does not exist', 16, 1)
      ROLLBACK
   END

/*  Does the employee.dept_id match the
    inserted.department.dept_id?  */
IF NOT EXISTS
   ( SELECT *
     FROM inserted
     WHERE dept_id = @emp_dept_id )
   BEGIN
     RAISERROR
       ('The dept head does not work in the right department',
        16, 1)
       ROLLBACK
   END
END
```

This trigger is for both the **INSERT** and **UPDATE** commands. **UPDATE** triggers provide both **INSERTED** and **DELETED** virtual tables, so you have access to both the before and after versions of the records being changed. This trigger also declares a local variable. Local variables are always preceded by an at sign (@) to distinguish them from table columns.

Triggers can implicitly invoke other triggers, and triggers can be recursive.

Within triggers, SQL Server extends **UPDATE** and **DELETE** syntax to allow the **INSERTED** and **DELETED** virtual tables to be accessed within a **FROM** clause. Observe the **UPDATE/FROM** statement below, which is executed within an **UPDATE** trigger on the **DEPARTMENT** table. When the department head changes, the trigger assigns everyone's manager in that department to be the new department head. **UPDATE** triggers can be used to create both the **INSERTED** and **DELETED** virtual tables:

```
CREATE TRIGGER sample
ON department
FOR UPDATE
AS
BEGIN
    IF ( SELECT i.dept_head_id FROM inserted i) <>
       ( SELECT d.dept_head_id FROM deleted d)
       UPDATE employee
       SET manager_id = i.dept_head_id
          FROM inserted i
       WHERE employee.dept_id = i.dept_id
END
```

Flow Control

Transact-SQL provides several flow-control statements. One of the more common is **IF-ELSE**. The syntax for an **IF** statement is:

```
IF  conditional_expression
   < statement >
ELSE
   < statement >
```

In Transact-SQL, as in C and C++, the truth portion of the **IF** statement is not followed by a **THEN** statement.

Conditional expressions cannot refer to table columns directly. However, the conditional expressions can contain **SELECT** subqueries. To test the **dept_id** just inserted in an insert-department trigger, you would have the following **IF** statement:

```
IF (SELECT dept_id FROM inserted) = 200 . . .
```

The **EXISTS** function returns True or False, based on whether a subquery returns any rows. As with other conditional logic, **NOT** can precede **EXISTS**.

A < **statement** > can be any number of statements surrounded with the keywords **BEGIN...END**.

```
BEGIN
   <statements>
END
```

The keywords **BEGIN...END** are optional if there is only one statement in the statement block.

A looping construct is available in this form:

```
WHILE conditional_expression
BEGIN
    <statements>
END
```

FOR iterative loops are not supported in Transact-SQL.

Stored Procedures

Where a trigger is event-driven, stored procedures are explicitly called from a client program, from another procedure, or from a trigger. Procedures are used to implement application-dependent transactions or algorithms. A procedure can return as many result sets, of any size, as needed.

When should application logic be implemented in a client program versus a database stored procedure? Two factors should be considered:

➤ *Performance*—Each SQL call from a client must be passed across the network, and the results must then be returned across the network. For complex transactions with multiple operations, the back-and-forth networking can add up to a sizable overhead. Migrating the transaction logic into a single server-based stored procedure will reduce network overhead to a minimum.

➤ *Portability*—Triggers and stored procedures do not follow an SQL standard, so vendor implementations have very little in common. For the highest degree of portability, do not use stored procedures or triggers at all.

Stored procedures may call other procedures, which may invoke triggers, which may call procedures, which may invoke triggers that invoke triggers, which may...well, you get the idea.

Creating Stored Procedures

Stored procedures may call other procedures residing in other SQL Servers. This technique is called a *remote procedure call (RPC)*. RPCs are often involved in the implementation of complicated, multisite, distributed transaction logic or data-replication scenarios. Although it's obviously a powerful feature, distributed processing is difficult to debug from a single seat, so caution should be exercised.

Consider this next stored procedure, which returns all the employees who work in a specific department. This procedure receives the department name, returning the employees as well as a count of the employees:

```
CREATE PROCEDURE get_emps
(@in_dept_name VARCHAR(20) , @out_num_emps INTEGER = 0 OUTPUT)
AS
DECLARE @my_num_emps INTEGER
BEGIN
   IF @in_dept_name IS NULL
      BEGIN
         RAISERROR('The dept name has not been supplied', 16, 1)
      END

   SELECT @my_num_emps = COUNT(*)
   FROM employee e , department d
   WHERE e.dept_id = d.dept_id
   AND dept_name = @in_dept_name

   IF @my_num_emps >= 1
   BEGIN
      /*  Return the employees to the client  */
      SELECT emp_id, e.dept_id, last_name, first_name
      FROM employee e , department d
      WHERE e.dept_id = d.dept_id
      AND dept_name = @in_dept_name

      /*  Load the output parameter  */
      SELECT @out_num_emps = @@rowcount
   END
RETURN
END
```

Local variables and procedure parameters are preceded with an at sign (@) to distinguish them from column names. The preceding procedure first loads the count of the number of employees for the given department into a variable called **@my_num_emps**. This variable is checked to see if there are any employees. If there are, then the employees are selected. Upon selection, SQL Server returns the rows to the client in a result set that can be interpreted via SQL Server's client interface.

SQL Server has a variety of system variables that can be referred to directly. By convention, system variables are preceded with a double at sign (@@). The system variable **@@rowcount** contains the number of rows selected in the prior **SELECT** statement. This system variable is loaded into the output parameter, and the procedure ends. This routine is purposely a little inefficient so that local and system variables can be demonstrated.

The stored procedure shown next removes an employee record. If the employee is a manager, the employee's department head is assigned as the manager until a suitable permanent manager can be found. The number of employees affected is returned. Here is the code:

```
CREATE PROCEDURE remove_employee
(@in_emp_id INTEGER , @out_num_emps INTEGER = 0 OUTPUT)
AS
DECLARE @my_num_emps INTEGER
BEGIN
    /*  See if the employee was a manager  */
    SELECT @out_num_emps = COUNT(*)
    FROM employee
<Cod   WHERE manager_id = @in_emp_id

    IF @out_num_emps >= 1
       BEGIN
          /*  For every person who reported to that manager,
              assign their department head to be their manager  */
          UPDATE employee managed_emp
          SET manager_id = ( SELECT dept_head_id
                             FROM department d
                             WHERE managed_emp.dept_id = d.dept_id )
          WHERE manager_id = @in_emp_id
       END

    /*  Remove the employee  */
    DELETE FROM employee
    WHERE emp_id = @in_emp_id

END
```

Calling Stored Procedures

A stored procedure is called with the **EXECUTE** command. The **EXECUTE** command can also be issued from any client programming interface, such as ODBC. The procedure just discussed could be called from another stored procedure or trigger, as shown in the following code:

```
DECLARE @my_out_num_emps INTEGER
   .
   .
   .
EXECUTE remove_employee  1234 , @my_out_num_emps OUTPUT
   .
   .
   .
```

System Stored Procedures

SQL Server ships with about 200 system stored procedures to assist with system management, data dictionary information, cursors, replication, and security. Many of these procedures have a visual front end through SQL Server's administrative interfaces. A few system procedures are listed here to give you a sense of what they do:

➤ *sp_configure*—Allows the setting of server configuration parameters.

➤ *sp_adduser*—Adds a new user to the system.

➤ *sp_help*—Displays definition information for a table or view.

➤ *sp_helpdb*—Displays database definition information.

➤ *sp_helptext*—Displays the textual definition of procedural objects, such as views, triggers, and procedures.

➤ *sp_who*—Displays statistics for users who are running in the server.

Cursors

A cursor is a pointer to a row in a result set. Within the result set, the cursor can be moved to the next row, previous row, nth row, first row, last row, etc. Although most SQL processing can be performed a set at a time, sometimes it's necessary to process data one row at a time. Cursors are commonly embedded in a client programming language or tool, such as C or Visual Basic, and may also be used within stored procedures and triggers. Note that these various programming interfaces have differing cursor syntax.

Creating Cursors

Consider this business request: At annual salary increase time, the salary increase for finance people (**dept_id** 100) is 5 percent, for marketing people (**dept_id** 200) is 6 percent, and for salespeople (**dept_id** 300) is 4 percent. One approach to coding this raise structure uses a brute-force strategy that scans the table three times and requires an exclusive table-level lock each time (significantly restricting multiuser concurrency):

```
UPDATE employee
SET salary = salary * 1.05
WHERE dept_id = 100

UPDATE employee
SET salary = salary * 1.06
WHERE dept_id = 200
```

```
UPDATE employee
SET salary = salary * 1.04
WHERE dept_id = 300
```

The other approach uses cursors. Each row is locked only as it is fetched from the cursor. The general flow of cursor code is as follows:

1. Declare the cursor: The **SELECT** statement is defined but not executed.

2. Open the cursor: The **SELECT** statement is executed.

3. Repeatedly fetch rows from the cursor, optionally updating or deleting a fetched row.

4. Close the cursor.

5. Deallocate the cursor.

The previous example can now be coded using more efficient cursors:

```
DECLARE my_cursor CURSOR FOR
SELECT dept_id
FROM employee e
FOR UPDATE
go

DECLARE @my_dept_id INTEGER

OPEN my_cursor

FETCH NEXT FROM my_cursor INTO @my_dept_id

WHILE @@fetch_status = 0   /* until there are no more rows... */
BEGIN
    IF @my_dept_id = 100
        UPDATE employee
        SET salary = salary * 1.05
        WHERE CURRENT OF my_cursor
    IF @my_dept_id = 200
        UPDATE employee
        SET salary = salary * 1.06
        WHERE CURRENT OF my_cursor
    IF @my_dept_id = 300
        UPDATE employee
        SET salary = salary * 1.04
        WHERE CURRENT OF my_cursor
    FETCH NEXT FROM my_cursor INTO @my_dept_id
END
```

```
CLOSE my_cursor
DEALLOCATE my_cursor
```

Cursor Options

A scrollable cursor allows a high degree of flexibility in placing the cursor within the result set. Without the ability to scroll, cursors can only move forward. The following code shows how to declare a scrollable cursor:

```
DECLARE cursor_name CURSOR SCROLL
FOR select_statement
```

 A scrollable cursor allows you to fetch the next, prior, first, or last row; an absolute row; or a row relative to the current row.

The cursor can also be declared as read-only, which enables efficient locking:

```
DECLARE cursor_name CURSOR READ_ONLY
FOR select_statement
```

Using Cursors Within Stored Procedures

It is sometimes desirable to use cursors within stored procedures to facilitate row-at-a-time processing. For example, graduated raises for a given department are granted based on salary ranges: 4 percent if the salary is less than $50,000, 5 percent if the salary is between $50,000 and $80,000, and 6 percent if the salary is more than $80,000. To set this scale of raises, you would implement the following code:

```
CREATE PROCEDURE annual_increase
(@in_dept_id INTEGER)
AS
DECLARE @my_salary MONEY
BEGIN
DECLARE my_cursor CURSOR FOR
SELECT salary
FROM employee e
WHERE dept_id = @in_dept_id
FOR UPDATE

OPEN my_cursor
```

```
FETCH NEXT FROM my_cursor INTO @my_salary

WHILE @@fetch_status = 0  /* until there are no more rows... */
BEGIN
    IF @my_salary < $50000
        UPDATE employee
        SET salary = salary * 1.04
        WHERE CURRENT OF my_cursor
    IF @my_salary >= $50000 and @my_salary <= $80000
        UPDATE employee
        SET salary = salary * 1.05
        WHERE CURRENT OF my_cursor
    IF @my_salary > $80000
        UPDATE employee
        SET salary = salary * 1.06
        WHERE CURRENT OF my_cursor
    FETCH NEXT FROM my_cursor INTO @my_salary
END

CLOSE my_cursor
DEALLOCATE my_cursor
END
```

Cursors can be nested inside one another. A variable loaded from an outer cursor **FETCH** can be used within the **WHERE** clause of an inner cursor declaration. This technique is commonly used for elaborate nested reports that gather totals and subtotals.

A variable can be declared as a **CURSOR** data type. A stored procedure can sift through various rows, find what it's looking for, and return the cursor to the calling routine. To continue its processing, the calling routine then uses the row to which the cursor is pointing.

Locking Strategies

One of the primary functions of a DBMS is to ensure that two or more users do not change the same data at the same time and potentially overwrite one another. For example, suppose that User A wants to add $500 into an account with $3,000, and User B wants to add $100 into the same account. User A reads $3,000, as does User B. User A adds $500 to $3,000 and writes $3,500 into the account. User B then adds $100 to $3,000 and writes $3,100 into the account. The customer won't be happy.

The situation described above is called a *buried update*. To prevent buried updates, the DBMS uses a *pessimistic locking strategy*, which ensures that two people cannot access and change the same data at the same time. Pessimistic locking ensures some level of transaction consistency. As described in this section, there are several *isolation levels* of locking, which enforce different user views of data but also restrict the degree of multiuser concurrency.

Ideally, the above scenario should work like this: User A reads $3,000 and indicates that he intends to update the amount. User B does the same, but is forced to wait until User A releases the "intent-to-update" lock. User A applies the change, at which time User B is allowed to proceed.

For some application situations, the developer knows that concurrency "collisions" are unlikely to occur and that locking is not necessary. In these situations, *optimistic locking* can be enabled to turn off DBMS locking. When a user tries to change data in a row, and the DBMS sees that any data in the row has changed since the user read it, the DBMS flags an error.

Isolation Levels

The four transaction isolation levels are:

➤ *Uncommitted Read: Level 0*—Optimistic locking. No locks are held. "Dirty" data being read and changed by users within their transactions can be read and changed by other users. Buried updates are possible.

➤ *Committed Read: Level 1*—SQL Server default. Within respective transactions for Users A and B, data that has been changed by User A can be read by User B. The issue is, if User B reads data within a transaction, User A changes it, and then User B rereads it, User B will likely see a new value.

➤ *Repeatable Read: Level 2*—Ensures that changes made by User A cannot be read by User B until User A commits (safe-stores) the transaction. If User B reads data within a transaction, User A changes it, and then User B rereads it, User B will see the original value. Less multiuser concurrency is available than with Levels 0 and 1. An issue remains: Entire rows of new data can be inserted, which User B will see (upon reread) and which weren't there before. These are called *phantom* rows.

➤ *Serializable: Level 3*—Prevents phantom rows (explained in previous bulleted item). This is the most restrictive isolation level.

Isolation level syntaxes are presented in Table 6.1.

Table 6.1   Isolation level syntax.

Level Number	Transaction Level	Table Level
Level 0	READ UNCOMMITTED	READUNCOMMITTED or NOLOCK
Level 1	READ COMMITTED	READCOMMITTED or READPAST (row)
Level 2	REPEATABLE READ	REPEATABLEREAD
Level 3	SERIALIZABLE	SERIALIZABLE or HOLDLOCK

Here are two examples of how to specify an isolation level:

```
SET TRANSACTION ISOLATION LEVEL REPEATABLE READ
```

or

```
SELECT *
FROM employee WITH (REPEATABLEREAD)
WHERE ...
```

Optimistic locking can be implemented with cursors by using the **OPTIMISTIC** keyword when the cursor is opened. **OPTIMISTIC** and **READ_ONLY** are mutually exclusive.

```
DECLARE cursor_name CURSOR SCROLL OPTIMISTIC
FOR select_statement
```

Practice Questions

Question 1

Which of the following statements regarding locking is false? [Check all correct answers]

☐ a. **UNCOMMITTED READ** prevents buried updates.

☐ b. **COMMITTED READ** prevents phantom records.

☐ c. Locking does not affect the workload throughput (transactions per second).

☐ d. Locking trades transaction consistency for multiuser concurrency.

☐ e. Optimistic locking should be used in all situations because it maximizes concurrency.

Answers a, b, c, and e are correct. This question is a trick because it asks for the statements that are false. Answer a is false because **UNCOMMITTED READ** is optimistic locking, which doesn't prevent buried updates. Answer b is false because it is isolation level 1, and isolation level 4, **SERIALIZABLE,** is required in order to prevent phantom records. Answer c is false because locking inherently causes transactions to wait until contentious resource locks are released. Answer e is false because optimistic locking assumes that very little, if any, resource contention will be present, and this is not always the case. Answer d is incorrect because it is a true statement. Pessimistic locking implements transaction consistency through the enforcement of a locking isolation level, where the levels are progressively more restrictive with regard to multiuser concurrency.

Question 2

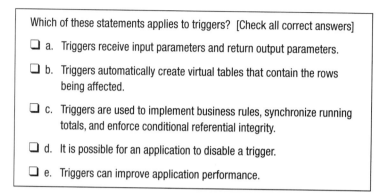

Which of these statements applies to triggers? [Check all correct answers]

❑ a. Triggers receive input parameters and return output parameters.

❑ b. Triggers automatically create virtual tables that contain the rows
being affected.

❑ c. Triggers are used to implement business rules, synchronize running
totals, and enforce conditional referential integrity.

❑ d. It is possible for an application to disable a trigger.

❑ e. Triggers can improve application performance.

Answers b, c, and e are correct. Answer b is correct because triggers use the inserted and deleted tables, which are logical tables that reside in RAM. Answer c is correct because triggers are used to extend the servers built-in integrity and data manipulation features. Answer e is correct because the alternative would be to embed the trigger's business-rule logic in the client, and doing so would incur significant network overhead. Answer a is incorrect because triggers do not have parameters. Answer d is incorrect because the whole idea of a trigger is to enforce logic based on data changes independent of the application causing the change to occur.

Question 3

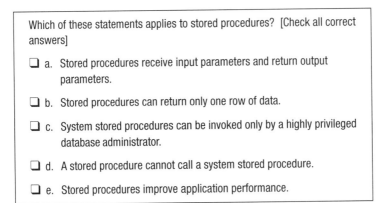

Which of these statements applies to stored procedures? [Check all correct answers]

❏ a. Stored procedures receive input parameters and return output parameters.

❏ b. Stored procedures can return only one row of data.

❏ c. System stored procedures can be invoked only by a highly privileged database administrator.

❏ d. A stored procedure cannot call a system stored procedure.

❏ e. Stored procedures improve application performance.

Answers a and e are correct. Stored procedures receive input parameters and return output parameters, and they imporove application performance. Answer b is not correct because, unlike other RDBMS products, SQL Server can return to a client as many rows within as many result sets as are needed. Answer c is not correct because anybody can call any system stored procedure as long as they have the privilege to do so; for example, most **sp_helpxxx** procedures are callable by anyone. Likewise, answer d is incorrect because a stored procedure can call any other stored procedure, regardless of whether it was supplied by the vendor or not.

Questions 4 through 10 use the following scenario: A bank maintains **AC-COUNTS**. There are checking and savings accounts. **CUSTOMERS** may have more than one account. **TRANSACTIONS** are processed for withdrawals from and deposits into any account. Tables are designed as shown below:

```
CREATE TABLE customers
( customer_id INTEGER NOT NULL ,
  first_name VARCHAR(15) NOT NULL ,
  last_name VARCHAR(20) NOT NULL ,
  street VARCHAR(30) NOT NULL ,
  city VARCHAR(20) NOT NULL ,
  state CHAR(2) NOT NULL ,
  zip CHAR(5) NOT NULL ,
  referred_by INTEGER NULL )

CREATE TABLE accounts
( account_id INTEGER NOT NULL ,
  customer_id INTEGER NOT NULL ,
  acct_type CHAR(1) NOT NULL ,
  opened_date DATETIME NOT NULL ,
  balance MONEY DEFAULT 0 NOT NULL ,
  CONSTRAINT chk_acct_type CHECK (acct_type IN ('S','C') )
)
     /*  Savings, Checking  */

CREATE TABLE transactions
( txn_id INTEGER NOT NULL ,
  account_id INTEGER NOT NULL ,
  txn_date DATETIME NOT NULL ,
  txn_type CHAR(1) NOT NULL ,
  amount MONEY NOT NULL ,
  CONSTRAINT chk_txn_type CHECK (txn_type IN ('D','W') )
  )
    /*  Deposit, Withdrawal  */
```

Question 4

Refer to the scenario that precedes this question. Which of the following triggers implements the business rule "When an account transaction occurs, modify the account balance appropriately"?

○ a.
```
CREATE TRIGGER modify_balance
ON transactions
FOR INSERT
AS
BEGIN
    IF (SELECT txn_type FROM inserted) = 'W'
        UPDATE accounts a
        SET balance = balance + i.amount
        FROM inserted i
        WHERE a.account_id = i.account_id
    IF (SELECT txn_type FROM inserted) = 'D'
        UPDATE accounts a
        SET balance = balance - i.amount
        FROM inserted i
        WHERE a.account_id = i.account_id
END
```

○ b.
```
CREATE TRIGGER modify_balance
ON transactions
FOR INSERT
AS
BEGIN
    IF (SELECT txn_type FROM inserted) = 'W'
        UPDATE accounts a
        SET balance = balance - i.amount
        FROM inserted i
        WHERE a.account_id = i.account_id
    IF (SELECT txn_type FROM inserted) = 'D'
        UPDATE accounts a
        SET balance = balance + i.amount
        FROM inserted i
        WHERE a.account_id = i.account_id
END
```

(continued)

Question 4 (continued)

```
○ c. CREATE TRIGGER modify_balance
     ON accounts
     FOR UPDATE
     AS
     BEGIN
         IF (SELECT acct_type FROM inserted) = 'C'
             UPDATE accounts a
             SET balance = balance - i.amount
             FROM inserted i
             WHERE a.account_id = i.account_id
         IF (SELECT acct_type FROM inserted) = 'S'
             UPDATE accounts a
             SET balance = balance + i.amount
             FROM inserted i
             WHERE a.account_id = i.account_id
     END
```

Answer b is correct. An account needs to be changed when a new transaction record is inserted. A withdrawal needs to be subtracted from the account's balance, and a deposit needs to be added to the balance.

Question 5

Refer to the scenario that precedes Question 4. Which of the following triggers implements the business rule "When a customer closes an account, remove the transactions as well"?

○ a.
```
CREATE TRIGGER close_account
   ON accounts
   FOR DELETE
   AS
   BEGIN
      DELETE FROM transactions t
      FROM inserted i
      WHERE t.account_id = i.account_id
   END
```

○ b.
```
CREATE TRIGGER close_account
   ON transactions
   FOR DELETE
   AS
   BEGIN
      DELETE FROM transactions t
      FROM deleted d
      WHERE t.account_id = d.account_id
   END
```

○ c.
```
CREATE TRIGGER close_account
   ON accounts
   FOR DELETE
   AS
   BEGIN
      DELETE FROM transactions t
      FROM deleted d
      WHERE t.account_id = d.account_id
   END
```

Answer c is correct. An account is closed when the account is deleted. A **DELETE** trigger generates the **DELETED** virtual table.

Question 6

Refer to the scenario that precedes Question 4. Which of the following triggers implements the business rule "If a new customer is referred to the bank by an existing customer, give the existing customer a $100 gift, placed in the customer's savings account (we'll assume the customer has a savings account)"?

○ a.
```
CREATE TRIGGER customer_referral
ON customers
FOR INSERT
AS
BEGIN
    IF (SELECT referred_by FROM inserted) IS NOT
NULL
        UPDATE accounts a
        SET balance = balance + 100
        FROM inserted i
        WHERE a.customer_id = i.referred_by
        AND a.acct_type = 'S'
END
```

○ b.
```
CREATE TRIGGER customer_referral
ON customers
FOR INSERT
AS
BEGIN
    IF (SELECT referred_by FROM inserted) IS NOT
NULL
        UPDATE accounts a
        SET balance = balance + 100
        FROM inserted i
        WHERE a.customer_id = i.customer_id
        AND a.acct_type = 'S'
END
```

(continued)

Question 6 (continued)

```
○ c.  CREATE TRIGGER customer_referral
      ON customers
      FOR INSERT
      AS
      BEGIN
          IF (SELECT referred_by FROM inserted) IS NOT
      NULL
              UPDATE accounts a
              SET balance = balance + 100
              FROM inserted i
              WHERE a.referred_by = i.customer_id
              AND a.acct_type = 'S'
      END
```

Answer a is correct. Each trigger is identical except for the **WHERE** clause of the **UPDATE**. You want to **UPDATE** the account with the **customer_id** of the customer who referred the new customer, as indicated by the **referred_by** column. The **WHERE** clause in answer a reads "where the account's **customer_id** equals the inserted customer's **referred_by** [customer] id". Answer b reads "where the account's **customer_id** equals the inserted customer's id"—which isn't what you want. Answer c reads "where the account's **referred_by** equals the inserted customer's id"—which is incorrect because the account table does not have a **referred_by** column.

Question 7

Refer to the scenario that precedes Question 4. Which of the following triggers implements the business rule "If a transaction overdraws an account, do not let the transaction happen"?

○ a.
```
CREATE TRIGGER check_balance
ON accounts
FOR UPDATE
AS
BEGIN
    IF ( SELECT acct_type FROM inserted ) = 'C'
        AND ( SELECT a.balance - i.amount
                FROM accounts a , inserted i
                WHERE a.account_id = i.account_id
            ) < 0
        BEGIN
            raiserror('Account is overdrawn',16,1)
            ROLLBACK
        END
END
```

○ b.
```
CREATE TRIGGER check_balance
ON transactions
FOR INSERT
AS
BEGIN
    IF ( SELECT txn_type FROM inserted ) = 'W'
        AND ( SELECT i.amount - a.balance
                FROM accounts a , inserted i
                WHERE a.account_id = i.account_id)
            < 0
        BEGIN
            RAISERROR('Account is overdrawn',16,1)
            ROLLBACK
        END
END
```

(continued)

Question 7 (continued)

```
○ c.  CREATE TRIGGER check_balance
      ON transactions
      FOR INSERT
      AS
      BEGIN
          IF ( SELECT txn_type FROM inserted ) = 'W'
                AND ( SELECT a.balance - i.amount
                      FROM accounts a , inserted i
                      WHERE a.account_id = i.account_id)
          < 0
            BEGIN
                RAISERROR('Account is overdrawn',16,1)
                ROLLBACK
            END
      END
```

Answer c is correct. The creation of a new transaction triggers this business rule, which must change the account balance associated with the transaction. You need to check only withdrawal transactions because withdrawals can cause an overdraft. The transaction amount needs to be subtracted from the account's balance. Answer c correctly verifies that the transaction is a withdrawal and correctly subtracts the new transaction amount from the account balance.

Question 8

Refer to the scenario that precedes Question 4. What business rule does the following trigger implement?

```
CREATE TRIGGER triggers_happen
ON customers
FOR INSERT
AS
BEGIN
    IF NOT EXISTS
        ( SELECT *
          FROM customers c , inserted i
          WHERE c.customer_id = i.referred_by )
        BEGIN
            RAISERROR('An error has occurred',16,1)
            ROLLBACK
        END
END
```

○ a. If the customer does not exist, raise an error.

○ b. If the customer has not been referred by another customer, raise an error.

○ c. If the customer who referred a new customer does not exist, raise an error.

○ d. If the customer has not been inserted, raise an error.

Answer c is correct. The inserted table contains the new customer. The **WHERE** clause says, "Where the customer id is equal to the newly inserted customer's **referred_by** customer id".

Need To Know More?

 Forta, Ben. *SAMS Teach Yourself SQL in 10 Minutes.* Indianapolis, IN: SAMS, 1999. ISBN: 0-672-31664-1. This book is easy to read and provides the right level of detail for an application developer.

 McEwan, Bennett William, and David Solomon. *Transact–SQL in 21 Days.* Indianapolis, IN: SAMS, 1997. ISBN: 0-672-31045-7. This book provides a good introduction to Transact-SQL at the right level of detail.

 Taylor, Allen G. *SQL For Dummies.* Foster City, CA: IDG Books Worldwide, 1998. ISBN: 0-7645-0415-0. This book is a good introduction to SQL, and its treatment of joins is first-rate.

 www.microsoft.com/backoffice/sql lets you download Microsoft SQL Server 7 evaluation software and peruse SQL Server books online.

Creating A
Physical Database

. . . .

Terms you'll need to understand:

√ Data model

√ Entity

√ Attribute

√ Relationship

√ Transaction log

√ Referential integrity

√ Restrictive integrity

√ Page

√ Master database

√ Index

√ Bulk load (bulk copy)

Techniques you'll need to master:

√ Defining a data model

√ Creating a database

√ Creating tables

√ Defining referential integrity

√ Defining business rules

√ Managing indexes

√ Loading and unloading the database

This chapter looks at what it takes to create a database. First, the issues that need to be considered when implementing a data architecture are addressed. Next, the process and SQL commands used to create an SQL Server database are presented.

Implementing A Data Storage Architecture

Several factors influence the choices made in implementing a data architecture. Ultimately, the data architecture is designed to support the requirements of the business. The business will require a certain level of reliability, availability, growth (scalability), distributed access, and, of course, performance. Each of these requirements is discussed briefly.

Reliability

Application reliability is directly proportional to the maturity of the system's hardware and software components. Older hardware and software are more reliable than newer technologies. A business must make a hard choice between the competitive advantage that a newer technology offers and the stability it provides. In database systems, relational technologies have matured into very stable and reliable systems, whereas newer object-relational features are likely to have the traps and pitfalls we all come to expect of newer software offerings.

Availability

Each application should have availability requirements clearly defined. What are its hours of operation—24×7, 12×5, or 8×5/12×2? Often, high availability is measured as a percentage. 99.99 percent translates to about 53 minutes of unscheduled downtime per year. Such highly available systems require a high degree of redundancy for expensive hardware and software components. Redundant components include power supplies, fans, disks, CPUs, memory, network cables, and special failover software. The software and database designs must take into account failure conditions that can occur at any time.

A "clustered" system is often configured for high-availability purposes, and then the entire configuration is duplicated for redundancy. This duplicate configuration is then duplicated in a remote location to avoid weather-related disasters. Off-site storage and other disaster measures are also considered. The cost of all this redundancy is weighed against the cost of downtime to the business, and often the numbers easily justify the added system expense.

Scalability

The system needs to be able to grow as the business grows. It is not unreasonable for data to expand at more than 100 percent per year. User population may increase significantly, particularly beyond the initial trial period. Transaction volumes typically increase nonlinearly as users become smarter and more comfortable in their use of the system. The hardware, software, and database design must be able to accommodate this growth over a projected period of time. From a hardware perspective, upgrade paths are examined. From a software perspective, process and data partitioning is employed. Complex yet intelligent software architectures—such as multithreading and parallel processing—are considered.

Distributed Application And Data Access

The performance or political (ownership) requirements often demand that data and processing be physically located in multiple places. The hardware and software must be able to accommodate the system's networking bandwidth requirements. Additionally, physically distributed data sometimes requires multisite transactions in which a database management system (DBMS) transaction changes data in more than one location and the data is committed or rolled back in an all-or-nothing fashion.

Technically, multisite transactions are extremely difficult to implement. Two approaches exist: two-phase commit, and replication.

➤ *Two-phase commit*—Assumes that all sites involved in the transaction are always available. It is unlikely that the business will tolerate a stoppage in transaction processing just because a site is down, so two-phase commit has very limited real-world applicability.

➤ *Replication*—Makes copies of data at multiple sites so it is available in more than one location should one site fail. Replication operates much like email, using a store-and-forward mechanism. Replication solves the system outage problem, but it is fraught with unusual failure conditions that require application-dependent recovery procedures implemented in software.

Performance

Performance, by far, has the biggest influence on physical database design. Database systems are at the mercy of disk speeds and data-transfer rates. Based on a detailed analysis of the application workload, the database designer spreads data across enough disks to accommodate the anticipated disk I/O (input/output) rates. In high-end OLTP (On-Line Transaction Processing) applications, transaction log files are especially prone to saturating disk I/O.

The designer must also examine multiuser locking issues for hotly contended data resources. Data prone to "hot spots" should be physically spread out to avoid locks that "stand in line" (queue), waiting for one another to be released.

Queries involving large volumes of data are analyzed to see if parallel processing across multiple CPUs may help meet response requirements. The query analysis is also used to identify data indexes that should be defined and memory that should be allocated.

Client/server network bandwidth issues must also be examined. Often, individual system performance is perfectly fine, but the network is woefully inadequate (as evidenced by the joke about "WWW" standing for "World Wide Wait").

Data Design

The previous sections provide some sense of how business requirements influence system/data architecture and design. But how do we ultimately decide what our tables should be? A methodology to derive a table design is outlined in this section. Development groups that deviate from this approach often end up with ill-defined, ill-performing data models. Successful data design requires the commitment of adequate time and resources toward rigorous system analysis and design. Without a proper analysis, system performance ultimately suffers.

Business Modeling And Data Normalization

The primary tool for data design methodology is a *model*. A model is a picture of our system, much like a road map is a picture of geography. Similarly, system and data models are "pictures worth a thousand words." There are many types of models, including architecture, process, technology, and organizational models. Models tend to be of two flavors: *as-is* (how the world works now), and *to-be* (how we would like the world to work).

The *business process model* (BPM) identifies the steps required to perform a business operation. Processes are stated in short, three-to-five-word sentences using a noun-verb-object format. The model shows how the process flows from one step to the next, how multiple processes flow into a single process, and what processes a given process may need to wait for in order to continue. Some software-based process models can be quantified with the time required to process individual steps. This quantified process model is then simulated. The simulation output shows how long the entire process will take, along with human resource costs, material costs, and so on.

A *data flow diagram* (DFD) is then manually generated from the BPM. This diagram incorporates the data elements that flow in and out of processes, so both process and data are represented. Data elements can be very high-level items—such as customers, parts, and orders—or very detailed low-level items—such as customer numbers, part numbers, and order quantities. These nouns, which were initially identified in the BPM, now become more concrete and more detailed.

A *business data model* is then manually generated from the DFD. The business data model is process-less. The model strictly represents our data entities, attributes, and relationships. An *attribute* is a fact about something. This fact cannot be described by anything else. For example, your last name is an attribute about you. An *entity* is something that can be described by attributes; the facts about an entity are its attributes. To continue the preceding example, you are an entity, and your last name is one of your attributes. Similarly, **EMPLOYEE** is an entity, and **Last_Name** is an attribute of (a fact about) **EMPLOYEE**.

Entities, attributes, and relationships between entities are often identified through a formal design methodology called *data normalization*, which is based on relational theory. The goal of normalization is to minimize the redundancy of attributes within entities. For example, your last name should appear only once in the entire database within the **EMPLOYEE** table, and not in any other entity, such as **PAY_CHECK**, where your last-name value might be stored many times. This design technique guarantees that if your last name changes (as might be the case after marriage), it will need to be modified only once and not hundreds of times.

As normalization and business analysis identify *relationships* between entities, the relationship's properties are also identified. Consider **DEPARTMENT**s and **EMPLOYEE**s. We ask the question, "For one department, will there be one or many employees?" The answer is many. There is a one-to-many relationship between **DEPARTMENT** and **EMPLOYEE**. The "many-ness" of a relationship is called its *cardinality*. **DEPARTMENT** is the parent entity (the "one" side), and **EMPLOYEE** is the child entity (the "many" side).

We also ask if the relationship is required or not. "Must a department have an employee?" Technically, no. This relationship is said to be "optional." If the answer had been "yes," the relationship would be called "mandatory." This question identifies the relationship's *optionality*.

"One department may employ many employees." Note the five parts to our sentence: the subject or parent—department; the object or child—employee; the relationship—employ; the optionality—may; the cardinality—many. EMPLOY is the name of the relationship from **DEPARTMENT** to **EMPLOYEE**. All relationships are *unidirectional* and *named*. These sentences are read straight off the model.

There will always be at least two relationships between two related entities—in this example, from **DEPARTMENT** to **EMPLOYEE** and, as we'll see now, from **EMPLOYEE** to **DEPARTMENT**. "For one employee, will there be one or many departments?" One. "Must an employee have a department?" Yes. "One employee must work in one department." The name of this relationship is WORK IN.

The relationship also supports some level of *referential integrity (RI)*. RI asks if a child entity is allowed to be an orphan (have no parent). "Is an employee allowed to have no department?" RI is examined from parent to child and from child to parent in the following manner:

➤ *Parent to child*—If we delete a parent, should we also delete its children? If yes, this operation is called a *cascading delete*. If no, then we don't allow the parent delete to happen. This situation is called *restrictive* integrity.

➤ *Child to parent*—If we insert a child, and the child has no parent, should we let the insert happen? If the answer is no (which it is 99.9 percent of the time), then we restrict the child insert from happening (R). Every now and then, we let the child insert happen and cascade the insert to create a dummy parent. (Those of us who are parents can relate to this phenomenon.)

➤ If some other action is required, we implement *other exceptional* integrity. For example, if a department is deleted, we don't want to delete the associated employees; rather, we want to reassign them to some other department by some business algorithm.

➤ Every once in a while, leaving an orphan child record is allowed. This situation is denoted as *OK* integrity.

Data normalization has many stages, or forms. *First normal form* (1NF) identifies child entities. Second and third normal forms identify parent entities. A design in third normal form (3NF) has identified all one-to-many relationships. Fourth and fifth normal forms identify many-to-many relationships. Beyond this, normalization becomes esoteric.

You should have a good understanding of normalization and be able to explain the first, second, and third normal forms.

In a business model, entities may be related to one another in a variety of manners. Earlier, we identified a one-to-many relationship between **DEPARTMENT** and **EMPLOYEE**. **STUDENTS** and **COURSES** are related to each other in a many-to-many fashion: One student takes many courses; one course is taken by many students. Another type of relationship is one-to-one. In addition to **DEPARTMENT** and **EMPLOYEE**'s one-to-many relationship, there is also a one-to-one relationship here. One department must be managed by one **department_head** employee, and one employee may be employed as one department's **department_head**.

The business analysis and logical data model may also show that some entities are special cases, or subtypes, of other entities. For example, the supertype **EMPLOYEE** can be specialized as **SALES_PEOPLE** and **NON_SALES_PEOPLE**, **EXEMPT_EMPS** and **NON_EXEMPT_EMPS**, **MANAGERS** and **NON_MANAGERS**, and so on.

A business data model often cannot be implemented in a relational database. As we'll see, an RDBMS understands only one-to-many relationships, yet the business data model may contain many-to-many and one-to-one relationships. Additionally, an RDBMS does not understand subtypes and supertypes (which are actually special one-to-one relationships).

Logical Data Modeling

Database designers use data modeling techniques to resolve all these special types of objects and relationships in order to create a *logical data model*. A logical data model contains no specialized entities (no subtypes or supertypes) and has only one-to-many relationships.

The logical data model can be implemented in a relational database, though it is not in a form that can take advantage of vendor-specific features. The logical model is fully normalized, and, ideally, all cross-column, cross-row, cross-table, and temporal (time-based) data interdependencies are addressed.

Physical Data Modeling

Physical data modeling takes into account real-world aspects of the database system. The database design is modified to facilitate client-screen-to-database-object mappings, security issues, business rules, transactions and associated locking issues, physical locations of distributed data, and, of course, performance requirements. Additionally, subtypes and supertypes are manifested through relational views (see "Creating Views" in Chapter 7).

Upon completion, the physical data model can be implemented in a vendor-specific relational database. The remainder of this chapter describes the features available in defining the database and its tables by using SQL Server's Data Definition Language (DDL).

Whenever possible, we will present the SQL or system stored procedure syntax used for database definition and management. Though it is not possible within this space to describe each and every option in detail, the most important features are presented.

Creating Databases

There are a variety of interfaces for managing SQL Server, including:

➤ Wizards from an application using the SQL-NameSpace client object (new in SQL Server 7)

➤ Menu interface in SQL Enterprise Manager

➤ SQL Enterprise Manager wizards

➤ SQL statements within the Query Analyzer

➤ The good old isql interactive command utility

One SQL server may have up to 32,767 databases. Each database has a transaction log. SQL Server 7 incorporates the ability to create database-related files within the NT file system (previous versions created SQL Server–specific "devices"). Files must be on disks with controllers that do not perform write-through caching. File types include:

➤ *Primary data files*—Use an .mdf extension.

➤ *Secondary files*—Used if the primary file fills up; use an .ndf extension.

➤ *Log files for the transaction log*—Use an .ldf extension. To facilitate recovery in the event of a primary-file disk failure, the log should be on a separate physical disk.

SQL Server ships with a set of databases. Notably, the system catalog is in a database called "master." Several DDL commands, such as creating a database, require you to initially establish context in the master database.

To create a database and take defaults, simply state:

```
USE master
go     /* by default, isql commands are run by entering "go"  */
CREATE DATABASE my_database
go     /* from now on, we will eliminate the "go" command  */
```

To spread the database across multiple disks, you can use a more complete syntax:

```
USE master
go
CREATE DATABASE my_database
```

```
ON PRIMARY
    ( FILENAME = 'D:\SQL7\DATA\file1.mdf' ,
      SIZE = 16000 MB ) ,
    ( FILENAME = 'E:\SQL7\DATA\file2.ndf' ,
      SIZE = 16000 MB ) ,
    ( FILENAME = 'F:\SQL7\DATA\file3.ndf' ,
      SIZE = 16000 MB )
LOG ON
        ( FILENAME = 'F:\SQL7\LOG\log1.ldf' ,
          SIZE = 8000 MB )
```

Databases have options that may be set through various interfaces, including the system stored procedure **sp_dboption**. Some of these options include making the database read-only, truncating the transaction log periodically, enabling DBO (database owner) use only, allowing nonlogged bulk load operations, enabling single-user use, and setting the database offline.

Creating Database Tables

One database may have up to 2 billion tables. One table may have up to 1,024 columns. The basic format for a table definition is:

```
USE my_database   /*  Context is established in your database  */
go
CREATE TABLE table_name
( column_name  datatype  [NOT] NULL [,...] )
```

Each column should be explicitly defined to be **NULL** or **NOT NULL**. Different database products implement the default in a different manner, so it's always best to be explicit, especially if the database will be ported to different products.

Some representative SQL Server data types are:

➤ *char(n)*—Where n <= 8,000. Strings are delimited with single quotes.

➤ *varchar(n)*—Where n <= 8,000

➤ *integer*—4 byte

➤ *smallint*—2 byte

➤ *tinyint*—1 byte

➤ *numeric(p,s)*—negative $10^{38} - 1$ through positive $10^{38} - 1$ when maximum precision is used

➤ *float*—Exponents of + or -308

➤ *money*—Plus or minus 922 quadrillion with 4 decimal places

➤ *datetime*—1,753 to 9,999, to the thousandths of a second

➤ *binary(n)*—Where n <= 8,000

➤ *varbinary(n)*—Where n <= 8,000

➤ *text*—A character string up to 2GB in size

➤ *image*—A binary string up to 2GB in size

We will build on the following example:

```
CREATE TABLE department
( dept_id INTEGER NOT NULL ,
  dept_name VARCHAR(20) NOT NULL ,
  cost_center CHAR(3) NULL ,
  dept_head_id INTEGER NULL
)

CREATE TABLE employee
(
  emp_id INTEGER NOT NULL ,
  dept_id INTEGER NOT NULL ,
  first_name VARCHAR(15) NOT NULL ,
  last_name VARCHAR(20) NOT NULL ,
  phone CHAR(18) NULL ,
  manager_id INTEGER NULL ,
  salary MONEY NULL
)
```

Enforcing Data Integrity

By using the **DEFAULT** clause, you can give a column an initial default value when none is supplied. You can also define a column as being **UNIQUE**—values are not allowed to repeat:

```
CREATE TABLE department
(
  dept_id INTEGER NOT NULL ,
  dept_name VARCHAR(20) DEFAULT 'UNKNOWN' NOT NULL ,
  cost_center CHAR(3) NULL UNIQUE ,
  dept_head_id INTEGER NULL
)
```

Next you'll see how column domains are defined using a **CHECK** constraint. A domain defines the allowable values for a specific column. Any conditional expression that can be used in a **WHERE** clause can also be used in the **CHECK** constraint. Here is the previous example with a **CHECK** constraint added:

```
CREATE TABLE department
(
  dept_id INTEGER NOT NULL ,
  dept_name VARCHAR(20) DEFAULT 'UNKNOWN' NOT NULL ,
  cost_center CHAR(3) NULL UNIQUE ,
  dept_head_id INTEGER NULL ,
  CONSTRAINT check_cost_center
      CHECK (cost_center LIKE '[A-Z][0-9][A-Z]' OR
            cost_center = 'X99')
)
```

Enforcing Referential Integrity

Finally, primary and foreign keys are defined using constraints. Foreign key constraints always define at least restrictive integrity from child to parent, and may optionally define cascading integrity (see the "Business Modeling And Data Normalization" section earlier in this chapter). Foreign keys are specified on previously defined primary keys.

Assume that in the **DEPARTMENT** table you have a primary key called **dept_id** and in the **EMPLOYEE** table you have a foreign key, also called **dept_id**. (The foreign key column name could be anything, but for consistency this is a good convention to follow.) The table definitions become:

```
CREATE TABLE department
(
  dept_id INTEGER NOT NULL ,
  dept_name VARCHAR(20) DEFAULT 'UNKNOWN' NOT NULL ,
  cost_center CHAR(3) NULL UNIQUE ,
  dept_head_id INTEGER NULL ,
  CONSTRAINT check_cost_center
   CHECK ( cost_center LIKE '[A-Z][0-9][A-Z]' OR
          cost_center = 'X99') ,
  CONSTRAINT dept_pk PRIMARY KEY (dept_id)
)

CREATE TABLE employee
(
  emp_id INTEGER NOT NULL ,
  dept_id INTEGER NOT NULL ,
  first_name VARCHAR(15) NOT NULL ,
  last_name VARCHAR(20) NOT NULL ,
  phone CHAR(18) NULL ,
  manager_id INTEGER NULL ,
```

```
   salary MONEY NULL ,
   CONSTRAINT emp_pk PRIMARY KEY (emp_id) ,
   CONSTRAINT dept_emp_fk FOREIGN KEY (dept_id)
      REFERENCES department (dept_id)
)
```

If the relationship from **DEPARTMENT** to **EMPLOYEE** needs to implement cascading deletes, the syntax for the foreign key definition is:

```
CONSTRAINT dept_emp_fk FOREIGN KEY (dept_id)
         REFERENCES department (dept_id)
         ON DELETE CASCADE
```

If the primary and foreign keys consist of more than one column (a situation called a *composite key*), these columns are listed inside their respective parentheses.

Recall that sometimes our referential integrity is neither restrictive nor cascading; rather, some other exceptional processing is required. In this case, a trigger is created to implement these special processing requirements. Suppose we have a business rule that says when an employee's manager leaves, find everyone who reported to the manager and assign their new manager to be their department head (until a permanent person can be found). A foreign key constraint between **DEPARTMENT** and **EMPLOYEE** must *not* be defined because this business rule requires neither restrictive nor cascading integrity. The table definitions and the associated trigger to enforce this business rule are presented here:

```
CREATE TABLE department
(
  dept_id INTEGER NOT NULL ,
  dept_name VARCHAR(20) DEFAULT 'UNKNOWN' NOT NULL ,
  cost_center CHAR(3) NULL UNIQUE ,
  dept_head_id INTEGER NULL ,
  CONSTRAINT check_cost_center
     CHECK (cost_center LIKE '[A-Z][0-9][A-Z]' OR
            cost_center = 'X99') ,
  CONSTRAINT dept_pk PRIMARY KEY (dept_id)
)

CREATE TABLE employee
(
  emp_id INTEGER NOT NULL ,
  dept_id INTEGER NOT NULL ,
  first_name VARCHAR(15) NOT NULL ,
  last_name VARCHAR(20) NOT NULL ,
```

```
   phone CHAR(18) NULL ,
   manager_id INTEGER NULL ,
   salary MONEY NULL ,
   CONSTRAINT emp_pk PRIMARY KEY (emp_id)
)

CREATE TRIGGER temp_manager
ON employee
FOR DELETE
AS
BEGIN
/*  Was this person a manager?  */
IF EXISTS
      ( SELECT *
        FROM employee e , deleted old_mgr
        WHERE e.manager_id = old_mgr.emp_id )
    BEGIN
       UPDATE employee e
       SET manager_id = (SELECT dept_head_id
                         FROM department
                         WHERE d.dept_id = e.dept_id)
       WHERE manager_id IN (SELECT emp_id
                            FROM deleted)
    END
END
```

 Be sure you know how to create tables and how to apply constraints.

Indexes

Before reading this section, please review "The Importance Of Indexes" in Chapter 7.

By way of background, data and indexes are physically stored on *pages* where every page is 8,000 bytes. Each access to a page results in one logical disk I/O. If the page is not already in memory when it is accessed, then a physical disk I/O (expensive disk head movement) is required to access the data.

RDBMSs provide a fast access mechanism called an *index*. An index works much like looking up a word in a dictionary: You begin by opening the book to the vicinity of the word in question, and then you narrow your search many pages at a time. The DBMS performs all the search logic for you.

Indexes are placed on a column or combination of columns in one table. The index sorts (in ascending or descending order) the values found in each row for the column(s), and places these values into a special disk-based structure. So, although there is disk-space overhead with an index, access time is often instantaneous.

It makes sense to place indexes on columns that are frequently present in **WHERE, GROUP BY, HAVING,** and **ORDER BY** clauses, as well as on primary and foreign keys. An index is most useful for columns where a small number of values are being searched. For example, an equality such as **id='123'** is most restrictive. An inequality such as **id<10000** is unlikely to benefit from an index because the search involves so many pages of the table that it's more efficient for the DBMS to sweep through the entire table using multipage disk I/Os.

There are two kinds of indexes: clustered and nonclustered. A *clustered index* defines the sort order of the table's physical storage, so there can be only one clustered index per table. *Nonclustered indexes* are maintained in a balance tree, where a leaf node contains the key value and a row locator.

As with data, indexes are stored on pages. In essence, the lowest level of the index is the actual data row, so clustered indexes nearly always require one less logical I/O to search. In a child table, a good clustered index is often the foreign key followed by the primary key. In this way, all the children for a given parent are physically stored next to one another on the same page or neighboring pages, so less logical I/O is needed for searches from parent to child.

It is possible for table access to "pile up" in one section of the table. This often happens at the end of a table, where the most recent data tends to accumulate (called *monotonically increasing data*). A clustered index can be defined on a more random column to physically spread the data across multiple pages, thereby spreading out the physical access and associated locking.

Each table can have up to an additional 249 nonclustered indexes. In a child table, it is possible that a given parent's children are each physically on a different page. So, in the worst case, each child may require a separate physical I/O. For this reason, our choice of clustered versus nonclustered indexes is very important.

Creating Indexes

The syntax for creating an index is:

```
CREATE [UNIQUE] [CLUSTERED | NONCLUSTERED]
INDEX index_name ON table (column [,...n])
```

For this example, the indexes can be:

```
CREATE INDEX dept_name_idx ON department (dept_name)

CREATE INDEX emp_dept_fk_idx ON employee (dept_id , emp_id)
  /*  An index with more than one column
      is called a composite index  */

CREATE INDEX emp_lname_idx ON employee (last_name)
```

Both tables already have a clustered index, which was created because of the primary key constraint. If they didn't, here is the code you could use to create clustered keys:

```
CREATE CLUSTERED INDEX dept_pk_idx ON department (dept_id)
CREATE CLUSTERED INDEX emp_pk_idx ON employee (emp_id)
```

Maintaining Indexes

When SQL Server compiles a query, it examines how the query may make use of available indexes. For example, the indexes just defined would be useful for **WHERE** clauses such as the following:

```
WHERE emp_id = 1234

WHERE last_name BETWEEN 'Johnson' AND 'Jones'

WHERE dept_id = 101 AND emp_id IN (1234, 2345, 3456)
```

To see what indexes are on a table, enter:

```
sp_help table_name
```

SQL Server provides a utility called *showplan* that shows which indexes are being used for a given query. Showplan is very useful for identifying large tables in a query that are inefficient at table scanning and could benefit from an index.

SQL Server keeps data-value-distribution statistics for indexes. These statistics are not maintained over time. So, as data is deleted and inserted over time, the statistics need to be recalculated. The command to refresh statistics is:

```
UPDATE STATISTICS table_name
```

This command can be time consuming to use on large tables, so it is best to run it off-hours.

To remove an index, enter:

```
DROP INDEX table_name.index_name
```

 Be sure you understand the concept of indexes and are aware of advantages and disadvantages in using them.

Populating The Database

After the database and its tables are defined, data is loaded into the tables. The primary mechanism for doing so is SQL Server's Bulk Copy Program utility, called *BCP*. A bulk copy is a high-performance "streaming" load of data. The utility is designed to run at the disk's peak throughput rate, and it allows multiple disks to be writing in parallel at the same time. For efficiency reasons, bulk copies are not logged. If a bulk copy were logged, the log could become larger than the table itself. Because a log of the newly inserted rows is not available, it is important to back up the database immediately after the load concludes.

The BCP utility has several interfaces, including an interactive utility (the most common interface), a callable interface through ODBC enhancements, and an SQL-based **BULK INSERT** command.

First, the database must be set to enable bulk copying:

```
USE database_name
go
sp_dboption database_name, 'select into/bulkcopy', 'true'
go
```

To invoke BCP's interactive interface, enter this command (place everything on one line; here it appears on two lines because of line count restraints) as superuser "sa":

```
bcp database_name..table_name in c:\path\my_file.dat
    -Sserver_name -Usa -Ppassword
```

For each column, a series of questions is asked. These questions tell BCP what your input data file looks like. The defaults for each question are taken from the table definition (as represented in the system catalog). Here are four representative questions:

```
Enter the file storage type of field last_name [char]:
Enter prefix length of field last_name [0]: /* use default */
Enter length of field last_name [20]:
Enter field terminator [none]:
```

It is likely that the fields in the input data file will be separated by a character or a tab. A tab is indicated with a "\t". The last column is likely to be terminated with a Return, which is indicated with a "\n". After the information for the last column is entered, BCP asks if you want to save your responses in a format file:

```
Do you want to save this format information in a file? [Y/n] y
Host filename: [my_bcp.fmt]
```

Saving responses in a format file is recommended so that as new loads are performed, you can use the –f option in BCP to refer to the format file. The following command (again, it should all be on one line) refers to the format file from the previous example:

```
bcp database_name..table_name in c:\path\my_file.dat
      -fc:\path\my_bcp.fmt -Sserver_name -Usa -Ppassword
```

Alternatively, SQL has a **BULK INSERT** command. As an example:

```
BULK INSERT my_database.dbo.my_table
FROM 'c:\path\my_file.dat'
WITH (FORMATFILE = 'c:\path\my_bcp.fmt')
```

Practice Questions

Question 1

> Which of the following does a physical data model represent? [Check all correct answers]
>
> ❏ a. Entities
>
> ❏ b. Processes
>
> ❏ c. Relationships
>
> ❏ d. Attributes
>
> ❏ e. Files

Answers a, c, and d are correct. A physical data model represents entities, relationships, and attributes. Answer b is incorrect because a physical data model is process-independent. Answer e is incorrect because the physical file layout is determined by a database administrator after the data model has been developed.

Question 2

> Which of the following violates referential integrity?
>
> ○ a. A child is inserted, having a foreign key value that exists in the parent table.
>
> ○ b. A parent that has no children is deleted.
>
> ○ c. A child's foreign key value is changed to a value that exists in the parent.
>
> ○ d. A child that has a parent is deleted.
>
> ○ e. None of the above.

Answer e is correct. None of the above scenarios leaves an orphan record—that is, a child record with no parent. An orphan record would violate referential integrity.

Question 3

Which of the following tables has been incorrectly designed?

○ a. CREATE TABLE customers
        (customer_id INTEGER NOT NULL ,
          company_name VARCHAR(20) NOT NULL ,
          address VARCHAR(30) NULL ,
          city VARCHAR(20) NULL ,
          state CHAR(2) NULL ,
          zip CHAR(5) NULL)

○ b. CREATE TABLE products
        (product_id INTEGER NOT NULL ,
          product_name VARCHAR(15) NOT NULL ,
          qty_on_hand INTEGER NOT NULL ,
          order_date DATETIME NOT NULL ,
          description VARCHAR(100) NULL)

○ c. CREATE TABLE loans
        (loan_id INTEGER NOT NULL ,
          cust_id INTEGER NOT NULL ,
          loan_type INTEGER NOT NULL ,
          approval_date DATETIME NOT NULL ,
          amount MONEY NOT NULL ,
          balance MONEY NOT NULL)

Answer b is correct. The **order_date** is not a fact about a product; rather, it is a fact about an **ORDER**. Because **order_date** has nothing to do with the primary key, it is not normalized. Answers a and c are incorrect because all the other attributes are facts about their respective entities and are normalized.

Question 4

Which table below has been incorrectly defined? [Check all correct answers]

❑ a. CREATE TABLE customers
(customer_id INTEGER NOT NULL UNIQUE ,
company_name VARCHAR(20)
DEFAULT 'UNKNOWN' NOT NULL ,
address VARCHAR(30) NULL ,
city VARCHAR(20) NULL ,
state CHAR(2) NULL ,
zip CHAR(5) NULL ,
CHECK (state IN
('ME' , 'NH' , 'VT' , 'MA' , 'CT' , 'RI')))

❑ b. CREATE TABLE products
(product_id INTEGER,
product_name VARCHAR(15),
qty_on_hand INTEGER,
order_date DATETIME,
description VARCHAR(100)
CONSTRAINT prod_pk PRIMARY KEY (product_id))

❑ c. CREATE TABLE loans
(loan_id INTEGER NOT NULL ,
cust_id INTEGER NOT NULL ,
loan_type INTEGER NOT NULL ,
approval_date DATETIME NOT NULL ,
amount MONEY NOT NULL ,
balance MONEY NOT NULL ,
CONSTRAINT loan_pk
PRIMARY KEY (loan_id, cust_id) ,
CONSTRAINT cust_loan_fk
FOREIGN KEY (cust_id) ,
REFERENCES customers (cust_id))
/* the PK in Customer is cust_id */

This is a nasty, trick question. First, you need to very carefully examine the code to find the problem. Then, because each definition is incorrect, answers a, b, and c are all correct answers to this question. In answer a, the **CONSTRAINT** keyword and the constraint name are missing from the **CHECK** clause. In answer b, though it is not good practice to omit the **NULL** or **NOT NULL**, SQL Server will default to **NOT NULL**; however, what's more important, the comma is missing after the last column definition. In answer c, it is okay to have a composite primary key, and it is okay that one of those columns is a foreign key; however, there is an extra comma after the foreign key column and before the **REFERENCES** keyword.

Question 5

An order has any number of line items. Each line item is associated with a product being ordered. A line item can be uniquely identified by the combination of an order number, product number, and line number. Each line item is associated with an order. If an order is removed from the system, we also remove its line items. If a product is removed from the system, we keep its line items for historical analysis. Assume that the primary key of **ORDERS** is **order_id**, and the primary key of **PRODUCTS** is **product_id**. Which of the following single table definitions implements this design?

○ a.
```
CREATE TABLE line_items
  ( order_id INTEGER NOT NULL ,
    product_id INTEGER NOT NULL ,
    line_num INTEGER NOT NULL ,
    quantity INTEGER DEFAULT 0 NOT NULL ,
    ship_date DATETIME NOT NULL ,
    CONSTRAINT li_pk PRIMARY KEY
      (order_id, product_id, line_num) ,
    CONSTRAINT ord_li_fk FOREIGN KEY (order_id)
            REFERENCES orders (order_id)
            ON DELETE CASCADE ,
    CONSTRAINT prod_li_fk
        FOREIGN KEY (product_id)
          REFERENCES products (product_id) )
```

(continued)

Question 5 (continued)

```
○ b. CREATE TABLE line_items
      ( order_id INTEGER NOT NULL ,
        product_id INTEGER NULL ,
        line_num INTEGER NOT NULL ,
        quantity INTEGER DEFAULT 0 NOT NULL ,
        ship_date DATETIME NOT NULL ,
        CONSTRAINT li_pk PRIMARY KEY
            (order_id, product_id, line_num) ,
        CONSTRAINT ord_li_fk FOREIGN KEY (order_id)
                REFERENCES orders (order_id)
                ON DELETE CASCADE )


○ c. CREATE TABLE line_items
      ( order_id INTEGER NOT NULL ,
        product_id INTEGER NOT NULL ,
        line_num INTEGER NOT NULL ,
        quantity INTEGER DEFAULT 0 NOT NULL ,
        ship_date DATETIME NOT NULL ,
        CONSTRAINT li_pk PRIMARY KEY
            (order_id, product_id, line_num) ,
        CONSTRAINT ord_li_fk FOREIGN KEY (order_id)
                REFERENCES orders (order_id) ,
        CONSTRAINT prod_li_fk
            FOREIGN KEY (product_id)
                REFERENCES products (product_id)
                ON DELETE CASCADE )
```

Answer b is correct. **ON DELETE CASCADE** implements the rule that when an order is removed, the line items are removed. Per the original question, when products are removed, we must keep the line items. This means that a line item is allowed to exist without a parent product, so no constraint is defined for the product relationship. Additionally, if the line item has no associated product, the **product_id** will be **NULL**, so the **product_id** is defined to be **NULL** allowed.

Question 6

Which of the following statements regarding BCP is *false*? [Check all correct answers]

❏ a. BCP is a high-performance data-loading mechanism.

❏ b. BCP has interactive and programmable interfaces.

❏ c. BCP is a valuable utility for a data warehouse that requires periodic massive data loads.

❏ d. BCP is a valuable tool for transaction processing environments that require periodic archival of transaction data.

❏ e. None of the above are false.

Answer e is correct. All of these statements are true.

Question 7

Consider the three queries:

```
SELECT *    /* Query 1 */
FROM customers c , orders o
WHERE c.cust_id = o.cust_id
AND c.company_name = 'ACME'

SELECT *    /* Query 2 */
FROM product p , line_items li , orders o
WHERE p.product_id = li.product_id
AND li.order_id = o.order_id
AND o.order_total > 2

SELECT *    /* Query 3 */
FROM orders o, line_items li
WHERE o.order_id = li.order_id
AND o.order_date = '22-APR-99'
```

Which indexes on **ORDERS** will most assist these queries? [Check all correct answers]

❑ a. CREATE CLUSTERED INDEX ON orders (order_id, cust_id)

❑ b. CREATE CLUSTERED INDEX ON line_items (cust_id, order_id)

❑ c. CREATE INDEX ON orders (order_date)

❑ d. CREATE INDEX ON orders (order_total)

Answers a, b, and c are correct. Query 1 will benefit most from index b because both the **cust_id** and **order_id** are available, and for the given customer, all the customer's orders will be physically next to one another. Query 2 will benefit most from index a because it needs the **order_id**; the **cust_id** portion of this index will not be used for this query, but that's okay (this is called index coverage). Query 3 will benefit most from index a and index c. Answer d is incorrect because query 2 will likely *not* benefit from index d; the majority of all records could have an **order_total** greater than two dollars, so the index will not be useful because all the pages need to be searched.

Need To Know More?

 Forta, Ben. *SAMS Teach Yourself SQL in 10 Minutes*. SAMS Publishing, Indianapolis, IN, 1999. ISBN: 0-672-31664-1. This book is easy to read and provides the right level of detail for an application developer.

 McEwan, Bennett William, and David Solomon. *Transact-SQL in 21 Days*. SAMS, Indianapolis IN, 1997. ISBN: 0-672-31045-7. This book provides a good introduction to Transact-SQL at the right level of detail.

 Otey, Michael, and Paul Conte. *SQL Server 7 Developer's Guide*. Osborne McGraw-Hill, Berkely, CA, 1999. ISBN: 0-07-882548-2. This book is half database administrator's manual and half developer's primer. It is easy to read, well organized, and has some good examples. Whether you're a DBA or a developer, this is a good book to own.

 Taylor, Allen G. *SQL For Dummies*. IDG Books Worldwide, Foster City, CA, 1998. ISBN: 0-7645-0415-0. This book is a good introduction to SQL, and its treatment of joins is first-rate.

 www.microsoft.com/backoffice/sql lets you download Microsoft SQL Server 7 evaluation software and peruse SQL Server books online.

Data Services

Terms you'll need to understand:

√ Open Database Connectivity (ODBC)

√ Data Access Objects (DAO)

√ Remote Data Objects (RDO)

√ Universal Data Access (UDA)

√ The Microsoft Data Access Components (MDAC)

√ ActiveX Data Objects (ADO)

√ OLE DB

Techniques you'll need to master:

√ Determining the appropriate database access model (ODBC, DAO, RDO, or ADO) to use in your application

√ Describing the role of ADO in applications that require database access

√ Describing the ADO programming model

√ Describing the role of OLE DB in applications that require database access

√ Describing the roles of ODBC, ADO, and OLE DB as they relate to MDAC

√ Using ADO controls in a C++ program

√ Implementing an application that uses ODBC

√ Implementing an application that uses ADO

√ Implementing an application that uses OLE DB

Many different database management systems (DBMSs) can be used with an application. Each DBMS comes with its own API (application programming interface). The benefit of a native interface is that a developer can take advantage of the special features of a particular DBMS. The shortcoming is that the developer must learn a different API for each DBMS. Therefore, the decision as to which DBMS will be used with an application is driven more by familiarity than by price, performance, and support. In addition, after a DBMS is selected, it's difficult to change to another one. SQL, which is used in more than 100 software products, was an attempt to standardize the database programming interface. However, because the SQL specification is only a guideline, each vendor—in an effort to differentiate its product from the competition's—provides its own unique flavor of SQL. To allow standardized access to many different database systems, Microsoft has, over the years, introduced a number of application layers, such as Visual Basic SQL (VBSQL), Open Database Connectivity (ODBC), Data Access Objects (DAO), and Remote Data Objects (RDO).

In the past, organizations used databases and mainframes to store their data. Today, however, an organization's data might also be found in file systems, in mail stores, in Web-based text, and more. Universal Data Access (UDA), shown in Figure 10.1, is Microsoft's strategy for providing access to this information, no matter where it might be—from the desktop to the enterprise. Microsoft Data Access Components (MDAC) are a collection of the key technologies that Microsoft is using to deliver UDA. These components are as follows:

➤ *OLE (Object Linking and Embedding) DB*—An open specification for a set of COM-based low-level system interfaces designed for both relational and nonrelational information sources. Everything that is specific to a data source is hidden by the OLE DB interface and represented in a general format that an application can always access in the same manner. OLE DB is the foundation of the UDA architecture.

➤ *ADO*—An open specification for a set of COM-based application-level interfaces designed to support a variety of development needs. ADO uses OLE DB to access the data. ADO presents developers with an interface that is easy to use and that will feel comfortable to developers familiar with DAO or RDO.

➤ *ODBC*—A proven API that makes it possible for an application to access relational data from a variety of database management systems.

Because Microsoft wants to eventually replace DAO and RDO with ADO, it is encouraging customers and developers to move to OLE DB and ADO. ODBC is part of MDAC, which provides backward compatibility. This chapter covers ODBC, ADO, and OLE DB.

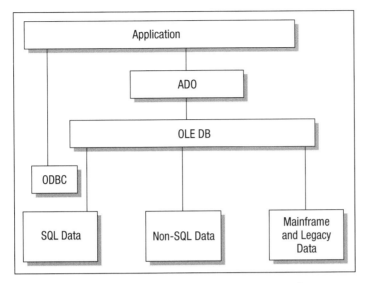

Figure 10.1   The Universal Data Access (UDA) architecture.

In the short term, you will probably need to understand DAO and RDO. Three key points to remember are:

➤ DAO is an object model for accessing local or SQL data through the Microsoft Jet database engine.

➤ RDO is an object model for accessing relational data through ODBC.

➤ Both are COM interfaces.

Open Database Connectivity

Open Database Connectivity (ODBC) was Microsoft's first cohesive effort to design an API that could be used by C programmers. ODBC provides its own flavor of SQL. The application passes ODBC SQL to ODBC, which translates the ODBC SQL into the flavor of SQL that is appropriate for the DBMS being used. ODBC is a proven interface that makes it possible for an application to access relational data from a variety of database management systems.

The ODBC architecture consists of a top-level driver manager (odbc32.dll) and many DBMS-specific DLLs, known as *drivers*. The driver manager loads and unloads the native drivers, receives requests from the application, and manages the subsequent driver actions. The driver handles the communication between the driver manager and the data source. See Figure 10.2.

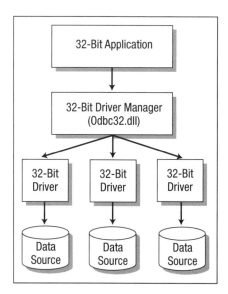

Figure 10.2 The ODBC architecture.

ODBC SDK Programming

You must know about and manage three key ODBC elements: the environment, the connection, and the statement. Each of these elements is accessed through *handles*. The *environment* establishes the link between your application and the ODBC system. The *connection* provides an association to a specific driver and a data source. The *statement* can be any valid SQL statement. Using the ODBC SDK consists of connecting to the data source; allocating a statement handle; preparing and executing an SQL statement; processing the data, which can involve database queries and database updates; committing or rolling back the transactions; and disconnecting from the data source.

Connecting To A Data Source

First, you must obtain an environment handle. You do this by calling **SQLAllocHandle()**. An application normally has only one environment handle. After you have an environment handle, you need to set the **SQL_ATTR_ ODBC_VERSION** environment attribute. You do this by calling **SQLSetEnvAttr()**. Next, you again call **SQLAllocHandle()**, but this time you're allocating a connection handle. Now, with all of the preliminaries out of the way, you call **SQLConnect()** to establish a connection. An environment can have multiple simultaneous connections.

Minus error checking, here's what the code might look like if you wanted to connect to the SQL Server **pubs** database:

```
SQLHENV hEnv = SQL_NULL_HENV;
SQLAllocHandle(SQL_HANDLE_ENV, SQL_NULL_HANDLE, &hEnv);
SQLSetEnvAttr(hEnv,
              SQL_ATTR_ODBC_VERSION,
              reinterpret_cast<SQLPOINTER>(SQL_OV_ODBC3),
              SQL_IS_INTEGER);
SQLHDBC hDBC = SQL_NULL_HDBC;
SQLAllocHandle(SQL_HANDLE_DBC, hEnv, &hDBC);
SQLConnect(hDBC,
      reinterpret_cast<SQLCHAR *>("pubs\0"), SQL_NTS,
      reinterpret_cast<SQLCHAR *>("sa\0"), SQL_NTS,
      reinterpret_cast<SQLCHAR *>("\0"), SQL_NTS);
```

SQLAllocHandle() is an ODBC 3 generic function that replaces the ODBC 2 functions **SQLAllocEnv()**, **SQLAllocConnect()**, and **SQLAllocStmt()**. All three of these functions can take an assortment of parameters. Use the "Platform SDK, Data Access Services" subset of the MSDN to familiarize yourself with these functions.

Allocating A Statement Handle

Think of a statement in ODBC as being an SQL statement with attributes. These attributes are stored in a structure to which a statement handle is pointing. Each statement requires its own handle and is associated with a single connection. The generic **SQLAllocHandle()** is used to allocate a statement handle, as shown here:

```
SQLHSTMT hSTMT = SQL_NULL_HSTMT;
SQLAllocHandle(SQL_HANDLE_STMT, hDBC, &hSTMT);
```

Preparing And Executing An SQL Statement

Now you have a number of choices. At runtime, you can choose to prepare and execute an SQL statement in a single step or to prepare it once and execute it multiple times. Other choices available are database stored procedures and driver functions that can be called. Here's an example of an SQL statement that is prepared and executed at runtime in a single step:

```
SQLExecDirect(hSTMT,
        reinterpret_cast<SQLCHAR *>("SELECT * FROM authors"),
        SQL_NTS);
```

The preceding SQL statement defines a query that returns a block of data, called a *rowset*. This rowset consists of all columns of all rows in the **authors** table.

Note: Visual Basic and Access use the term recordset instead of rowset. Probably to be consistent with VB and Access, much of the Visual C++ documentation also uses the term recordset. However, the VC++ documentation is not consistent, and both terms are used. The VC++ glossary makes a subtle distinction between them. It defines a rowset as "in ODBC, one or more rows returned by a single fetch operation," and it defines a recordset as "a set of records selected from a data source. The records can be from a table, a query, or a stored procedure that accesses one or more tables." The term result set is also used. It is defined as "a collection of data returned by an SQL query on a database."

Processing The Data

After the preceding SQL statement has been executed, you need to get the results. You have three options involving the use of **SQLBindCol()** and **SQLGetData()**. Assume that you don't want to bind each column in the result set to a program variable. You would first call **SQLFetch()** to retrieve a row of information and then call **SQLGetData()** from each data item you wish to retrieve. **SQLGetData()** copies the data from a specific result-set column to a specific program variable. Here's a snippet of code that retrieves the information and prints the first name, last name, and phone number for each entry in the **authors** table:

```
for(RETCODE rCode = SQLFetch(hSTMT);
    SQL_SUCCEEDED(rCode);
    rCode = SQLFetch(hSTMT))
{
  char szLastName[MAXLASTNAME];
  char szFirstName[MAXFIRSTNAME];
  char szPhone[MAXPHONE];
  SQLINTEGER len;
  SQLGetData(hSTMT, 2, SQL_C_CHAR,
             szLastName, MAXLASTNAME, &len);
  SQLGetData(hSTMT, 3, SQL_C_CHAR,
             szFirstName, MAXFIRSTNAME, &len);
  SQLGetData(hSTMT, 4, SQL_C_CHAR,
             szPhone, MAXPHONE, &len);
  Display(szFirstName, szLastName, szPhone);
}
```

Committing Or Rolling Back The Transactions

Because no statements were executed that would change the database, this step is not needed here. However, if you executed a statement that changed, deleted, or added data to the database, you would need to call **SQLEndTran()** to commit or roll back the transaction.

Disconnecting From The Data Source

After you are finished with the database, you need to disconnect and free all of the handles:

```
SQLFreeHandle(SQL_HANDLE_STMT, hSTMT);
SQLDisconnect(hDBC);
SQLFreeHandle(SQL_HANDLE_DBC, hDBC);
SQLFreeHandle(SQL_HANDLE_ENV, hEnv);
```

> *Note: SQLFreeHandle() is an ODBC 3 generic function that replaces the ODBC 2 functions SQLFreeEnv(), SQLFreeConnect(), and SQLFreeStmt().*

ODBC MFC Programming

MFC (Microsoft Foundation Classes) provides two wrapper classes for the ODBC API. The **CDatabase** class represents the database source, and the **CRecordset** class represents the data itself. Two other classes can also be used with ODBC MFC applications. **CDBException** objects are thrown by almost all of the **CDatabase** classes' member functions if an exception condition occurs. **CRecordView**, which is derived from **CView**, is directly connected to a **CRecordset** object and can display database records using dialog controls. All four classes are defined in afxdb.h.

The **CDatabase** Class

Although a **CDatabase** object can be used by itself, it is normally used with one or more **CRecordset** objects. Because a **CDatabase** class object represents a connection to a data source, very seldom will you need to derive a class from **CDatabase**. Here's a snippet of code that inserts a new author into the **pubs** database:

```
CDatabase db;
try
{
  db.Open(_T("ODBC;DSN=pubs;UID=sa;PWD="));
  db.ExecuteSQL(_T("INSERT INTO authors "
    "(au_id, au_lname, au_fname, phone, "
    "address, city, state, zip, contract)"
    "VALUES ('404-24-4472', 'James', 'Jesse', "
    "'908 840-4098', '1231 First Street', 'Boston', "
    "'MA', '01052', 1)"));
  db.Close();
}
```

```
catch(CDBException *pe)
{
  MessageBox(pe->m_strError, "Database Error");
  pe->Delete();
}
```

The **CRecordset** Class

A **CRecordset** object represents a set of records retrieved from a data source. The **CRecordset** class supports several types of recordsets, but two are generally used: snapshots and dynasets. A *snapshot* is a static picture of the data taken when the recordset was filled; a snapshot is not affected by changes made by other users of the data source. A *dynaset*, on the other hand, is dynamic; it stays synchronized with changes made by other users.

The easiest way to create a recordset class is to use the ClassWizard to generate a class. The ClassWizard will display the Database Options dialog box, shown in Figure 10.3, so that you can specify many of the characteristics that will be used to define your **CRecordset**-derived class. For this data source, two additional dialog boxes are displayed. The first lets you specify login information, and the second lets you select the data source.

After you have a **CRecordset**-derived class, you can use it to execute SQL statements against the data source. Here's a snippet of code that retrieves the **authors** table and displays the first name, last name, and phone number for each entry in the table:

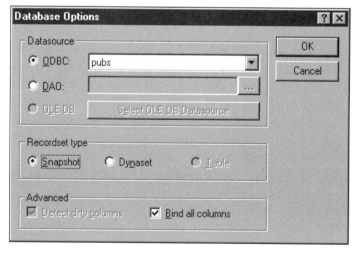

Figure 10.3   The Database Options dialog box.

```
CDatabase db;
try
{
  if(db.Open(_T("ODBC;DSN=pubs;UID=sa;PWD=")))
  {
    CAuthorsSet authorset(&db);
    authorset.Open(CRecordset::snapshot,
            _T("SELECT * FROM authors ORDER BY au_lname"));
    for( ; ! authorset.IsEOF(); authorset.MoveNext())
    {
      Display(authorset.m_au_fname,
              authorset.m_au_lname,
              authorset.m_phone);
    }
    db.Close();
  }
}
catch(CDBException *pe)
{
  MessageBox(pe->m_strError, "Database Error");
  pe->Delete();
}
```

The **CRecordset** class provides a number of features that make queries easier to perform. First, if you don't pass a **CDatabase** object to the **CRecordset** constructor, **CRecordset::Open()** will create a **CDatabase** object, call the **CRecordset** virtual function **GetDefaultConnect()** to get the data-source connection string, and then pass the string to **CDatabase::Open()**. The ClassWizard provides this function for your **CRecordset**-derived class. You might want to modify the ClassWizard-provided connect string to include the user ID and password.

The ClassWizard also provides your **CRecordset**-derived class with a **GetDefaultSQL()** function, which the framework calls. You can edit this function as you see fit. For example, you can use a **CALL** statement to specify a predefined query: {**CALL GetAuthorizationByUserID**}. When the ClassWizard generates your **CRecordset**-derived class, it provides a data member for each of the columns in the data source. These data members are tied to the corresponding columns in the data source by the **DoFieldExchange()** function. The framework calls this function to move data from the data source to your data members or vice versa. This partial implementation of a **CRecordset**-derived class is used to query the **authors** table for the first name, last name, and phone columns. Here's the code for this example:

```
CNameAndPhone::CNameAndPhone(CDatabase* pdb)
  : CRecordset(pdb)
{
  //{{AFX_FIELD_INIT(CNameAndPhone)
  m_au_lname = _T("");
  m_au_fname = _T("");
  m_phone = _T("");
  m_nFields = 3;
  //}}AFX_FIELD_INIT
  m_nDefaultType = snapshot;
}


CString CNameAndPhone::GetDefaultConnect()
{
  return _T("ODBC;DSN=pubs;uid=sa;pwd=");
}


CString CNameAndPhone::GetDefaultSQL()
{
  return _T("[dbo].[authors]");
}


void CNameAndPhone::DoFieldExchange(CFieldExchange* pFX)
{
  //{{AFX_FIELD_MAP(CNameAndPhone)
  pFX->SetFieldType(CFieldExchange::outputColumn);
  RFX_Text(pFX, _T("[au_lname]"), m_au_lname);
  RFX_Text(pFX, _T("[au_fname]"), m_au_fname);
  RFX_Text(pFX, _T("[phone]"), m_phone);
  //}}AFX_FIELD_MAP
}
```

The frequently used **CRecordset** data members are **m_strFilter** and **m_strSort**. These data members are used to specify, respectively, the selection criteria and how the records are to be sorted. Following is a snippet of code that returns the first name, last name, and phone number of the authors with an area code of 415. The recordset is sorted by last name in ascending alphabetical order.

```
try
{
  CNameAndPhone authorset;
  authorset.m_strFilter = "phone LIKE '415 %'";
  authorset.m_strSort = "au_lname ASC";
  authorset.Open();

  for( ; ! authorset.IsEOF(); authorset.MoveNext())
```

```
  {
    Display(authorset.m_au_fname,
            authorset.m_au_lname,
            authorset.m_phone);
  }
}
catch(CDBException *pe)
{
  MessageBox(pe->m_strError, "Database Error");
  pe->Delete();
}
```

ActiveX Data Objects

ActiveX Data Objects (ADO) are a collection of dual-interface objects used to connect to and manipulate data. The ADO model, shown in Figure 10.4, consists of seven objects (**Connection, Command, Recordset, Error, Property, Parameter,** and **Field**) and four collections (**Errors, Properties, Parameters,** and **Fields**), making it fairly simple to understand. ADO is housed in

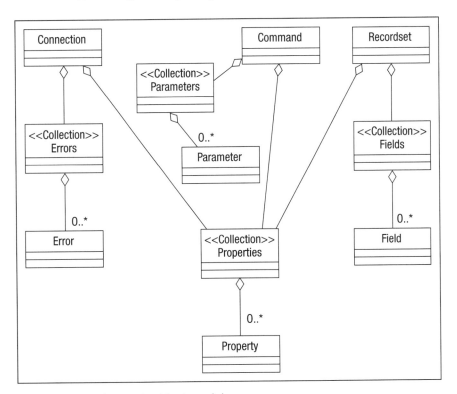

Figure 10.4   The ADO object model.

msado15.dll and has a type library that you can view with the OLE/COM Object Viewer. See Figure 10.5.

> *Note: As of this writing, the MDAC 2.5 SDK Beta documentation indicates that two additional objects will be added to the model: **Record** and **Stream**.*

You bring ADO into your program by using the **#import** directive, like this:

```
#import "c:\Program Files\Common Files\System\ADO\msado15.dll"
```

The type library contained in msado15.dll is defined in the ADODB namespace. If you want, you can place it in another namespace by using the **rename_namespace** attribute. Or you can use the **no_namespace** attribute, which tells the compiler to not generate a namespace at all.

The preceding **#import** statement has a potential problem. The type-library header generated will contain a definition of EOF, which will conflict with an EOF definition in ios.h. To avoid this conflict, you need to use the **rename** attribute. Here's one possible way you might change the **#import** directive:

```
#import "C:\Program Files\Common Files\system\ado\MSADO15.DLL" \
    rename_namespace("ADOCG") rename("EOF", "EndOfFile")
using namespace ADOCG;
```

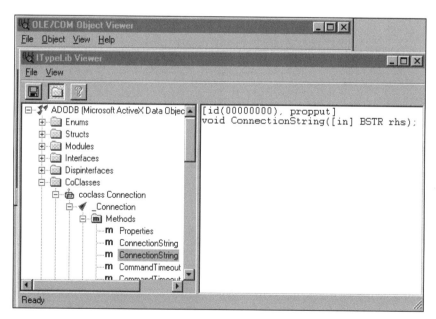

Figure 10.5   Viewing the ADO type library.

The **Connection** Object

The **Connection** object has one primary purpose: to manage a physical connection to the database. With the **Connection** object, you can access simple nonrelational data, such as files on a server, or more robust data, such as a relational database. The **Connection** object allows you to:

➤ Open a connection to a data source.

➤ Execute SQL statements or database stored procedures.

➤ Establish transactions for data updates.

Although it's not required that you establish a connection first, it's usually the wise thing to do because significant overhead is involved in connecting to a data source. Creating the **Connection** object is very simple when you use the type-library–produced smart pointer. You only have to declare a smart pointer and pass the **Connection** object's **CLSID** into its constructor:

```
_ConnectionPtr spConn(__uuidof(Connection));
```

To initiate the connection, you call **Open()**, passing a connection string to specify the data source, the user ID, and the password required for the connection. The connection string can be as simple as the ODBC data source name, or it can contain extra parameters separated by semicolons. For example, to connect to an SQL Server database named **Development** located on a server named **Appleseed**, you could use the following string:

```
"driver={SQL Server};server=Appleseed;database=Development"
```

When you are finished with the data source connection, you simply call **Close()**. When the smart pointer goes out of scope, it will release the **Connection** object. The **Connection** object's methods are described in Table 10.1.

The **Connection** object's **Execute()** method is used to directly execute a query and return a minimally featured **Recordset** object. The method prototype (taken from .tlh) looks like this:

```
_RecordsetPtr Execute (_bstr_t CommandText,
                       VARIANT * RecordsAffected,
                       long Options );
```

CommandText is an SQL statement, table name, stored procedure, or some other provider-specific command text. **RecordsAffected** returns the number of records that were affected by the command. (It returns −1 if an error occurred.) **Options** indicates how the provider should evaluate the **CommandText** argument. It can be one or more of **CommandTypeEnum** or **ExecuteOptionEnum** values.

Table 10.1   The Connection object's methods.

Method	Description
BeginTrans	Assists in transaction management. Use this method when you want to group a series of data-source changes into a single unit.
Cancel	Cancels the current asynchronous operation (**Execute()** or **Open()**).
CommitTrans	Assists in transaction management. Use this method to make permanent all changes within the current transaction.
Execute	Executes a **Connection** object's command directly.
Open	Establishes the connection to the data source.
OpenSchema	Returns schema information, such as table structures, from the database.
RollbackTrans	Assists in transaction management. Use this method to undo all changes within the current transaction.

The possible values for **CommandTypeEnum** are as follows:

➤ **adCmdUnspecified**—Not specified.

➤ **adCmdUnknown**—An unknown command type (default).

➤ **adCmdText**—A simple SQL command or query.

➤ **adCmdTable**—A database table name.

➤ **adCmdStoredProc**—A database stored procedure.

➤ **adCmdFile**—The name of a file that is a persistent recordset.

➤ **adCmdTableDirect**— A table with all columns selected.

The possible values for **ExecuteOptionEnum** are as follows:

➤ **adOptionUnspecified**—How the provider should execute the command is unspecified.

➤ **adAsyncExecute**—Indicates that the command should execute asynchronously.

➤ **adAsyncFetch**—After the initial rows are fetched, the remaining rows will be fetched asynchronously.

➤ **adAsyncFetchNonBlocking**—The main thread will never block.

➤ **adExecuteNoRecords**—Discards the recordset normally returned from Execute().

The **Connection** object's properties are described in Table 10.2.

Here's a snippet of code that uses a smart pointer to create a **Connection** object and then opens the **pubs** database:

```
_ConnectionPtr spConn(__uuidof(Connection));
spConn->ConnectionString = "Data Source=pubs;uid=sa;pwd=";
spConn->Open("", "", "", adConnectUnspecified);
```

Rather than using the **ConnectionString** property, the information can be passed as arguments, like so:

```
spConn->Open("pubs",                    // Using a DSN
             "sa",                      // User ID
             "",                        // Password
             adConnectUnspecified);     // Options
```

The last parameter can be one of two values: **adConnectUnspecified** opens the connection synchronously, and **adAsyncConnect** opens it asynchronously.

Table 10.2 The Connection object's properties.	
Property	**Description**
Attributes	Used to change the type of transactions used in the session.
CommandTimeout	Specifies the number of seconds to wait before a command times out and generates an error. The default is 30 seconds.
ConnectionTimeout	Specifies the number of seconds to wait before a connection attempt times out and generates an error. The default is 15 seconds.
ConnectionString	The session's connection string.
CursorLocation	Indicates whether recordset cursors (indicating the current record) should reside with the client or with the server. The default is **adUseServer**, which specifies that the server will manage the cursor. For large recordsets, this is more efficient, and the cursor is more sensitive to changes made by other users. The value **adUseClient** specifies that the local (client-side) cursor will be used. The local cursor provides the most flexibility of the two.

(continued)

Table 10.2	The Connection object's properties (continued).
Property	**Description**
DefaultDatabase	Indicates the default database of a connection. This property is not available with all OLE DB providers.
IsolationLevel	An enumerated value that lets you change the isolation level. The most frequently used values are **adXactCursorStability**, which specifies that your transaction can't see the uncommitted changes of other transactions, and **adXactChaos**, which specifies that your transaction can't overwrite pending changes of more highly isolated cursors. Other values are **adXactUnspecified, adXactReadUncommitted, adXactBrowse, adXactReadCommitted, adXactRepeatableRead, adXactIsolated**, and **adXactSerializable**.
Mode	An enumerated value that lets you set (or find) a set of permissions. The possible values are **adModeUnknown, adModeRead, adModeWrite, adModeReadWrite, adModeShareDenyRead, adModeShareDenyWrite, adModeShareExclusive, adModeShareDenyNone**, and **adModeRecursive**.
State	Indicates the state of the connection, such as open (**adStateOpen**) or closed (**adStateClosed**).
Version	The ADO version.

The **Command** Object

The **Command** object is one of the most useful ADO objects. With it you can do a number of necessary and powerful tasks. For instance, you can do the following:

➤ Execute SQL statements or stored procedures.

➤ Define and execute repetitive SQL commands that require a set of SQL parameters.

➤ Use a **Command** object to source a recordset.

You must set some properties before you can execute a command; others are optional. Table 10.3 describes the **Command** object's properties.

The **Command** object has several methods, and, like the **Connection** object, it has an **Execute()** method. However, their signatures are different. Look at the

Table 10.3   The Command object's properties.

Property	Description
ActiveConnection	A mandatory pointer to the **Connection** object associated with the current session.
CommandText	A mandatory text string that contains the SQL statement to be executed. **CommandText** can also be a table name, a stored procedure, or some other command recognized by the data provider.
CommandTimeout	Specifies how many seconds the command can execute before generating an error. A value of zero specifies that there is no timeout. Defaults to 30 seconds.
CommandType	A value that describes the type of command that the **CommandText** property contains. The possible value can be one or more **CommandTypeEnum** values and **adExecuteNoRecords** from the **ExecuteOptionEnum**. Refer to the **Connection** object's **Execute()** method in Table 10.1.
Name	Indicates a name for a command.
Parameters	A pointer to the **Parameters** collection, which can be used to set up SQL parameters for the command.
Prepared	True causes the data provider to prepare (compile) the command on the first invocation and then use the compiled command subsequently.
State	Indicates the object's current state. **adStateClosed** indicates that the object is closed, whereas **adStateOpen** indicates that it is open. **adStateConnecting** indicates that the object is connecting, and **adStateExecuting** indicates that an asynchronously executing command is still executing. **adStateFetching** indicates that the rows of the object are being fetched. The **State** property can have a combination of values. The default state is **adStateClosed**.

Connection object's Execute() method, shown previously, and compare it to the following prototype for the Command object's Execute() method:

```
_RecordsetPtr Execute(VARIANT * RecordsAffected,
                      VARIANT * Parameters,
                      long Options );
```

The first parameter, **RecordsAffected**, is used to receive the number of rows affected by the command. The second parameter is used to pass an array of SQL parameters stored in a **Variant**-filled **SafeArray** wrapped by a **Variant**. Setting this up is not trivial. Fortunately, an easier method exists. First, store each parameter in a **Parameter** object and add the **Parameter** objects to the **Command** object's **Parameters** collection object. Then, pass **NULL** as the second parameter, indicating that the parameters to the SQL statement are to be taken from the **Parameters** collection object. (The **Parameters** collection object and the **Parameter** object are discussed next.)

In case you didn't set the **CommandType** property, you can use the last parameter to indicate the command type. The value can be one or more of **CommandTypeEnum** or **ExecuteOptionEnum** values.

The **Parameters** Collection And The **Parameter** Object

A **Parameter** object is used to specify information about the data transferred to or from the data source when your command object is executed. Suppose you have the following query:

```
SELECT * FROM authors WHERE state = ?
```

The question mark is a placeholder for a parameter to be supplied as a property of a **Command** object, as seen in this example:

```
_CommandPtr spCmd("ADODB.Command");
spCmd->ActiveConnection = spConn;
spCmd->CommandText = "SELECT * from authors WHERE state = ?";

_ParameterPtr spState = spCmd->CreateParameter("state",
                                               adChar,
                                               adParamInput,
                                               2,
                                               "KS");
spCmd->Parameters->Append(spState);
```

First, using a smart pointer, you create a **Command** object, and then you assign the active connection. Next, the query statement is stored in the **Command** object's **CommandText** property. After that, a **Parameter** object is created and added to the **Command** object's **Parameters** collection with the **Append()** method.

The **Command** object's **CreateParameter()** method takes five arguments. Its prototype looks like this:

```
_ParameterPtr CreateParameter (
        _bstr_t Name,
        enum DataTypeEnum Type,
        enum ParameterDirectionEnum Direction,
        long Size,
        const _variant_t & Value = vtMissing );
```

The **Parameters** collection has two other methods besides **Append()**. One is **Delete()**, which does just what its name indicates. The other, **Refresh()**, tells ADO to examine both the query and the database to determine what data type to use.

The **Parameters** collection has only two properties: **Count** and **Item**. **Count** contains the number of **Parameter** objects that the collection contains, and **Item** is an array that contains the **Parameter** objects.

The **Parameter** object has only one method: **AppendChunk()**. The first time you call this method, any data in the **Parameter** object is overwritten. Subsequent calls add data to the end of the existing data. You use this method to fill the **Parameter** object with a large binary object. Be sure that the **Attributes** property has **adParamLong** set before you use **AppendChunk()**. The **Parameter** object's properties are described in Table 10.4.

Table 10.4 The Parameter object's properties.	
Property	**Description**
Attributes	Describes whether the parameter can be **NULL** (**adParamNullable**), signed (**adParamSigned**), or long binary object (**adParamLong**).
Direction	Specifies the direction of transfer or specifies whether the parameter is a return value. Can be **adParamInput**, **adParamOutput**, **adParamInputOutput**, or **adReturnValue**.
Name	Indicates a name for a parameter.

(continued)

Table 10.4 The Parameter object's properties (continued).	
Property	**Description**
NumericScale	Indicates the number of digits to the right of the decimal place.
Precision	Indicates the number of digits used to represent a numeric value.
Size	Indicates the maximum size of the parameter.
Type	An enumerated value that specifies the type of data. Common types are **adBinary**, **adBoolean**, **adBSTR**, **adChar**, **adCurrency**, **adGUID**, **adDBTimeStamp**, **adDouble**, **adNumeric**, **adInteger**, **adVarChar**, and **adWChar**.
Value	Indicates the actual value held by the parameter.

The **Recordset** Object

Although you can carry out all your database operations using discrete SQL statements, doing so would become very laborious. Instead, use the ADO **Recordset** object, which is specifically designed to manipulate data held in a data source. The **Recordset** object—the most robust of all the ADO objects—represents a set of records from the data provider. This object provides the ability to scroll through the records, as well as add, edit, and delete them. Each record consists of one or more fields. If the data source is a database, then the records represent table rows and the fields represent columns.

The **Recordset** object works by retrieving records and then letting you manipulate each specific record indicated by a cursor position. You can access a record's data by using the **Recordset** object's **Fields** collection. ADO provides four types of recordset cursors; each type affects the way that your data is updated. A **CursorTypeEnum** value specifies the cursor type. Table 10.5 describes the four cursor types.

Make sure you understand the various cursors. If you wererepresented with a set of requirements, be sure you'd be able to select a cursor type.

The **Recordset** object has a number of properties and methods. Table 10.6 presents the **Recordset** object's key properties, and Table 10.10 presents some of the more common methods. Table 10.7 describes the **FilterGroupEnum** values, Table 10.8 describes the **LockTypeEnum** values, and Table 10.9 describes the **RecordStatusEnum** values.

Table 10.5   ADO cursor types.

Cursor Type	CursorTypeEnum	Description
Dynamic	**adOpenDynamic**	Allows unrestricted movement through the recordset. You can add, modify, or delete records. Records added, modified, or deleted by other users are visible. Depending on the data provider, you may or may not be able to use bookmarks. A bookmark allows you to easily and quickly move to a row.
Keyset	**adOpenKeyset**	Similar to dynamic. Changes made by other users are incorporated into your recordset, but additions and deletions aren't.
Forward	**adOpenForwardOnly**	Identical to dynamic, except it allows only forward movement through the records. This speeds up access to the data. This is the default cursor type.
Static	**adOpenStatic**	Allows you to add, modify, or delete records. However, changes made by other users are not visible.

Table 10.6   The Recordset object's properties.

Property	Description
BOF	If true, the current cursor position is at the start of the recordset. If there are no records, BOF is still true.
Bookmark	Identifies the current cursor position. You can save a bookmark in a variable and then later use it to quickly return to that record after moving to a different record.
CursorLocation	Sets the client-side or server-side cursor (**adUseClient** or **adUseServer**).
CursorType	Sets the recordset type. Must be one of the **CursorTypeEnum** values specified in Table 10.5.

(continued)

Table 10.6 The Recordset object's properties (continued).

Property	Description
EditMode	Indicates the current record's editing mode: **adEditNone, adEditInProgress, adEditAdd**, or **adEditDelete**.
EOF	If true, the current cursor position is at the end of the recordset. If there are no records, EOF is still true. You will normally need to rename this property in the **#import** directive. **EndOfFile** and **adoEOF** are commonly used.
Fields	Accesses the **Fields** collection for manipulating the data in the current record.
Filter	Allows you to specify which records in a recordset can become current. You can use a filter such as "state = 'CA' or state = 'OR'" to cause only records meeting the criterion to be displayed. You can also set **Filter** to one of the **FilterGroupEnum** values shown in Table 10.7.
LockType	Sets the type of record locking by using one of the **LockTypeEnum** values shown in Table 10.8.
MaxRecords	Limits the maximum number of records retrieved.
RecordCount	Returns the number of records in the recordset. Will be −1 if ADO cannot determine the number of records.
Sort	Allows you to sort the recordset by any field after retrieval. You can optionally use **ASC** or **DESC** to specify the sort order. The default sort order is ascending.
Source	Contains the source of the data, such as the **SQL SELECT** statement or the name of the stored procedure.
State	Indicates the current state of the recordset. It can be any of the **ObjectStateEnum** values: **adStateClosed, adStateOpen, adStateConnecting, adStateExecuting**, or **adStateFetching**.
Status	Returns a combination of **RecordStatusEnum** values. Refer to Table 10.9.

Table 10.7   The FilterGroupEnum values.

Value	Description
adFilterNone	Removes all filtering.
adFilterPendingRecords	Used to view only records changed but not yet saved to the server. Used only in batch mode.
adFilterAffectedRecords	Used to view only records affected by the last **CancelBatch**, **Delete**, **Resync**, or **UpdateBatch** method.
adFilterFetchedRecords	Used to view only the most recently cached records.
adFilterConflictingRecords	Used to view only records that failed the last **UpdateBatch** attempt.

The **Filter** and **Sort** properties affect the data in the recordset; they don't modify the SQL statement. The **Filter** property is not the same as the SQL **WHERE** clause, nor is the **Sort** property the same as the SQL **ORDER BY** clause.

Table 10.8   The LockTypeEnum values.

Value	Description
adLockReadOnly	The data can't be altered. This is the default.
adLockPessimistic	The record is locked as soon as you start to edit it.
adLockOptimistic	The record is locked only as it is sent back to the database.
adLockBatchOptimistic	The records are locked when a batch of records is updated.

Be sure you understand the different locking types. Give special attention to **adLockPessimistic** and **adLockOptimistic**. Know when the lock starts and when it's released.

Table 10.9 The RecordStatusEnum values.

Value	Description
adRecOK	The record was successfully updated.
adRecNew	The record is new.
adRecModified	The record was modified.
adRecDeleted	The record was deleted.
adRecUnmodified	The record was not modified.
adRecInvalid	Because its bookmark is invalid, the record was not saved.
adRecMultipleChanges	Because it would have affected multiple records, the record was not saved.
adRecPendingChanges	Because it refers to a pending insert, the record was not saved.
adRecCanceled	Because the operation was canceled, the record was not saved.
adRecCantRelease	Because of existing record locks, the record was not saved.
adRecConcurrencyViolation	Because optimistic concurrency was in use, the record was not saved.
adRecIntegrityViolation	Because the user violated integrity constraints, the record was not saved.
adRecMaxChangesExceeded	Because there were too many pending changes, the record was not saved.
adRecObjectOpen	Because of a conflict with an open storage object, the record was not saved.
adRecOutOfMemory	Because the computer ran out of memory, the record was not saved.
adRecPermissionDenied	Because the user has insufficient permissions, the record was not saved.
adRecSchemaViolation	Because it violates the structure of the underlying database, the record was not saved.
adRecDBDeleted	The record has already been deleted.

Table 10.10   The Recordset object's methods.

Method	Description
AddNew	Adds a new record. You can optionally specify some or all of the **Fields** and **Values** arguments.
CancelUpdate	Cancels pending changes.
Clone	Creates a copy of a recordset.
Close	Closes the **Recordset** object.
Delete	Deletes the current record. Pass it to **adAffectGroup** to delete all the records that meet the current **Filter** criteria.
Find	Starting at the current record, searches for a record that satisfies the specified criteria. The criteria are specified in a valid SQL **WHERE** clause.
Move	Allows you to move an absolute number of records forward or backward.
MoveFirst	Allows you to move to the first record in the recordset.
MoveLast	Allows you to move to the last record in the recordset.
MoveNext	Allows you to move forward by one record in the recordset.
MovePrevious	Allows you to move backward by one record in the recordset.
Requery	Refreshes the recordset by reissuing the query.
Resync	Refreshes the recordset to reflect the changes made by any other users.
Save	Allows you to persist the recordset (save it to a file).
Update	Saves changes made to the current record. As with the **AddNew** method, you can optionally set values by using the **Fields** and **Values** arguments.

The **Fields** Collection And The **Field** Object

Each recordset has a **Fields** collection that contains **Field** objects. Each **Field** object represents an individual field in the recordset. The **Field** object contains basic information about the field, such as value, data type, and size. The **Field** object has only two methods: **GetChunk** and **AppendChunk**. Both are used to manipulate long binary data. The **Field** object's properties are described in Table 10.11.

When you create a new **Recordset** object, its **Fields** collection will be empty. **Field** objects can then be appended to the **Fields** collection. This will happen automatically when you call the **Recordset** object's **Open()** method. You can also append **Field** objects programmatically by calling the **Fields** collection's **Append()** method. Before calling **Append()**, you must set the **Recordset** object's **CursorLocation** property to **adUseClient**.

In addition to the **Append()** method, the **Fields** collection has two other methods: **Delete()** and **Refresh()**. The **Fields** collection has two properties: **Count** and **Item**.

Table 10.11 The Field object's properties.	
Property	**Description**
ActualSize	Returns the number of bytes actually stored in the **Field** object.
Attributes	Describes characteristics of the **Field** object. The **Attributes** property can hold one or more **FieldAttributeEnum** values.
DefinedSize	Returns the maximum number of bytes that can be stored in the **Field** object.
Name	Provides the name of the field as stored in the database or as specified in the command that retrieved the data.
NumericScale	Indicates the number of digits to the right of the decimal place.
OriginalValue	Contains the value of **Field** when first retrieved from the database.
Precision	Indicates the number of digits used to represent a numeric value.
Type	Contains one of the **DataTypeEnum** values.
UnderlyingValue	Returns the current data value.
Value	Indicates the actual value held by the **Field** object.

The **Recordset** object and its associated **Fields** collection provide you with a flexible data structure that you can use for buffering and saving (persisting) data, which can really simplify the task of moving legacy data, stored in flat files, into a database.

Here's a snippet of code that opens a recordset on a client-side cursor. The code then sorts the records by last name in ascending alphabetical order. Finally, it moves through the recordset one record at a time and displays the first name, last name, and phone number for each of the authors in the recordset.

```
_RecordsetPtr spRs(__uuidof(Recordset));
spRs->CursorLocation = adUseClient;
spRs->Open((IDispatch *) spCmd, vtMissing,
       adOpenStatic, adLockBatchOptimistic, adCmdUnspecified);

spRs->Sort = "au_lname ASC";

for(spRs->MoveFirst(); !spRs->EndOfFile; spRs->MoveNext())
{
   _bstr_t bstrFirstName =
             spRs->GetFields()->GetItem("au_fname")->Value;

   _bstr_t bstrLastName =
             spRs->GetFields()->GetItem("au_lname")->Value;

   _bstr_t bstrPhone =
             spRs->GetFields()->GetItem("phone")->Value;
   Display(bstrFirstName, bstrLastName, bstrPhone);
}
```

Exceptions And Error Processing

Most database operations are capable of throwing a number of errors. ADO stores each of these errors in the **Errors** collection. You can obtain these errors from your **Connection** object by calling the **GetErrors()** method. After you have the **Errors** collection object, you can iterate through the **Error** objects. The **Error** object has several properties and no methods. The properties are described in Table 10.12.

The **Description** and **Number** properties are probably the most useful because you can use them to find out what caused the error and then take the appropriate action. Here's an example of how you might catch and report errors:

Table 10.12	The Error object's properties.
Property	**Description**
Description	A text description of the error.
HelpContextID	A context ID identifying the help topic.
HelpFile	A Windows help file associated with the error.
NativeError	Specifies the data provider's own error number.
Number	A unique numeric error code.
Source	The name of the object that caused the error.
SQLState	Corresponds to the ODBC SQL state, as documented in the ANSI SQL standards.

```
...
_ConnectionPtr spConn(__uuidof(Connection));
  try
  {
    // your code goes here
  }
  catch (_com_error &e)
  {
    DumpComError(e);
    DumpADOError(spConn->GetErrors());
  }

  // more code here

void DumpComError(_com_error &e)
{
  cout << "\nCOM Error:\nCode = " << hex << e.Error()
       << "\nCode meaning = " << e.ErrorMessage()
       << "\nSource = "
       << static_cast<LPCSTR>(e.Source())
       << "\nDescription = "
       << static_cast<LPCSTR>(e.Description())
       << endl;
}

void DumpADOError(ErrorsPtr spErrors)
{
  for(int i = 0; i < spErrors->GetCount(); i++)
  {
    _variant_t vtItem((long) i);
    ErrorPtr spError(spErrors->Item[vtItem]);
```

```
   cout << "\nADO Error:\nCode = "
        << hex << spError->GetNumber()
        << "\nSource = "
        << static_cast<LPCSTR>(spError->GetSource())
        << "\nDescription = "
        << static_cast<LPCSTR>(spError->GetDescription())
        << endl;
   }
   cout << endl;
}
```

OLE DB

OLE DB is the underpinning of UDA. OLE DB is the protocol used to communicate with a data source, whether it's a relational database or a nonrelational source, such as a spreadsheet, a flat file, or an email message. OLE DB components are one of two basic types: data providers and data consumers. An OLE DB data provider retrieves information from a data source and returns it to a data consumer in a usable tabular form. Each data provider is written to provide access to a particular data source. An OLE DB data consumer is an application or COM component that uses a specific data provider to access information regardless of where it is stored.

Another OLE DB component is the service provider. This is a hybrid component that acts as a consumer of raw OLE DB data sources and as a provider to other OLE DB components. As a middleman, a service provider can supply functionality that extends a data provider. When a data consumer requests some functionality that a data provider doesn't support, the Service Component Manager will automatically step in and invoke the proper service component.

OLE DB consists of eight COM objects:

➤ **Enumerator** objects

➤ **Data Source** objects

➤ **Session** objects

➤ **Command** objects

➤ **Rowset** objects

➤ **View** objects

➤ **Transaction** objects

➤ **Error** objects

For each of these COM objects, OLE DB defines a cotype. A *cotype* defines a group of COM objects that have similar characteristics. Each cotype specifies a set of mandatory interfaces that must be exposed, as well as a set of optional interfaces.

The **Enumerator** Object

The **Enumerator** object allows you to traverse the Registry for provider-specific information. The OLE DB SDK provides an enumerator, known as the *root enumerator*, that allows you to locate and retrieve information regarding the OLE DB providers on your system. The **CLSID** of this root enumerator is **CLSID_OLEDB_ENUMERATOR**. Alternatively, the MSDASQL enumerator (**CLSID_MSDASQL_ENUMERATOR**) will search for ODBC data sources. All enumerators are of the cotype TEnumerator, which must expose the interfaces described in Table 10.13.

The **Data Source** Object

The **Data Source** object does just what you think: It provides a session in which a data consumer can connect to a data repository via a data provider. You can create the **Data Source** object by calling **CoCreateInstance()** or by binding a moniker returned by an **Enumerator** object. Table 10.14 presents the required interfaces exposed by the TDataSource cotype.

The **Session** Object

The **Session** object provides a context for transactions and commands. The **Session** object can be used to create a rowset. Additionally, depending on the interfaces supported, a **Session** object can be used to create a **Command** object, to create or modify tables and indexes, and to create various other objects. Table 10.15 presents the required interfaces exposed by the TSession cotype.

Table 10.13 The TEnumerator cotype's mandatory interfaces.	
Interface	**Description**
IParseDisplayName	Used to convert a displayable name string to a moniker. Provides one method: **ParseDisplayName()**.
ISourcesRowset	Used to access rowset data from data sources and enumerators. Provides one method: **GetSourcesRowset()**.

Table 10.14 The TDataSource cotype's mandatory interfaces.	
Interface	**Description**
IDBCreateSession	Creates a new session with a data source, which provides a mechanism for creating commands and rowsets. Provides one method: **CreateSession()**.
IDBInitialize	Provides two methods, **Initialize()** and **Uninitialize()**, which do just what their names imply—they initialize and uninitialize a data source object.
IDBProperties	Used to get and set the properties of a data source object. Provides three methods: **GetProperties()**, **GetPropertyInfo()**, and **SetProperties()**.
IPersist	The base interface for other persist-type interfaces, such as **IPersistStream** and **IPersistFile**.

Table 10.15 The TSession cotype's mandatory interfaces.	
Interface	**Description**
IGetDataSource	Used to access a data source object. Provides one method: **GetDataSource()**.
IOpenRowset	Used to access a rowset from a data source that doesn't support commands. Provides one method: **OpenRowset()**.
ISessionProperties	Used to get and set the properties of a Session object. Provides two methods: **GetProperties()** and **SetProperties()**.

The **Command** Object

Command objects perform commands that the provider supports—for example, SQL statements. OLE DB data providers are not required to support commands. Table 10.16 presents the required interfaces exposed by the TCommand cotype.

The **Rowset** Object

The **Rowset** object is used to provide access to data-source data in a tabular form. A *rowset* is a set of rows in which each row has fields or columns of data. Table 10.17 presents the required interfaces exposed by the TRowset cotype.

Table 10.16 The TCommand cotype's mandatory interfaces.	
Interface	**Description**
IAccessor	Used to manage the buffer in which retrieved rowsets or command parameters are stored. Provides four methods: **AddRefAccessor()**, **CreateAccessor()**, **GetBindings()**, and **ReleaseAccessor()**.
IColumnsInfo	Used to get information about the rowset's columns. Provides two methods: **GetColumnInfo()** and **MapColumnIDs()**.
ICommand	Used to execute and manage executing commands. Provides three methods: **Cancel()**, **Execute()**, and **GetDBSession()**.
ICommandProperties	Used to get and set properties for the command. Provides two methods: **GetProperties()** and **SetProperties()**, which you can use to get and set the properties on the rowset.
ICommandText	Used to get and set the actual command text, which specifies the data source command to execute. Provides two methods: **GetCommandText()** and **SetCommandText()**.
IConvertType	Used to find out if a command can convert data types. Provides one method: **CanConvert()**.

The **View** Object

The **View** object allows providers to expose simple operations, such as sorting or filtering. The TView cotype is only required to expose one interface: **IColumnsInfo**. Refer to Table 10.16 for a description of the **IColumnsInfo** interface.

Transactions

A *transaction* is an atomic unit of work. Transactions control the operations on a data source. All of the operations in a transaction must be completed successfully or the transaction fails. A transaction starts before an operation begins and ends when the changes to the data source are committed or aborted. Table 10.18 presents the required interfaces exposed by the TTransaction cotype.

The **Session** object can also provide support for transactions by exposing any of four optional interfaces: **ITransaction, ITransactionJoin, ITransactionLocal**, and **ITransactionObject**.

Table 10.17	The TRowset cotype's mandatory interfaces.
Interface	**Description**
IAccessor	Used to manage the buffer in which retrieved rowsets or command parameters are stored. Provides four methods: **AddRefAccessor()**, **CreateAccessor()**, **GetBindings()**, and **ReleaseAccessor()**.
IColumnsInfo	Used to get information about the rowset's columns. Provides two methods: **GetColumnInfo()** and **MapColumnIDs()**.
IConvertType	Used to find out if a command can convert data types. Provides one method: **CanConvert()**.
IRowset	Used to access rowsets and the data they contain. Provides five methods: **AddRefRows()**, **GetData()**, **GetNextRows()**, **ReleaseRows()**, and **RestartPosition()**.
IRowsetInfo	Used to obtain information about a rowset, such as how many modifications can be buffered. Provides three methods: **GetProperties()**, **GetReferencedRowset ()**, and **GetSpecification()**.

Table 10.18	The TTransaction cotype's mandatory interfaces.
Interface	**Description**
IConnectionPointContainer	A standard COM interface that is used when connecting data to other COM objects. Provides two methods: **EnumConnectionPoints()** and **FindConnectionPoint()**.
ITransaction	Used to control a transaction: It commits transactions, aborts transactions, and obtains the current transaction status. Provides three methods: **Abort()**, **Commit()**, and **GetTransactionInfo()**.

The **ITransactionJoin** interface supports distributed transactions. It can be used to retrieve distributed transaction options and to join a distributed transaction. It has two methods: **GetOptionsObject()** and **JoinTransaction()**.

The **ITransactionLocal** interface can be used to start a transaction or to specify transaction options. **ITransactionLocal** supports two methods: **StartTransaction()** and **GetOptionsObject()**. The **GetOptionsObject()** method retrieves a pointer to the **ITransactionOptions** interface. This interface is used to get and set transaction-level options. The **ITransactionOptions** interface provides two methods: **GetOptions()** and **SetOptions()**.

Error Handling

For many of the OLE DB objects, the **ISupportErrorInfo** interface is an optional interface. If it's supported, the client can use it to determine if the **IErrorInfo** interface is supported. The **IErrorInfo** interface is a generic COM interface that can be used to retrieve extended information about a single error. However, OLE DB needs to provide addition error information that can't be provided by the **IErrorInfo** interface. OLE DB needs to return provider-error information and multiple error values simultaneously. To accomplish this, OLE DB defines three additional interfaces: **IErrorLookup**, **IErrorRecords**, and **ISQLErrorInfo**.

➤ The **IErrorLookup** interface is mandatory for all data providers that return OLE DB error objects. The **IErrorLookup** interface provides three methods: **GetErrorDescription()**, **GetHelpInfo()**, and **ReleaseErrors()**.

➤ The **IErrorRecords** interface is used to manage multiple errors. It provides six methods: **AddErrorRecord()**, **GetBasicErrorInfo()**, **GetCustomErrorObject ()**, **GetErrorInfo()**, **GetErrorParameters()**, and **GetRecordCount()**.

➤ The **ISQLErrorInfo** interface is used to retrieve SQL state and native error codes. This interface has one method: **GetSQLInfo()**.

Developing OLE DB data consumers by using the SDK can be a daunting task. However, developing an OLE DB data consumer with either MFC or ATL is remarkably easy. In fact, it's easier than building ADO clients, because both MFC and ATL provide wizards to help you with OLE DB data consumers, but not with ADO clients.

Be sure you can use MFC and ATL to develop an OLE DB data consumer. Also, you should be able to use ATL to build an OLE DB data provider.

Practice Questions

Question 1

Which of the following methods opens a transaction?

○ a. **ITransaction::Open()**

○ b. **ISession::BeginTrans()**

○ c. **ITransactionLocal::StartTransaction()**

○ d. **ICommand::StartTransaction()**

Answer c is correct. The **ITransactionLocal::StartTransaction()** method begins a set of operations that will be enveloped by a transaction. The transaction ends when either the **ITransaction::Commit()** method or the **ITransaction::Abort()** method is invoked. Answers a, b, and d are incorrect because they are not valid methods.

Question 2

Which of the following statements are true? [Check all correct answers]

❑ a. RDO is an object model for accessing local and SQL data through Microsoft Jet.

❑ b. The MDAC toolkit includes DAO, ADO, OLE DB, and ODBC.

❑ c. ADO is an object model for accessing all types of data through OLE DB.

❑ d. DAO is an object model for accessing relational data through ODBC.

Answer c is correct. ADO is a collection of COM objects that use OLE DB to access relational and nonrelational data. Answer a is incorrect because RDO accesses data through ODBC, not through Microsoft Jet. Answer b is incorrect because MDAC consists of the latest versions of ADO, OLE DB, and ODBC, as well as ODBC drivers and OLE DB providers. DAO is not part of MDAC. Answer d is incorrect because DAO accesses data through Microsoft Jet, not through ODBC. This is a trick question because you are told to check all correct answers, but only one answer is correct.

Question 3

You are writing an OLE DB consumer application. After calling **ICommandText::SetCommandText()**, which of the following macros can you use to check the returned **HRESULT** value? [Check all correct answers]

- ❑ a. **INVALID**
- ❑ b. **SUCCEEDED**
- ❑ c. **ISERROR**
- ❑ d. **FAILED**

Answers b and d are correct. The **SUCCEEDED** and **FAILED** macros provide generic tests on any **HRESULT** value. These two macros are the only two that provide this functionality. Answers a and c are incorrect because they are not valid COM macros.

Question 4

Assume that you are developing a geophysical application and you need to store a number of large bitmaps in the database. Which ADO method would you use?

- ○ a. **AppendBlob()**
- ○ b. **PutData()**
- ○ c. **AppendChunk()**
- ○ d. **AppendLongBinary()**

Answer c is correct. The **AppendChunk()** method is used to store large binary objects in a **Field** object. Answers a, b, and d are incorrect because they are not valid methods.

Question 5

Which of the following ADO objects have an **Open()** method? [Check all correct answers]

- ❑ a. **Connection**
- ❑ b. **Command**
- ❑ c. **Recordset**
- ❑ d. **Field**

Answers a and c are correct. Answer a is correct because the **Connection** object's **Open()** method is used to open a connection to a data source. Answer c is correct because the **Recordset** object's **Open()** method is used to open a cursor that represents records of a data source. Answer b is incorrect because the **Command** object is used to define a command that can be executed against a data source. Answer d is incorrect because a **Field** represents a column of data.

Question 6

> Which of the following are valid ways to populate an ADO **Recordset** object? [Check all correct answers]
>
> ❏ a. Pass an SQL statement to the **Recordset** object's **Open()** method.
>
> ❏ b. Pass an SQL statement to the **Connection** object's **Open()** method.
>
> ❏ c. Store an SQL statement in the **Command** object's **CommandText** property and then call its **Execute()** method.
>
> ❏ d. Store an SQL statement in the **Recordset** object's **Source** property and then call its **Execute()** method.

Answers a and c are correct. The **Recordset** object's **Open()** method and the **Execute()** method for either the **Command** object or the **Connection** object can be used to populate a **Recordset** object. The method you use depends on the type of recordset you wish to create. For example, when calling the **Recordset** object's **Open()** method, you can pass it an SQL statement, a table name, a stored procedure call, a valid **Command** object, or even a URL. You can also pass it a string, in which case it will use the **Source** property, which must contain a string or a valid **Command** object. When calling the **Connection** object's **Execute()** method, you can pass it the same things you can pass to the **Recordset** object's **Open()** method, plus you can pass it provider-specific text to execute. The **Command** object's **Execute()** method always executes what is stored in the **CommandText** property, which can be an SQL statement or any other type of command statement recognized by the provider.

Answer b is incorrect because you cannot pass an SQL statement to the **Connection** object's **Open()** method. Answer d is incorrect because the **Recordset** object doesn't have an **Execute()** method. However, it does have a **Source** property, which is used with its **Open()** method as described in the previous paragraph.

Question 7

Which of the following are valid ADO collections? [Check all correct answers]

❑ a. **Field**

❑ b. **Parameters**

❑ c. **Properties**

❑ d. **Connections**

Answers b and c are correct. **Parameters** and **Properties** are valid collections (as are **Errors** and **Fields**). Answer a is incorrect because **Fields** is the collection, not **Field**. Answer d is incorrect because **Connection** is a standalone object; **Connections** does not exist.

Question 8

Which of the following statements are true? [Check all correct answers]

❑ a. ATL's **CDataSource** class represents a logical connection to a data source.

❑ b. ATL's **CTable** class can be used instead of SQL commands to insert, delete, and modify rows in a database.

❑ c. ATL's **CCommand** class can be used to execute an SQL command.

❑ d. ATL's **CSession** class represents a physical connection to a data source.

All answers are correct. This question is a trick because all of the answers are correct.

Need To Know More?

 Esposito, Dino. "With Further ADO: Coding Active Data Objects 2.0 with Visual Studio 6.0." *Microsoft Systems Journal,* February 1999. This is a well-written article that provides a good overview of ADO and quite a bit of detail on the **Recordset** object.

 Kruglinski, David J., George Shepherd, and Scot Wingo. *Programming Microsoft Visual C++, 5th ed.* Microsoft Press, Redmond, WA, 1998. ISBN 1-57231-857-0. Chapter 32 provides good introductory coverage of ODBC with MFC. If you are interested in DAO, Chapter 32 provides a good introduction.

 Robison, Lyn. *Teach Yourself Database Programming with Visual C++ 6 in 21 Days.* Sams Publishing, Indianapolis, IN, 1999. ISBN 0-672-31350-2. This is a well-written book that does a good job of showing how to use Visual C++ to write database programs. It's easy to follow, and the example code works. It's a good introductory book to get you started.

 Sussman, Dave. *ADO 2.1 Programmer's Reference.* Wrox Press Ltd., Birmingham, UK, 1999. ISBN 1861002688. This is a handy reference book to own. It's well organized and easy to use. Each of the major ADO objects is given its own chapter. Although, like Microsoft's online documentation, all code in the book is in Visual Basic, it provides a convenient source of information on methods, properties, and **enum** values.

 MSDN Library, Platform SDK\Data Access Services\Microsoft Data Access Components (MDAC) SDK\Microsoft ActiveX Data Objects (ADO). This provides the best coverage of ADO that I know about. The Programmer's Reference provides a good description of the features and is a very good API reference. A number of good samples are provided, and there is a tutorial to get the beginner started. Although the API reference is aimed at a Visual Basic programmer, there are sample programs for VC++.

 MSDN Library, Platform SDK\Data Access Services\Microsoft Data Access Components (MDAC) SDK\Microsoft Data Access Technical Articles. This subset of the MSDN Library provides a number of good articles. It includes articles on ODBC, UDA, ADO, and OLE DB.

MSDN Library\Technical Articles. There are a number of good articles on UDA and ADO. Many of them are somewhat dated, but because they deal mostly with strategy more than with implementation, they are still relevant.

 www.microsoft.com/data, Microsoft's Universal Data Access Web site, provides a wealth of information on ODBC, ADO, and OLE DB. You'll find links to articles, sample code, and downloads to the most current releases of the MDAC components.

Debugging And Testing Your Application

Terms you'll need to understand:

√ Breakpoint

√ Memory leak

√ Assertion

√ Exception

√ Unit test

√ Regression test

√ Integration test

√ Stress test

Techniques you'll need to master:

√ Building a debug version of your program

√ Using the debug libraries to locate memory leaks

√ Performing remote debugging

√ Understanding the differences between unit, integration, regression, stress, and beta testing

Congratulations are in order when you reach the point when you're ready to start debugging your project. From the perspective of the four-step process—design, code, debug, and test—it may appear that you're halfway to delivering a product. If it were only that simple. Just be thankful that you probably have to deal only with 32-bit operating systems. This chapter will lead you through a review of some debug topics that you're probably already familiar with and perhaps a few that are new.

Debugging And The IDE

The Visual C++ application incorporates a powerful debugging environment. The debugger supports the various executable forms that the development environment can create, including DLLs and COM components.

Creating A Debug Build

The first step in debugging an application is creating a debug build of the project. A *debug build* generally is different from a *release build* in two ways: the debug build contains symbolic debug information; and the compiler does not optimize the code.

The following characteristics generally apply to debug builds of your program:

➤ Compiler optimization is not enabled.

➤ The _DEBUG symbol is defined.

➤ Your program is linked with debug versions of the runtime and/or MFC libraries.

➤ Symbolic debugging information is produced for the project.

Commands Used In Debugging

The Visual C++ IDE (Integrated Development Environment) incorporates a sophisticated source-level debugger. This debugger has a graphical user interface, offering windows, menus, and toolbars. In addition, direct interaction between UI components is supported with drag-and-drop capability. Thus, memory-address locations may be dragged among Watch, Variable, and Memory windows.

When you're debugging your application, you'll use the following commands:

➤ *Go*—Begins the debugging process. This process continues to the end of the program, until a breakpoint is encountered, or until you issue the break command from the debugger to suspend execution.

➤ *Step Over*—This is the most common debug command, allowing you to proceed to the next statement.

➤ *Step Into/Out*—Instructs the debugger to enter the pending function or step out of the function.

➤ *Run To Cursor*—Similar to the Go command, this command instructs the debugger to stop at the cursor location.

Windows In The Visual C++ Debugger

The Visual C++ Debugger is composed of a number of windows. Each window can either float within the IDE frame window or be docked in almost any configuration imaginable.

Registers

The Registers window is not displayed by default when you first debug a project. After it's displayed, however, it becomes part of your project settings for your debug session and is subsequently displayed for future debugging. You can directly edit register values by typing over the displayed contents. You can also drag register contents to the Watch or Memory windows for viewing.

 You can change the **EIP** (instruction pointer) register during a debugging session to jump around code you do not wish to execute. The return value of a function is often placed in the **EAX** register. You may change this value and affect program flow accordingly.

Although it is technically not a register, the Visual C++ debugger offers a *pseudoregister*, labeled **ERR**, to view the last error code for the current thread. Enter this label in a Watch window, using the **hr** format specifier, as shown:

```
ERR, hr
```

Memory

The Memory window allows you to view the contents of large portions of contiguous memory. This is useful when you want to inspect large character buffers or string contents. The default is to view the memory contents in base 10; however, you can set an option to view the buffer as Unicode.

Watch

The Watch window consists of four tab views into which you may either type the name of variables to display or drag variable labels from other debug windows. The debugger allows you to supply a format argument to ease interpretation of watch variables.

 Variables and expressions in the Watch window can operate on any variable or object that is in scope. The syntax for formatting a variable requires you to place a comma and then the format symbol after the variable. Hence, the line

```
result, hr
```

formats the variable named **result** as an **HRESULT**. A value of 0x00000000L will appear as the "decoded" text **S_OK**. Similarly, formatting a variable with the Window message flag will display a 0x000F value as **WM_PAINT**.

The following list summarizes common Watch formatting codes.

➤ **d,i**—Signed decimal integer

➤ **u**—Unsigned decimal integer

➤ **o**—Unsigned octal integer

➤ **x,X**—Hexadecimal integer

➤ **l,h**—Long or short prefix for: d, i, u, o, x, X

➤ **f**—Signed floating-point numeric

➤ **e**—Signed scientific notation

➤ **g**—Signed floating-point numeric or signed scientific notation, whichever is shorter

➤ **c**—Single character

➤ **s**—String

➤ **su**—Unicode string

➤ **st**—Unicode string or ANSI string, depending on Unicode Strings setting in autoexp.dat

➤ **hr**—**HRESULT** or Win32 error code

➤ **wc**—Window class flag

➤ **wm**—Windows message numbers

The autoexp.dat file contains rules for expanding variables in the Data Tips, Variable, and Watch windows.

QuickWatch

The QuickWatch window is a valuable tool when you don't want to occupy screen real estate with a docked Watch window. This window is similar to the Watch window except that the QuickWatch window can display only a single variable or evaluate only a single expression.

Disassembly

The Disassembly window can be used to view the optimizations that may cause problems in release builds and that are not seen in nonoptimized debug projects. Additionally, you may step between statements that appear on a single line of C/C++ source code.

Call Stack

The Call Stack window displays those functions through which the program has entered and not yet returned.

 The Call Stack window allows you to set breakpoints by using exactly the same commands as in the editor.

Variables

The Variables window is a tabbed display that contains a view to variables that are in scope. The tabs further classify context variables in the following manner:

➤ *Auto*—Displays variables for the previous and current statement. This is the default view.

➤ *Locals*—Displays all variables that have context for the current function.

➤ *This*—Displays only class variables.

Output

The Output window includes Build, Debug, Results, and SQL Debugging tab views. To navigate quickly to the lines that contain compiler errors or warnings, you can double-click on the build entry. In addition, you can click on build error numbers in the Output window and display a description of the error by pressing F1.

Data Tips

The Visual C++ IDE allows you to "hover" over variables and expressions to display a pop-up window containing the appropriate values. This feature is available when you have stopped at a breakpoint and the values and expressions are in scope.

Threads

A thread management dialog box is available from the Debug menu and is available if your project is multithreaded. Using the Threads dialog box, you can set focus on a thread and suspend and resume thread operations.

File Types Used In Debugging

Two file types are instrumental in debugging your project; these are the program database files and the debug files.

The debug (.dbg) files that Visual C++ creates are in the Portable Executable (PE) format. In addition to CodeView information, this file also contains COFF (Common Object File Format) and FPO (Frame Pointer Optimization) symbol data.

The program database (.pdb) file contains the following information:

➤ Debugging data

➤ Project state information

➤ Incremental link data

The **AfxDumpStack** Function

The **AfxDumpStack** function is new to Visual C++ 6. This function allows you to obtain stack information about misbehaving MFC programs built in release mode and without the need for a debugger. This function sounds like a programmer's dream come true, and it is, considering how easy it is to implement. The function accepts a single argument, indicating the target, and its function prototype appears here:

```
void AFXAPI AfxDumpStack(DWORD dwTarget =
AFX_STACK_DUMP_TARGET_DEFAULT);
```

The **dwTarget** argument is defined as any of the following constants (combinations of these options may be supplied using the bitwise-**OR** operation):

➤ AFX_STACK_DUMP_TARGET_DEFAULT—This is the default value defined in the function prototype, sending dump output to the default output context. The output for debug builds utilizes the **TRACE** macro, whereas release builds utilize the clipboard.

➤ AFX_STACK_DUMP_TARGET_TRACE—This option directs all output to the **TRACE** macro for both release and debug builds. Thus, there is no output context for release builds because **TRACE** is ignored.

➤ AFX_STACK_DUMP_TARGET_CLIPBOARD—Output is always directed to the clipboard by using the **CF_TEXT** format.

➤ AFX_STACK_DUMP_TARGET_BOTH—This option provides dump information to both the clipboard and the **TRACE** macro.

➤ AFX_STACK_DUMP_TARGET_ODS—The ODS abbreviation identifies the **OutputDebugString** Win32 function. This option supplies debug information to both release and debug builds, either of which may be attached to a debugger.

For each stack entry that this method generates, the following information will be provided:

➤ The return address of the last function call

➤ The module and full path containing the function

➤ The function's prototype

➤ The offset in bytes from the function prototype to the return address

> *Note: To function properly, this feature requires the imagehlp.dll file to be installed; otherwise, an error message will be displayed when this function is called.*

Edit And Continue

New to Visual C++ 6 is the Edit And Continue debug option. As the name says, you can change your code while debugging and then continue running (or debugging) your program on the fly. To use this feature, you must be running your project in the debugger; however, your program need not be stopped in the debugger. Use the editor to change the code as necessary (see the limitations below), and then select the Apply Code Changes option from the Debug menu. The Output window will display output similar to the following:

```
Compiling...
mfc.cpp
Applying Code Changes...
Edit and Continue - 0 error(s), 0 warning(s)
```

Assuming that you receive no errors, your program will execute according to the changes you implemented.

Although Edit And Continue is a powerful extension of the development environment, it will not allow you to perform every code change you want and still be able to continue executing your program. Here are the limitations of the Edit And Continue option:

➤ Exception handling blocks cannot be modified.

➤ You cannot change data types or introduce new data types.

➤ You cannot remove or change function prototypes.

➤ Changes are not permitted on global or static code.

➤ You cannot make changes to resource and read-only files.

➤ You cannot change code using any optimization settings, including /O1, /O2, /Og, /Ox, /Ob1, and /Ob2.

Breakpoints

A *breakpoint* pauses execution of a program in the debugger. When the program is paused, the current stack, registers, and function variables may be inspected and/or modified.

 If you are having problems setting breakpoints or they are not behaving as expected, you might want to check the procedures and operations covered in this section.

A breakpoint can be set from source only if its symbolic data is available to the debugger. First, make sure that the code you are attempting to debug was compiled with the debug flag or that you have symbolic information available. Second, if the code is contained in a DLL or ActiveX component, the symbolic information might not be loaded yet. Specify additional DLLs and COM servers in the Additional DLLs field of the Debug Options dialog box.

You should already be familiar with common breakpoint operations, including those in which a variable or expression changes value. However, it may be important to review some advanced breakpoint settings, especially those set from the Data tab:

➤ *Array Element*—To break when any element in an array changes, enter the *first* element of the array in the Expression field and enter the number of elements in the Number Of Elements field.

➤ *Pointer*—To break at the address pointed to by a pointer requires a de-reference of the pointer name in the Expression field, whereas the location value of a pointer simply requires the pointer's name.

➤ *Conditional Breakpoints*—Using the Conditional Breakpoints option, you may debug conditions in which a function fails after succeeding many times prior. You can set the Skip Count value to indicate the number of times the debugger passes over the breakpoint before stopping.

The Breakpoint dialog box also supports breaking at specific memory addresses, and a specific **WndProc** receives designated Windows messages.

COFF And Exports

The default setting for the Visual C++ debugger is to utilize debug information in a CodeView-compatible format. However, the debugger offers debug support to programs that provide either COFF or Export information, as follows:

➤ *COFF*—The COFF debug format is used by other debuggers.

➤ *Export*—Symbolic information may be acquired by analyzing the export tables of a DLL.

The Debug tab of the Options dialog box provides a Load COFF & Exports checkbox to enable this feature.

Just-In-Time Debugging

The Just-In-Time debug option refers to the ability to debug a program that you are not currently working on in the Visual C++ environment. When an application faults on your computer, the Visual C++ debugger will be started automatically. This option is available from the Debug command in the Tools menu.

Symbols

The _DEBUG symbol is defined when the /Mtd or /Mdd compiler options are specified. Code blocks that appear between **#ifdef _DEBUG** and **#endif** are compiled.

Debugging Strategies

Describing all of the ways a developer can wreak havoc inside a program's process space would consume too many pages, so I have narrowed the list to some of the more common programming errors and ways to debug them.

Detecting MFC Memory Leaks

A *memory leak* occurs when heap memory is allocated and then is not deallocated before the program ends. Although it is normally simple to identify those cases that allocate memory in your program's **InitInstance** function and free the memory in **ExitInstance**, memory that is continually recycled during program operation can be difficult to track and cause you to exhaust the heap.

Tracking memory allocation in MFC programs can be made simpler, and the wizards do this for you automatically by defining the **DEBUG_NEW** macro, as shown here:

```
#define new DEBUG_NEW
```

By defining the macro at the top of your source files, you can track the file and line number of each allocation. Use the **DumpAllObjectsSince** function to output all of the objects that are currently allocated. MFC uses the same debug heap and memory allocator as the C runtime library does.

Although identifying memory allocations may be appropriate for some situations, MFC offers more powerful functions—**Checkpoint** and **Difference**—to build on memory tracking and help pinpoint leaks. Used in conjunction with the **CMemoryState** object, these functions allow you to take a "snapshot" of memory and identify memory allocation differences at a later time.

Assertions

Many programmers place assertion statements at the top of their functions under the assumption that the arguments that are being passed exist and/or are correct according to some constraint. For instance, if a function is designed to draw a line, and one argument is a handle to a device context (hDC), an **AS-SERT** statement may be placed at the top of the function verifying that a non-**NULL** value is passed in. **ASSERT** statements that fail result in the display of a message box. Visual C++ supports three general categories of **ASSERT** statements:

➤ C runtime library **ASSERT** statements

➤ MFC **ASSERT** macros

➤ ANSI C/C++ **ASSERT** functions

Any flavor of assertion compiles only when the **_DEBUG** flag is defined. Otherwise, the compiler treats the assertion as a null statement, introducing no additional overhead.

Common uses for ASSERT statements include:

➤ Verifying input parameters

➤ Testing for error conditions

➤ Validating operation results

Programs that employ objects that derive from **CObject** can benefit from the use of an **ASSERT_VALID** macro. This macro checks the object's internal consistency; as with the traditional **ASSERT** statements, this statement has no effect in a release build. MFC offers programmers an **ASSERT** statement that outputs file and line-number information when an expression evaluates to zero.

The **VERIFY** macro is similar to the MFC **ASSERT** macro, with the exception that the **VERIFY** macro evaluates the expression in release builds as well as in debug builds.

Threads

The Threads command in the Debug menu opens the Threads dialog box. Using this dialog box, you can set focus on a thread and suspend or resume thread execution.

Exceptions

Execution of code outside the normal flow of control identifies an exception. By default, the Visual C++ debugger writes exception messages to the Output window. However, your program is not halted unless a handler is not provided for the exception. The Exceptions dialog box—available from the Tools menu—allows you to specify either of two states—Stop Always or Stop If Not Handled—for nearly 30 exception conditions.

Debugging Without The Project

It is possible to debug both DLLs and EXEs even if you don't have the project or workspace in which they were built. As long as you have the source code for the module you are trying to debug, the steps to debug DLLs and EXEs are essentially the same. A temporary workspace is created when you debug in this manner. You have the option of saving the project settings when you leave Visual C++.

Debugging An EXE

To begin debugging an executable, choose Open or Open Workspace from the File menu and select the executable you wish to debug. The executable should have been compiled with debug information that resides either in the EXE or in a program database file. Activate the debugger in the same manner you would if you had a project workspace: Choose Start Debug from the Build menu, or click on the Go button in the Debug toolbar.

Debugging A DLL

To begin debugging a DLL, choose Open or Open Workspace from the File menu. Specify the executable you want to load the DLL using the Executable For Debug Session field in the Debug tab of the Project Settings dialog box. Choose Start Debug from the Debug menu.

Remote Debugging

Visual C++ supports a debug mode called *remote debugging*. Using this option, you can run the program that is being debugged on one computer while the IDE debugging the application runs on a different computer. You might want to use this mode for the following reasons: The failure that is being flushed out is not present on the debug machine; the target machine doesn't possess the resources to run the IDE; a local IDE interferes with the UI; or the target machine is in a different locale but is visible on a LAN.

The target machine—the one that is going to run the program being debugged (not the debugger)—must have access to the msvcmon.exe utility. This utility provides a dialog box in which you identify the debugging host.

The machine that contains the Visual C++ IDE must have the Debugger Remote Connection specified from the Build menu. In addition, you must identify the target machine. The debugger's Go command will cause the application being tested to launch on the target machine.

Active Process Debugging

It is possible to attach the Visual C++ debugger to any process running locally on the machine, including services, although you have to have the proper permissions. From the Build menu, choose the Start Debug option, which displays a submenu containing four items; one of these submenu items is Attach To Process. Choosing this option displays an Attach To Process dialog box, containing a list of processes and (optionally) system processes running on the computer. Selecting a process and clicking on the OK button is all that is required to begin a debugging session.

Debugging SQL Code

Visual C++ offers a debugging environment for client/server and n-tier solutions. The Enterprise edition of Visual C++ provides the ability to debug SQL Server stored procedures. Before debugging SQL code, you must have a number of DLLs and executables installed (and in the path) on both the client and server machines.

On the server machine, you need the following installed:

➤ autprx32.dll

➤ autmgr32.exe

➤ sdi50.dll

On the client machine, you need the following installed:

➤ autmgr32.exe

➤ autprx32.dll

Upon installation of these files, a client may trace calls made to SQL Server via ODBC or DBLib connections. The debugger will automatically step into and out of SQL Server code at the appropriate points while debugging your application.

The following limitations apply to debugging SQL:

➤ SQL statements must reside in a stored procedure.

➤ Expression breakpoints and other advanced breakpoints cannot be applied.

➤ A Data View must be present in the current workspace.

➤ SQL memory windows are not supported.

➤ Extended stored procedure (DLL) debugging is not supported.

➤ Modification to cached values or stored procedures is not allowed.

Debugging ActiveX Controls

Although ActiveX controls may be debugged in the Visual C++ IDE, the Test Container utility that Microsoft provides is a perfect example of a container application to use to exercise your control. Menus are provided to invoke methods, change properties, and fire events on your control.

If you are on the other side of the fence, writing an ActiveX container, your job is simpler because you can debug the container as you would any MFC application.

Debugging Optimized Code

A number of compiler options are available to optimize code. During this process, the compiler rearranges machine instructions to make better use of the processor's available registers and/or to attempt to produce code that can remain in cache.

Although you should make every attempt to debug code that has not been optimized, there are situations in which optimization can result in runtime errors. In such cases, it is recommended that you:

➤ Use the /Zi compiler switch to obtain symbolic information of variable names and types, as well as function and line numbers.

➤ Display the Registers and Disassembly windows to set breakpoints and analyze the resulting machine code for the best place to set breakpoints.

Debugging DLLs

When debugging a DLL, you might encounter different debug configurations. These include:

➤ *Calling program and DLL projects and source*—Load the calling program's project and set breakpoints in the DLL as you normally would for the project. If you load the DLL dynamically, you must specify the DLL by using the Additional DLLs field in the Debug Options dialog box.

➤ *DLL project and source*—You must fill in the Executable For Debug Session field in the Debug Options dialog box.

The Debug Heap

When you're writing C++ code, there is nothing more tedious than keeping track of memory allocation and release with the **new** and **delete** commands. For C++ projects, defining the **_CRTDBG_MAP_ALLOC** symbol will direct heap functions to their corresponding debug versions, outputting source file and line number information.

The debug heap adds some overhead in both performance and resource consumption by performing various overwrite checks and allocating more memory than that which was requested. The compiler "marks" memory on either side of an allocation request with a *no man's land*, filling this area with 0xFD bytes. An operation that causes a memory overrun will venture into this marked area, thus allowing the detection of faulty code. New memory requests are populated with 0xCD bytes, and memory-free operations are filled with 0xDD bytes.

 You can validate the integrity of the heap at any time, from within your code, by calling **_CrtCheckMemory**. In addition, a number of heap-checking properties may be set using the **_CrtSetDbgFlag** function.

Tips For Debugging MFC-Based Applications

When you're debugging an MFC-based application, you can do several things that can make your task easier. These methods are described in the following sections.

Window Arrangement

If possible, you should try to arrange the windows of your debugger and the application being debugged so that they don't overlap. This is important when you're attempting to solve focus issues and identifying the contents of a device context during GDI development.

Tracing

The MFC **TRACE** macros can be instrumental in identifying program problems, especially those where timing is involved and breakpoints hamper the natural flow of the code. There are four trace macros: **TRACE0, TRACE1, TRACE2,** and **TRACE3**. The macros take zero to three arguments, respectively, in a manner similar to **printf**.

Two global variables modify the **TRACE** macro behavior: **afxTraceEnabled** and **afxTraceFlags**.

➤ The first variable may be set to **TRUE** or **FALSE** depending on whether you want to produce trace output.

➤ The second variable may be set under program control, but is more easily set using the tracer.exe utility, which offers a user-friendly description of the possible bit-field options.

Object Dump

It is possible to dump the state of any **CObject**-derived object during a debug session by calling its **Dump** function. The **CObject** class provides a virtual function, **Dump**, that you should override to provide state information. The state information is written to a **CDumpContext** stream, which is passed into the function as an argument.

Afx Diagnostic Functions

Although more than a dozen **Afx** routines offer debugging services, you should be aware of some of the more commonly used functions:

➤ **AfxCheckError**—This method accepts a single argument, an **SCODE**, and is used to check OLE function-call return codes and throw the appropriate MFC exception as required.

➤ **AfxCheckMemory**—This is an expensive function that validates the available heap, printing inconsistency messages to the debugger's output window. This function accepts no arguments and returns a Boolean status value.

➤ **AfxEnableMemoryTracking**—This function accepts a single Boolean argument. You may use this function to enable memory tracking in the Debug version of the MFC library.

➤ **AfxIsMemoryBlock**—This diagnostic function verifies that the supplied pointer and block-length arguments are consistent with those of an allocation that occurred using the debug version of the **new** operator.

➤ **AfxIsValidAddress**—Among the most common MFC diagnostic functions, **AfxIsValidAddress** accepts a pointer and a number of bytes to test as valid within the calling program's process space. An optional third argument specifies whether the memory is accessed for reading and writing or is accessed just for reading.

➤ **AfxIsValidString**—This function verifies that the supplied pointer is a valid string. A second argument, indicating the length of the string, defaults to –1, identifying the string as null terminated.

➤ **AfxSetAllocHook**—This function accepts a single argument of type **AFX_ALLOC_HOOK**. Use this function to specify a callback function that is called before memory allocation takes place. The prototype for the callback function follows:

```
BOOL AFXAPI AllocHook(size_t nSize, BOOL bObject, LONG
lRequestNumber);
```

Debugging Tools

Over the years, Microsoft has provided a number of tools designed to help locate programming problems, test program features, or identify differences among the various supported platforms. Programs that were used for 16-bit development, such as HeapWalker and Shaker, have been gracefully retired, leaving room for a new breed of debugging and testing tools.

The Dependency Walker Utility

The purpose of the Dependency Walker utility is to investigate recursively all the DLLs or modules that make up an executable. The utility then produces a report that contains the following information:

➤ *Missing Files*—Generally indicates that the DLL is not in the path and cannot be located.

➤ *Invalid Files*—Indicates that the format of the file is not compatible with the Windows operating system.

➤ *Unresolved External*—Checks to make sure that function import requirements are addressed as exports of the specified module.

➤ *Circular Dependency*—Identifies forward-referenced functions that may cause problems under some circumstances.

➤ *Machine Build Mismatch*—Detects instances where DLLs built for one processor architecture are attempted to be loaded by a different type of machine.

The Spy++ Utility

One of the most useful tools for performance tuning is the Spy++ utility. This update of the original Spy program (which allowed you to monitor window activity and messages) allows you to view system processes and threads. The Spy++ utility is an MDI application, allowing you to open one or more windows in the messages, windows, processes, and threads.

Spying on windows or messages requires you to drag a locator icon out of the Find dialog box and onto a window to identify the source application.

When you are spying on windows, you can define the scope and origin of window messages.

When you are spying on messages, you can do the following:

➤ Define the scope of messages you want to view.

➤ Identify messages registered with the **RegisterWindowMessage** function.

➤ View "unknown" messages.

Debugging COM Clients And Servers

The process of debugging client/server applications can be trying at best. Microsoft's RPC debugger option removes some of the pain by allowing you to step between client and server code without effort. For in-process servers, your debugger switches between client and server debugging; for out-of-process servers, a second instance of the debugger is launched.

Before you can use Remote Procedural Call (RPC) debugging for client/server applications that employ COM, you must enable the option. The Options dialog box, available from the Tools menu, contains a Debug tab. The OLE RPC debugging option must be checked.

Testing

If there is one rule that summarizes the testing process, it is that it becomes increasingly (near exponentially) more expensive to identify and correct program flaws the further on in the design-code-debug-test life cycle that they are identified.

There are five common stages of testing: unit, integration, regression, stress, and Beta.

Unit Testing

Unit testing is generally the easiest testing to perform and is probably the most overlooked. Simply stated, a unit test exercises a small piece of code, usually a function. When you're dealing with MFC, OLE, and Windows, however, this may be a test of a message event or an ActiveX property or method.

Such tests, in a formal sense, are generally ignored—that is, most developers do not build test harnesses or expose entry points to a test program for the purpose of exercising single functions. Also, it may be difficult to exercise functions that rely on a certain state or complex data arguments because reconstituting the necessary state or building the required data parameters may be extremely difficult for a test program. Proper unit testing strives to execute every code path that exists in a function.

Integration Testing

The purpose of integration testing is to validate the correct operation of components, which may behave correctly in a standalone manner, but operate inappropriately when working together. Thus, functions and events that pass unit testing may fail during integration testing because certain function outputs feed other methods unexpected data values.

Regression Testing

Regression testing strives to identify seemingly unrelated bugs that are introduced during a code-build-debug-release cycle. Regression testing runs tests that encompass not only those areas into which change was introduced, but other parts of the application as well. A regression test suite is usually performed as a "smoke test" before the program is released to a larger testing audience.

Stress Testing

Stress testing refers to application testing that is performed while operating system resources are consumed in a manner that taxes the machine. Stress-testing an application may attempt to exhaust the following resources:

➤ Global heap

➤ Windows GDI resources

➤ File handles

➤ Available disk space

➤ Network bandwidth and other resources

The purpose of such testing is to cause the program to execute exception or other fault-protection logic if it exists. Otherwise, such testing results in the identification of conditions that cause the program to fail in an unrecoverable manner. Microsoft offers a utility named stress.exe that can exercise an operating system in many of the ways listed above.

Beta Testing

The Beta test stage opens the testing process to a larger audience and usually begins when the product's features are complete and when the product is stable enough to be made available to persons not in the quality assurance department.

Practice Questions

Question 1

Which is not a limitation of SQL debugging? [Check all correct answers]

❑ a. Expression breakpoints cannot be applied.

❑ b. Advanced-style breakpoints cannot be applied.

❑ c. SQL statements must reside in a stored procedure.

❑ d. Extended stored procedures must reside in a DLL.

Answers a, b, and c are correct. Answer d is incorrect because there is no support for debugging extended stored procedures.

Question 2

What does the Dependency Walker utility do?

○ a. Identifies parent/child window relationships in an application.

○ b. Converts an application's DLLs to work with a different processor architecture.

○ c. Walks SQL statements and identifies the table relationships.

○ d. Produces a report of the DLLs and modules that make up an executable.

Answer d is correct. The Dependency Walker utility recursively investigates all of the DLLs that make up an executable and produces a comprehensive report. This report includes missing and invalid files, unresolved externals, circular dependencies, and machine build mismatches.

Question 3

Which cannot be monitored by Spy++?

○ a. Threads

○ b. System processes

○ c. Window activity

○ d. Disk activity

Answer d is correct. The Spy++ utility monitors threads, system processes, window activity, and messages. The program does not monitor disk activity.

Question 4

Which are common test stages? [Check all correct answers]

❑ a. Unit

❑ b. Regression

❑ c. Compilation

❑ d. Integration

Answers a, b, and d are correct. Unit testing, regression testing, and integration testing are common test practices. There is no such thing as a compilation test.

Question 5

Which resource would probably not be included in a stress test?

○ a. Available disk space

○ b. File handles

○ c. Processor speed

○ d. Global heap

Answer c is correct; processor speed would probably not be included in a stress test. A number of factors can limit the speed at which a program executes; these factors include processor speed, RAM access time, and the types of devices plugged into the computer's bus. However, unless the application has realtime requirements, the application's response time is generally not something that is stress-tested.

Question 6

Window arrangement when using Spy++ may be important when debugging which messages? [Check all correct answers]

❑ a. Paint

❑ b. Dynamic Data Exchange

❑ c   Focus

❑ d. Timer

The correct answers are a and c. If the Spy++ program obscures the application under test, debugging paint or focus messages will be complicated. Answers b and e are incorrect because DDE and timer messages would not be affected by activation messages.

Question 7

Creating a *no man's land* around allocation requests serves what purpose?

○ a. Tracks memory access.

○ b. Identifies buffer overwrites.

○ c. Ensures proper byte alignment.

○ d. Provides space for inserting debug code.

The correct answer is b. The area surrounding memory allocation (no man's land) is populated with 0xFD bytes allowing overwrites to be identified. Answers a, c, and d are incorrect because this extra allocated space has nothing to do with tracking memory access, the structure's byte alignment, or debugging code.

Need To Know More?

 Box, Don, Keith Brown, Tim Ewald, and Chris Sells. *Effective COM: 50 Ways to Improve Your COM and MTS-Based Applications*. New York, NY: Addison Wesley Longman, Inc., 1999. ISBN 0-201-37968-6. This book contains all you need to know to create optimized COM objects. The "Transactions" section is especially relevant to the material covered in this chapter.

 Kruglinski, David J., George Shepherd, and Scot Wingo. *Programming Microsoft Visual C++*, *5th ed*. Redmond, WA: Microsoft Press, 1998. ISBN 1-57231-857-0. This book strikes a good balance between theory and practical application. It is divided into six parts and covers nearly every aspect of MFC programming, from the basics to database management and the Internet. Chapters 1 and 26 are especially relevant to this chapter.

 White, David, Kenn Scribner, and Eugene Olafsen. *MFC Programming with Visual C++ 6 Unleashed*. Indianapolis, IN: Sams Publishing, 1999. ISBN 0-672-31557-2. This text describes many aspects of MFC programming, as well as use of the Visual C++ tools. Chapter 8, "Advanced MFC," offers a comprehensive description for building and debugging DLLs.

Deploying Your Application

Terms you'll need to understand:

√ Files and file groups

√ Components and subcomponents

√ Systems Management Server (SMS)

√ Package Definition File (PDF)

√ "Zero Administration" Initiative for Windows (ZAW)

√ Total cost of ownership (TCO)

√ Cabinet

√ Sign

√ Certificate

√ Distributed Component Object Model (DCOM)

√ <Object> tag

Techniques you'll need to master:

√ Using InstallShield to create installation scripts

√ Identifying when to use Systems Management Server (SMS) to distribute applications

√ Using the design goals of the "Zero Administration" Initiative for Windows

√ Constructing and signing CAB files for Internet code deployment

√ Configuring clients and installing components for DCOM activation

The major motivation of application developers, who spend a tremendous amount of time behind their text editors and debuggers toiling long hours and eating only junk food, is a paycheck at the end of the week. Unfortunately, customers or clients don't like to pay programmers until they actually receive and/or install their software. This chapter covers the final stage in an application's life cycle: packaging and deployment.

InstallShield Packaging Concepts

Applications created using Visual C++ can be deployed using InstallShield, which ships on the Visual C++ disk but must be installed separately. You should be familiar with InstallShield's packaging scheme before generating a setup script. The building blocks for a setup script are files and file groups, and components and subcomponents.

Files And File Groups

Files identify any file that you wish to ship as part of the installation set, such as executables, dynamic link libraries, and help files. File groups are defined as sets of files with similar characteristics, including shared/not shared, compressed/ uncompressed, or NT only/Windows 95/98 only/Windows 2000 only.

Components And Subcomponents

The other packaging building blocks are components and subcomponents, which most closely relate to the installable items that the user checks or unchecks during the setup program, identifying what is to be installed during the setup process. Thus, components of an office productivity suite might include a word processor, a spreadsheet, and a database, whereas subcomponents might include sample files, tutorials, and templates for one of those components.

InstallShield Package And Deployment Wizard

The Package And Deployment Wizard simplifies the creation of an InstallShield installation script. A series of wizard steps guides you through the process of defining installation categories, collecting user information, and identifying the language or languages the user interface supports.

Setup Panel One

The wizard's first step captures basic information regarding your application and company:

➤ *Application name*—The application name appears in the title and caption bar of the setup window. The name also appears in the base Registry key under which additional information regarding this application's setup procedure is stored.

➤ *Company name*—The company name also appears in registry entries for the application.

➤ *Development environment*—InstallShield for Visual C++ provides only a single selection: Visual C++.

➤ *Application type*—The application type identifies common product categories, including database applications and Internet applications.

➤ *Application version*—The version number of the program is provided in an edit field and is available at runtime from the file's property sheet, available from Explorer.

➤ *Application executable*—The setup script must know the name of your executable, thus identifying the program to be run at the completion of the client installation procedure.

Choose Dialogs Panel

The resulting installation script will appear as a wizard with one or more dialog-box steps. Use the Choose Dialogs panel to select the steps that you want to include as part of your setup procedure:

➤ *Welcome message*—As the first page of the setup wizard, the welcome message identifies the application being installed, specifies the manufacturer, and displays copyright warnings.

➤ *Software license agreement*—A paragraph that explains your license agreement is displayed in this dialog box. Typically, the user is prompted either to agree with the terms, in which case the next step of the wizard is presented, or to cancel the installation.

➤ *Readme*—The Readme panel allows you to paste into a scrollable edit box the text of the readme.txt file that usually ships with your application.

➤ *User information*—This section contains fields for the end user to enter his or her name, company, and product serial number.

➤ *Install location*—The default installation location uses the company name that you entered in the first panel; the company name is used as a subdirectory name under the C:\Program Files directory.

➤ *Setup type*—A typical installation kit contains Typical, Compact, and Custom setup configurations. This panel offers these three common choices. If the user selects the Custom option, the next wizard step will be one that allows the selection of installable components.

➤ *Destination folder*—This standard step allows the end user to define the name of the desktop folder into which the program icons will be placed.

➤ *Summary*—The summary panel generally contains a paragraph that describes the selected options, installation directory, program folder, and so on.

➤ *Complete*—The last panel offers to view the Readme file and/or launch the successfully installed application.

Target Platform

The third step in the Package And Deployment Wizard is to identify the platform(s) that the setup script will target. Such targets include:

➤ Windows 95/98

➤ Windows NT 3.51 (Intel, MIPS, Alpha)

➤ Windows NT 4 (Intel, MIPS, Alpha)

> *Note: InstallShield for Visual C++ does not allow the creation of setup scripts for 16-bit Windows operating systems.*

Languages

The Languages panel of the Package And Deployment Wizard allows you to define the language(s) that you want the resulting setup to support. InstallShield for Visual C++ allows only English as the language, but you may purchase dozens of languages and dialects.

Setup Types

The next panel of the Package And Deployment Wizard allows you to select one or more setup types to include in your installation script. By default, Compact, Typical, and Custom are selected, but you can also choose one or more of the others, including:

➤ Network

➤ Administrator

➤ Network (Best Performance)

➤ Network (Efficient Space)

Components

The next step is the Specify Components panel, allowing you to select the components that constitute your setup types. Components can be changed at any stage of the install definition process. Typical components include:

➤ Program files

➤ Example files

➤ Help files

➤ Shared DLLs

File Groups

The second-to-last panel allows you to select the file groups—which you defined earlier—to be included in the installation set. Typical file groups include:

➤ Program executable files

➤ Program DLLs

➤ Example files

➤ Help files

➤ Shared DLLs

Summary

The final panel offers a summary of all of the wizard selections that you made to define the setup script for this project.

Systems Management Server (SMS)

Microsoft offers the Systems Management Server (SMS) product to provide centralized distribution and monitoring of workstation and server software. SMS is tightly integrated with Microsoft SQL Server and NT Server, using the Microsoft Management Console (MMC) as an administrative user interface. SMS adheres to industry-standard data formats: Desktop Management Task Force (DMTF) and Management Information Format (MIF).

Identifying Features

Systems Management Server offers a number of features that extend "Zero Administration" Initiative for Windows (ZAW) beyond those features offered by the operating system. These additional features include:

➤ *Configuration discovery*— SMS can "discover" information regarding the hardware and software that is on the network.

➤ *Granular software distribution*—SMS can be used to create sophisticated scripts that define the distribution of software based on hardware configuration and software inventory properties.

➤ *Unattended configuration*—Allows remote, synchronized, and timed distribution of client and server software.

➤ *Dry-run*—This unique feature allows an administrator to test the likelihood of installation success on machines under management, without actually disturbing the operating behavior of the target machines.

➤ *Roll-back*—If a software roll-out doesn't work correctly, SMS can be instructed to roll back all or specified clients.

➤ *Patch*—Rather than having to download an entire software component, you can use a patch to transmit just the binary's "delta" to a target machine.

➤ *Heterogeneous interoperability*—SMS is capable of managing hardware on and distributing software to platforms other than Intel and Windows.

➤ *Remote diagnostics*—Client machines that are experiencing trouble can be remotely diagnosed, and necessary configuration changes can be made accordingly.

Ease Of Use

SMS addresses the ZAW ease-of-use requirement by leveraging the Microsoft Management Console (MMC). MMC centralizes system-administration tasks by offering an extensible architecture into which applications supply *snap-ins* (plug-in components). Management snap-ins exist for most BackOffice products, including SMS, MTS (Microsoft Transaction Server), and SQL Server.

System Requirements

Microsoft recommends a Pentium II computer with 128MB of RAM and 1GB of hard-disk space as the hardware platform for SMS. The host operating system must be a minimum of NT 4 with Service Pack 4 installed. Additionally, SMS requires SQL Server to be present. The minimum configuration is SQL Server 6.5 with Service Pack 4, although SMS 2 is also compatible with SQL Server 7.

Software Distribution With SMS

Using SMS to distribute software requires a setup script that provides a Package Definition File (PDF). The PDF file is an ASCII text file that defines a software package that is to be distributed by the server. The PDF file, in conjunction with information that is stored in the SMS database, is used by the Package Control Manager (PCM) to execute software installations.

Package Definition File (PDF)

The PDF file contains information in name-value pair format that identifies properties that define a package. This file contains three predefined package settings:

➤ Workstation

➤ Sharing

➤ Inventory

SMS API

By programming to the SMS API (application programming interface), you can design your application to take advantage of the services that SMS offers. An SMS-aware application can use SMS to do the following:

➤ Find out the properties of any object in SMS inventory.

➤ Create, modify, or delete software-distribution packages.

➤ Create, modify, or delete software-distribution command jobs.

➤ Create, modify, or delete SMS object queries.

➤ Access existing machine and site groups, which act as aliases for groups of target machines and sites for software distribution.

"Zero Administration" Initiative For Windows

From a business-operations perspective, purchasing a computer involves two costs. The first—the actual cost of the computer hardware itself—continues to fall. The second cost—which may not be immediately apparent to software developers—is the price to support the computer after it is purchased and placed on a user's desk. In addition to the licensing fees that must be paid for the user's software, there are costs involved in setting up network access, establishing an email account, and providing training and help-desk services.

Microsoft's "Zero Administration" Initiative for Windows (ZAW) is an attempt to lower what is commonly referred to as *total cost of ownership (TCO)*. One of the most significant reductions of TCO for an enterprise's computer network will be the savings resulting from being able to perform common configuration tasks for client computers from a central location, instead of having to interact physically with each computer.

> *Note: ZAW is a superset of Microsoft's current ZAK (Zero Administration Kit) procedures. Although some of the goals of ZAK are common to ZAW, ZAK's technology is based on the Windows 95/98 and NT 4 platform offerings, whereas a fuller realization of ZAW will appear on the Windows 2000 operating system.*

Design Goals

ZAW has several design goals:

➤ *Ease of use*—Creating software and systems that are easy to use has been a design goal for almost every piece of hardware and software ever created. In the ZAW context, this goal implies software that can detect its environment and configure itself based on a set of provided rules.

➤ *Remote management*—By far the most ambitious goal set to reduce ownership cost is the remote management and configuration of hardware and software. This means that scripts can be defined that identify the applications, desktop settings, and data files that should be installed on a machine, regardless of which computer a user logs in on.

➤ *Transparency*—A final goal of ZAW is to integrate seamlessly with existing hardware and software. It would be senseless to offer a technology that is supposed to decrease TCO if the technology itself requires a steep learning curve and additional user training.

Core OS Features

The following core features will appear in Windows 2000 to support the ZAW initiative:

➤ Remote, centralized, policy-based management

➤ Simplified installation and maintenance of the Windows operating system

➤ Application management and deployment

➤ Support for mobile and roaming users

➤ Side-by-side machine replacement with no loss of user data

➤ Remote boot

➤ Improved supportability

 Active Directory solves the location transparency issues that face many of the ZAW initiatives. Active Directory service—included with Windows 2000 Server—provides secure, distributed, partitioned, and replicated storage objects. With Active Directory, the construction of the directory tree is performed from the "bottom up." This feature—which is different from traditional directory services—allows the construction of a large tree with domains subdivided into organization units (OU) for the purposes of administration.

Internet/Intranet Delivery

If you want to deploy your application or control by using a Web-based delivery mechanism, such as embedding the object in a Web page, you will need to understand Microsoft's CAB file architecture. In a nutshell, the steps to creating and signing a CAB file are as follows:

1. Acquire a certificate, either by purchasing one from a Certificate Authority (CA) or generating a test certificate.

2. Create the CAB file containing the files that you want to distribute.

3. Sign your files.

CAB File

The CAB (cabinet) file format is useful when you want to deliver code to an end user's computer in a single package, via the Internet or company intranet, and have the code automatically install and register itself. The CAB file format is a perfect vehicle for delivering MFC and ATL projects that you create using Visual C++. A CAB file contains all of an executable's components in a compressed form, as well as the instructions necessary to perform the installation. Cabinet files can contain an inventory file that has an .osd extension. The OSD file tells Internet Explorer's Package Manager how to install the cabinet's contents.

Signing And Certificates

Having executables download, install, and execute on your computer is an obvious security concern. One way to protect your computer from malicious programs is to allow only those programs that are signed and verified by a trusted source to execute on your computer. Although a programmer may "sign" individual DLLs and EXEs, it is more common to create a CAB file and sign this single file. Signing a file associates it with a digital certificate and ensures that the code that the end user receives has not been tampered with.

A certificate, provided by a Certificate Authority (CA), must be obtained before you can sign your code. The CA acts as a trusted intermediary between the software publisher and the end user. (Verisign is a well-known CA.) The certificate issued by the CA is called a Software Publisher Certificate, and it must conform to the X.509 standard, employing public key encryption. The certificate consists of two parts: the certificate file and the private key. You sign your files with the private key, and the user verifies the authenticity of the received file by obtaining the public key from the CA. It is also possible to generate a test certificate by using the MAKECERT utility provided with the Platform SDK or available on Microsoft's Web site.

A certificate contains the following information:

➤ *Version*— Identifies the format of the certificate.

➤ *Serial number*—A unique value assigned by the CA.

➤ *Algorithm identifier*—Identifies the algorithm used to sign the certificate.

➤ *Issuer*—Identifies the CA.

➤ *Period of validity*—The date the certificate is valid and the date the certificate expires.

➤ *Subject*—The name of the user.

➤ *Subject's public key*—Contains the public-key algorithm name and the public key.

➤ *Signature*—The CA's signature.

INF File

The INF file identifies the components of the installation set for the CAB file. These components may include DLLs, EXEs, help files, and others. The INF file instructs the CAB extraction utility how to deal with platform differences and file version issues. By default, newer versions of files on the target system overwrite older files.

Note: An INF file is not a CAB file requirement. Its purpose is to tell a Windows operating system how to load and register a bundled control. An OSD file may be present in the CAB instead of an INF file, identifying the various bundled components and their installation.

The INF file below defines a cabinet that contains two files: mycomponent.dll and additional.dll. The file identifies mycomponent.dll as a COM server, specifying a CLSID and requiring registration:

```
; Sample INF file for MYCOMPONENT.DLL
[version]
; version signature (same for both NT and Win95) do not remove
signature="$CHICAGO$"
AdvancedINF=2.0
[Add.Code]
mycomponent.dll=mycomponent.dll
additional.dll=additional.dll
; needed DLL
[additional.dll]
file-win32-x86=thiscab
FileVersion=1,0,1,1
DestDir=10
RegisterServer=yes
[mycomponent.dll]
file-win32-x86=thiscab
clsid={632BBD12-11EE-1220-A97A-000000001231}
FileVersion=1,0,0,1
RegisterServer=yes
; end of INF file
```

The following section definitions appear in a CAB file:

➤ *Version*—The version tag identifies the operating system(s) that the CAB is compatible with. These options include Windows 95/98, Windows NT 4, and Windows 2000 or later.

➤ *Add.Code*—The Add.Code section contains a list of files that are contained in the CAB and associates each file with a subsection in the INF file.

➤ *Subsection*—Each subsection must be associated with a file (defined in the section above). Values tags that may appear in this section include the CLSID of the control, the component's version number, and a flag that indicates that the component requires OLE registration.

Cabinetry

The files necessary to create, view, and sign CAB files are available in Microsoft's Cabinet Software Development Kit. The SDK includes the following:

➤ Utilities to create and extract CAB files

➤ Compression and decompression libraries and header files

➤ Documentation and code samples

Creating A CAB

If you have installed the SDK and have created an INF file, you can create a CAB file. The following line uses the cabarc.exe utility and the INF file defined above to create a CAB file named my.cab, containing a compressed Intel-compatible binary allowing 6,248 bytes for the digital certificate:

```
Cabarc.exe -s 6144 N My.cab MyComponent.dll additional.dll My.inf
```

Signing A CAB

Signing CAB files requires tools that are part of Microsoft's CryptoAPI Tools and Authenticode technology. The utilities that are part of this suite include those that can digitally sign files, view certificates, and modify certificates.

The first step of signing CAB files requires the makecert.exe program. This utility creates a key pair, consisting of a private key and a public key. Additionally, the key pair is associated with an X.500 distinguished name, and the resulting X.509 certificate is signed by the private key:

```
Makecert.exe -u:mykey -n:CN=strattonassociates cert.cer
```

The final step is use the signcode.exe utility to sign the CAB file and embed a PKCS7 certificate:

```
Signcode -spc cert.spc -k mykey mycab.cab
```

> *Note: The Certification File Validity Utility (chktrust) is a useful tool to have in your Internet-development arsenal, allowing you to extract certificates from signed objects.*

DCOM

DCOM, or Distributed Component Object Model, is commonly described as "COM over a longer wire." DCOM extends the notion of location transparency. Where local COM servers prove that components can lie outside of a program's process space, DCOM moves components outside of the physical machine.

Platform

The DCOM extensions have existed since NT 4 shipped, so Windows 2000 will also be DCOM-compliant. Windows 95 requires the DCOM extensions to be installed. You can do this by downloading the specific setup kit or any version of IE since version 4. Windows 98 contains DCOM support.

DCOM for Windows 95/98 will not automatically launch a server to create object instances. For this reason, programs that act as COM servers must be launched manually before they can be accessed remotely.

For DCOM to operate in a Windows peer-to-peer environment, the following operations must be performed:

➤ Enable File and Print Sharing from the Network icon in the Control Panel.

➤ To allow the machine to accept remote DCOM calls, set the following Registry key: \HKEY_LOCAL_MACHINE\SOFTWARE\ Microsoft\OLE\EnableRemoteConnect = 'Y'

➤ To enable DCOM, set the following Registry key: \HKEY_LOCAL_ MACHINE\SOFTWARE\Microsoft\OLE\EnableDCOM = 'Y'

Note: The Service Control Manager (SCM) locates or creates the object, across a network if necessary.

Installing

To configure a client/server application that employs DCOM technology, follow the steps explained next.

Server

Before you can access a COM server on a remote machine, you must register the server. Follow these steps:

1. Copy the COM server and any other necessary files to the target machine.

2. Register the server. If this is a local server, run the EXE with the /RegServer argument; otherwise, use regsvr32.exe followed by the DLL or OCX of the in-process server you want to register.

Windows 95/98 cannot automatically launch COM servers. Therefore, this platform supports only local servers, which you must start manually followed by the **Server** argument:

```
myserver.exe /Server
```

Client

Configuring the client can be done one of two ways, regardless of the Windows operating system you are using:

➤ Start the oleview.exe utility and locate the server class that you just registered on the target machine. Select the Activation tab in the workspace tabbed view and enter the IP address of the target machine in the Remote Machine Name field. Next, switch to the Implementation tab and remove the local server path in the Path To Implementation field. This effectively removes the server path key for this class in the Registry of the client machine (if it was so registered).

➤ Use the Distributed COM Configuration Properties utility (dcomcnfg.exe). This application offers a tabbed dialog box that allows you to identify remoteable components and set activation security attributes.

Network Dispersal

Now that your component has been created, signed, and packaged, it needs to get to its intended audience of users. One of the simplest and most common dispersal mechanisms is embedding a component in a Web page.

ActiveX

Distributing components for remote activation or for use by remote clients can easily be done using ActiveX technology. ActiveX was Microsoft's answer to a competing component technology in Java known as JavaBeans. The original ActiveX specification was a variation, actually a superset, of OLE Control functionality. For a COM server to consider itself an OLE Control, it had to implement a dozen or so interfaces. This specification has since been revised to categorize an ActiveX control as one that performs self-registration and exposes **IUnknown**. This relaxation of the ActiveX definition identifies almost any COM server as an ActiveX component. Therefore, it is now possible to distribute any COM server using ActiveX technology and to use DCOM for these components to communicate with each other.

The key to delivering ActiveX-enabled content within standard HTML pages is the <Object> tag. The <Object> tag, whose origin may have been well intentioned, has become a catchall for data types that were not envisioned during the design of HTML. The object used to embed an ActiveX control appears here:

```
<OBJECT
    ID=MYCONTROL
    TYPE="application/x-oleobject"
    CLASSID="clsid:ADD870B6-A8EE-11AF-9377-00BB004A7F12"
    CODEBASE="http://websvr/MYCONTROL. CAB"
    WIDTH=12
    HEIGHT=12>
    <PARAM NAME="Start Command" VALUE="Index">
    <PARAM NAME="Result Set Size" VALUE="100">
    <PARAM NAME="Query" VALUE="Author=Olafsen">
</OBJECT>
```

Although the <Object> tag supports almost two dozen modifiers, it is important to understand those that are necessary for ActiveX creation and initialization:

➤ **CODEBASE**—Identifies the path used to retrieve the object.

➤ **CLASSID**—Contains the CLSID for the object.

➤ **TYPE**—The MIME-type for ActiveX controls is "**application/x-oleobject**".

➤ **PARAM NAME**—Arguments that are passed to the component are prefaced by this tag.

Practice Questions

Question 1

> Which statement is not true about Systems Management Server?
>
> ○ a. SMS may roll a machine back to its previous state if a problem is encountered.
>
> ○ b. A "patching" mechanism allows just upgrade deltas to be sent to necessary machines.
>
> ○ c. Software must be specifically tailored for use in an SMS environment.
>
> ○ d. SMS can discover hardware and software on the network.

Answer c is correct. It is not necessary for an application to be modified in order to be used in an SMS environment. Deployment scripts describe the packaging and versioning that SMS uses to push software to clients and servers.

Question 2

> SMS requires which of the following software packages and/or technologies? [Check all correct answers]
>
> ❑ a. Microsoft Management Console (MMC)
>
> ❑ b. Distributed COM (DCOM)
>
> ❑ c. SQL Server (6.5+)
>
> ❑ d. NT 4 with Service Pack 4

Answers a, c, and d are correct. Systems Management Server requires Microsoft Management Console, SQL Server (6.5+), and NT 4 with Service Pack. Answer b is incorrect because SMS does not rely on DCOM to manage remote machines. SMS can be used in heterogeneous environment with machines that do not employ this technology.

Question 3

Which is not a predefined Package Definition File (PDF) setting?

○ a. Workstation

○ b. Network

○ c. Sharing

○ d. Inventory

Answer b is correct. The SMS server requires a network to communicate workstation and server changes, but is not designed to participate in network management. Answers a, c, and d are incorrect because workstation, sharing, and inventory are predefined PDF settings.

Question 4

Which are operations that are performed by Active Directory for storage objects? [Check all correct answers]

❑ a. Distributing

❑ b. Securing

❑ c. Replicating

❑ d. Validating

Answers a, b, and c are correct. Active Directory provides distributed, secure, replicated, and partitioned storage objects. Answer d is incorrect because this service is not responsible for validating the contents of these items.

Question 5

What information is part of a X.509 certificate?

○ a. Expiration information

○ b. Certificate destination

○ c. Issuer identification

○ d. A serial number

Answer b is correct. The certificate is issued to the entity that creates either the message or code. The issuing CA does not have to know who is going to receive the signed data.

Question 6

Which are valid ways to register a COM server? [Check all correct answers]

❏ a. Use the regsvr32.exe.

❏ b. Run the executable with the /Register switch.

❏ c. Run the executable.

❏ d. Write a custom registration routine.

Answers a and c are correct. MFC applications register server objects when they start up. The regsvr32.exe is necessary to register in-process object servers. Answers b and d are invalid answers.

Question 7

ActiveX components may be embedded in an HTML page with what tag?

○ a. <Insert>

○ b. <Object>

○ c. <Component>

○ d. <Field>

Answer b is correct. The <Object> tag provides a way for you to include ActiveX controls on an HTML page. Answers a, c, and d are incorrect because <Insert>, <Component>, and <Field> are not valid HTML tags.

Need To Know More?

 Li, Sing, and Panos Economopoulos. *Professional Visual C++ 5 ActiveX/COM Control Programming*. Olton, Birmingham, Canada: Wrox Press Ltd., 1997. ISBN: 1-861000-37-5. This book offers comprehensive discussions on developing and deploying ActiveX components.

 Pinnock, Jonathan. *Professional DCOM Application Development*. Olton, Birmingham, Canada: Wrox Press Ltd, 1998. ISBN: 1-861001-31-2. Chapters 9 and 10 of this book explain digital certificate technology as well as the various mechanisms available to deploy distributed applications.

Sample Test

In this chapter, I provide pointers to help you develop a successful test-taking strategy, including how to choose proper answers, how to decode ambiguity, how to work within the Microsoft testing framework, how to decide what you need to memorize, and how to prepare for the test. At the end of the chapter, I include 57 questions on subject matter pertinent to Microsoft Exam 70-015, "Designing and Implementing Distributed Applications Using Microsoft Visual C++ 6.0." In Chapter 14, you'll find the answer key to this test. Good luck!

Questions, Questions, Questions

There should be no doubt in your mind that you are facing a test full of specific and pointed questions. If the version of the exam that you take is fixed-length, it will include 50 questions, and you will be allotted 90 minutes to complete the exam. If it's an adaptive test (the software should tell you this as you begin the exam), it will consist of somewhere between 25 and 35 questions (on average) and take somewhere between 30 and 60 minutes.

Whichever type of test you take, exam questions will belong to one of five basic types:

➤ Multiple choice with a single answer

➤ Multiple choice with multiple answers

➤ Multipart with a single answer

➤ Multipart with multiple answers

➤ Simulations whereby you click on a GUI screen capture to simulate using the Visual C++ interface

You should always take the time to read a question at least twice before selecting an answer, and you should always look for an Exhibit button as you examine each question. Exhibits include graphics information related to a question. An *exhibit* is usually a screen capture of program output or GUI information that you must examine to analyze the question's contents and formulate an answer. The Exhibit button displays graphics and charts used to help explain a question, provide additional data, or illustrate page layout or program behavior.

Not every question has only one answer; many questions require multiple answers. Therefore, you should read each question carefully, determine how many answers are necessary or possible, and look for additional hints or instructions when selecting answers. Such instructions often appear in brackets immediately following the question itself (for multiple-answer questions).

Picking Proper Answers

Obviously, the only way to pass any exam is to select enough of the right answers to obtain a passing score. However, Microsoft's exams are not standardized like the SAT and GRE exams; they are far more diabolical and convoluted. In some cases, questions are strangely worded, and deciphering them can be a real challenge. In those cases, you may need to rely on answer-elimination skills. Almost always, at least one answer out of the possible choices for a question can be eliminated immediately because it matches one of these conditions:

➤ The answer does not apply to the situation.

➤ The answer describes a nonexistent issue, an invalid option, or an imaginary state.

➤ The answer may be eliminated because of information in the question itself.

After you eliminate all answers that are obviously wrong, you can apply your retained knowledge to eliminate further answers. Look for items that sound correct but refer to actions, commands, or features that are not present or not available in the situation that the question describes.

If you're still faced with a blind guess among two or more potentially correct answers, reread the question. Try to picture how each of the possible remaining answers would alter the situation. *Be especially sensitive to terminology*; sometimes the choice of words ("remove" instead of "disable") can make the difference between a right answer and a wrong one.

Only when you've exhausted your ability to eliminate answers but remain unclear about which of the remaining possibilities is correct should you guess at an answer. An unanswered question offers you no points, but guessing gives you at least some chance of getting a question right; just don't be too hasty when making a blind guess.

If you're taking a fixed-length test, you can wait until the last round of reviewing marked questions (just as you're about to run out of time or out of unanswered questions) before you start making guesses. If you're taking an adaptive test, you'll have to guess in order to move on to the next question (if you can't figure out an answer some other way). Either way, guessing should be a last resort.

Decoding Ambiguity

Microsoft exams have a reputation for including questions that can be difficult to interpret, confusing, or ambiguous. In my experience with numerous exams, I consider this reputation to be completely justified. The Microsoft exams are tough, and they're deliberately made that way.

The only way to beat Microsoft at its own game is to be prepared. You'll discover that many exam questions test your knowledge of things that are not directly related to the issue raised by a question. This means that the answers you must choose from, even incorrect ones, are just as much a part of the skill assessment as the question itself. If you don't know something about most aspects of Visual C++ 6, you may not be able to eliminate answers that are wrong because they relate to an area of Visual C++ other than the one that's addressed by the question at hand. In other words, the more you know about the software, the easier it will be for you to tell right from wrong.

Questions often give away their answers, but you have to be Sherlock Holmes to see the clues. Often, subtle hints appear in the question text in such a way that they seem almost irrelevant to the situation. You must realize that each question is a test unto itself and that you need to inspect and successfully navigate each question to pass the exam. Look for small clues, such as the mention of times, group permissions and names, and configuration settings. Little things such as these can point to the right answer if they're properly understood; if missed, they can leave you facing a blind guess.

Another common difficulty with certification exams is vocabulary. Microsoft has an uncanny knack for naming some utilities and features entirely obviously in some cases and completely inanely in other instances. Be sure to brush up on the key terms presented at the beginning of each chapter of this book. You may also want to read the glossary at the end of this book the day before you take the test.

Working Within The Framework

The test questions appear in random order, and many elements or issues that are mentioned in one question may also crop up in other questions. It's not uncommon to find that an incorrect answer to one question is the correct answer to another question, or vice versa. Take the time to read every answer to each question, even if you recognize the correct answer to a question immediately. That extra reading may spark a memory or remind you about a Visual C++ 6 feature or function that helps you on another question elsewhere in the exam.

If you're taking a fixed-length test, you can revisit any question as many times as you like. If you're uncertain of the answer to a question, check the box that's provided to mark it for easy return later on. You should also mark questions that you think may offer information you can use to answer other questions. On fixed-length tests, I usually mark somewhere between 25 and 50 percent of the questions. The testing software is designed to let you mark every question if you choose; use this framework to your advantage. Everything you'll want to see again should be marked; the testing software can then help you return to marked questions quickly and easily.

For fixed-length tests, I strongly recommend that you first read the entire test quickly, before getting caught up in answering individual questions. Doing this will help jog your memory as you review the potential answers and can help you identify questions that you want to mark for easy access to their contents. You can also identify and mark the tricky questions for easy return. The key is to make a quick pass over the territory to begin with—so that you know what you're up against—and then survey that territory more thoroughly on a second pass, when you can begin to answer all questions systematically and consistently.

If you're taking an adaptive test and you see something in a question or in one of the answers that jogs your memory on a topic, or that you feel you should record if the topic appears in another question, write it down on your piece of paper. Just because you can't go back to a question in an adaptive test doesn't mean you can't take notes on what you see early in the test in hopes that it might help you later in the test.

 For adaptive tests, don't be afraid to take notes on what you see in various questions. Sometimes, what you record from one question can help you on other questions later on, especially if it's not as familiar as it should be or it reminds you of the name or use of some utility or interface details.

Deciding What To Memorize

The amount of memorization you must undertake for an exam depends on how well you remember what you've read and how well you know the software by heart. If you're a visual thinker and can see the drop-down menus and dialog boxes in your head, you won't need to memorize as much as someone who's less visually oriented. However, the exam will stretch your abilities to memorize product features and functions, interface details, and proper application design, development, and maintenance approaches, as well as how they all relate to Visual C++ 6.

At a minimum, you'll want to memorize the following kinds of information:

➤ MFC

➤ COM components

➤ ATL

➤ ActiveX

➤ ADO

➤ SQL

➤ DLLs

➤ Debugging

➤ Development tools

If you work your way through this book while sitting at a machine with Visual C++ 6 installed and try to manipulate this environment's features and functions as they're discussed throughout, you should have little or no difficulty mastering this material. Also, don't forget that The Cram Sheet at the front of the book is designed to capture the material that's most important to memorize; use this to guide your studies as well.

Preparing For The Test

The best way to prepare for the test—after you've studied—is to take at least one practice exam. I've included one here in this chapter for that reason; the test questions are located in the pages that follow. (Unlike the questions in the preceding chapters in this book, the answers don't follow the questions immediately; you'll have to flip to Chapter 14 to review the answers separately.)

Give yourself 105 minutes to take the exam, and keep yourself on the honor system—don't look at earlier text in the book or jump ahead to the answer key. When your time is up or you've finished the questions, you can check your work in Chapter 14. Pay special attention to the explanations for the incorrect answers; these can also help reinforce your knowledge of the material. Knowing how to recognize correct answers is good, but understanding why incorrect answers are wrong can be equally valuable.

Taking The Test

Relax. Once you're sitting in front of the testing computer, there's nothing more you can do to increase your knowledge or preparation. Take a deep breath, stretch, and start reading that first question.

You don't need to rush, either. You have plenty of time to complete each question, and if you're taking a fixed-length test, you'll have time to return to the questions that you skipped or marked for return. On a fixed-length test, if you read a question twice and you remain clueless, you can mark it; if you're taking an adaptive test, you'll have to guess and move on. Both easy and difficult questions are intermixed throughout the test in random order. If you're taking a fixed-length test, don't cheat yourself by spending too much time on a hard question early in the test, thereby depriving yourself of the time you need to answer the questions at the end of the test. If you're taking an adaptive test, don't spend more than five minutes on any single question—if it takes you that long to get nowhere, it's time to guess and move on.

On a fixed-length test, you can read through the entire test, and, before returning to marked questions for a second visit, you can figure out how much time you've got per question. As you answer each question, remove its mark. Continue to review the remaining marked questions until you run out of time or complete the test.

On an adaptive test, set a maximum time limit for questions, and watch your time on long or complex questions. If you hit your limit, it's time to guess and move on. Don't deprive yourself of the opportunity to see more questions by taking too long to puzzle over questions, unless you think you can figure out the answer. Otherwise, you're limiting your opportunities to pass.

That's it for pointers. Here are some questions for you to practice on. Good luck!

Sample Test

Question 1

Which Visual C++ edition allows only static linking to the MFC libraries?

○ a. Standard

○ b. Professional

○ c. Enterprise

○ d. Personal

Question 2

MTS is middleware that provides scalability to components built on which component architectures?

○ a. JavaBeans

○ b. SOM

○ c. COM

○ d. OpenDoc

Question 3

Which of the following scenarios violates referential integrity (leaves an orphan)?

○ a. Delete a child record that has an associated parent.

○ b. Change a child's foreign key value to a value that exists in the parent's primary key.

○ c. Remove a parent record that has only one child.

○ d. Insert a child record for a parent that already has children.

○ e. Insert a parent record that has no children yet.

Question 4

SMS requires which products or utilities to operate? [Check all correct answers]

❑ a. SQL Server

❑ b. NT Server

❑ c. MMC

❑ d. MTS

Question 5

Which of the following are valid ADO cursor values? [Check all correct answers]

❑ a. **adOpenStatic**

❑ b. **adOpenDynamic**

❑ c. **adOpenForwardOnly**

❑ d. **adOpenKeyset**

Question 6

Which of the following does MDAC (Microsoft Data Access Components) provide support services for? [Check all correct answers]

❑ a. ADO

❑ b. OLE DB

❑ c. DCOM

❑ d. ODBC

Question 7

Pick the relational construct you would use to answer this request: "Show the customers who have not placed any orders."

○ a. Union

○ b. Join

○ c. Outer join

○ d. Difference

Question 8

The **LockType** property must be set to which value in order to do batch updates?

- ○ a. **adLockBatchPessimistic**
- ○ b. **adLockBatchOptimistic**
- ○ c. **adLockPessimistic**
- ○ d. **adLockBatch**

Question 9

Which of the following can perform a query? [Check all correct answers]

- ❑ a. **Recordset::Open()**
- ❑ b. **Command::Open()**
- ❑ c. **Connection::Execute()**
- ❑ d. **Command::Execute()**

Question 10

Which security concept masks information in a way that makes it unintelligible to anyone other than the intended recipient?

- ○ a. Authentication
- ○ b. Encryption
- ○ c. Auditing
- ○ d. Certificate

Question 11

Which of the following can be used in a **WHERE** clause? [Check all correct answers]

- ❑ a. **IN**
- ❑ b. **BETWEEN**
- ❑ c. Aggregate functions
- ❑ d. **LIKE**
- ❑ e. **DISTINCT**

Question 12

Which register can you modify to change the next instruction that is to be executed?

○ a. ERR

○ b. EIP

○ c. EAX

○ d. EBX

Question 13

Which one of the following statements regarding reference counting is true?

○ a   **QueryInterface()** always initializes the reference count by setting it to one.

○ b. After calling **Release()**, the client can continue to safely use the interface pointer until the pointer goes out of scope.

○ c. If the client deletes a non-null interface pointer, the object's destructor must call **Release()**.

○ d. The client should call **AddRef()** whenever it makes a copy of a non-null interface pointer.

Question 14

Which statement best describes the purpose of a firewall?

○ a. A firewall isolates two networks by blocking all traffic.

○ b. A firewall inspects each packet entering or leaving a network and allows it to pass based on security configuration rules.

○ c. A firewall is a piece of software that runs on a computer connected to two networks.

○ d. A firewall filters HTTP, FTP, and Telnet traffic.

Question 15

Which watch window formatting codes can be used for a signed decimal integer? [Check all correct answers]

❑ a. **d**

❑ b. **u**

❑ c. **i**

❑ d. **f**

Question 16

Which two of the following statements are false?

❑ a. Given a class that can be aggregated, when created as a nonaggregated component, the constructor must ensure that the **IUnknown *** member variable is **NULL**.

❑ b. When the outer object in an aggregation queries an interface belonging to the inner object, the reference count belonging to the outer object is incremented.

❑ c. One of the advantages of containment over aggregation is that, when you're using containment, the interface can be extended by adding code to an existing interface.

❑ d. A client can determine if a component is using aggregation.

Question 17

What is the relational construct that compares rows of a given table to other rows in the same table?

○ a. Join

○ b. Self-join

○ c. Outer join

○ d. Intersection

Question 18

Which information is not contained in a certificate?

- ○ a. The activation date
- ○ b. An expiration date
- ○ c. A field that indicates the validity of the certificate
- ○ d. A unique identifier given by the issuer

Question 19

Which of the following can you do with the DCOMCNFG utility? [Check all correct answers]

- ❑ a. Set default security values that apply to all DCOM applications on a machine.
- ❑ b. Allow clients on other machines to access COM objects on this machine.
- ❑ c. Set security values that apply to a particular application.
- ❑ d. Specify where an application should run when a client calls **CoCreateInstance()**.

Question 20

What does ATL stand for?

- ○ a. ActiveX Tool Library
- ○ b. Active Template Library
- ○ c. Action Template Library
- ○ d. ActiveX Template Library

Question 21

Which of the following statements regarding indexes is false?

○ a. Indexes use disk space to improve performance.

○ b. Index design is based on an analysis of the workload's queries.

○ c. Inserts and deletes will take longer if the affected table has indexes.

○ d. An equi-join **SELECT** will always benefit from an index on the equi-joined columns.

○ e. **INSERT**, **UPDATE**, and **DELETE** statements cannot use indexes.

Question 22

Which are two valid ways of acquiring a certificate?

❑ a. Generate a test certificate by using the MakeCert utility.

❑ b. Purchase a certificate from a CA.

❑ c. Use any certificate that is posted publicly.

❑ d. Create a certificate by using the ChkTrust utility.

Question 23

Which two of the following statements are true?

❑ a. ATL's **CDataSource** OLE DB template class represents a physical connection to a data source.

❑ b. ATL's **CSession** OLE DB template class represents a physical connection to a data source.

❑ c. ATL's **CSession** OLE DB template class represents a logical connection to a data source.

❑ d. ATL's **CDataSource** OLE DB template class represents a logical connection to a data source.

Question 24

Which of the following statements is true regarding the creation of a dockable toolbar?

○ a. You need to enable docking for only the frame window.

○ b. You do not need to enable docking for the frame window; however, you must enable docking for each toolbar that you want to be dockable, and you must add code to dock the toolbar to a frame window.

○ c. You must enable docking for the frame, enable docking for each toolbar that you want to be dockable, and dock the toolbar to the frame window.

○ d. You must enable docking for the frame and add code to dock the toolbar to the frame, but you do not need to enable docking for the toolbar you want to dock.

Question 25

Which components or applications are required for MTS operation on NT 4? [Check all correct answers]

❑ a. MSMQ

❑ b. MMC

❑ c. IE 4.01 (or higher)

❑ d. SQL Server

Question 26

Which of the following are features of SMS operation? [Check all correct answers]

❑ a. Dry run

❑ b. Roll-back

❑ c. Virus detection

❑ d. Patch

Question 27

Which of the following pairs of macros does MFC use to define the COM interface map?

○ a. **BEGIN_INTERFACE_MAP** and **END_INTERFACE_MAP**

○ b. **BEGIN_OBJECT_MAP** and **END_OBJECT_MAP**

○ c. **BEGIN_INTERFACE_PART** and **END_INTERFACE_PART**

○ d. **BEGIN_COM_MAP** and **END_COM_MAP**

Question 28

Which of the following statements concerning views are true? [Check all correct answers]

❑ a. Views must be uniquely named.

❑ b. Views cannot be indexed, but they can have triggers and default values associated with them.

❑ c. Views improve performance by caching data.

❑ d. Views can simplify complex SQL operations.

Question 29

Visual C++ organizes projects in what?

○ a. A collection

○ b. A workspace

○ c. A file

○ d. A project with subprojects

Question 30

Which of the following functions must be implemented by all in-process servers? [Check all correct answers]

❑ a. **DllCanUnloadNow()**

❑ b. **DllGetClassObject()**

❑ c. **DllRegisterServer()**

❑ d. **DllUnregisterServer()**

Question 31

What is the result of the following code?

```
CDataSource ds;
HRESULT hr;
hr = ds.OpenFromInitializationString(
            OLESTR("PROVIDER=SQLOLEDB;")
            OLESTR("DATABASE=pubs;")
            OLESTR("UID=sa;PWD="));
```

○ a. It will return an error code because the string passed to **OpenFromInitializationString()** is not valid.

○ b. It won't compile because **OpenFromInitializationString()** is not a member of **CDataSource**.

○ c. It will open the **pubs** database as a data source.

○ d. None of the above because not enough information is provided.

Question 32

In which debug windows may you set breakpoints? [Check all correct answers]

❑ a. Source

❑ b. QuickWatch

❑ c. Call Stack

❑ d. Output

Question 33

You are implementing an MFC application (myapp.exe) that supports printing and persistence. You used AppWizard to generate an SDI application, and in Step 4 of 6, you selected Context-Sensitive Help and accepted all of the defaults, including Printing and Print Preview. You want your online help to cover all aspects of your application. When you distribute your application, which of the following files would not be included as part of the installation? [Check all correct answers]

❏ a. myapp.exe

❏ b. myapp.hlp

❏ c. myapp.cnt

❏ d. afxprint.rtf

Question 34

Which core features appear in Windows 2000 to support the ZAW initiative? [Check all correct answers]

❏ a. Support for mobile and roaming users

❏ b. Side-by-side machine replacement with no loss of user data

❏ c. Remote, centralized, policy-based management

❏ d. Hardware upgrade capability

Question 35

Look at the following code:

```
pCnn1.CreateInstance(__uuidof(Connection)));
pCnn1->Open(strCnn, "", "",
            adConnectUnspecified);
pCmdChange.CreateInstance(__uuidof(Command)));
pCmdChange->ActiveConnection = pCnn1;
pCmdChange->CommandText = strSQLChange;

pRstTitles.CreateInstance(
            __uuidof(Recordset)));
pRstTitles->Open(
        "Titles",
        _variant_t((IDispatch *) pCnn1, true),
        adOpenForwardOnly, adLockOptimistic,
        adCmdTable);
```

Which of the following lines of code could be added to make a record the current record? [Check all correct answers]

❏ a. **pRstTitles->MoveNext();**

❏ b. **pRstTitles->MovePrevious();**

❏ c. **pRstTitles->MoveFirst();**

❏ d. **pRstTitles->MoveLast();**

Question 36

What business rule does the following trigger implement?

```
CREATE TRIGGER triggers_happen
ON transactions
FOR DELETE
AS
BEGIN
   IF (SELECT txn_type FROM deleted ) = 'D'
      UPDATE accounts a
      SET balance = balance - d.amount
      FROM deleted d
      WHERE a.account_id = d.account_id
   ELSE IF (SELECT txn_type FROM deleted ) = 'W'
      UPDATE accounts a
      SET balance = balance + d.amount
      FROM deleted d
      WHERE a.account_id = d.account_id
END
```

○ a. When a deposit or a withdrawal occurs, update the account appropriately.

○ b. If the plus and the minus in the **SET** clauses are interchanged, then when a deposit or a withdrawal occurs, update the account appropriately.

○ c. When a deposit or withdrawal is canceled, update the account appropriately.

○ d. If the plus and the minus in the **SET** clauses are interchanged, then when a deposit or withdrawal is canceled, update the account appropriately.

Question 37

Visual C++ supports which three character-mapping modes?

- ❏ a. Single-byte
- ❏ b. Multibyte
- ❏ c. Variable-byte
- ❏ d. Unicode

Question 38

Which types of COM servers operate under the MTS environment?

- ○ a. In-process
- ○ b. Local
- ○ c. Dual interface
- ○ d. Single apartment

Question 39

Which are tabbed panes in the Variables debug window? [Check all correct answers]

- ❏ a. Auto
- ❏ b. Local
- ❏ c. This
- ❏ d. Globals

Question 40

Which of the following statements regarding ATL's object map are true? [Check all correct answers]

❑ a. It exposes your custom interfaces.

❑ b. It controls the class factories and registration for the coclasses in your project.

❑ c. The **DECLARE_OBJECT_MAP** and **IMPLEMENT_OBJECT_MAP** macros are used to declare and implement the object map.

❑ d. The **BEGIN_OBJECT_MAP** and **END_OBJECT_MAP** macros define the start and end of the object map.

Question 41

Which of the following are **IObjectContext** interface methods?

○ a. **SetComplete()**, **SetAbort()**, **EnableCommit()**, and **DisableCommit()**.

○ b. **SetCommit()**, **SetAbort()**, and **SetRollback()**.

○ c. **SetCompletionStatus()**, and **SetCommitStatus()**.

○ d. **Complete()**, **Abort()**, **Commit()**, and **Rollback()**.

Question 42

What business rule does the following trigger implement?

```
CREATE TRIGGER check_balance
ON transactions
FOR INSERT
AS
BEGIN
   IF ( SELECT txn_type FROM inserted ) = 'W'
        AND ( SELECT acct_type
               FROM account a , inserted i
               WHERE a.account_id = i.account_id ) = 'C'
        AND ( SELECT a.balance - i.amount
               FROM accounts a , inserted i
               WHERE a.account_id = i.account_id ) < 0
      BEGIN
        UPDATE account a
        SET balance = balance - 200
        FROM account aok , inserted i
        WHERE aok.account_id = i.account_id
        AND   aok.customer_id = a.customer_id
        AND   a.acct_type = 'S'

        UPDATE account a
        SET balance = balance + 200
        FROM inserted i
        WHERE a.account_id = i.account_id

        RAISERROR("An error has occured",16,1)
      END
END
```

(continued)

Question 42 (continued)

○ a. If a withdrawal overdraws a checking account, transfer $200 from the customer's savings account to his checking account and raise an error.

○ b. If there are no withdrawals from the checking account, transfer $200 from the customer's savings account to his checking account and raise an error.

○ c. If a withdrawal overdraws a checking account, penalize the customer $200 and raise an error.

○ d. If a withdrawal overdraws any account, penalize the customer $200 and raise an error.

Question 43

Which debug utility is especially useful for debugging and testing ActiveX controls?

○ a. Spy++

○ b. OLE View

○ c. Test Container

○ d. ZoomIn

Question 44

Which ADO objects can be created independently? [Check all correct answers]

❑ a. **Recordset**

❑ b. **Error**

❑ c. **Connection**

❑ d. **Command**

Question 45

Which **IObjectContext** interface method indicates a successful completion of the object's participation in a transaction?

○ a. **Commit**

○ b. **EnableCommit**

○ c. **SetComplete**

○ d. **Complete**

Question 46

Which function does the framework call to initialize data in a dialog box or to retrieve and validate dialog box data?

○ a. **CWnd::DoDataExchange()**

○ b. **CDataExchange::UpdateData()**

○ c. **CWnd::OnInitDialog()**

○ d. **CWnd::UpdateData()**

Question 47

Which statement is correct?

○ a. An ActiveX control must support at least the **IDispatch** interface and be self-registering.

○ b. An ActiveX control must support at least all of the interfaces that an OLE control must support.

○ c. An ActiveX control must support at least the **IDispatch::Invoke()** method and the **IErrorInfo** interface.

○ d. An ActiveX control must support at least the **IUnknown** interface and be self-registering.

Question 48

What is the term used by MTS to identify collections of components that together perform a task or a set of related tasks?

○ a. Bundle

○ b. Package

○ c. Super-component

○ d. Application

Question 49

Which SQL construct allows the result of an inner query to be passed to an outer query?

○ a. Outer join

○ b. Inner join

○ c. Subquery

○ d. Union

Question 50

You have created a toolbar and have placed three buttons on it. Now you want to add a text label to each of the buttons. Which of the following functions would you use?

○ a. **CToolBar::SetButtonText()**

○ b. **CToolBar::SetButtonLabel()**

○ c. **CToolBar::SetText()**

○ d. **CToolBar::SetCaption()**

Question 51

Which operating systems are DCOM compliant or can be made DCOM compliant? [Check all correct answers]

❑ a. Windows 2000

❑ b. Windows 98

❑ c. Windows 95

❑ d. Windows NT 4 Workstation

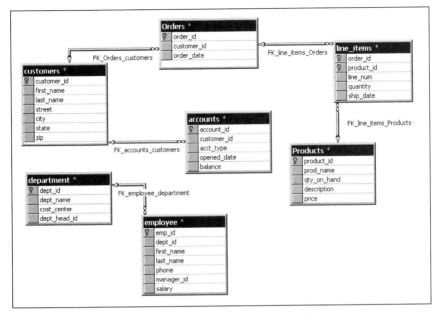

Figure 13.1   Use this figure for Questions 52 through 57.

Question 52

Based on the scenario depicted in Figure 13.1, what business request does the following SQL query implement?

```
SELECT customer_id
FROM orders o , line_items li , products p
WHERE li.product_id = p.product_id
AND    prod_name = 'Widget'
AND    order_date < ship_date
GROUP BY customer_id
HAVING COUNT(*) >= 5
```

- ○ a. Show the customers who have purchased five or more Widgets on the Widgets' ship date.
- ○ b. Show the customers who have five or more orders for Widgets that were not shipped on the dates they were ordered.
- ○ c. Show the customers who bought five or more products that were ordered before Widgets were shipped.
- ○ d. Show the customers who bought five or more Widgets before the Widgets were shipped.

Question 53

Based on the scenario depicted in Figure 13.1, what business request does the following SQL query implement?

```
SELECT customer_id , p.product_id , COUNT(*)
FROM   orders o , line_items li , products p
WHERE o.order_id = li.order_id
AND    li.product_id = p.product_id
GROUP BY customer_id , p.product_id
HAVING SUM(quantity*price) > 1000
```

○ a. For customers who have bought more than $1,000 of a product, display the customer, the product, and the number of units of the product that the customer has purchased.

○ b. For orders worth more than $1,000, display the customer, the products purchased, and the number of units of each product.

○ c. For customers who have bought more than $1,000 of a product, display the customer, the product, and the number of orders for the product by that customer.

○ d. For orders worth more than $1,000, display the customer, the product, and the number of orders for the product by that customer.

Question 54

Based on the scenario depicted in Figure 13.1, what business rule does the following trigger implement?

```
CREATE TRIGGER triggers_happen
ON transactions
FOR INSERT
AS
BEGIN
   IF (SELECT SUM(amount)
      FROM transactions t , inserted i
      /* Assume this has only date, not time */
      WHERE t.txn_date = i.txn_date
      AND t.account_id = i.account_id
      AND txn_type = 'W' ) > 350
     BEGIN
       RAISERROR("An error has occurred",16,1)
       ROLLBACK
     END
END
```

○ a. If more than 350 withdrawals have happened today, raise an error.

○ b. If more than $350 has been withdrawn from this account today, raise an error.

○ c. If more than $350 has been withdrawn from the bank today, raise an error.

○ d. If more than 350 days' worth of withdrawals exist, raise an error.

Question 55

Based on the scenario depicted in Figure 13.1, what business request does the following SQL query implement?

```
UPDATE orders
SET order_total =
  ( SELECT SUM(quantity*price)
    FROM line_items li , products p, orders
    WHERE li.product_id = p.product_id
    AND li.order_id = orders.order_id )
WHERE orders.order_id IN
  ( SELECT li.order_id
    FROM line_items li , products p
    WHERE li.product_id = p.product_id
    AND prod_name = 'Widget' )
```

○ a. Add up the order total for all orders with Widgets.

○ b. Add up the order total for all orders without Widgets.

○ c. Change the order total for all orders with a product that changed its name to Widget.

○ d. Recalculate the order total if Widgets are added to the order.

Question 56

Based on the scenario depicted in Figure 13.1, a view has been defined as indicated here:

```
CREATE VIEW my_stuff
AS
SELECT li.order_id , COUNT(*) AS num_lines ,
     SUM(quantity*price) AS total
FROM line_items li , products p
WHERE li.product_id = p.product_id
GROUP BY li.order_id
```

What business request does the following SQL query implement?

```
SELECT customer_id , SUM(total)
FROM orders o , my_stuff m
WHERE o.order_id = m.order_id
GROUP BY customer_id
HAVING COUNT(*) >= 2  OR  AVG(num_lines) = 1
```

- ○ a. Display the total value of all orders for each order with two or more line items or with an average of one line item on each order.
- ○ b. Display the total value of all orders for each product that's on two or more orders or that's on an average of one line item on each order.
- ○ c. Display the total value of all orders for each customer who has two or more orders or who has an average of one line item on each order.
- ○ d. Display the total value of all orders for each customer who has two or more products on an order or who has an average of one line item on each order.

Question 57

Based on the scenario depicted in Figure 13.1, what business request does the following SQL query implement?

```
INSERT INTO products
SELECT MAX(product_id)+1, 'THIS ONE' ,
            -(quantity) , NULL , 0
FROM line_items
WHERE product_id NOT IN
   ( SELECT product_id FROM products )
```

○ a. For products that have not been sold, tag them as requiring further attention.

○ b. For line items with an unknown product, create a dummy product placeholder.

○ c. For products that have been sold, tag them as requiring further attention.

○ d. Create a line item for any products that have not been sold.

Answer Key

1. a	20. b	39. a, b, c
2. c	21. e	40. b, d
3. c	22. a, b	41. a
4. a, b, c	23. b, d	42. a
5. a, b, c, d	24. c	43. c
6. a, b, d	25. b, c	44. a, c, d
7. d	26. a, b, d	45. b
8. b	27. a	46. a
9. a, c, d	28. a, d	47. d
10. b	29. b	48. b
11. a, b, d	30. a, b, c, d	49. c
12. b	31. c	50. a
13. d	32. a, c	51. a, b, c, d
14. b	33. d	52. b
15. a, c	34. a, b, c	53. c
16. a, d	35. a, c	54. b
17. b	36. c	55. a
18. c	37. a, b, d	56. c
19. a, b, c, d	38. a	57. b

Question 1

Answer a is correct. The Standard edition allows only static linking. Answers b and c are incorrect because the Professional and Enterprise editions allow a program to be linked to both the static and dynamic libraries. Answer d is incorrect because there is no Personal edition.

Question 2

Answer c is correct. The Component Object Model (COM) is Microsoft's preferred component software architecture, and it is both language and platform independent. Answer a is incorrect because JavaBeans and Enterprise JavaBeans are Java-only component architecture. Answer b is incorrect because System Object Model (SOM) is a component architecture developed by IBM. Answer d is incorrect because OpenDoc is a component architecture developed by Apple.

Question 3

Answer c is correct. This is a tough question because the discussion of parent-child relationships and referential integrity is spread throughout Chapter 9. Fundamentally, this question is asking which of these operations may cause a child record to have no associated parent record. Only answer c causes this to happen.

Question 4

Answers a, b, and c are correct. Systems Management Server (SMS) is tightly integrated with Microsoft SQL Server and NT Server, using the Microsoft Management Console (MMC) as an administrative user interface. Answer d is incorrect because SMS does not require MTS (Microsoft Transaction Server).

Question 5

Answers a, b, c, and d are correct. All of these are valid ADO cursor values. **adOpenStatic** allows you to add, modify, or delete records. However, changes made by other users are not visible. **adOpenDynamic** allows unrestricted movement through the recordset. You can add, modify, or delete records. Records added, modified, or deleted by other users are visible. **adOpenForwardOnly** is identical to **adOpenDynamic**, except that **adOpenForwardOnly** allows only forward movement through the records. This speeds up access to the data.

This is the default cursor type. **adOpenKeyset** is similar to **adOpenDynamic**. Changes made by other users are incorporated into your recordset, but additions and deletions aren't.

Question 6

Answers a, b, and d are correct. The MDAC package provides support for ActiveX Data Objects (ADO), OLE DB, and ODBC drivers and services. Answer c is incorrect because DCOM services are either included in the operating system (Windows 98, NT 4, 2000) or available as a service pack for Windows 95.

Question 7

Answer d is correct. The relationship between a customer and an order is one-to-many. The data would tell us the customers who *have* placed orders, and would tell us who all the customers are. When we subtract (difference) the list of who has placed an order from the list of everybody, we would be left with the list of who has *not* placed an order. Answer a is incorrect because a union adds all the elements of the second set to the first set. Answer b is incorrect because a join extracts data by relating columns in one table to columns in another table. Answer c is incorrect because an outer join includes rows from one table that have no related rows in the other table.

Question 8

Answer b is correct. The **LockType** property must be set to **adLockBatchOptimistic** in order to do batch updates. Answers a and d are incorrect because **adLockBatchPessimistic** and **adLockBatch** are not valid **LockTypeEnum** values. Answer c is incorrect because **adLockPessimistic** is used for record-by-record editing.

Question 9

Answers a, c, and d are correct. Answer a is correct because you can pass a query string for execution to the **Recordset::Open()** method. Answers c and d are correct because both **Connection::Execute()** and **Command::Execute()** execute the query specified in the **CommandText** property and return a **Recordset** object. Answer b is incorrect because the **Command** object does not have an **Open()** method.

Question 10

Answer b is correct. Encryption allows information to be masked such that only the intended recipient can view the actual contents. Answers a and d are incorrect because authentication involves the concept of verifying authenticity; this may or may not involve certificates. Answer c is incorrect because auditing is the process of logging and/or reviewing the logs of system activity.

Question 11

Answers a, b, and d are correct. **IN, BETWEEN,** and **LIKE** can all be used in a **WHERE** clause. Answer c is incorrect because aggregate functions cannot be used in a **WHERE** clause but can be used in **HAVING** clauses. Answer e is incorrect because **DISTINCT** is used in the **SELECT** list to display unique occurrences of the result rows.

Question 12

Answer b is correct. You can change the EIP (instruction pointer) register during a debugging session to jump around code that you don't want to execute. Answer a is incorrect because ERR is a pseudoregister that displays the last error code for the current thread. Answers c and d are incorrect because EAX and EBX are general-purpose registers.

Question 13

Answer d is correct. The client should call **AddRef()** whenever it makes a copy of a non-null interface pointer. Answer a is incorrect because successful calls to **QueryInterface()** will cause the object's reference count to be increased by one, not set to one. Answer b is incorrect because when the client calls **Release()**, it is telling the object that it is no longer needed. The client must then assume that the interface pointer is invalid. From a practical standpoint, an object's reference count can theoretically fall to zero after any call to **Release()**; therefore, an interface pointer should never be used after calling **Release()**. Answer c is incorrect because the client should not **delete** a COM object; instead, the client calls **Release()**, and if the reference count goes to zero, the object can self-destruct by performing **delete this**.

Question 14

Answer b is correct. A firewall is a device that isolates two networks, such as isolating a corporate LAN from the Internet or some other potentially malicious network. Answer c is incorrect because a firewall may either be software that runs on a general-purpose computer or it may be a specialized piece of hardware. Answers a and d are incorrect because a firewall may be configured to accept or block all (or specific) types of packets that appear on computers' socket ports.

Question 15

Answers a and c are correct. The **d** and **i** codes can be used for a signed decimal integer. Answer b is incorrect because the **u** code is for an unsigned decimal integer. Answer d is incorrect because the **f** code is used for a signed floating-point value.

Question 16

Answers a and d are correct. This is a nasty question. It provides two true statements and two false statements and then asks that you mark the false statements as the correct answers to the question. Answer a is correct because it is false. The inner object's **IUnknown *** member variable must be initialized to point to the outer unknown or the inner unknown. At no time should it be NULL. Answer d is correct because it is false. The inner component's **IUnknown** is hidden from the client. When the client queries for **IUnknown**, it is always presented with the outer component's **IUnknown**. Answers b and c are incorrect because they are both true statements. When queried, the inner object delegates the **AddRef()** call to the outer unknown. The result is that the outer object component's reference count—and not the inner object component's reference count—is incremented. One of the major uses of containment is to extend an interface by adding your own code, which you can't do when you use aggregation.

Question 17

Answer b is correct. A self-join compares rows of a given table to other rows in the same table. A restrictive self-join usually compares one row of the given table to all other rows in the same table. One must take care not to join a row to itself. Answer a is incorrect because a join associates different tables. Answer c is incorrect because an outer join is used to include rows from one table that have no related rows in the other table. Answer d is incorrect because an intersection presents the elements that are common to the two sets. In SQL Server, intersection is written as a join.

Question 18

Answer c is correct. A certificate in and of itself offers proof of authentication. Using a certificate issued by a trusted third party (Certificate Authority) and verified by this issuer is generally the best way to authenticate the contents of a file signed by a certificate. The other answers are incorrect because the activation date, expiration date, and unique identifier are components of a certificate.

Question 19

Answers a, b, c, and d are all correct. The DCOMCNFG utility allows you to configure DCOM-specific Registry settings. These settings include settings for a particular COM object, default permissions for all local COM objects, and default permissions for clients on another machine.

Question 20

Answer b is correct. ATL stands for Active Template Library. Unlike MFC, which is an application framework, ATL is a component framework, designed for the construction of efficient COM objects. The other answers are wrong.

Question 21

Answer e is correct (meaning, it's false). **INSERT, UPDATE,** and **DELETE** statements will use indexes to find the rows being affected and will then apply the change. All the other statements are true, so they're incorrect.

Question 22

Answers a and b are correct. Generating a test certificate with the MakeCert utility and purchasing a certificate from a CA are both valid ways to acquire a certificate. Answer c is incorrect because using a publicly posted certificate (if you can find one) is not a wise idea, because the private-key information must be posted to be of any use, and once that is posted, there is very little value in having the certificate. Answer d is incorrect because the ChkTrust utility is used to check the validity of a signed file.

Question 23

Answers b and d are correct. The **CSession** class represents a physical connection to a data source, and the **CDataSource** class represents a logical connection to a data source.

Question 24

Answer c is correct. To create a dockable toolbar, you must complete all three steps: enable docking for the frame, enable docking for each toolbar that you want to dock, and add code to dock the toolbar to the frame window.

Question 25

Answers b and c are correct. MTS depends on the Microsoft Management Console (MMC) to create and manage MTS components and packages. IE 4.01 (or higher) is also required because it contains some libraries that MTS requires to operate. Answers a and d are incorrect because the Microsoft Message Queue Server (MSMQ) and SQL Server are not necessary for MTS operation.

Question 26

Answers a, b, and d are correct. Answer a is correct because a dry-run feature allows an administrator to test the likelihood of installation success. Answer b is correct because a roll-back can be performed if software installation doesn't work correctly. Answer d is correct because using a patch avoids having to download an entire application or component. Answer c is incorrect because SMS does not provide virus-detection capabilities.

Question 27

Answer a is correct. The **BEGIN_INTERFACE_MAP()** and **END_INTER-FACE_MAP()** macros are used in the implementation file to define the interface map. Answer c is incorrect because these macros are placed in the header file to create an interface as a nested class, create an instance of the interface, and generate function prototypes for **QueryInterface()**, **AddRef()**, and **Release()**. Answers b and d are incorrect because they are ATL macros.

Question 28

Answers a and d are correct. Answer a is correct because views, like tables, must be uniquely named. Answer d is correct because one of the most common uses of views is to hide complex SQL. Answer b is incorrect because triggers and default values can't be associated with views. Answer c is incorrect because one of the drawbacks of views is that they can degrade performance, not improve it.

Question 29

Answer b is correct. Visual C++ defines a workspace when you create a project. You may add additional projects to this workspace, and they are identified in the DSW workspace file. Answers a and c are incorrect because Visual C++ does not organize projects in files or collections. Answer d is incorrect because project folders within project folders are not supported in Visual C++.

Question 30

Answers a, b, c, and d are all correct. **DllCanUnloadNow()**, **DllGetClass-Object()**, **DllRegisterServer()**, and **DllUnregisterServer()** must be implemented by all in-process servers. This question is trying to trick you by providing only answers that are correct.

Question 31

Answer c is correct. The code will open the **pubs** database as a data source. Answer a is incorrect because ODBC-style strings can be used with OLE DB to open databases; therefore, an error code will not be returned. Answer b is incorrect because **OpenFromInitializationString()** is a member of **CDataSource**. Answer d is incorrect because sufficient information is provided to determine that answer c is correct.

Question 32

Answers a and c are correct. You can set breakpoints in the Source and Call Stack windows. Answers b and d are incorrect because you cannot set breakpoints in the Watch windows or the Output window.

Question 33

Answer d is correct. This question tries to trick you in two ways. First, you are directed to check all correct answers, but only one is correct. Second, it refers to printing and then provides an answer that has "print" in its name; this answer is correct because the afxprint.rtf file is used in the creation of myapp.hlp during development, but it doesn't need to be installed on the user's machine. Answer a is incorrect because it is the application itself, so naturally it must be installed. Answer b is incorrect because it is the help file, so it too must be installed. Answer c is incorrect because it is the contents file and must be installed in order for WinHelp to provide a tree-view table of contents.

Question 34

Answers a, b, and c are correct. To support the ZAW initiative, Windows 2000 has support for mobile and roaming users, side-by-side machine replacement with no loss of user data, and remote, centralized, policy-based management. Answer d is incorrect because Windows 2000 does not have a provision to upgrade the physical hardware of a computer over the network.

Question 35

Answers a and c are correct. The **MoveNext()** and **MoveFirst()** methods can both be called on a forward-only **Recordset** object. Answers b and d are incorrect because **MovePrevious()** and **MoveLast()** will both return an error when called on a forward-only **Recordset** object.

Question 36

Answer c is correct. The trigger fires when a transaction is deleted (canceled). If the canceled transaction was a deposit, you need to subtract the amount out of the account; if the canceled transaction was a withdrawal, you need to add the amount back in.

Question 37

Answers a, b, and d are correct. The Visual C++ compiler supports three character-mapping modes: single-byte (default), multibyte (_MBCS), and Unicode (_UNICODE). Answer c is incorrect because variable-byte is not on the list of character-mapping modes supported by Visual C++.

Question 38

Answer a is correct. COM objects that need to participate in an MTS environment must be in-process (DLL-based) servers. Answer b is incorrect because a local server is contained in an executable. Answer c is incorrect because a dual interface is one that supports automation through **IDispatch** and allows binding directly to the vtable. Answer d is incorrect because apartments (single, multiple, and free) refer to the threading model that the component supports.

Question 39

Answers a, b, and c are correct. Auto, Local, and This are all tabbed panes in the Variables debug window. Answer d is incorrect because a Globals tab is not offered.

Question 40

Answers b and d are correct. You use the **BEGIN_OBJECT_MAP**, **END_OBJECT_MAP**, and **OBJECT_ENTRY** macros to define your object map. **BEGIN_OBJECT_MAP** and **END_OBJECT_MAP** are used to define the start and end of a null-terminated array. **OBJECT_ENTRY** is used to place each of your externally creatable coclass entries in the map. Answer a is incorrect because your custom interfaces are exposed by the **COM_INTERFACE_ENTRY** macro as part of the COM interface map. Answer c is incorrect because **DECLARE_OBJECT_MAP** and **IMPLEMENT_OBJECT_MAP** are not valid ATL macros.

Question 41

Answer a is correct. **SetComplete()**, **SetAbort()**, **EnableCommit()**, and **DisableCommit()** are all **IObjectContext** interface methods. The other answers are incorrect because they are variations on these correct method names.

Question 42

Answer a is correct. The **IF** statement checks to see if the transaction was a withdrawal ('W'), if it was a checking account ('C'), and if the balance will be less than zero. If all of these requirements are true, remove $200 from the savings account that has the same customer ID as the overdrawn account, and add $200 to the overdrawn account.

Question 43

Answer c is correct. The ActiveX Control Test Container provides menus to invoke methods, change properties, and fire events on your control. Answer a is incorrect because the Spy++ utility is useful in viewing message activity. Answer b is incorrect because OLE View may be used to review a control's interface definitions. Answer d is incorrect because the ZoomIn utility is a graphical display capture tool.

Question 44

Answers a, c, and d are correct. The **Recordset, Connection,** and **Command** objects can be created independently of each other. Answer b is incorrect because the **Error** class is dependent on the **Connection** class.

Question 45

Answer b is correct. The **EnableCommit()** method is used to indicate a successful completion in a transaction. Answers a and d are incorrect because **Commit()** and **Complete()** are not **IObjectContext** methods. Answer c is incorrect because the **SetComplete()** method allows a component to identify its completion status to MTS.

Question 46

Answer a is correct. Answers c and d are added to confuse you. Note that the question asks which function the framework calls. When a dialog box is created, **CDialog::OnInitDialog** calls **UpdateData()** (inherited from **CWnd**) with a **FALSE** parameter to initialize the dialog box controls. **UpdateData()** creates a **CDataExchange** object and calls the dialog's **DoDataExchange()** function, passing it a pointer to the **CDataExchange** object. **DoDataExchange()**, in turn, calls one or more **DDX_** functions to initialize the dialog box controls. Later, when the user clicks on OK, **CDialog::OnOK()** calls **UpdateData()** with a TRUE parameter, causing the **DDX_** functions to transfer the data from the controls to the member variables. The **DDV_** functions will also validate the data values. If a data value fails the validation, a warning message is displayed and the dialog box remains on the screen with the input focus on the control that failed the validation.

Question 47

Answer d is correct. Technically, the only interface that an ActiveX control is required to support is **IUnknown**. The idea here is that an ActiveX control needs to support only the interfaces it needs—unlike an OLE control, which is required to support a minimum set of interfaces. For an ActiveX control to be useful—that is, one that can be used in a Web page, an MFC dialog, or a Visual Basic form—it needs to expose some number of methods and properties. It does this by implementing **IDispatch**. Additionally, it will usually have the ability to fire one or more events. Answers a, b, and c include interfaces that are often supported, but are not required.

Question 48

Answer b is correct. Packages is the term used by MTS. Answers a , c, and d are incorrect because they are not the terms used by MTS to identify collections of components that together perform a task or a set of related tasks.

Question 49

Answer c is correct. The output result set of a query can be passed as input to another query through subquery constructs. This question tries to confuse you by using the words "outer" and "inner" in answers a and b. Answer a is incorrect because an outer join includes rows from one table that have no related rows in the other table. Answer b is incorrect because an inner join extracts data by relating columns in one table to columns in another table. Inner joins are usually just called joins. Answer d is incorrect because a union adds all the elements of the second set to the first set.

Question 50

Answer a is correct. **SetButtonText()** is the only function of the four listed that is a member of the **CToolBar** class. **SetButtonText()** is called to set the text on a toolbar button. You need to be careful when you use **SetButtonText()** because the pane will not automatically resize. To resize the pane, you must use **CToolBar::SetSizes()**. Note that you must not use these functions if you want your toolbars to follow the *Windows Interface Guidelines for Software Design* recommendations for button and image sizes.

Question 51

Answers a, b, c, and d are all correct. By default, Windows 2000, Windows 98, and Windows NT 4 Workstation and Server are DCOM-compliant. Windows 95 requires DCOM extensions to be installed separately.

Question 52

Answer b is correct. The query first gets all line items for Widgets. The query then finds all those line items with a ship date greater than the order's order date; in other words, the order did not ship on the date it was ordered. The orders are grouped by customer. The **COUNT** counts the number of Widget line items for each customer; this number happens to be the same as the number of Widget orders for each customer. The list of customers with five or more Widget orders is displayed.

Question 53

Answer c is correct. The SQL query will display one row for each customer and each product purchased by that customer. The grouping occurs across all orders. For each customer, for each product, do certain task(s). In this case, we check how much the customer has spent on each product purchased. If this is more than $1,000, display the result. The **COUNT** displays the number of times the product was ordered (the number of line items—each line item will have one order and one product).

Question 54

Answer b is correct. The inserted table contains a new transaction. The **SELECT** statement adds up all the withdrawal transactions for that day for that account. So the trigger limits to $350 how much someone can withdraw from the account in one day.

Question 55

Answer a is correct. The update's **WHERE** clause finds all orders that include a Widget. For each order (o), the **SET** clause adds up the value of the order (via a correlated subquery). In practice, this query executes very slowly.

Question 56

Answer c is correct. The view creates one large row for each order. Each row in the view contains the number of line items for the order (**num_lines**) and the value of the order (total). The SQL query gathers all these rows for each customer. **COUNT(*) >= 2** looks for customers who have at least two orders. **AVG(num_lines)=1** checks to see if the average number of line items for all the orders for a customer is exactly one. If either one of these conditions is true, then the query displays the customer ID and the value of all of that customer's orders.

Question 57

Answer b is correct. The subquery finds all products, and the **NOT IN** finds any line-item product IDs that are not in that list of known products. For this list of unknown products, a dummy record is created and some initial values are loaded.

Glossary

ACID—An acronym that stands for the four properties of a transacional system: atomicity, consistency, isolation, and durability.

activation—The process of loading an object into memory, which puts the object into its running state.

ActiveX—A set of technologies that enables software components to interact with one another in a networked environment, regardless of the language in which they were created. ActiveX is built on the Component Object Model (COM).

ActiveX component—A physical file that contains classes, which are definitions of objects. Classes were formerly known as "OLE Automation servers" and "OLE Automation controllers."

ActiveX control—An object that you place on a form to enable or enhance a user's interaction with an application. ActiveX controls have events and can be incorporated into other controls.

ActiveX object—An object can meet the requirements of the ActiveX specification by implementing the **IUnknown** interface and being self-registering. In practical terms, however, one normally thinks of an ActiveX object as an object that is exposed to other applications or programming tools through Automation interfaces.

ADO (ActiveX Data Objects)—A collection of dual-interface objects and their properties, methods, and events that together allow you to connect to and manipulate data. ADO uses OLE DB to access the data and presents the developer with an easy-to-use interface. See also *OLE DB*.

aggregate function—In SQL, a function that operates on a set of rows to calculate and return a single value.

aggregate object—A COM object that is made up of one or more other COM objects. One object in the aggregate is designated as the controlling object, which controls which interfaces in the aggregate are exposed and which are private. This controlling object has a special implementation of **IUnknown** called the *controlling IUnknown*. All objects in the aggregate must pass calls to **IUnknown** methods through the controlling **IUnknown**. See also *aggregation*.

aggregation—A composition technique for implementing COM objects. Aggregation allows you to build a new object by using one or more existing objects that support some or all of the new object's required interfaces. The aggregate object chooses which interfaces to expose to clients, and the interfaces are exposed as if the aggregate object implemented them. Clients of the aggregate object assume they communicate only with the aggregate object. See also *aggregate object*.

ambient property—A runtime property that defines a container's surroundings, including default colors, fonts, and alignment. Controls use ambient properties to assume the look and feel of their surrounding environments.

apartment—In COM, objects with different concurrency semantics are separated into distinct execution contexts called apartments. Apartments help programmers manage thread concurrency with respect to their COM objects. COM's apartment model provides a simple set of rules that, when followed, give programmers the concurrency behavior they expect from the COM environment. See also *single-threaded apartment (STA) model* and *multithreaded apartment (MTA) model*.

apartment thread—See *main thread* and *single-threaded apartment (STA) model*.

apartment threading model—See *main thread* and *single-threaded apartment (STA) model*.

API (application programming interface)—A set of routines that an application uses to request and carry out lower-level services. The ODBC API is composed of the ODBC functions.

Automation—COM-based technology that enables interoperability among components. Automation is typically used to create applications that expose objects to programming tools and macro languages, to create and manipulate one application's objects from other applications, or to create tools for accessing and manipulating objects.

Automation object—An object that is exposed to other applications or programming tools through Automation interfaces.

bookmark—A value that identifies a row in a rowset. Bookmarks are saved by the consumer and used later in the life of the rowset to retrieve a particular row.

breakpoint—A location in a program at which execution is paused so that a programmer can examine the program's status, the contents of variables, and so on. A breakpoint is set and used within a debugger and is usually implemented by inserting some kind of jump, call, or trap instruction that transfers control to the debugger.

BSTR—Short for "Basic string" or "binary string." A pointer to a null-terminated wide character string in which the length is stored before the array of characters.

business rules—An organization's standard operating procedures, which require that certain policies be followed to ensure that the business is run properly. Business rules—as implemented in software—are carried out through a combination of validation edits, logon verifications, database lookups, policies, and algorithmic transformations that constitute an enterprise's way of doing business. Business rules ensure that the database maintains its conformance with business policies. Also known as "business logic."

cabinet file—A file that contains compressed files. The CAB file format is useful when you want to deliver code to an end user's computer in a single package, via the Internet or company intranet, and have it automatically install and register itself.

cache—A buffer used to hold data during input/output (I/O) transfers between disk and random access memory (RAM).

call-level interface (CLI)—The interface supported by ODBC for use by an application.

catalog—The Microsoft Transaction Server data store that maintains configuration information for components, packages, and roles. You can administer the catalog by using the Microsoft Transaction Server Explorer.

class—The formal definition of an object. The class acts as the template from which an instance of an object is created at runtime. The class defines the properties of the object and the methods used to control the object's behavior.

class factory—A COM object that implements the **IClassFactory** or **IClassFactory2** interface and that creates one or more instances of an object identified by a given class identifier (CLSID). See also *class identifier (CLSID)*.

class ID—See *class identifier*.

class identifier (CLSID)—A Globally Unique Identifier (GUID) that identifies a COM component. Each COM component has its CLSID in the Windows Registry so that it can be loaded by other applications. See also *Globally Unique Identifier*, *class*, and *class factory*.

class object—In object-oriented programming, an object whose state is shared by all the objects in a class and whose behavior acts on that class-wide state data. In COM, class objects are called "class factories" and typically have no behavior except to create new instances of the class. See also *class factory*.

client—An application or process that requests a service from some process or component.

client cursor—In database programming, a cursor implemented on the client. The entire result set is first transferred to the client, and the client API (application programming interface) software implements the cursor functionality from this cached result set. Client cursors typically do not support all types of cursors, just static and forward-only cursors. See also *server cursor*.

CLSID—See *class identifier (CLSID)*.

coclass—An IDL statement that describes a COM class in terms of the interfaces it supports.

collection—An object that contains a set of related objects.

column—In a relational database table, the area in each row that stores the data about an attribute of the entity represented by the table. Also called a "field." See also *table* and *row*.

column ID—A structure used to identify a column, primarily in a command where there are no stable ordinals or column names.

COM—See *Component Object Model (COM)*.

COM object—An object that conforms to the Component Object Model (COM) architecture. A COM object is an instance of an object definition (class), which specifies the object's data and one or more implementations of interfaces on the object. Clients interact with a COM object only through its interfaces. See also *Component Object Model (COM)* and *interface*.

command—An ADO object that encapsulates an SQL statement or a data provider's unique operation.

commit—The capability to persistently save any changes made to a database, or to a storage or stream object, since it was opened or since changes were last saved. An SQL **COMMIT** statement guarantees that either all or none of a transaction's modifications are made a permanent part of the database. See also *roll back.*

component—A discrete unit of code, built on COM technology, that provides a well-specified set of publicly available services through well-specified interfaces. Components provide the objects that clients request at runtime.

Component Object Model (COM)—A software architecture that allows components made by different software vendors to be combined into a variety of applications. COM defines a standard for component interoperability, does not depend on any particular programming language, is available on multiple platforms, and is extensible. COM is the programming model and binary standard on which ActiveX and Automation technologies are based. See also *interface.*

concurrency—A mode of operation that allows multiple users to access and change shared data at the same time.

connectable object—A COM object that implements, as a minimum, the **IConnectionPointContainer** interface for the management of connection-point objects. Connectable objects support communication from the server to the client. A connectable object creates and manages one or more connection-point objects, which receive events from interfaces implemented on other objects and send them on to the client. See also *connection-point object.*

connection—A particular instance of a driver and data source.

connection-point object—A COM object that is managed by a connectable object and that implements the **IConnectionPoint** interface. One or more connection-point objects can be created and managed by a connectable object. Each connection-point object manages incoming events from a specific interface on another object and sends those events on to the client. See also *connectable object.*

connection pooling—A cache of idle database connections maintained by Microsoft Transaction Server (MTS). MTS borrows a connection from the cache when creating a transactional context and releases the connection when the transaction finishes.

consistency—A state in which durable data matches the state expected by the business rules that modified the data.

container—An application or object that can contain other objects and that interacts with the contained objects through Automation.

container application—An application that supports compound documents. The container application provides storage for an embedded or linked object, a site for its display, access to the display site, and an advisory sink for receiving notifications of changes in the object.

control—An object that you can place on a window. A control has its own set of recognized properties and events. Controls can receive user input, display output, and trigger event procedures. You can manipulate most controls by using methods.

control container—An object that provides sites that can contain controls. Typically, these sites all exist on the same document or form. The control container implements entry points for controls and exposes ambient properties to them. In COM, a control container is an application that supports embedding of controls by implementing the **IOleControlSite** interface. See also *control*.

controlling IUnknown—A special instance of the **IUnknown** interface that is implemented in an aggregate object. See also *aggregate object* and *aggregation*.

current row—The row to which the cursor is currently pointing. Positioning operations act on the current row.

cursor—A database object used by applications to manipulate data by rows. Using cursors, multiple operations can be performed row by row against a result set—with or without returning to the original table.

custom interface—A user-defined COM (Component Object Model) interface that isn't defined as part of COM.

database—A collection of information, tables, and other objects organized and presented to serve a specific purpose, such as to facilitate searching, sorting, and recombining data. Databases are stored in files. A database is also a discrete collection of data in a DBMS (database management system).

database management system (DBMS)—A repository for the collection of computerized data files that enables users to perform a variety of operations on those files. Operations include retrieving, appending, editing, and updating data and generating reports. A DBMS provides a layer of software between the physical database and the user and manages all access to the database.

Data Control Language (DCL)—In SQL, commands used to control database operations. See also *Structured Query Language (SQL)*, *Data Definition Language (DDL)*, and *Data Manipulation Language(DML)*.

Data Definition Language (DDL)—In SQL, statements used to create database objects, such as tables and views. See also *Structured Query Language (SQL)*, *Data Control Language (DCL)*, and *Data Manipulation Language (DML)*.

Data Manipulation Language (DML)—In SQL, statements used to retrieve and modify data that's contained in the database. See also *Structured Query Language (SQL)*, *Data Control Language (DCL)*, and *Data Definition Language (DDL)*.

data source name (DSN)—The name assigned to an ODBC data source. Applications can use data source names (DSNs) to request a connection to a system ODBC data source, which specifies the computer name and (optionally) the database to which the DSN maps. A DSN can also refer to an OLE DB connection.

data transfer object—An object that implements the **IDataObject** interface and contains data to be transferred from one object to another through either the clipboard or drag-and-drop operations.

debugger—A program designed to help find errors in another program by allowing the programmer to step through the program, examine the data, and monitor conditions, such as the values of variables.

DELETE—In database programming, an SQL statement used to remove rows from a database table. See also *Structured Query Language(SQL)*, *INSERT*, *SELECT*, and *UPDATE*.

design-time object—An object used at design time within a host's development environment. See also *runtime object*.

document view—A particular presentation of a document's data. A single document object can have one or more views, but a single document view can belong to one (and only one) document object.

dynamic cursor—A mechanism that allows unrestricted movement through a recordset. Updates, deletions, and insertions done by users are reflected in the dynamic cursor. See also *keyset cursor*, *static cursor*, and *forward-only cursor*.

dynamic link library (DLL)—An executable file that contains one or more functions that are compiled, linked, and stored separately from the processes that use them. The operating system maps the DLLs into the address space of the calling process when the process is starting or while it's running.

enumerator—A COM object that searches for data sources and other enumerators.

equi-join—In databases, the joining of two or more tables based on the same number and types of columns common in both tables. Data rows with no matching rows in the other tables are not selected. See also *outer join*.

error code—A class of return code, of the type **HRESULT**, that begins with E_ or DB_E_ and indicates that the method failed completely and was unable to do any useful work.

error object—An object that contains detailed information about an error.

event sink—A mechanism that implements the member functions for a set of events.

event source—A mechanism that calls the interface that handles events.

exception—An abnormal condition or error that occurs during the execution of a program and that requires the execution of software outside the normal flow of control.

field—See *column*.

filter—A set of criteria applied to records to show a subset of the records.

forward-only cursor—A mechanism that can move only forward through the recordset; rows can be read only in sequence from the first row to the last row. See also *dynamic cursor*, *keyset cursor*, and *static cursor*.

free threading model—See *multithreaded apartment (MTA) model*.

Globally Unique Identifier (GUID)—In COM, a 16-byte (128-bit) value that uniquely identifies something—usually the software that implements one or more objects or an interface on one of those objects. Microsoft's implementation of the Open Software Foundation (OSF) distributed computing environment (DCE) Universally Unique Identifier (UUID).

HRESULT—A 32-bit integer value that provides error information. It consists of four parts: severity (bit 31), reserved (bits 29 and 30), facility code (bits 16 to 28), and return code (bits 0 to 15). The predefined severity constants are **SEVERITY_SUCCESS** (zero) and **SEVERITY_ERROR** (one).

In parameter—A parameter that is passed from the client to the server. **In** parameters are allocated, set, and freed by the caller of a function or interface method. An **In** parameter is not modified by the called function. Input parameters are always passed by value. See also *In/Out parameter* and *Out parameter*.

In/Out parameter—A parameter that is passed to the server that can be modified by the server. **In/Out** parameters are initially allocated and freed by the caller of an interface method. **In/Out** parameters are passed using a pointer. See also *In parameter* and *Out parameter*.

in-process server—A server implemented as a DLL that runs in the process space of the client. See also *out-of-process server*, *local server*, and *remote server*.

INSERT—In database programming, an SQL statement used to add new rows to a database table. See also *Structured Query Language (SQL)*, *DELETE*, *SELECT*, and *UPDATE*.

instance—An object for which memory is allocated or which is persistent.

instantiate—To create an instance of an object.

interface—A group of semantically related functions that provide access to a COM object. Each interface defines a contract that allows objects to interact according to the Component Object Model (COM). See also *Component Object Model (COM)* and *COM object*.

Interface Definition Language (IDL)—Used to specify a COM interface. The interface includes the set of data types and the set of functions to be executed. Interfaces specify the function prototypes for remote functions. These prototypes, in turn, define many aspects of the behavior interface that users can expect from these functions.

interface identifier (IID)—A Globally Unique Identifier (GUID) associated with an interface. Some functions take IIDs as parameters to allow the caller to specify which interface pointer should be returned. See also *Globally Unique Identifier*.

IPersistxxx object—A COM object that supports **IPersistStream, IPersistStreamInit**, or **IPersistStorage**.

keyset cursor—A mechanism that allows unrestricted movement through a recordset. The keyset cursor reflects updates made to the recordset's member rows by other users, but it doesn't show the effects of insertions or deletions. See also *dynamic cursor*, *static cursor*, and *forward-only cursor*.

left outer join—In databases, an outer join that retrieves all the rows in the table specified on the left side of the join command. See also *outer join* and *right outer join*.

license key—A string that, if present, allows a software component to be created.

licensing—A feature of COM that provides control over object creation. Only clients that are authorized to use licensed objects can create them. Licensing is implemented in COM through the **IClassFactory2** interface and by support for a license key that can be passed at runtime.

local server—An out-of-process server implemented as an EXE application running on the same machine as its client application. See also *in-process server*, *out-of-process server*, and *remote server*.

lock—A restriction on access to a resource in a multiuser environment. SQL Server automatically locks users out of a specific record, field, or file to maintain security or to prevent problems with concurrent data manipulation.

locking—The process by which a DBMS (database management system) restricts access to a row in a multiuser environment. The DBMS usually sets a bit on a row or on the physical page containing a row to indicate that the row or page is locked.

main thread—A single thread used to run all objects of components marked as "single threaded." See also *single-threaded apartment (STA) model.*

marshaling—The process of packaging and sending interface method calls across thread, process, or machine boundaries. See also *unmarshaling, proxy,* and *stub.*

method—A procedure (function) that acts on an object.

Microsoft ActiveX Data Objects (ADO)—An easy-to-use application programming interface (API) that wraps OLE DB for use in languages, such as Visual Basic, Visual Basic for Applications, Active Server Pages, and Microsoft Internet Explorer Visual Basic Scripting.

MIDL—Microsoft Interface Definition Language; a compiler (midl.exe).

moniker—An object that acts as the name that uniquely identifies a specific COM object instance. Each moniker knows how to create and initialize a COM object of the type it represents. A moniker object implements the **IMoniker** interface.

multithreaded apartment (MTA) model—In COM, the MTA model allows multiple threads to operate within the same thread-safe "box." This model is sometimes referred to as the *free threading model* and occasionally as a *worker thread.*

natural join—See *equi-join.*

object—A combination of code and data that can be treated as a unit. A class defines a specific kind of object. In object-oriented programming, an object is an entity that has state, behavior, and identity. An object's state consists of its attributes and the current values of those attributes. An object's behavior consists of the operations that can be performed on it and the corresponding changes in its state. An object's identity distinguishes it from other objects. In contrast, a COM object's behavior is defined by the interfaces it supports. A COM object's state is not explicitly specified, but is implied by its interfaces. A COM object is created by a component's class factory. See also *Component Object Model (COM), interface,* and *instance.*

Object Description Language (ODL)—Used to specify a COM interface. ODL was superseded by IDL. However, AppWizard still creates ODL files. See also *Interface Definition Language (IDL).*

Object Linking and Embedding (OLE)—A mechanism that allows users to place content objects created by one application in documents created by another application.

ODBC—See *Open Database Connectivity (ODBC)*.

ODBC driver—A dynamic link library (DLL) that an ODBC-enabled application can use to access an ODBC data source. Each ODBC driver is specific to a database management system (DBMS). See also *Open Database Connectivity (ODBC)*.

OLE—See *Object Linking and Embedding (OLE)*.

OLE DB—A COM-based application programming interface (API) for accessing data. OLE DB supports accessing any format of data storage (databases, spreadsheets, text files, and so on) for which an OLE DB provider is available.

Open Database Connectivity (ODBC)—A relational-database application programming interface (API) aligned with the American National Standards Institute (ANSI) and International Organization for Standardization (ISO) standards for a database call-level interface (CLI). ODBC supports access to any database for which an ODBC driver is available.

outer join—In databases, a join that retrieves all the rows in one of the tables involved in the join, whether or not there are matching rows in the other table. See also *equi-join*, *left outer join*, and *right outer join*.

out-of-process server—A server, implemented as an EXE application, that runs outside the process of its client, either on the same machine or on a remote machine. See also *local server* and *remote server*.

Out parameter—A parameter that is used to return data from the server. An Out parameter is freed by the caller, but has its value set by the method being called. Output parameters are always passed using a pointer. See also *In parameter* and *In/Out parameter*.

package—A set of components that perform related application functions. All components in a package run together in the same Microsoft Transaction Server (MTS) process. A package is both a trust boundary that defines when security credentials are verified and a deployment unit for a set of components. You can create packages with the Transaction Server Explorer.

package file—A file that contains information about the components and roles of a package. A package file is created by using the package export function of the Transaction Server Explorer. When you create a prebuilt package, the associated component files (DLLs, type libraries, and proxy-stub DLLs, if implemented) are copied to the same directory where the package file was created.

persist—To save the current state of an object, such as to a file.

persistent—Lasting between program sessions or renewed when a new program session is started.

persistent storage—Storage of a file or object in a medium, such as a file system or database, so that the object and its data persist when the file is closed and then later reopened.

programmatic identifier (progID)—A name that identifies a COM component.

property—A named attribute of an object. Properties define object characteristics (such as size, color, and screen location) or the state of an object (such as enabled or disabled).

property frame—The user-interface mechanism that displays one or more property pages for a control. A standard implementation of a property frame that can be accessed by using the **OleCreatePropertyFrame** helper function. See also *control* and *property page*.

property page—A group of properties presented as a tabbed page of a property sheet. In COM, an object with its own CLSID that is part of a user interface, that is implemented by a control, and that allows the control's properties to be viewed and set. Property page objects implement the **IPropertyPage** interface. See also *CLSID* and *control*.

property page site—The location within a property frame where a property page is displayed. The property frame implements the **IPropertyPageSite** interface, which contains methods to manage the sites of each of the property pages supplied by a control. See also *property frame*.

property set—A logically related group of properties that is associated with a persistently stored object. To create, open, delete, or enumerate one or more property sets, implement the **IPropertySetStorage** interface. If you are using compound files, you can use COM's implementation of this interface rather than implementing your own.

property set storage—A COM storage object that holds a property set. A property set storage is a dependent object associated with and managed by a storage object.

property sheet—A specialized window through which users can modify the attributes of an external object, such as the current selection in a view. A property sheet has three main parts: the containing window; one or more property pages, shown one at a time; and a tab (at the top of each page) that the user clicks on to select that page. See also *property page*.

proxy—In COM, an interface-specific object that provides the parameter marshaling and communication required for a client to call a server object that is running in a different apartment. A proxy runs in the address space of the client and communicates with a corresponding stub in the server's address space. See also *stub*, *marshaling*, and *unmarshaling*.

query—Any SQL statement. Usually used to mean a **SELECT** statement.

record—In ADO, the record object represents a row in a recordset, or a file or directory in a file system. See also *row*.

recordset—In ADO, represents the entire set of records from a base table, query, or view. See also *result set*.

reference counting—In COM, keeping a count of each interface pointer held on an object to ensure that the object is not destroyed before all references to it are released. See also *lock*.

Registry key—A unique identifier assigned to each piece of information in the system registration database.

remote component—A component used by a client on a different computer. See also *remote server*.

remote procedure call (RPC)—A standard that allows one process to make calls to functions that are executed in another process. The process can be on the same computer or on a different computer in the network.

remote server—A server application running on a different machine from the client application using it. See also *in-process server*, *local server*, and *out-of-process server*.

result set—The set of rows returned from a **SELECT** statement. The format of the rows in the result set is defined by the **column-list** parameter of the **SELECT** statement.

right outer join—In databases, an outer join that retrieves all the rows in the table specified on the right side of the join command. See also *outer join* and *left outer join*.

roll back—The capability to remove partially completed transactions after a database or other system failure. An SQL **ROLLBACK** statement discards all changes made to a database since the beginning of the transaction. See also *commit*.

row—Formally known as a tuple, a row is a data structure that is a collection of columns, each with its own name and type. A row can be accessed as a collective unit of elements, or the elements can be accessed individually. A row is also known as a "record." See also *table* and *column*.

Running Object Table (ROT)—A globally accessible table that's used to keep track of all COM objects in the running state that can be identified by a moniker. Moniker providers register an object in the table, which increments the object's reference count. Before the object can be destroyed, its moniker must be released from the table.

runtime object—An object created at runtime and used as part of an executable application. See also *design-time object*.

SCODE—A 32-bit integer value used to return detailed information to the caller of an interface method or function. See also *HRESULT*.

SELECT—In database programming, an SQL statement used to retrieve rows from one or more database tables. See also *Structured Query Language (SQL)*, *DELETE*, *INSERT*, and *UPDATE*.

self-registration—The process by which a server can perform its own Registry operations.

semaphore—A locking mechanism used inside resource managers or resource dispensers. Semaphores have no symbolic names, have only shared and exclusive-mode access, have no deadlock detection, and have no automatic release or commit.

server—A network computer that controls access to resources, such as files, printers, and communication devices. In COM, *server* is informal for "server application."

server application—An application that can create COM objects. Container applications can then embed or link to these objects. See also *container application*.

server cursor—A cursor implemented on the server. The cursor is built at the server, and only the rows fetched by an application are sent to the client. See also *client cursor*.

single-threaded apartment (STA) model—In COM, this model allows multiple threads to be created, where each thread will belong to only one apartment. When instantiated, the COM object is placed in its own apartment and will automatically be thread-safe because the same thread is always used to call its methods. This model is sometimes referred to as the *apartment threading model* and occasionally as a *user-interface-style thread*.

single threading model—All of a component's methods are executed on the main thread only.

SQL—See *Structured Query Language (SQL)*.

SQL-92—The version of the SQL standard that was published in 1992. The international standard is ISO/IEC 9075:1992 Database Language SQL. The American National Standards Institute (ANSI) also published a corresponding standard (Data Language SQL X3.135-1192), so SQL-92 is sometimes referred to as *ANSI SQL* in the United States.

static cursor—A mechanism that allows unrestricted movement through a recordset. Static cursors don't reflect updates, deletions, or insertions made in underlying data while the cursor is open. Sometimes called "snapshot cursors." See also *dynamic cursor, keyset cursor*, and *forward-only cursor*.

storage object—A COM object that implements the **IStorage** interface. A storage object contains nested storage objects or stream objects, resulting in the equivalent of a directory/file structure within a single file. See also *stream object*.

stored procedure—In database programming, a compiled collection of SQL statements stored within the database. Often used to encapsulate business rules. See also *Structured Query Language (SQL)*.

stream object—A COM object that implements the **IStream** interface. A stream object is analogous to a file in a directory/file system. See also *storage object*.

Structured Query Language (SQL)—A database query and programming language originally developed by IBM for mainframe computers. It is widely used for accessing data and for querying, updating, and managing relational database systems. There is now an ANSI-standard SQL definition for all computer systems. See also *SQL-92*.

structured storage—COM's technology for storing compound files in native file systems. See also *storage object* and *stream object*.

stub—In COM, an interface-specific object that unpackages the marshaled parameters and calls the required method. The stub runs in the receiver's address space and communicates with a corresponding proxy in the sender's address space. See also *proxy, marshaling*, and *unmarshaling*.

system Registry—A system-wide repository of information supported by Windows, the Registry contains information about the system and its applications, including COM clients and servers.

system stored procedure—A precompiled collection of SQL statements. System stored procedures are provided as shortcuts for retrieving information from system tables or as mechanisms for accomplishing database administration and other tasks that involve updating system tables. You can write stored procedures (called "user-defined stored procedures") that can be executed from any database. See also *Structured Query Language (SQL)*.

table—In databases, a structured collection of data of a specific type. It is composed of rows and columns. See also *row* and *column*.

thread—The basic entity to which the operating system allocates CPU time. A thread can execute any part of the application's code, including a part currently being executed by another thread. All threads of a process share the virtual address space, global variables, and operating-system resources of the process.

thread safe—A resource or process that internally handles synchronization. Threads that need to access thread-safe resources can do so as if they were in a single-threaded environment.

threading model, apartment—See *single-threaded apartment (STA) model*.

threading model, both—Objects that support the single-threaded apartment (STA) model and the multithreaded apartment (MTA) model.

threading model, free—See *multithreaded apartment (MTA) model*.

threading model, multithreaded—See *multithreaded apartment (MTA) model*.

threading model, single—See *single threading model*.

transaction—An atomic unit of work. The work in a transaction must be completed as a whole; if any part of the transaction fails, the entire transaction fails.

Transact-SQL—SQL Server's dialect of SQL. Transact-SQL is compliant with most ANSI SQL standards, but it also provides a number of extensions. See also *Structured Query Language (SQL)* and *SQL-92*.

trigger—In database programming, a stored procedure that is automatically executed when a database table is modified using an **UPDATE, INSERT,** or **DELETE** operation. See also *stored procedure*, *UPDATE, INSERT*, and *DELETE*.

type information—Information about an object's class provided by a type library. To provide type information, a COM object implements the **IProvideClassInfo** interface.

type library—A file or component within another file that contains standard descriptions of exposed objects, properties, and methods.

Unicode—Unicode defines a set of letters, numbers, and symbols in a worldwide encode scheme. Each symbol is represented by 16 bits. Unicode has more than 65,000 possible values and includes characters for most languages. Windows NT uses Unicode exclusively at the system level.

uniform data transfer—A model for transferring data via the clipboard, drag and drop, or Automation. Objects conforming to this model implement the **IDataObject** interface. This model replaces DDE (dynamic data exchange).

uniform resource locator (URL)—The identifier used by the Web for the names and locations of objects on the Internet.

Universally Unique Identifier (UUID)—See *Globally Unique Identifier (GUID)*.

unmarshaling—Unpacking parameters that have been sent across apartment boundaries. See also *marshaling*, *proxy*, and *stub*.

UPDATE—In database programming, an SQL statement used to modify column values in a database table's rows. See also *Structured Query Language (SQL)*, *DELETE, INSERT*, and *SELECT*.

view—In databases, an object that provides a logical table that consists of specific columns from one or more physical tables. See also *table* and *query*.

Virtual Table (VTBL or vtable)—An array of pointers to interface method implementations. See also *interface*.

warning code—A class of return code, of the type **HRESULT**, that begins with **S_** or **DB_S_** and that indicates success of the method but with a warning.

Index

Coriolis introduces

EXAM CRAM INSIDER™

A FREE ONLINE NEWSLETTER

Stay current with the latest certification information. Just email us to receive the latest in certification and training news for Microsoft, Java, Novell, A+, Linux, Cisco, and more! Read e-letters from the Publisher of the Exam Cram and Exam Prep series, Keith Weiskamp, and Exam Cram Series Editor, Ed Tittel, about future trends in IT training and education. Access valuable insider information on exam updates, new testing procedures, sample chapters, and links to other useful, online sites. Take a look at the featured program of the month, and who's in the news today. We pack all this and more into our *Exam Cram Insider* online newsletter to make sure *you* pass your next test!

To sign up for our twice monthly newsletter, go to www.coriolis.com and click on the sign up sheet, or email us at eci@coriolis.com and put "subscribe insider" in the body of the message.

EXAM CRAM INSIDER – Another reason Exam Cram and Exam Prep guides are *The Smartest Way To Get Certified*™ And it's free!

Look for All of the Exam Cram Brand Certification Study Systems

ALL NEW! Exam Cram Personal Trainer Systems

The Exam Cram Personal Trainer systems are an exciting new category in certification training products. These CD-ROM based systems offer extensive capabilities at a moderate price and are the first certification-specific testing product to completely link learning with testing.

This Exam Cram Study Guide turned interactive course lets you customize the way you learn.

Each system includes:

• A Personalized Practice Test engine with multiple test methods,

• A database of nearly 300 questions linked directly to the subject matter within the Exam Cram on which that question is based.

Exam Cram Audio Review Systems

Written and read by certification instructors, each set contains four cassettes jam-packed with the certification exam information you must have. Designed to be used on their own or as a complement to our Exam Cram Study Guides, Flash Cards, and Practice Tests.

Each system includes:

• Study preparation tips with an essential last-minute review for the exam

• Hours of lessons highlighting key terms and techniques

• A comprehensive overview of all exam objectives

• 45 minutes of review questions complete with answers and explanations

Exam Cram Flash Cards

These pocket-sized study tools are 100% focused on exams. Key questions appear on side one of each card and in-depth answers on side two. Each card features either a cross-reference to the appropriate Exam Cram Study Guide chapter or to another valuable resource. Comes with a CD-ROM featuring electronic versions of the flash cards and a complete practice exam.

Exam Cram Practice Tests

Our readers told us that extra practice exams were vital to certification success, so we created the perfect companion book for certification study material.

Each book contains:

• Several practice exams

• Electronic versions of practice exams on the accompanying CD-ROM presented in an interactive format enabling practice in an environment similar to that of the actual exam

• Each practice question is followed by the corresponding answer (why the right answers are right and the wrong answers are wrong)

• References to the Exam Cram Study Guide chapter or other resource for that topic